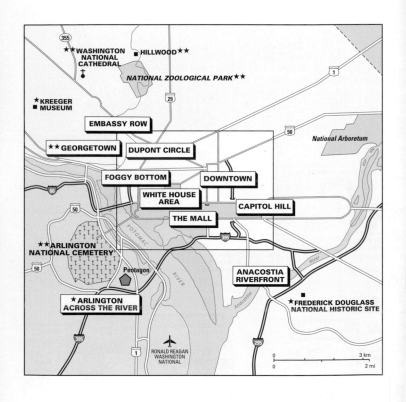

2 50

10. 21. 22

The**Green**Guide
Washington, DC

The Capitol ©Zain Deane/Michelin

THEGREENGUIDE **WASHINGTON, DC**

Editorial Director	Cynthia Clayton Ochterbeck
Editor	Gwen Cannon
Contributing Writers	Zain Deane, K. M. Kostyal
Production Manager	Natasha G. George
Cartography	Peter Wrenn
Photo Researcher	Nicole D. Jordan
Interior Design	Chris Bell
Layout	Michelin Travel Partner, Nicole D. Jordan
Cover Design	Chris Bell, Christelle Le Déan
Cover Layout	Natasha G. George

Contact Us Michelin Travel and Lifestyle North America
One Parkway South
Greenville, SC 29615
USA
travel.lifestyle@us.michelin.com
www.michelintravel.com

Michelin Travel Partner
Hannay House
39 Clarendon Road
Watford, Herts WD17 1JA
UK
℘01923 205240
travelpubsales@uk.michelin.com
www.ViaMichelin.com

Special Sales For information regarding bulk sales,
customized editions and premium sales,
please contact us at:
travel.lifestyle@us.michelin.com
www.michelintravel.com

Note to the reader Addresses, phone numbers, opening hours and prices
published in this guide are accurate at the time of press. We welcome
corrections and suggestions that may assist us in preparing the next edition.
While every effort is made to ensure that all information printed in this guide
is correct and up-to-date, Michelin Travel Partner accepts no liability for any
direct, indirect or consequential losses howsoever caused so far as such can
be excluded by law.

HOW TO USE THIS GUIDE

PLANNING YOUR TRIP
The blue-tabbed PLANNING YOUR TRIP section gives you **ideas for your trip** and **practical information** to help you organize it. You'll find tours, practical information, a host of outdoor activities, a calendar of events, information on shopping, sightseeing, kids' activities and more.

INTRODUCTION
The orange-tabbed INTRODUCTION section explores **Washington, DC Today** and its **History**, spanning the Colonial Period and the growth of the capital up to the present. The city's **Architecture** is summarized by century. The **Cultural Scene** focuses on DC's museums, modern sculpture and performing arts.

DISCOVERING
The green-tabbed DISCOVERING section features Principal Sights by area, describing the most interesting local **Sights**, **Walking Tours** and nearby **Excursions**. Admission prices shown are normally for a single adult.

ADDRESSES
We've selected the best hotels, restaurants, cafes, shops, nightlife and entertainment to fit all budgets. See the Legend on the cover flap for an explanation of the price categories. See Your Stay in Washington, DC for a list of hotels and restaurants.

Sidebars
Throughout the guide you will find blue, orange and green-colored text boxes with lively anecdotes, detailed history and background information.

😊 A Bit of Advice 😊
Green advice boxes found in this guide contain practical tips and handy information relevant to your visit or a sight in the Discovering section.

STAR RATINGS★★★
Michelin has given star ratings for more than 100 years. If you're pressed for time, we recommend you visit the ★★★ or ★★ sights first:

★★★	**Highly recommended**
★★	**Recommended**
★	**Interesting**

MAPS
⊚ Principal Sights map.
⊚ Two- and Four-days itinerary map.
⊚ Plans of Museums and Monuments.
⊚ Excursions map.

All maps in this guide are oriented north, unless otherwise indicated by a directional arrow. The term "Local Map" refers to a map within the chapter or Tourism Region. A complete list of the maps found in the guide appears at the back of this book.

PLANNING YOUR TRIP

©G. Cannon/Michelin

INTRODUCTION TO WASHINGTON, DC

DISCOVERING WASHINGTON, DC

CONTENTS

YOUR STAY IN WASHINGTON, DC

Welcome to Washington, DC

Washington's gleaming marble monuments, priceless museum collections and grand government buildings lure millions of visitors to the capital city each year who in turn fall in love with its stately charm. This guide will help you navigate DC's seemingly endless collection of historic sights as well as cast light on the city's off-the-beaten path gems waiting to be explored.

CAPITOL HILL (pp68-85)

Capitol Hill's most famous landmark gives the neighborhood its name and much of its charm. Many Hill staffers, lobbyists and others connected to the government live in the historic 19C row houses found here. Capitol Hill is also home to the Library of Congress, the Supreme Court and Union Station.

THE MALL (pp86-143)

Many of Washington's most recognizable sites line the National Mall including the vast majority of the world famous Smithsonian museums and many governmental institutions.

At the western end Washington's iconic memorials, stately and imposing, top the city's must see list. The nation's most recognizable memorials welcome the public free of charge.

The Mall also serves as the staging ground for a range of events, protests and celebrations.

WHITE HOUSE AREA (pp144-159)

The large white mansion at 1600 Pennsylvania Avenue, NW, stands as the city's most famous residence housing the first family and the presidential offices. A pedestrian walkway in front of the White House allows visitors to snap photos and admire the facade. Nearby is the massive Eisenhower Executive Office Building (formerly known as the Old Executive Office Building) and the Corcoran Gallery of Art.

DOWNTOWN (pp160-175)

Washington's downtown area comes alive during the workday abuzz with lobbyists, lawyers and other professionals who fill its abundance of office buildings. Many of the town's associations and not-for-profit groups have their headquarters and administrative offices here. Downtown is also home to a variety of restaurants, hotels and shops.

FOGGY BOTTOM (pp176-183)

The Foggy Bottom area is nestled along the tree-lined banks of the Potomac River. It is at once a residential, business and a college neighborhood housing George Washington University, the Kennedy Center, the Department of State and a collection of row houses and apartment buildings, with the infamous Watergate complex among them.

GEORGETOWN (pp184-193)

Tony Georgetown with its upscale restaurants, boutiques and town homes has long been the "see and be seen" DC neighborhood. Shoppers fill the streets here during the day, and at night the bars, clubs and fine dining establishments are the big draw. The picturesque streets here are home to prestigious Georgetown University, estate museums and gardens.

ARLINGTON ACROSS THE RIVER *(pp194-201)*

Although the famous sights that sit on the other side of the Potomac are not technically part of DC, they still are very much part of the Washington experience. The Marine Corps War Memorial (better known as the Iwo Jima Memorial), Arlington National Cemetery and the Pentagon are all found here.

DUPONT CIRCLE *(pp202-209)*

The hip and trendy gravitate toward DC's Dupont Circle neighborhood and its mix of popular clubs, bars, coffee shops and stores. Its side streets are lined with historic townhouses, many of which have been converted into apartments. Several smaller but noteworthy museums and galleries can also be found in Dupont Circle.

EMBASSY ROW *(pp210-215)*

Just about every country on the map operates an embassy or consulate in DC. The highest concentration of these regal residences—and many of the most impressive ones architecturally—line the pretty, tree-shaded part of town known as Embassy Row. A stroll down this famous street helps provide a sense of the city's global and political significance.

THE ANACOSTIA RIVERFRONT *(pp216-220)*

Anacostia began as one of DC's first suburbs in the mid 1800s before eventually becoming part of the city itself. In 2000 the riverfront section of the Southwest Washington neighborhood became the focus of a development project aimed at revitalizing the waterfront.

Smithsonian Institution Building–The Castle

©Gwen Cannon/Michelin

The area is now home to the city's new baseball stadium, the Smithsonian's Anacostia Community Museum and the Frederick Douglass National Historic Site.

ADDITIONAL SIGHTS IN WASHINGTON, DC *(pp221-235)*

Although the sights most readily associated with Washington, DC tend to be downtown or on the Mall, the city also boasts numerous world-class museums, galleries, parks, gardens, architectural treasures and historical sights away from the typical tourist trail.

EXCURSIONS *(pp236-257)*

The Washington experience is hardly limited to what can be found within the city limits. Cross the border to find many significant historical destinations worth exploring like Mount Vernon, Gunston Hall and the Woodlawn estate. These historic sites give visitors an opportunity to glimpse into the past. Often a couple of the these attractions can be visited as part of a one-day excursion.

Towpath along the C & O Canal in Georgetown
© World Pictures/Photoshot

When and Where to Go

WHEN TO GO
CLIMATE

Generally speaking, there isn't a bad time of year to come and explore Washington DC, and visit its famed sights. The capital city enjoys a mild climate pretty much year-round. Along with Maryland and Virginia, the city falls into the **humid subtropical** climatic zone that defines the lower half of the eastern US. In summer, DC is subject to high humidity and temperatures of at least 75ºF (24ºC). The average high in July in DC is 88ºF (31ºC), while the average low is 70ºF (21ºC). Precipitation is typically highest in summer (July averages 3.9in/10cm) when afternoon thunderstorms are common. The winter months, especially January and February, can witness ups and downs in terms of temperatures. January's average high is 43ºF (6ºC), and the average low is 28ºF (-2ºC). The District, on the whole, experiences little snowfall compared to its more northern neighbors but the occasional blizzards are not unheard of here. But be warned: When it does snow, even a modest storm can bring the capital to a virtual standstill closing offices, attractions, and, if the weather is severe enough, the federal government. **Spring** is Washington's **peak tourist season**. The mild temperatures and the blossoming of the famous cherry trees *(late Mar–early Apr)* attract the greater part of the capital's 15 million annual visitors. Hotel reservations should be made well in advance, and long lines are to be expected. The hot and humid **summer** weather can make touring uncomfortable but the season's long days, extended operating hours for some sights and numerous outdoor events are a major draw. **Fall** is a pleasant season to visit DC. Temperatures are moderate, the crowds have thinned out and the display of autumn foliage is often spectacular. **Winter** months are unpredictable, with temperatures ranging from the high 40s Fahrenheit (up to 9ºC) to well below freezing. Despite the cold, every four years on 20 January crowds gather in front of the US Capitol to watch the president take the oath of office. If you want to come to watch this historic moment, make hotel and other travel-related reservations well in advance.

WEATHER FORECASTS

The website of *The Washington Post* newspaper *(www.washingtonpost.com)* shows (under Local) the current weather and the six-day outlook for the capital. The Weather Channel *(www.weather.com)* gives current conditions and other forecasts.

WHAT TO PACK

Pack as little as possible. But always take an umbrella or hooded jacket in case of rain and for touring inside air-conditioned buildings. Sunglasses, a hat and sunscreen are also recommended for the warmer months. A sweater or light jacket is useful for evenings. Some dressier clothes are suggested for evening activities. Take a tote bag for a picnic lunch or as an extra carry-on to hold your souvenirs. (Most stores in DC charge 5 cents for plastic bags.) A pair of comfortable walking shoes will also be needed.

WHERE TO GO
PLANNING TIPS

The fast-paced itineraries below and shown on the map on pages 13-15 are designed for visitors pressed for time. It is best to reserve popular tours in advance *(see Reservations for Sights)*. Purchasing advance tickets for the Holocaust and Spy museums is advised. **Shuttle buses** – Partial travel by **Old Town Trolley** tour bus is incorporated into the second day. Grayline's **Big Bus Tours** also serve many of the sights below.

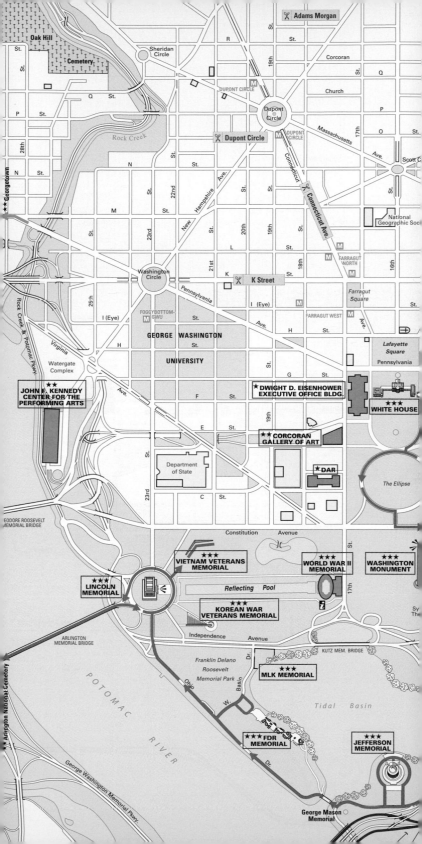

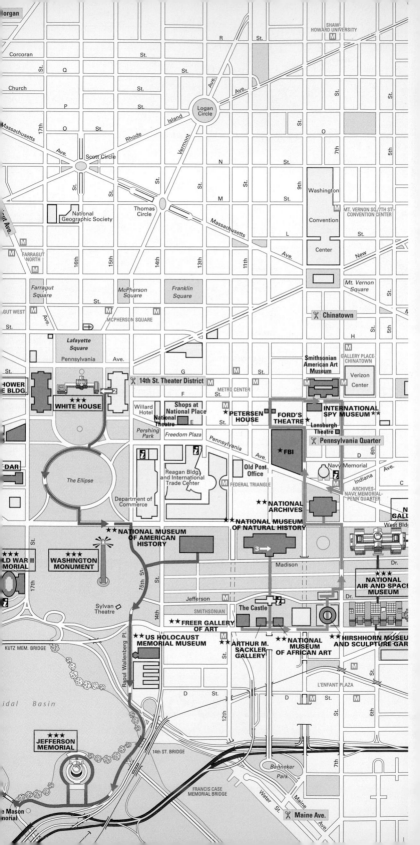

TWO-DAY ITINERARY

FIRST DAY - Itinerary in red ➡
Morning The Capitol★★★
  Library of Congress★★
Lunch Supreme Court★★
  Supreme Court★★ or National
  Air and Space Museum★★★
Afternoon National Air and
  Space Museum★★★
  National Gallery of Art★★★
Evening John F. Kennedy Center★★

SECOND DAY - Itinerary in purple
(partially with Old Town Trolley) ➡
Morning White House★★★
  National Museum of American
  History
Lunch National Museum of
  American History★★★ National
  Air and Space Museum★★★
Afternoon US Holocaust Memorial
  Museum★★
  Jefferson Memorial★★★
  MLK Memorial★★★
  FDR Memorial★★★
  Lincoln Memorial★★★
  Vietnam Veterans Memorial★★★
  Arlington National Cemetery★★
Evening City lights. Tour by car the
  illuminated sights shown on
  the map.

FOUR-DAY ITINERARY

*(For the first two days, follow the
itinerary described opposite.)*

THIRD DAY - Itinerary in green ➡
Morning National Museum of Natural
  History★★
  Arthur M. Sackler Gallery★★ or
  Freer Gallery of Art★★
  National Museum of African
  Art★★ or Hirshhorn Museum and
  Sculpture Garden★★
Lunch On the Mall
Afternoon National Archives★★
  ★ Ford's Theatre and Petersen
  House★ International Spy
  Museum★★ (return to
  Pennsylvania Ave. and take bus 31,
  32, or 36 to Georgetown)
Late Afternoon/Evening Tour
  and dinner in Georgetown

FOURTH DAY
(👣See Excursion Map p238)
Morning Mount Vernon★★★,
  Woodlawn★
Lunch Mount Vernon★★★
Afternoon/Evening Gunston Hall★★
  Alexandria Walking Tour of Old
  Town★★ and dinner in Alexandria

What to See and Do

SIGHTSEEING
GENERAL INFORMATION

Free publications such as *Where
Washington* and the *Washington Flyer*
magazine (the latter available at
local airports) offering information
on events, attractions, shopping and
dining can be found at hotels and
visitor information kiosks. Contact
Destination DC , 901 7th St. NW,
Fourth Floor, Washington, DC 20001
(✆202-789-7000; http://washington.
org) to obtain a free *Official Visitors
Guide*, or visit the **Washington, DC
Visitor Information Center** in the
DC Chamber of Commerce office, 506

9th St. NW (✆866-324-7386; www.
dcchamber.org). The **Smithsonian
Information Center** is located at
1000 Jefferson Dr. SW in the Castle
(open year-round daily 8:30am–5:30pm;
closed Dec 25; ✆202-633-1000; www.
si.edu). This state-of-the-art visitor
center (complete with interactive
touch screens and electronic wall
maps) is the place to plan your
visit to the world's largest museum
complex and research organization.
The **White House Visitor Center** on
Pennsylvania Ave. between 14th and
15th Sts. provides information about
the White House and displays exhibits
about the famous first residence.
Tours are free but limited and must be
arranged in advance. Call ✆ 202-456-
7041 for current tour information and

scheduling procedures (⏰*open year-round daily 7:30am–4pm; closed Jan 1, Thanksgiving Day, Dec 25; ✆202-208-1631; www.whitehouse.gov).*

The **Capitol Visitor Center** provides information, maps and exhibits *(entrance at First St. and E. Capitol St.; open year-round Mon–Sat 8:30am–4:30pm; closed Jan 1 & 20, Thanksgiving Day, Dec 25; ✆202-226-8000; www.visitthecapitol.gov).*

For visitors with limited time, we recommend following the two- or four-day itineraries on p16. Addresses, opening hours, admission charges and other information designed to help you organize your visit are included with each of the sight descriptions in this guide. A variety of guided tours (sightseeing buses, walking tours, cruises and special tours) are available to the visitor. For principal tours, see Sightseeing Tours and Cruises.

⚠**Be aware:** *Security is tight at many tourist sights. Many attractions require visitors to pass through metal detectors and have their bags searched prior to admission. Some high-profile sites also limit which personal items may be carried inside. Check websites for the most current restrictions.*

RESERVATIONS FOR SIGHTS

It is wise to make reservations in advance for guided tours of certain popular Washington sights. Due to increased security in the capital city, several sights, like the White House, Congress, the Pentagon and the Washington Navy Yard, require advance reservations and strictly limit personal items that can be carried into the buildings. Consult the admission information that accompanies the sight descriptions in this guide for details on the attractions you intend to visit and check web sites for up-to-date security restrictions and guidelines.

Tickets for **congressional visits** (special tours of some of the more popular sights, such as the White House, Capitol, and the Bureau of Engraving and Printing) may be

obtained by writing to your senators or representative *(below)*. Tours of the Capitol building can also be reserved in advance online (http://tours.visitthecapitol.gov). Additionally, each member of Congress is allotted a limited number of tickets, which can be requested up to six months in advance in most cases.

VISITING YOUR SENATORS OR REPRESENTATIVES

If you would like to meet the elected officials who represent you in Congress, you should write several months prior to your trip to request an appointment. Call the Capitol (✆202-226-8000) or write:

- ◆ **US Senate**
  Washington, DC 20510
- ◆ **US House**
  Washington, DC 20515

SIGHTSEEING TOURS

ANC Tours – *✆202-488-1012; www.anctours.com.* This company takes visitors to several monuments on **the Mall** as well as through Arlington National Cemetery. ANC offers **express shuttle-bus service** from Union Station to the World War II Memorial, Lincoln Memorial, Arlington National Cemetery, Martin Luther King, Jr. Memorial and the Smithsonian Metro Station and back daily 9am–6:30pm (Oct–Feb based on demand). Tickets *($5 per boarding)* can be purchased at Union Station *(on the bus level of the parking garage)* and online at www.graylinedc.com.

Tours within **Arlington National Cemetery** leave from the cemetery's visitor center daily 8:30am–6:30pm (Oct–Mar til 4:30pm). Last tour departs 30min before the cemetery closes. Tours include the Kennedy gravesites, the Tomb of the Unknowns and Arlington House. Buy tickets on-site from the visitor center: $8.75, children $4.50 (ages 3-11).

Big Bus Tours – *✆877-332-8689; www.opentopsightseeing.com.* Grayline operates open-top buses for hop-on, hop-off tours of major DC sights *(daily every 20min)* 9am–6pm, 5pm Oct–Mar; *$25-$35, children $15-$20, depending upon route)*. Evening 3hr tour $25 *(children $15; reservations required; ℘202-408-4717)*. Purchase tickets onboard, at Union Station, Ford's Theatre, Mall kiosks or online.

Old Town Trolley – *℘202-832-9800, 888-910-8687; www.trolleytours.com*. Tours of DC run daily 9am–5:30pm (except Marine Corps Marathon day, Thanksgiving Day, Sun before Memorial Day, Jul 4 and Dec 25). Visitors can board the orange and green trolleys every 30min at several locations around town. The complete itinerary lasts 3hrs and the same ticket *($39 or $35.10 online)* allows free reboarding the entire day. The Moonlight Night Tour (2hrs; ℘202-438-1433) departs Union Station at 7:30pm *($39 or $35.10 online)*.

Bike and Roll Washington DC – Day and evening guided tours around the National Mall and historic old town Alexandria are offered Mar–Dec. Also night tours of the monuments and capital sights as well as a self-guided bike tour of Mt. Vernon are also offered; dates vary. Bicycles, helmets, water and a snack are included in the cost of the tour *(call or check website for tour availability; $35–$89; ℘202-842-2453; www.bikethesites.com)*.

Spy City Tours – Sponsored by the International Spy Museum and Grayline, these 2.5hr tours visit more than 25 of downtown Washington's notable and notorious espionage sites and include an interactive "mission" for each participant. The tour is held Fridays at 10am. Ticket includes same-day admission to the International Spy Museum *($58.95; ℘800-472-9546; www.grayline.com)*.

City Segway Tours – Step on a segway for the opportunity to roll through the city on a variety of guided tours, including a 3hr National Mall Segway Tour and a 2hr Segway Experience Tour *(call for times; $65-$75; ℘202-626-0017, 877-734-8687; http://citysegwaytours.com/washington-dc)*. The company will also arrange private tours upon request.

SIGHTSEEING CRUISES
Departing from DC
Tours along the Potomac River offer views of the capital city by day and by night, when many sights are illuminated. Some companies offer dinner/dance cruises in addition to lunch and party tours. All cruises are round-trip. Below are the principal boat cruises operating on the river. **DC Ducks** takes occupants in amphibious open-air "boats" on a 90-minute land and sea tour of major sights, followed by a cruise

Tour the city on a segway

©Gwen Cannon/Michelin

on the Potomac *(departs from Union Station Mar–Nov daily 10am–4pm on the hour; $39, or $35.10 online; 202-832-9800, 855-323-8257; www.dcducks.com); no tours on the Sunday of Memorial Day, Jul 4 and Marine Corps. Marathon day.* **Spirit Cruises** offers lunch, dinner and party cruises in addition to seasonal cherry blossom sightseeing cruises and midnight cruises. *(depart from Pier 4, 6th & Water Sts. SW; year-round daily 6:30pm; 3hrs; $44–$111).* The *Spirit of Mount Vernon* cruises to **Mount Vernon** *(departs from Pier 4, Mar–Oct, days vary 8am; $43 and up. Several cruises also depart from National Harbor, Maryland, at the Pier & Terminal; 866-835-8851; www.cruisetomountvernon.com). Reservations recommended for all cruises (866-302-2469; www.spiritofwashington.com).*
Odyssey offers year-round dinner cruises to Georgetown aboard the glass-atrium yacht *Odyssey III (departs from 600 Water St. SW; check for current departure times; 3hrs; coat and tie recommended; board 1hr before departure time; $52-$114).* Lunch and brunch cruises are also available. Reservations required for all cruises (866-306-2469; www.odysseycruises.com).

Departing from Alexandria
 see Excursions map. **Dandy Restaurant Cruises** offers lunch, brunch and dinner cruises that leave from Alexandria, sail past the monuments, cruise over to Georgetown and then return to Old Town *(depart from Prince St. and the National Harbor year-round; call for times and dates; $47-$98).* Reservations are required. Dinner jackets for men are recommended but not required for evening cruises, and "dressy casual" attire is recommended for other excursions. (703-683-6076; www.dandydinnerboat.com). The **Potomac Riverboat Co.** features a variety of narrated sightseeing cruises, including a Washington monuments tour, Mount Vernon cruise, Alexandria seaport cruise, pirates cruise, and sailing aboard the Skipjack *Minnie V. (depart from City Marina, Cameron and Union Streets year-round but days vary by season; 40min; $12-$40; phone for departure times: 703 684-0580; www.potomacriverboatco.com).*

WALKING TOURS

Cultural Walking Tours – This non-profit organization offers an array of guided walking tours sponsored by the many local cultural groups who belong to this umbrella organization. Offerings include a "DC in Black" African American History Tour, an Anecdotal History Tour, and a Civil War Sites Tour. *(202-661-7581; www.culturaltourismdc.org).*
Washington Walks – Licensed guides walk you through the DC area while sharing anecdotes and local lore. The company's popular ghost tour explores famous sites in town said to be haunted by the spirits of DC past. Other offerings include neighborhood walking tours and a Christmas tour during the holiday season. Regularly scheduled tours are available throughout the week and private tours may be available by advance request. *(Call for tour times and departure locations; $15; 202-484-1565; www.washingtonwalks.com).*

OUTDOOR FUN

The District's two main recreational areas are the National Mall and Rock Creek Park, both in the northwest quadrant and administered by the National Park Service. The **Mall**, with its sprawling lawns and planted gardens is well suited to jogging, biking, picnicking, paddleboating and a variety of sports (tennis, baseball, softball, football, volleyball, soccer and polo). Covering some 2,100 acres along scenic Rock Creek, the rugged terrain of **Rock Creek Park** is crossed by a network of paved roads, trails, and bicycle and bridle paths. Facilities include picnic areas, playgrounds, tennis courts, a golf course and stables.

BIKING

There are many bike routes in and around Washington. Parts of **Potomac Park** are designated for cyclists. The picturesque **Chesapeake and Ohio Canal towpath,** which meanders 184mi from Georgetown to Cumberland, Maryland, is very popular with cyclists and hikers. Extending 17mi from the Arlington Bridge to George Washington's estate in Virginia, the **Mount Vernon Trail** borders the western shore of the Potomac River alongside the George Washington Memorial Parkway.

Bike Rentals

Bike shops and boating centers offering bike rentals and trail information include:

- **Big Wheel Bikes**
  road, hybrid, mountain, tandem
  1034 33rd St. NW
  ℘202-337-0254
  www.bigwheelbikes.com
- **Bike and Roll Washington DC**
  Trek comfort hybrids, performance, road, tandem, cruisers, kids bikes, attachments
  1100 Pennsylvania Ave. NW (also at Union Station and Alexandria)
  ℘202-842-2453
  www.bikethesites.com
- **Capital Bike Share**
  Rent a bike at any one of 140 stations across DC and Arlington and return it at any station.
  ℘877-430-2453
  www.capitalbikeshare.com
- **Fletcher's Boat House**
  landcruisers
  4940 Canal Rd. NW
  ℘202-244-0461
  www.fletchersboathouse.com
- **Thompson's Boat Center**
  landcruisers
  Rock Creek Parkway & Virginia Ave.
  ℘202-333-9543
  www.thompsonboatcenter.com
- **Washington Sailing Marina**
  landcruisers
  One Marina Dr., Alexandria, VA
  ℘703-548-9027.
  www.washingtonsailing marina.com

Cycling Events

For information concerning cycling events and bike routes, contact:

- **National Park Service**
  (bike-route maps)
  www.nps.gov
- **District Dept of Transportation**
  ℘202-673-6813
  http://ddot.dc.gov
- **Potomac Pedalers Touring Club**
  ℘703-241-9113
  www.bikepptc.org
- **Washington Area Bicyclist Assn**
  ℘202-518-0524
  www.waba.org

Bike and Roll Washington DC bike tours

Snow Photography

- **Maryland National Capital Parks & Planning Commission**
  ℘301-699-2255
  www.mncppc.org
- **Alexandria Department of Recreation & Parks**
  ℘703-838-4343
  http://alexandriava.gov/recreation
- **Arlington County Department of Parks & Recreation**
  ℘703-228-7529
  www.co.arlington.va.us

BOATING

For sightseeing and dining cruises on the **Potomac** *⌕ see Sightseeing Cruises, above.* Because of its location on the Potomac River and its proximity to the Chesapeake Bay, Washington offers a range of activities for boating enthusiasts. Renting a paddleboat on the Tidal Basin is a classic DC activity and a favorite with children. Boats can be rented by the hour from Tidal Basin Paddleboats *(photo ID required; 1501 Maine Ave. SW; ℘202-479-2426; www.tidalbasinpaddleboats.com).* Canoes and rowboats can be rented from **Fletcher's Boat House** or **Thompson's Boat Center** *(⌕ see Bike Rentals above).* Sailboats can be rented from **Washington Sailing Marina** *(Alexandria, VA ℘703-548-9027; www.washingtonsailingmarina.com).*
For information on sailing and boating events on Chesapeake Bay, contact the **Chesapeake Bay Yacht Racing Assn**, 612 Third St., Suite 401, Annapolis MD 21403; ℘410-990-9393; www.cbyra.org.

Marinas
(docking facilities only – no rentals)
- **Buzzard Point Boat Marina**
  Half & V Sts. SW
  ℘202-488-8400
- **Capital Yacht Club**
  1000 Water St. SW
  ℘202-488-8110
  www.capitalyachtclub.net

- **Washington Marina**
  1300 Maine Ave. SW
  ℘202-554-0222
  www.washingtonmarina.com

GOLF

The following public golf courses are maintained by the **National Park Service** *(www.nps.gov);* all of them rent clubs and other equipment.

Public and Private Courses
There are more than 100 public golf courses in DC, Virginia and Maryland.
- **East Potomac Park (par 65)**
  972 Ohio Dr. SW ℘202-554-7660
- **Langston Park (par 72)**
  26th St. & Benning Rd. NE
  ℘202-397-8638
- **Rock Creek Park (par 71)**
  16th & Rittenhouse Sts. NW
  ℘202-882-7332
In addition, numerous country-club courses in the District welcome only members or guests of members to play, including the well-known **Congressional Country Club** in Bethesda, MD (par 72 and 70, 8500 River Road; ℘301-469-2000; www.ccclub.org).

Golf DC
Golf DC provides information on three public courses maintained by the National Park Service, as well as news and information about events, workshops and promotions. Go online to www.golfdc.com.

HIKING

Rock Creek Park offers year-round hikes and nature walks guided by US park rangers. Favorite walks within the District include a 5mi loop around Hains Point and the Tidal Basin, especially when the famous Japanese cherry trees are in bloom in early April. For information: ℘202-895-6070.
Theodore Roosevelt Island, located off the banks of Foggy Bottom, has 2.5mi of footpaths through woods, swamp and marshland with a variety of native plants and animals. A footbridge on the Virginia side is the

only way to access the islands. Free parking is available. For information: ℰ703-289-2500; www.nps.gov/this. For a hike outside city limits, take the Chesapeake and Ohio Canal towpath to Old Anglers Inn (12.5mi), Great Falls Park (14mi), or Violettes Lock (22mi). Hikers to Glen Echo Park (7mi) have the option of returning to Washington by Metrobus. The trail system provides scenic but sometimes rugged hiking terrain. Maps and books about the canal are sold at some visitor centers along the trail. For further information, call the **C&O Canal National Historical Park** (*ℰ301-739-4200*). The Mount Vernon Trail is also designed for bikers. *For more information on hiking in the metropolitan area:*

- **National Park Service**
  Access each park online for routes and specific information.
  www.nps.gov
- **Sierra Club**
  ℰ202-548-4581
  www.sierraclub.org
- **Maryland National Capital Parks & Planning Commission**
  ℰ301-454-1740
  www.mncppc.org

HORSEBACK RIDING

There are many stables in and near the city that provide mounts and riding instruction. Rock Creek Park has miles of designated bridle paths. **Rock Creek Park Horse Center**, managed by the National Park Service, offers trail rides, lessons and boarding year-round (*ℰ202-362-0117; www.rockcreekhorsecenter.com*). Full riding and horse-care facilities are offered by **Meadowbrook Stables**, 8200 Meadowbrook Lane, Chevy Chase MD; ℰ301-589-9026; www. meadowbrookstables.com. The city's main equestrian event is the Washington International Horse Show held yearly at the end of October at the Verizon Center; *ℰ202-525-3679; www.wihs.org).*

ICE-SKATING

The two major outdoor skating rinks in DC *(skates are available to rent)* are:

- **National Gallery of Art Sculpture Garden and Ice Rink**
  On the Mall at 7th St and Constitution Ave. NW
  ℰ(202) 216-9397
  www.nga.gov/skating
- **Pershing Park Ice Rink**
  Pennsylvania Ave. and 14th St. NW
  ℰ202-737-6938
  www.pershingparkicerink.com

SWIMMING

Hotel pools typically are reserved for guests only. Some private clubs with pools offer short-term memberships. The DC Department of Recreation operates several outdoor pools in the summer *(mid-Jun–Labor Day)*. For locations and hours, call the DC Department of Recreation (*ℰ202-673-7647; www.dpr.dc.gov).*

TENNIS

About 150 public courts are available on a first-come, first-served basis at no charge. For information, contact the DC Department of Recreation *(open year-round Mon–Fri 8:30am–6:30pm ℰ202-673-7647; www.dpr.dc.gov).* The National Park Service maintains the following courts:

- **East Potomac Tennis Center**
  (indoor and outdoor courts)
  Hains Point. SW, ℰ202-554-5962
  www.eastpotomactennis.com
- **Rock Creek Park Tennis Center**
  (outdoor) 16th & Kennedy Sts. NW
  ℰ202-722-5949
  www.rockcreektennis.com
- **Montrose Park court** *(outdoor)*
  R St. between 30th and 31st Sts. NW, Georgetown

ACTIVITIES FOR KIDS

Throughout this guide, sights of particular interest to children are indicated with a symbol. Many museums and other attractions offer special family programs. Most attractions in Washington offer discounted admission to visitors younger than 18. Many hotels also offer family discount packages, and some restaurants provide children's menus. 🍂 *See sidebar on page 27.*

BOOKS
REFERENCE

Above Washington, Robert Cameron (1989). Historical and architectural descriptions of DC's landmarks.

Washington DC: Then and Now. Alexander D. Mitchell IV (1999). A collection of black-and-white photographs of the capital city, some dating to the mid-19C.

AIA Guide to the Architecture of Washington, D.C. G. Martin Moeller Jr. (2006). Historical and architectural descriptions of DC's many landmarks.

BIOGRAPHY

Grand Avenues: The Story of Pierre Charles L'Enfant. Scott W. Berg. (2008). The story of the Frenchman who designed DC.

George Washington Carver. John Perry (2011). The chronicle of the former slave who dedicated his life to teaching poor black students.

Narrative of the Life of Frederick Douglass. Frederick Douglass. (1845; reprinted 2004). The autobiography of America's famous orator and abolitionist, a former slave himself.

Personal History. Katharine Graham. (1998). The author's memoirs detailing her stint as head of the *Washington Post.*

FICTION

Clear and Present Danger. Tom Clancy. (1989). The presidency, politics, drugs and covert CIA operations steer this thriller.

Kill Alex Cross. James Patterson (2011). Detective Alex Cross must solve the kidnapping of the President.

Murder at the Watergate. Margaret Truman. (1999). One of President Truman's daughter's many Capital Crimes Mysteries.

FOR CHILDREN

Underground Train. Mary Quattlebaum. (1999). A rhythmic ride aboard DC's Metro.

Good Night Washington, DC. Adam Gamble. (2006). One in a series of stories, surveying the attractions of each destination.

We're There! Washington, DC. Elizabeth Skinner Grumbach. (2005). A fun, interactive, guide to the city's major sights.

The People in Pineapple Place. Anne Lindbergh Roy. (2003). A boy adjusts to his new home in DC with the help of invisible friends who live in Pineapple Place.

The Capital Mysteries series. Ron Roy. (2001-present). Whodunits for elementary school readers, based on DC lore and backdropped by the city's famous sights.

FILMS

Mr. Smith Goes to Washington (1939). Frank Capra's film starring Jimmy Stewart defending his ideals amid DC's corrupt politicians.

All the President's Men (1976). Dustin Hoffman and Robert Redford star as *Washington Post* reporters who uncover the Watergate break-in.

First Monday in October (1981). The first appointment of a woman to the US Supreme Court sparks a liberal vs. conservative standoff.

In the Line of Fire (1993). Clint Eastwood is an aging Secret Service presidential bodyguard.

The American President (1995). A widowed president falls in love in this romantic comedy.

Legally Blond 2 (2003). Postgrad learns DC's workings in an attempt to legislate a bill.

Breach (2007). True story of CIA agent Robert Hanssen's betrayal of his country.

State of Play (2009). Political thriller in which journalist Russell Crowe investigates the suspicious death of congressman Ben Affleck's mistress.

Calendar of Events

Below is a selection of DC's popular annual events. Some dates may vary from year to year; consult the quarterly Calendar of Events available from Destination DC (☏202-789-7000; http://washington.org). See Alexandria for its events. Unless otherwise specified, the area code for all phone numbers is 202.

SPRING

MID MAR

National Capital Boat Show— Dulles Expo Center, Chantilly VA ☏(800) 441-0013. www.gsevents.com

St. Patrick's Day Parade — Constitution Ave. NW. ☏670-0317. www.dcstpatsparade.com

Washington Home and Garden Show — Washington Convention Center. ☏(703) 823-7960. www.washingtonhomeand gardenshow.com

LATE MAR–APR

National Cherry Blossom Festival — Tidal Basin. ☏(877) 442-5666. www.national cherryblossomfestival.org

Parade, National Cherry Blossom Fesitval

Easter Sun

Easter Sunrise Service — Arlington National Cemetery. ☏(703) 607-8000. www.arlingtoncemetery.org

Easter Mon

Easter Egg Roll and Egg Hunt — White House. ☏456-7041. www.whitehouse.gov

EARLY APR

Spring Garden Tours — White House. ☏456-7041. www.whitehouse.gov

LATE APR

Shakespeare's Birthday — Folger Shakespeare Library. ☏544-4600. www.folger.edu

Georgetown House Tour — Georgetown. ☏338-1796. www.georgetownhousetour.com

EARLY MAY

Flower Mart — Washington National Cathedral. ☏537-3185. www.cathedral.org

MID MAY

Spring Wine Festival — Mt. Vernon, VA. ☏(703) 780-2000. www.mountvernon.org

LATE MAY

Memorial Day Weekend Concert — US Navy Memorial. ☏737-2300. www.navylog.org

MAY–JUN

Twilight Tattoo — (military parade/ show). Washington Monument. ☏685-2888. http://twilight.mdw.army.mil

SUMMER

EARLY JUN

Dance Africa DC — Dance Place. 3225 8th St. NE ☏269-1600. www.danceplace.org

DC Jazz Festival — Citywide ☏457-7628. www.dcjazzfest.org

Courtesy of National Cherry Blossom Festival

Safeway Barbecue Battle

Courtesy of Safeway Barbecue Battle

US Military Concerts

Washington, DC's tradition of live military music continues each summer. Free concerts are held on alternating days from **Memorial Day to Labor Day**, usually at 8pm. For information contact: US Army Band (*☎703-696-3399; www. usarmyband.com*); US Marine Band (*☎202-433-4011; www.marineband. usmc.mil*); US Navy Band (*☎202-433-2525; www.navyband.navy.mil*) and US Air Force Band (*☎202-767-4310; www.usafband.com*).

Dupont-Kalorama Museum Walk — Dupont Circle. ☎347-3168 ext. 137. www.dkmuseums.com

LATE JUN

Safeway Annual Barbecue Battle — Pennsylvania Ave. NW at 9th St. NW. ☎828-3099. www.bbqdc.com

LATE JUN–EARLY JUL

Smithsonian Folklife Festival — Mall. ☎633-6440. www.folklife.si.edu

4 JUL

National Independence Day Parade — Constitution Ave. NW. ☎619-7222. www.july4thparade.com

MID JUL

Capital Fringe Festival — Downtown. ☎737-7230. www.capfringe.org

MID AUG

US Army Band's 1812 Overture Concert — Sylvan Theatre, Mall. ☎(703) 696-3399. www.usarmyband.com

FALL

EARLY SEPT

National Symphony Orchestra Labor Day Concert — Capitol (west lawn). ☎416-8100. www.kennedy-center.org

Adams Morgan Day Festival — Between Columbia Rd. & Florida Ave. NW. ☎232-1960.

National Black Family Reunion — Mall. ☎(301) 390-8408. www. ncnw.org/events/reunion.htm

MID SEPT

Arts on Foot Festival — Downtown, 8th & F Sts. L St. NW. ☎638-3232. www.artsonfoot.org

LATE SEPT

National Book Festival— Mall. ☎(888)-714-4696. www.loc.gov/bookfest

OCT–DEC

US Army Band Fall Concert Series — Brucker Hall, Fort Myer, Arlington. ☎(703) 696-3399. www.usarmyband.com

MID OCT

Fall Garden Tours — White House. ☎208-1631. www.whitehouse.gov

Washington International Horse Show — Verizon Center, Downtown. ☎525-3679. www.wihs.org

LATE OCT
Marine Corps Marathon — Marine
Corps War Memorial, Downtown
DC, and northern VA.
☎800-786-8762.
www.marinemarathon.com

MID NOV
Veterans Day Ceremonies —
Arlington National Cemetery
☎(703) 607-8000.
www.arlingtoncemetery.org
Vietnam Veterans Memorial
☎426-6841. www.nps.gov/vive

WINTER

DEC–1 JAN
**National Christmas Tree Lighting
& Christmas Pageant of Peace** —
The Ellipse. ☎208-1631.
http://thenationaltree.org

EARLY DEC
Wolf Trap Holiday Sing-A-Long —
Filene Center.
☎(703) 255-1900.
www.wolftrap.org
US Army Band Holiday Festival —
DAR Constitution Hall.
☎(703) 696-3399.
www.usarmyband.com

U. S. Capitol
Christmas Tree

© svetlana larina/Fotolia.com

MID DEC
People's Christmas Tree Lighting —
Capitol (west lawn). ☎225-6827.
http://capitolchristmastree.org

24 AND 25 DEC
Christmas Celebration Services —
Washington National Cathedral.
☎537-6200.
www.cathedral.org

LATE DEC
Christmas Candlelight Tours—
White House.
☎456-7041.
www.whitehouse.gov

1ST WEEK JAN
Congress convenes — Capitol.
www.senate.gov
www.house.gov

MID JAN
**Martin Luther King Jr. Birthday
Observance & National Day of
Service** ☎426-6841. www.nps.gov
and www.mlkday.gov

FEB
Date Nights DC —
Citywide promotions for
couples. http://datenightsdc.
washington.org
Chinese New Year Celebration —
Chinatown. ☎342-2580.
www.chineseparadedc.com

12 FEB
**Abraham Lincoln Birthday
Celebration** — Lincoln Memorial.
☎426-6841. ww.nps.gov

MID FEB
**Washington, DC International
Wine & Food Festival** —
International Trade Center.
☎505-4933.
www.wineandfooddc.com

21 FEB
Presidents' Day —
Various locations. ☎(800) 422-
8644. http://washington.org

Washington, DC
FOR KIDS

♔♙ WHERE TO EAT

♦ **Air and Space Museum Shop**   ☎ 202-633-1000
Astronaut Food
On the Mall

♦ **Hard Rock Cafe**   ☎ 202-737-7625
Rockin' hamburgers and ribs.
999 E St. NW; www.hardrock.com

♦ **Mitsitam Cafe**   ☎ 202-633-1000
Buffalo burgers and other Native American food.
National Museum of the American Indian (on the Mall)

♔♙ WHAT TO SEE

♦ **Bureau of Engraving and Printing** – Watch money being made.

♦ **Mount Vernon** – See staff in colonial clothes or visit the baby animals on the farm just like the one that was here in Washington's day.

♦ **National Air and Space Museum** – Gaze at the stars in the Albert Einstein Planetarium and take a ride in a flight simulator.

♦ **National Archives' Charters of Freedom** - See the original copies of the Declaration of Independence, Constitution and the Bill of Rights.

♦ **National Aquarium** – You can get an up-close look at marine life including alligators, eels and frogs at this small aquarium, which is a good size for toddlers.

♦ **National Gallery of Art** – Free art-themed stories followed by a hands-on project every weekend *(ages 4-7)*.

♦ **National Museum of Natural History** – Have you ever seen a tarantula eat?

♦ **National Postal Museum** – Make a postcard and send yourself a message.

♦ **National Zoological Park** – Visit the pandas, learn about a rainforest in Amazonia and check out orangutans crossing overhead on the "O Line."

♦ **US Navy Museum** – Look at the world through a real submarine periscope.

♦ **The Castle** – Explore the Haupt Garden behind the castle.

♦ **The Smithsonian's Discovery Theater** (located in the Ripley Center) – Watch history come alive during performances for school-aged children.

♔♙ PLANNING YOUR TRIP

Children's Concierge – Consultants help you organize your trip from where to stay and where to go. They even provide a Kidspack with age-appropriate supplies to enhance your children's visit. *($120/hr; ☎877-888-5462; www.childrensconcierge.com)*

♔♙ WHAT TO DO

"Goodnight Mr. Lincoln" – Put on your PJs and go to the Lincoln Memorial with your friends. Private parties of up to 20 *($250; reserve ahead)* experience the life of Abraham Lincoln through stories, games and music offered by Children's Concierge *(☎877-8885462; www.childrensconcierge.com)*.

Carousel Ride – Ride an old-fashioned carousel on the Mall *($3.50; 900 Jefferson Dr. SW)*.

Carriages of the Capital – Hire a horse-drawn Cinderella-style carriage or fringed surrey *($175/hr; 6 riders max.; ☎841-7401; www.carriagesofthecapital.com)*.

♔♙ ONLINE INFORMATION

www.nga.gov/kids ♦ www.our-kids.com ♦ http://kids.dc.gov

Know Before You Go

USEFUL WEBSITES

Here are several websites to help you plan your trip or find out information once you get to Washington, DC:

www.thecapitol.net –
A good resource for business professionals visiting the DC area. Includes a legislative glossary.

www.culturaldc.org –
Information on the DC area's art exhibits, cultural events and activities. Festivals and little-known treasures can be found on this online "Insider's Arts Guide."

www.dcchamber.org
The DC's Chamber of Commerce informational site. Business-oriented events and topics.

www.dc.gov – The government of DC's official website, including city services, and resources for visitors.

www.downtowndc.org – What to do and how to get there for Downtown DC, provided by the Business Improvement District.

www.firstgov.gov – All you need to know about the nation's government.

www.washingtonian.com – The magazine's online version, with restaurant and theater reviews, events and more.

http://washington.org – Official visitors' guide for Washington, DC.

www.washingtonpost.com –
Current events from what's in the news to where to see your favorite band in DC.

www.where-events.com–
Where magazine online: dining, entertainment, etc.

www.whitehouse.gov – White House events, history, past and present residents.

www.wmata.com – Official site of Washington Metropolitan Area Transit Authority, including bus and Metro.

www.dccirculator.com – About bus travel within the city's central core.

www.fly2dc.com – *Washington Flyer* magazine online, a free publication.

TOURIST OFFICES
LOCAL

Visitors may contact the following agencies to obtain maps and information on points of interest, accommodations and seasonal events:

- ◆ **Destination DC**
  901 7th St. NW, Fourth Floor Washington, DC 20001.
  ☎202-789-7000.
  http://washington.org

- ◆ **Washington, DC Visitor Information Center**
  DC Chamber of Commerce, 506 9th St. NW, Washington, DC 20054. ☎866-324-7386.
  www.dcchamber.org

- ◆ **Alexandria Convention and Visitors Association**
  221 King St., Suite 300 Alexandria VA 22314.
  ☎703-746-3301.
  http://visitalexandriava.com

- ◆ **Arlington Visitors Center**
  1100 N. Glebe Road, Suite 1500 Arlington VA 22201.
  ☎800-296-7996.
  www.stayarlington.com

OTHER

- ◆ **Annapolis Visitors Bureau**
  Annapolis and Anne Arundel Visitors Bureau
  26 West St. Annapolis, MD 21401.
  ☎410-280-0445
  www.visitannapolis.org

EMBASSIES AND CONSULATES			
Country	Address	✆	Website
Australia	1601 Massachusetts Ave. NW	202-797-3000	www.usa.embassy.gov.au
Britain	3100 Massachusetts Ave. NW	202-588-7800	http://ukinusa.fco.gov.uk/en
Canada	501 Pennsylvania Ave. NW	202-682-1740	www.canadainternational.qc.ca/washington
France	4101 Reservoir Rd. NW	202-944-6000	www.info-france-usa.org
Germany	2300 M St. NW	202-298-4000	www.germany.info
India	2107 Massachusetts Ave. NW	202-939-7000	www.indianembassy.org
Ireland	2234 Massachusetts Ave. NW	202-462-3939	www.embassyofireland.org

INTERNATIONAL VISITORS

For tourist information, visitors from outside the US can contact the US embassy in their country and the organizations listed under Tourist Offices above.

EMBASSIES AND CONSULATES

Since Washington, DC is the nation's capital, all embassies and many consulates are located here. International visitors may contact the consulate or embassy of their country of residence for information. Below are addresses and phone numbers of several. To obtain the phone numbers of others, call the information line for Washington, DC (✆202-555-1212) or go online to www.embassy.org.

ENTRY REQUIREMENTS

Citizens of countries participating in the Visa Waiver Pilot Program (VWPP) are not required to obtain a visa to enter the US for visits of fewer than 90 days. Rules require that residents of visa-waiver countries must apply ahead for travel authorization online through the **ESTA program** *(www. cbp.gov/esta)*. Travelers may apply any time ahead of their travel; at least three days before departure is strongly recommended. Beware private sites charging extravagant fees. Though they look official, these are not affiliated with the US government. Citizens of nonparticipating countries must have a visitor's visa. Upon entry, nonresident foreign visitors must present a valid passport and round-trip transportation ticket. Canadian citizens traveling by air will need a valid passport to enter the US; if entering by land or sea, Canadian citizens must present one of the following documents: a valid passport, enhanced driver's license/enhanced identification card, NEXUS, FAST/EXPRES or SENTRI enrollment card. Inoculations are generally not required, but check with the US embassy or consulate before departing.

HEALTH

The US does not have a national health program that covers foreign nationals. Before departing, visitors from abroad should check their health care insurance to determine if doctors' visits, medication and hospitalization in the US are covered. Prescription drugs should be properly identified, and accompanied by a copy of the prescription. Hotel staff can often make recommendations for doctors and other medical services.

CUSTOMS

All articles brought into the US must be declared at the time of entry. **Exempt** from customs regulations: personal effects; one liter (33.8 fl oz) of alcohol (for visitors at least 21 years old); 200 cigarettes or 100 cigars (for pipe or loose tobacco, contact port of entry directly); and gifts (to persons in the US) that do not exceed $100 in value. **Prohibited items** are plant material, firearms and ammunition (if

Wheelchair access on Metrobus

© WMATA/Larry Levine

not intended for sporting purposes) and meat and poultry. For more information, contact the US embassy or consulate, or the US Department of Homeland Security, 1300 Pennsylvania Ave. NW, Washington, DC 20229 (☎202-282-8000; www.cbp.gov).

DRIVING IN THE US

Visitors with valid driver's licenses issued by their country of residence do not need an International Driver's License. Drivers must always carry vehicle registration, rental contract, and proof of insurance. Most rental car companies require drivers to be at least 25 years old but will sometimes rent to younger drivers for an additional charge. U.S. rental cars typically have automatic transmissions and rental rates tend to be lower than overseas. Gasoline is sold by the gallon (1 gallon = 3.8 liters) and tends to be cheaper than in many other countries. Most service stations sell car maintenance items but do not do repairs. Vehicles are driven on the right side of the road. Distances are posted in miles (1 mi = 1.6 km).

ACCESSIBILITY   ♿

Throughout this guide, wheelchair access is noted on floor plans and in the admission information accompanying sight descriptions with the ♿ symbol. Handicap parking is available at most sites throughout the city. The Smithsonian has many services for disabled visitors. To obtain a copy of Smithsonian Access (large-type edition available), call or write Smithsonian Institution, SI Building, Room 153, Washington, DC 20560 ☎202-633-2921.
The Transit Authority offers **MetroAccess**, a shared-ride, door-to-door paratransit service (☎301-562-5360) as well as reduced fares for disabled Metro and bus riders. For information call ☎202-637-7000, TTY ☎202-633-4353; or go online to www.wmata.com.
Disabled travelers using **Amtrak** and **Greyhound** should call in advance of their trip to make special arrangements.
For information about travel for individuals or groups, contact the Society for Accessible Travel & Hospitality, 347 Fifth Ave., Suite 605, New York NY 10016; ☎212-447-7284; www.sath.org.

SENIOR CITIZENS

Most attractions, hotels and theaters offer discounts to visitors age 62 and older. Photo ID may be required. Discounts on other travel-related items may be available to members of AARP, 601 E St. NW, Washington, DC 20049; ☎202-434-3525 or 888-687-2277; www.aarp.org.

Getting There

BY PLANE

Washington is served by three major airports.

RONALD REAGAN WASHINGTON NATIONAL AIRPORT (DCA)

℘703-417-8000 (information), ℘703-417-8600 (corporate offices). www.metwashairports.com. 4.5mi south of downtown DC, across the Potomac in Virginia. Domestic and commuter flights arrive at and depart from National. **Traveler's Aid Booths** *(open Mon–Fri 9am–9pm, weekends 9am–6pm)* are located near baggage claim. **Smoking** is prohibited except in designated outdoor areas.
Sit-down **restaurants** are located in all terminals.
Free shuttle buses operate *(daily 6am–1am)* to and from all terminals, the satellite parking lots, garages, and the Metro station. Most **public transportation** departs from the curbside in front of each terminal.

Taxis

Taxis are available at the exits of Terminal A and the baggage-claim levels of Terminals B and C. Passengers are required to wait in line and take the dispatched cab. Taxi service to downtown takes about 15min and costs about $20, plus an airport fee of $2.50.

Fares are increased by 25 percent when the city declares a snow emergency.

Shuttles

For transport to residences, businesses and hotels throughout the greater DC area, **SuperShuttle** provides shared-ride, door-to-door service year-round 24hrs daily *(℘800-258-3826; www. supershuttle.com).* Telephones for hotel courtesy shuttles are located on the baggage-claim levels.

Rental Cars

Rental car company counters are located on the lower level of Parking Garage A opposite Terminal A *(free shuttle buses stop at the garage).* At the airport, a sales tax of 10 percent plus an airport fee of $2.50 per day are added to the rental rate.

Public Transportation

The airport is served by the Blue and Yellow **Metrorail** lines. The Metro station is adjacent to Terminals B & C. Buses serve areas Metrorail does not. The **Metrobus** stop is located at the base of the station *(℘202-637-7000; www.wmata.com).*

DULLES INTERNATIONAL AIRPORT (IAD)

℘703-572-2700. www.metwash airports.com. 26mi west of downtown DC, in Loudoun County, VA.

Departure Hall, Ronald Reagan Washington National Airport

© Brigitta L. House/Michelin

International flights and domestic flights arrive at and depart from Dulles. A **Traveler's Aid Booth** *(open Mon–Fri 8am–9pm, weekends 8am–7pm)* is located on the lower level of the Main Terminal. Smoking is prohibited except in **smoking rooms** located in each of the concourses *(open 24hrs daily)*. Sit-down **restaurants** are located on the upper level of the Main Terminal and in the concourses. **Public transportation** departs from the lower level of the Main Terminal.

Taxis

Taxis are available at the exits of the baggage-claim level of the Main Terminal. Passengers must wait in line and take the dispatched cab. Taxi service to downtown DC takes about 45min and averages between $56–$64. Fares are increased by 25 percent when the city declares a snow emergency. *Washington Flyer Taxicabs; ℘703-661-6655.*

Shuttles

For transport throughout the greater DC area, **SuperShuttle** provides shared-ride, door-to-door service year-round, 24hrs daily *(℘800-258-3826)*. Telephones for hotel courtesy shuttles are located on the Main Terminal lower level.

Rental Cars

Rental car company courtesy telephones are located on the Main Terminal's lower level. A 10 percent sales tax is added and some car companies add a 10 percent airport access fee or a daily surcharge.

Public Transportation

An airport–Metro shuttle operates between Dulles and West Falls Church **Metro** station (Orange line). *Shuttles run daily 5:45am–10:15pm, weekends 7:45am–10:15pm; every half hour; 25min; $10 one way/$18 round-trip; ℘888-927-4359.* Public buses serve areas Metrorail does not. The **Metrobus** stop is located at the base of the Metro station.

BALTIMORE-WASHINGTON INTERNATIONAL AIRPORT (BWI)

℘800-I FLY BWI. www.bwiairport.com. 28mi north of Washington and 8mi south of Baltimore with domestic, commuter and international flights. **Airport Information Booths** are located on the upper level ticketing area before Concourses C and D, as well as the lower level of Concourses C, D, and International. Smoking is prohibited except in designated outdoor areas. Sit-down **restaurants** are found in all terminals. Free airport shuttle buses operate 24hrs daily to and from short-term parking and the BWI rail station. **Public transportation** departs from the lower level.

Taxis

Taxis are available at the exits of the lower level of the terminal. Taxi service to downtown DC takes about 50min and costs about $90. *(BWI Airport Taxi Management; ℘410-859-1100).*

Shuttles

SuperShuttle services BWI and downtown DC 24/7. Counters are located in the airport's baggage claim areas 1 and 10. *℘800-258-3826. www.supershuttle.com. About $15 one way.*

Rental Cars

Free shuttles take passengers to and from the rental areas. An 11.5 percent sales tax is added to the rental rate; some car companies add a 10 percent airport access fee as well as a $3 daily facility charge.

Trains

See Additional Sights in DC for Map. Maryland Rail Commuter Service (**MARC**) provides commuter service between the airport and DC's Union Station Mon–Fri 5:30am–10:30pm *(1hr; $6 one way; ℘800-325-7245; http://mta.maryland.gov/marc-train).* **Amtrak** offers daily service between Baltimore and DC *(45min)*. For fares and schedules: *℘800-USA-RAIL; www.amtrak.com.*

Aerial view of Union Station, the Potomac River in the background

© WMATA/Larry Levine

BY TRAIN

Union Station is DC's only railroad station and offers **Amtrak** and other rail services. Located near Capitol Hill at Massachusetts and Delaware Aves. NE, the station is accessible by Metro (Red line). Amtrak provides daily service between DC and major destinations throughout the Northeast, the Midwest and the South. The Acela Express is the high-speed link between DC and Boston via Baltimore, Philadelphia and New York. Amtrak's longer routes include those from Atlanta *(13hrs 30min)*, Chicago *(20hrs)* and Miami *(22hrs)* Advance reservations are recommended. Amtrak also offers daily services between Baltimore and DC. Maryland Rail Commuter Service (**MARC**) operates trains between the two cities on weekdays.

The **USA RailPass** *(not for US & Canadian citizens or legal residents)* offers unlimited travel at a discount. For schedules and routes, call ℘*800-872-7245 (toll-free in North America only; outside North America, contact a travel agent)* or visit www.amtrak.com.

www.seat61.com offers advice on routes and fares (including passes) and has timetable and map information.

BY BUS/COACH

Greyhound provides access to Washington DC, at fares that tend to be lower than air and rail. The **Discovery Pass** *(www.discoverypass.com)* allows unlimited travel for 4 to 60 days. Advance reservations are suggested. For information, call ℘800-231-2222 or visit www.greyhound.com. The capital's main bus terminal *(℘202-289-5160)* is located at 1005 1st St. NE, a short walk from Union Station.

BY CAR

♿ *See Additional Sights in DC for Map.*
Washington is at the crossroads of several major interstates: I-95 (north–south), I-66 (east), Rte. 50 (west) and I-270 (north–west). These and other roads leading to the capital connect with the Capital Beltway (I-495), which encircles the city about 12mi from the center.

33

Getting Around

LAY OF THE LAND
DC STREET SYSTEM

From the beginning, Pierre Charles L'Enfant envisioned DC as a capital city that would at once impress and intimidate foreign dignitaries, royalty and world leaders. The result is a system where a series of intersecting diagonal avenues are superimposed over a grid system with the grand Capitol building serving as its impressive focal point. From this prominent landmark, the two cardinal axes—North Capitol and South Capitol streets, and East Capitol Street and the Mall—divide the city into four quadrants: Northwest, Northeast, Southeast and Southwest.

Numbered streets running north-south are laid out in ascending order on either side of North and South Capitol streets, while **lettered streets** running east-west begin on either side of the Mall/East Capitol axis. Since the same address may be found in each of the four quadrants, it is imperative that the appropriate designation (NE, SE, SW, NW) be attached to the address to avoid confusion. **Avenues** bearing the names of the states of the Union run diagonally across the grid pattern and generally radiate from **circles** named after prominent Americans such as Washington, Sheridan and Dupont.

Note the following particularities: in the NW and SW quadrants there is no A Street, owing to the location of the Mall; B Street is replaced by Constitution Avenue (NE and NW) and Independence Avenue (SE and SW); there is no J Street; and I Street is commonly spelled Eye Street. The lettered streets end at W Street, beyond which a new alphabetical series begins with two-syllable names (Adams, Bryant, Channing, etc.).

HOW TO FIND AN ADDRESS

Once you understand the city's rational street layout, you should be able to locate an address in central DC with ease. Bear in mind that the quadrant designation (NW, NE, SE, SW) indicates the location in relation to the Capitol and that building numbers run in series of 100 per block. The odd-even numbering of buildings in each of the four quadrants follows a distinct pattern according to the street's orientation in relation to the Capitol. As a general rule, in the **Northwest quadrant**, the north and east sides of streets and avenues are odd-numbered, while the south and west sides are even-numbered. Some examples:

1. The intersection of 2nd and C streets SE is two streets east of the Capitol and (C being the 3rd letter of the alphabet) three streets south of East Capitol Street.

2. The Hart Senate Office Building, located at the intersection of 2nd and C streets NE, is two streets east of the Capitol and three streets north of East Capitol Street.

3. Ford's Theatre at 511 10th Street NW is ten numbered streets west of the Capitol and five lettered streets north of the Mall between E (the 5th letter of the alphabet) and F streets. The number 511 indicates that the theater is located on the east side of 10th Street.

4. The Martin Luther King Library at 901 G Street NW is located on G Street in the northwest quadrant between 9th and 10th streets. The odd-numbered street address (901) indicates that the library stands on the north side of G Street.

A CITY FOR WALKERS

The principal sights, government buildings, and entertainment and business centers are concentrated in the northwest quadrant and on Capitol Hill. The logical street layout, the well-manicured appearance and the abundant greenery of this quadrant make orientation easy and walking a pleasure. Since parking can

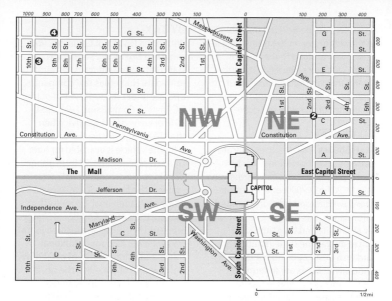

be severely limited and traffic tends to be heavy, walking is also the most efficient choice for getting where you want to go in many situations.

The city's most heavily visited areas, such as the Mall, Capitol Hill and Georgetown, where parking is limited, are best visited on foot. However, some visitors will find walking uncomfortable and tiring during the summer months, when temperatures and humidity are high. Remember to carry water and stay well hydrated when walking during the heat of the day.

⊘*It is advisable to remain in the northwest quadrant of the city after nightfall and to always use caution wherever you happen to be.*

During **rush hours**—the peak transit times for business commuters *(Mon-Fri 7am–9:30am and 4pm–6:30pm)*—when no street parking is permitted, visitors should be aware of fast-moving vehicles in traffic lanes close to the sidewalks. Compliance with pedestrian walking signs is expected. Violators may be fined for crossing in the middle of the block rather than at corners.

A new DC **streetcar** line is slated to open in summer 2013 (the city's streetcar service ended in 1962).

BY PUBLIC TRANSPORTATION

The **Washington Metropolitan Area Transit Authority** (*202-637-7000; www.wmata.com*) operates a public rapid transit (Metrorail) and bus system (Metrobus) that links Washington, DC and areas of Maryland and northern Virginia. Other bus services are provided by Alexandria's **DASH** buses (*703-746-3274; www.dashbus.com*) and Fairfax County's Fairfax Connector buses (*703-339-7200; www.fairfaxconnector.com*), both of which join with Metrobuses and Metrorail (*service to Mount Vernon, see Sightseeing Tours*). Montgomery County's **Ride On** buses also connect to Metrorail and Metrobuses (*240-777-0311; www.montgomerycountymd.gov*).

RAPID TRANSIT SYSTEM

The Metrorail subway system, known locally as the **Metro**, is efficient, clean and dependable. The Metro carries commuters to and from the suburbs during rush hour *(7am–9:30am and 4pm–6:30pm)* and is convenient and inexpensive for sightseeing in the city. Stations are open Mon–Thu 5:30am–midnight, Fri 5am–3am, Sat 7am–3am, and Sun 7am–midnight. ⊘Eating and drinking are prohibited on the Metro and riders can be ticketed for doing so in the stations or on the trains. Please remember to stand to the right on Metro escalators. *You'll find a Metro system map and information about fares, ticket purchase and transit lines inside the back cover of this guide.*

CITY BUSES

Metrobuses – These buses operate daily; hours of operation differ by route, please contact the information line (*202-637-7000*) or the website *(www.wmata.com)* for more detailed information. Bus stops are indicated by red, white and blue signs. The buses display the route number and final destination above the windshield. **Fares** are determined by the time of day and length of trip. The base fare for most rides is $1.70. Exact fare is required. Some surcharges and transfer fees may apply. For free transfers from bus-to-bus within a two-hour period, reduced fare transfers to express buses, and reduced fare transfers from bus to Metro, you must use a **SmarTrip** card, a permanent, rechargeable fare card (*$5; purchase online or at Metro sales offices and other stations that have parking*). **SmarTrip** card users also pay discounted fares on the Metrorail as well as Metrobuses. Many routes are accessible to riders with disabilities. To request a *Metro Visitor's Kit*, *202-962-2733* or consult the website www.wmata.com.

DC Circulator – Buses operate daily within DC's central core every 10min along five main routes: Dupont Circle/Rosslyn, Georgetown/Union Station, Potomac Avenue Metro/Skyland, Union Station/Navy Yard Metro and Woodley Park/McPherson Square. Bus stops are identifiable by a red, white and yellow flag bearing the name Circulator. The **fare** is $1 (exact change required). SmarTrip fare cards can be used, and passes (1-day, 3-day, weekly or monthly) are available for purchase. For schedules, call *202-962-1423* or go online to www.dccirculator.com.

BY TAXI

Within the District of Columbia, you can hail a taxi on the street or at taxi stands at hotels and transportation terminals. Numerous taxi companies operate under the supervision of the DC Taxicab Commission (*202-645-6018 or www.dctaxi.dc.gov*). When the "TAXI" sign on the roof of the cab is lit, the vehicle is available for hire. DC taxis recently moved from a zone system to a more traditional meter system. The first 1/6 of a mile costs $3 while each additional 1/6 mile after that costs 25 cents. Additional charges are listed in the cab and include extra fees for large luggage, additional riders and animals. A list of passenger rights is also displayed in the car. It is not unusual for the driver to request payment before setting out or to pick up another passenger en route. A rider can expect additional charges for radio-dispatched telephone requests, multiple stops, waiting time, rush-hour travel, more than one piece of luggage, oversized luggage, special assistance. Fares are increased by 25 percent when the city declares a snow emergency. The maximum fare within DC, before surcharges, is $19.

BY CAR

Given the efficiency of the public transportation system, the availability of taxis and the ease with which many sights can be reached on foot, a car is not necessary to visit Washington. Street parking is limited and rush-hour traffic is heavy. Visitors are encouraged to avoid driving during **rush hours**: Mon–Fri 7am–9:30am and 4pm–6:30pm.

If you are staying outside DC, consider leaving your car at the parking lots at the fringe Metro stations (*see Metro map on the inside back cover*) and taking the Metro into the city (arrive early on weekdays, as these parking lots fill up quickly).

For excursions outside the city, a vehicle is highly recommended.

ROAD REGULATIONS

Talking on a hand-held cell phone while driving in DC is punishable by a $100 fine as is sending text messages while driving. The maximum **speed limit** on major expressways is 55 mph. The speed limit within the city is 25mph unless otherwise posted. **Seat belts** are mandatory for drivers and passengers. Child safety seats are required for children younger than 8 years old. Drivers must always yield the **right of way** to pedestrians. DC law requires motorists to bring vehicles to a full stop when school bus warning signals are flashing. Unless posted, drivers may turn right at a red light after coming to a complete stop. Drivers are required to wear seatbelts at all times.

PARKING

Parking in DC is limited and regulations are strictly enforced. Some metered parking is available. Arterial streets have posted **rush-hour restrictions** that generally prohibit parking from 7am–9:30am and 4pm–6:30pm. Parking in some residential areas is by permit only. Nonresidents may park in these areas for up to 2 hours between 7am and 8:30pm on weekdays and longer on weekends in some neighborhoods. Always check the signs first as restrictions vary from street-to-street in some cases. Parking signs are color-coded: **green and white** signs indicate when parking is allowed; **red and white** signs indicate when parking is prohibited. Parking spaces reserved for specific use by permit only (e.g., diplomatic or government vehicles) are reserved 24hrs daily unless noted. Parking spaces identified with ♿ are reserved for people with disabilities; anyone parking in these spaces without proper ID is subject to heavy fines and towing. Private parking garages are found throughout downtown and many popular restaurants offer valet service during the dinner rush and on weekends.

RENTAL CARS

Major rental-car agencies have offices downtown and at the airports. In most cases you must be at least 25 years old, although some companies rent to younger drivers for an additional fee. A major credit card and valid driver's license are required (some also require proof of insurance). The daily rate for a compact car averages $58. A 10 percent sales tax and a 11.10 percent concession recoup fee are added to the daily rate in DC. There is also a per-day contract fee added to the total charge.

♿ See the chart of rental companies below *(toll-free numbers may not be accessible outside North America)*. The car sharing company Zipcar allows you to hire vehicles on a pay-as-you go basis by the hour or day., with rates inclusive of fuel, insurance, maintenance and parking (☎ 1-866-494-7227, www.zipcar.com).

RENTAL COMPANY	☎ RESERVATIONS	WEBSITE
Alamo	800-462-5266	www.alamo.com
Avis	800-331-1212	www.avis.com
Budget	800-527-0700	www.budget.com
Dollar	800-800-3665	www.dollar.com
Enterprise	800-264-6350	www.enterprise.com
Hertz	800-654-3131	www.hertz.com
National	800-227-7368	www.nationalcar.com
Thrifty	800-847-4389	www.thrifty.com

Basic Information

BUSINESS HOURS

Most businesses operate Monday to Friday 9am–5pm. Banks are generally open Monday to Thursday 9am–3pm with longer hours on Friday; some banks offer limited Saturday service. Department stores and shopping centers operate Monday to Saturday 10am–9pm, and many are open Sunday noon–5pm or 6pm; some extend their hours on Saturday.

COMMUNICATIONS

A local call generally costs 50¢ from a pay phone. Most calls within a distance of 12mi of the Capital Beltway *(Interstate 495)* are charged as local calls, but dial 1 and the area code. SIM cards for GSM mobile phones are available for purchase at T-Mobile and AT&T retail locations, as well as many electronics stores throughout the city. Note that GSM phones must be unlocked to use a SIM card for a North American network.

Free Wi-Fi is available throughout DC.

AREA CODES

- 📞 Washington, DC 202
- 📞 Suburban Virginia 703, 571, 434
- 📞 Eastern Maryland 410, 443
- 📞 Suburban Maryland 301, 240

Instructions for using public telephones are listed on or near the telephone. Some **public telephones** accept credit cards, and all will accept **long-distance** calling cards. Post offices, convenience stores and supermarkets sell pre-paid phone cards for long-distance and international calls. For long-distance calls in the US and Canada, dial 1+area code+number. To place an **international call**, dial **011**+country code+number. A list of country codes can be found in the Yellow Pages and online. To place a **collect call** (person receiving call pays charges) dial 0+area code+number and tell the operator

you are calling collect. For international calls, ask for the overseas operator. The cost for a local call from a pay phone is generally 50¢ (any combination of nickels, dimes or quarters is accepted but not pennies). Most phone numbers in this guide that start with **800**, **866**, **877** or **888** are toll-free (no charge) in the US only and may not be accessible outside of North America. Dial 1 before dialing an 800 or 888 number in the US. The charge for numbers preceded by **900** can range from 50¢ to $15 per minute. Most hotels add a surcharge for local and long-distance calls. For further information dial 0 for operator assistance.

You can send a **telegram** or money, or have money telegraphed to you, via the Western Union system 📞800-325-6000 or www.westernunion.com.

ELECTRICITY

The voltage in the US is 110 volts AC, 60 Hz. Foreign-made appliances may need voltage transformers and North American flat-blade adapter plugs (available at specialty travel and electronics stores).

EMERGENCIES

In all major US cities you can call the police, ambulance or fire service by dialing **911**. Another way to report an emergency is to dial **0** for the operator.

IMPORTANT NUMBERS

- ✚ **Emergency Police/Ambulance/ Fire Department (24hrs)** 📞911
  Police (non-emergency) 📞311
- ✚ **Inn House Doctors (24hrs)**
  www.innhousedoctor.com
  📞202-216-9100
- ✚ **Dental Referral**
  (Mon–Fri 8am–4pm)
  📞202-547-7613
- ✚ **Pharmacies (24hrs)**
  CVS, 6 Dupont Cir. NW
  📞202-785-1466
  CVS, 2240 M St. NW
  📞202-296-9876
- ✚ **Poison Control Center (24hrs)**
  📞800-222-1222

LIQUOR LAW

The legal minimum age for purchase and consumption of alcoholic beverages is 21. Proof of age (photo ID) is normally required. Establishments can serve alcoholic beverages Monday to Thursday 8am–2am, Friday to Saturday 8am–3am and Sunday 10am–2am. Beer and wine can be purchased in some convenience and grocery stores seven days a week. Liquor stores are closed on Sunday except on 24 and 31 December when those dates fall on a Sunday. A DC law requires all city stores that sell food or food products to charge 5 cents for bags.

MAJOR HOLIDAYS

Most banks and government offices in the District are closed on the following legal holidays:

1 January	New Year's Day
Every four years on 20 January	Inauguration Day
3rd Monday in January	Martin Luther King Jr.'s Birthday
3rd Monday in February	Presidents' Day
Last Monday in May	Memorial Day
4th July	Independence Day
1st Monday in September	Labor Day
2nd Monday in October	Columbus Day
11 November	Veterans Day
4th Thursday in November	Thanksgiving
25 December	Christmas

MAIL/ POST

National Capitol Station Post Office, at Capitol St. and Massachusetts Ave. NE (next to Union Station) is open Monday to Friday 9am–7pm and Sat–Sun 9am–5pm. For location and hours of local post offices and other information, contact the Postal Service Customer Call Center (✆ 800-275-8777; www.usps.com). First-class rates within the US: letter 44¢ (1oz), postcard 28¢. Overseas rates are calculated based on the country where the letter is being sent. Letters can be mailed from most hotels. Stamps and packing material may be purchased at post offices, grocery stores, CVS stores and businesses offering postal and express shipping services located throughout the city (*see the Yellow Pages of the telephone directory under "Mailing Services" or "Post Offices" or go online to www.usps.com).*

MONEY

The majority of banks are members of the network of Automatic Teller Machines (ATMs), which allows visitors from around the world to withdraw cash using bank cards and major credit cards 24hrs a day, 7 days a week. ATMs can usually be found in banks, airports, grocery stores, hotel lobbies and shopping malls. Networks (Cirrus, Plus) serviced by the ATM are indicated on the machine. To inquire about ATM service, locations and transaction fees, contact your local bank, Cirrus ✆ 800-424-7787 or Plus ✆ 800-847-2911. Traveler's checks are accepted in banks and some stores, restaurants and hotels. To report a lost or stolen credit card: American Express ✆ 800-528-4800; Diners' Club ✆ 800-234-6377; MasterCard ✆ 800-307-7309 or the issuing bank; Visa ✆ 800-336-8472. American Express Travel Service offices are 1501 K St. NW ✆ 202-457-1300.

CREDIT CARDS AND TRAVELER'S CHECKS

Rental car agencies and many hotels require credit cards. Most banks will cash brand-name traveler's checks and give cash advances on major credit cards (American Express, Visa, MasterCard/Eurocard) with correct ID.

CURRENCY EXCHANGE

Foreign currency exchange, traveler's checks and wire transfers are available at many banks in town, including **PNC Bank**, 1919 Pennsylvania Ave. NW (and other branch locations); ☏888-762-2265; www.pnc.com. Private companies offering exchange services include **American Express Travel Service**, 1501 K St. NW; ☏202-457-1300 or www.americanexpress.com. Visitors can also exchange currency at Reagan National Airport (at Customer Service Centers in Terminals B and C and at Travelex Currency Services, Inc. in Terminal C, ☏703-417-3201); Dulles International Airport (exchange is located in the Business Service Center on the ticketing level of the Main Terminal; exchange centers also in the Upper Level of the Main Terminal, East and West Ticketing Levels and Concourse B, C and D. Travelex Foreign Currency ATM are found near Gates D23 and C28); and BWI (in the upper level concourse of the Main Terminal between C and D).

NEWSPAPERS AND MAGAZINES

The city's leading daily paper, *The Washington Post* (established 1877), known for its investigative reporting, is one of the country's most influential newspapers, providing local, national and international coverage. The weekend section in the Friday edition lists entertainment, special events, reviews and activities for children. The Sunday edition contains a section highlighting the performing arts. *The Post* lists the day's congressional and Supreme Court schedules (www.washingtonpost.com). *The Post* also publishes Express, a free daily newspaper handed out to commuters or in news boxes found at many of the city's Metro stations. Its website, www.expressnightout.com, gives overviews of nightlife and events in town. Another daily, the *Washington Times* was established in 1982 *(www.washingtontimes.com)*. The *Washingtonian*, a monthly magazine, lists events and features stories about the city *(www.washingtonian.com)*. The *City Paper (www.washingtoncitypaper.com)* is a free alternative weekly *(distributed Thursday)*. The *Washingon Blade* focuses on the GLBT community (www.washingtonblade.com).

SMOKING

It is prohibited to smoke any tobacco product in most indoor spaces in DC including hotels, bars, sports arenas, restaurants and offices but allowed in some outdoor spaces attached to restaurants, bars and hotels. Fines for smoking in non-smoking areas range from $100 to $1,000. Maryland and Virginia have similar smoking restrictions in place.

TAXES AND TIPPING

In Washington, DC the general sales tax is 6 percent. The hotel tax is 14.5 percent. The rental-car tax is 10 percent. The food and beverage tax (restaurants) is 10 percent. Sales taxes in neighboring areas outside DC vary depending on the state and city. In restaurants it is customary to tip the server 15-20 percent of the bill. Taxi drivers usually receive 15 percent of the fare. Skycaps and porters are generally tipped $1 per bag and hotel maids $1 per night.

TEMPERATURE AND MEASUREMENT

In the US, temperatures are measured in degrees Fahrenheit and measurements are expressed according to the US Customary System of weights and measures.

TIME

Washington, DC is located in the Eastern Standard Time (EST) zone, which is five hours behind Greenwich Mean Time. Daylight Saving Time *(clocks advanced 1hr)* is in effect for most of the US from the second Sunday in March until the first Sunday in November.

CONVERSION TABLES

Weights and Measures

1 kilogram (kg)	**2.2 pounds (lb)**	**2.2 pounds**	*To convert kilograms to pounds, multiply by 2.2*
6.35 kilograms	14 pounds	1 stone (st)	
0.45 kilograms	16 ounces (oz)	16 ounces	
1 metric ton (tn)	**1.1 tons**	**1.1 tons**	
1 litre (l)	**2.11 pints (pt)**	**1.76 pints**	*To convert litres to gallons, multiply by 0.26 (US) or 0.22 (UK)*
3.79 litres	1 gallon (gal)	0.83 gallon	
4.55 litres	1.20 gallon	1 gallon	
1 hectare (ha)	**2.47 acres**	**2.47 acres**	*To convert hectares to acres, multiply by 2.4*
1 sq kilometre (km²)	**0.38 sq. miles (sq mi)**	**0.38 sq. miles**	
1 centimetre (cm)	**0.39 inches (in)**	**0.39 inches**	*To convert metres to feet, multiply by 3.28; for kilometres to miles, multiply by 0.6*
1 metre (m)	**3.28 feet (ft) or 39.37 inches or 1.09 yards (yd)**		
1 kilometre (km)	**0.62 miles (mi)**	**0.62 miles**	

Clothing

Women	⭐	🇺🇸	🇬🇧
	35	4	2½
	36	5	3½
	37	6	4½
Shoes	38	7	5½
	39	8	6½
	40	9	7½
	41	10	8½
	36	6	8
	38	8	10
Dresses	40	10	12
& suits	42	12	14
	44	14	16
	46	16	18
	36	6	30
	38	8	32
Blouses &	40	10	34
sweaters	42	12	36
	44	14	38
	46	16	40

Men	⭐	🇺🇸	🇬🇧
	40	7½	7
	41	8½	8
	42	9½	9
Shoes	43	10½	10
	44	11½	11
	45	12½	12
	46	13½	13
	46	36	36
	48	38	38
Suits	50	40	40
	52	42	42
	54	44	44
	56	46	48
	37	14½	14½
	38	15	15
Shirts	39	15½	15½
	40	15¾	15¾
	41	16	16
	42	16½	16½

Sizes often vary depending on the designer. These equivalents are given for guidance only.

Speed

KPH	10	30	50	70	80	90	100	110	120	130
MPH	6	19	31	43	50	56	62	68	75	81

Temperature

Celsius (°C)	0°	5°	10°	15°	20°	25°	30°	40°	60°	80°	100°
Fahrenheit (°F)	32°	41°	50°	59°	68°	77°	86°	104°	140°	176°	212°

To convert Celsius into Fahrenheit, multiply °C by 9, divide by 5, and add 32.
To convert Fahrenheit into Celsius, subtract 32 from °F, multiply by 5, and divide by 9.
NB: Conversion factors on this page are approximate.

View of the Lincoln Memorial, Washington Monument, the Capitol and
Arlington Memorial Bridge over the Potomac River
©PhotoDisc

The City Today

The seat of the nation's government occupies a relatively small amount of real estate, yet with its height restrictions and well-planned development, the capital often does not feel overly crowded. Yes, there is traffic, but sweeping green spaces, monumental buildings, parks and two water bodies make the city a desirable, if costly, place to live. An international populace peppers the mix of neighborhoods. The capital city is remarkably accessible, opening the doors of Congress, the White House and other federal institutions to hosts of visitors who come to witness democracy in progress.

LOCATION AND CLIMATE

Washington, DC lies approximately in the middle of the eastern seaboard of the US, about 90 miles inland from the Atlantic Ocean. Situated on the northern banks of the Potomac River, the city rises from low bottomland along the riverfront to a series of hills in the north. At its highest elevation in the Northwest quadrant of the city, it is 390ft above sea level. Rock Creek, a tributary of the Potomac, follows a shallow, wooded valley extending through the heart of the city from north to south. Located at 39° north latitude and 77° west longitude, the city has a temperately continental climate. Winds are generally from the west, and humidity is often high because of proximity to the ocean and the Chesapeake Bay, 25 miles east of the city. In the vicinity of Washington, the Potomac River has an average channel depth of about 14ft, making it unnavigable for large cargo-carrying vessels.

SIZE AND POPULATION

Shaped like a truncated diamond, each side measuring 10 miles, the city is carved out of Maryland and separated from Virginia by the Potomac. It covers 67 square miles and is divided into four quadrants: **Northwest** (NW), **Northeast** (NE), **Southeast** (SE) and **Southwest** (SW). The longest distance from its southern to its northern tip is 12 miles. The official 2010 census count of 601,723 was a population increase of about 2,000 from 2009, making Washington the 24th largest city in the US.

The Northeast, Southeast and Southwest quadrants have large African-American communities while the Northwest quadrant is largely white although by no means exclusively. The neighborhood known as Adams Morgan, concentrated mainly in the area of Columbia Road and 18th Street NW, has been the hub of Washington's growing Latino community, which constitutes

Pennsylvania Avenue

©Gwen Cannon/Michelin

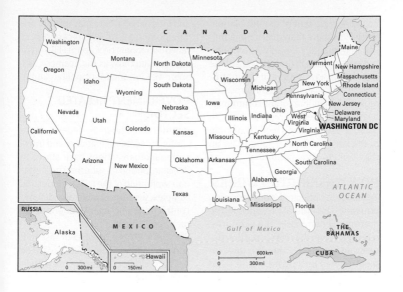

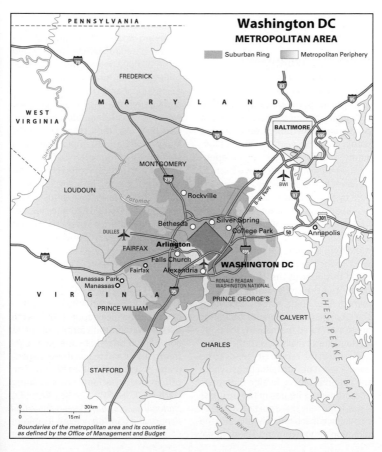

Washington DC
METROPOLITAN AREA

Suburban Ring   Metropolitan Periphery

Boundaries of the metropolitan area and its counties as defined by the Office of Management and Budget

nearly nine percent of the population. Since 1990 more than quarter of a million immigrants, primarily Asians who compose more than three percent of the population, have settled in the metropolitan area, mainly in the suburbs. The region's Indian immigrant community has also experienced rapid growth, in part due to the region's high-tech boom of the late 1990s that helped build up the Northern Virginia corridor.

HOW WASHINGTON WORKS

Washington's principal industry is government. The federal presence in the metropolis dominates the economy, directly through the civil service bureaucracy and indirectly through government-related businesses. Politics and government also influence the social climate of the capital city. With less than two percent of its work force involved in manufacturing, Washington functions like a white-collar town.

FEDERAL GOVERNMENT

Some 350,000 people living in the metropolitan area are on the federal payroll, from the president to park rangers, custodians to museum curators. Most permanent government positions are within the purview of the Office of Personnel and Management, an independent agency of the Executive branch. However, higher-level jobs are generally held by presidential appointment, and new appointees are customarily brought in with each change of administration. Every day hordes of employees commute from the surrounding suburbs to work in the government offices scattered throughout the city. About 23 percent of the city's land is federally owned. After hours, whole corridors of the city where government buildings are concentrated (particularly in Foggy Bottom) are virtually deserted.

Social life in the capital city tends to be conducted at private gatherings, where the nation's leaders, foreign diplomats and prominent figures in the business world informally share political and economic ideas that ultimately influence the direction of government. The national and international elite may meet in private homes, at embassy receptions, in reception rooms on Capitol Hill and in such private clubs as the Cosmos Club, Sulgrave Club and Metropolitan Club.

GOVERNMENT-RELATED SECTOR

In order to be near the federal nerve center, hundreds of national and international organizations have offices in Washington and its suburbs. The Pentagon, wellspring of the military industrial complex, supports innumerable defense contracting companies throughout the metropolitan area.

Since the 1970s a number of research and development complexes have been built around the Capital Beltway. Their fortunes are very much dependent on the political climate and the congressional appropriation of federal resources. As many as 40,000 people engage in lobbying work in the capital. Washington-based **lobbyists** representing some 23,000 special interest groups, political action organizations (PACs), professional and trade associations, and foreign countries and businesses, work to persuade legislators to support laws helpful to their clients' interests. Many organizations employ their own staff lobbyists, but often such work is undertaken by well-connected attorneys at DC firms. The term "lobbyist" derives from the 19C, when such influence peddlers would haunt the lobbies of public buildings where politicians congregated. Today lobbyists conduct their business at fine restaurants and well-orchestrated social gatherings.

PRIVATE SECTOR

Exerting a powerful influence on the city's sociopolitical fabric is the **fourth estate**. Washington's formidable press corps is comprised of correspondents from national and regional newspapers, many of whom maintain Washington offices in the National Press Building (14th and F Sts. NW). The New Republic, National Geographic, US News and World Report, and USA Today (with its parent company, newspaper and media giant

Gannett), are among the publications with their headquarters in or near the capital. Dominated by the *Washington Post,* one of the country's most influential newspapers, the press has become a major player in shaping public opinion. The *Post's* involvement in uncovering the Nixon-Watergate debacle in the mid-1970s broke new ground in investigative reporting.

The District also serves as headquarters for large corporations, such as Marriott; and for more than a thousand associations and interest groups, such as the America's Union Movement (AFL-CIO) and the over 50s organisation, AARP.

TOURISM

Attracted by the capital's renowned monuments and museums and by the numerous conventions held in the area, some 14.8 million visitors came to Washington in 2009. Tourism, the city's second-largest industry, brought in about $5.2 billion in 2009 to hotels, restaurants and other service-related businesses that cater to visitors. Traditionally a place of pilgrimage for Americans, in recent years the capital has begun to draw more foreign tourists.

THE INTERNATIONAL ELEMENT

Once a rather provincial town with only a small contingent of foreigners, Washington has become, in recent decades, a cosmopolitan city. More than 150 foreign missions maintain embassies and consulates here, and such international organizations as the World Bank, International Monetary Fund and Organization of American States are based in the city.

The influx of Asian, Middle Eastern and African immigrants that began in the late 1970s has given the city a distinctly international flavor. Washington's shops, restaurants and festivals reflect this urban mix of cultures. Dining in the District has become a global experience, from Adams Morgan's Ethiopian and Mexican eateries and Downtown's Spanish and Indian restaurants, to Chinatown's Asian cuisines and nearby Arlington's Vietnamese dining spots. French, Italian and American fare have long been staples of the city's dining scene.

THE METROPOLITAN AREA

The Washington, DC metropolitan area comprises 18 counties in Maryland, Virginia and West Virginia, and the District of Columbia itself. The total metropolitan area encompasses 6,510 square miles. With a population of 5,582,000 (601,723 in DC), it ranks seventh among the nation's 361 metropolitan areas.

Continued growth has drawn many of the outlying towns and villages into a steadily expanding ring of suburban settlements. The municipalities bordering the Capital Beltway (Interstate 495), which encircles the District at a distance of approximately 12 miles from the center, tend to be suburban "bedroom" communities closely attached to Washington culturally and economically. As the suburban reach of Washington extends farther west and south into the hinterland, more distant and traditionally more rural counties in Virginia and West Virginia—as well as independent cities of Virginia, such as Fairfax, Manassas and even more remote Fredericksburg—serve as commuter communities as well.

NATIONAL CAPITAL PLANNING COMMISSION

The National Capital Region covers the District of Columbia, the city of Alexandria and Maryland's Prince George's and Montgomery counties as well as Virginia's Arlington, Fairfax, Prince William and Loudoun counties. First established in 1924 by Congress, the National Capital Planning Commission (NCPC) was authorized to acquire land for a park and recreation system for the nation's capital. Major federal laws underpinning the commission's decisions include the Height of Buildings Act of 1910, the Commission of Fine Arts Act of 1910 and the Commemorative Works Act of 1986. It is the central planning agency of the federal government in the Capital Region.

Responsibilities include approving new federal building plans in the District, reviewing plans for federal structures and preparing a yearly analysis of all federal agency capital project proposals in the Region.

In 1997 NCPC released its Extending the Legacy Plan—measures for preserving and enhancing the city's Monumental Core, from the Mall to the Potomac and Anacostia rivers, as well as 22 miles of waterfront from Georgetown to the National Arboretum.

More recently, NCPC and the Commission of Fine Arts launched the National Capital Framework Plan, an initiative to relieve pressure on the Mall by enhancing its surroundings. More detailed than the Legacy plan, it seeks to focus on underused federal lands.

THE DISTRICT GOVERNMENT

After a century of congressional rule, in 1973 Washington was given the federally mandated authority to govern itself. Headed by an elected mayor and a 13-member legislative council, the city government, by merit of the District's unique status, undertakes all local, county, and state government responsibilities—the schools, the police, the courts, the department of motor vehicles, etc. Though the city functions somewhat independently of the federal legislature, Congress retains veto power over bills passed by the District council. In addition, many federal agencies and commissions exercise oversight jurisdiction in District matters. The National Capital Planning Commission, a 12-member body appointed by the president and the mayor, reviews city development plans, while the Commission of Fine Arts oversees the design of buildings, parks and monuments. Congress itself sets height restrictions on all District buildings, and the president's Office of Management and Budget establishes limits for the city budget.

Historically, suffrage has been a matter of concern to the citizens of Washington. In 1964 they were allowed to vote in the presidential election for the first time.

As part of the 1973 Home Rule Act, they were also allowed to elect one delegate to the House of Representatives. The delegate serves a two-year term and, though not granted a vote on the floor of Congress, is allowed to vote on issues within the congressional committees on which he or she serves. Unbowed by the failure of a proposed constitutional amendment in 1978, the defeat in the House of DC statehood legislation in 1993, and the denial of a voting-rights lawsuit by the Supreme Court in 2000, DC residents continue to push for a voice in Congress.

THE FEDERAL GOVERNMENT

Under the system of checks and balances established by the US Constitution, the federal government is composed of three branches: the **Legislative** (both houses of Congress), the **Executive** (the president and the Executive Office) and the **Judicial** (the Supreme Court and all other federal courts). All three branches of US government are housed in Washington, DC, and in nearby Arlington, the command center for the entire American military establishment that sprawls over 6.5 million square feet.

The White House, seat of the Executive branch, is situated within a mile of Capitol Hill, where the Capitol, home of Congress, and the Supreme Court building are located. Each of these branches fulfils specific functions and duties of its own, as well as overseeing and keeping in check the powers exercised by the other two branches.

THE LEGISLATIVE BRANCH

Conceived by the Founding Fathers as a bicameral system of government, the Congress comprises two bodies: the Senate and the House of Representatives. Jointly they are responsible for drafting and passing laws; for handling matters of national finance, such as setting and collecting taxes and coining money; for ensuring, in conjunction with the president, the defense of the nation; for regulating commerce; and for admitting new states to the Union.

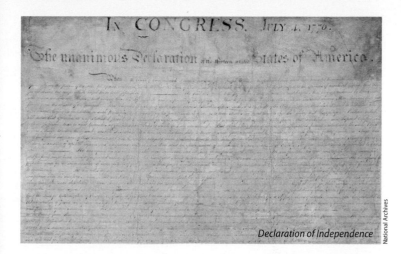

Declaration of Independence

National Archives

Within these broadly defined powers, each body has separate duties, as described below.

A specific Congress serves for two years (the 111th Congress convenes from 2009 to 2011), beginning new sessions each year in late January and generally recessing in August and again in the fall.

The **Senate** is composed of 100 senators, two from each of the 50 states in the Union. Senators are elected to six-year terms by popular vote, in accordance with the 17th Amendment, which was added to the Constitution in 1913 (originally, the Constitution required that senators be elected by state legislatures).

Senate terms are staggered so that no more than one-third of the Senate seats are renewed each year. The vice president is the official presiding officer of the Senate, but in his or her absence, senators elect a president pro tempore from among their ranks. The Senate's specific duties include approving presidential appointments; ratifying foreign treaties by a two-thirds majority (a power now little used); and trying federal officials impeached by the House. (Only two US presidents have stood trial before the Senate: Andrew Johnson in 1868, and Bill Clinton in 1999. Both presidents were acquitted.)

The **House** is composed of 435 representatives (often referred to as congressmen and congresswomen), with the number of representatives per state based on population. California has the most representatives (53). The District of Columbia and the US territories of Guam, the Virgin Islands and American Samoa are represented by nonvoting delegates to the House, and the commonwealth of Puerto Rico sends a nonvoting resident commissioner.

Members of the House serve two-year terms, and their presiding officer is the Speaker of the House, elected anew with each Congress. Under the Constitution the House is responsible for originating all bills relating to taxes; impeaching (that is, charging federal officials with criminal actions); and determining the outcome of a presidential election if there is no clear electoral majority.

Historically Congress has been dominated by two opposing political parties, whose names and policies have changed over time. Today the major parties are Democratic and Republican, though nothing prevents "independents" or members of smaller parties from running for office.

In both houses, the dominant party elects a **majority leader** and a deputy, the **majority whip**. The minority party, likewise, elects its own leader and whip. If the majority party in one or both houses of Congress is different from the party of the president, legislation may bog down, as Congress votes against

President Barack Obama delivers the State of the Union address on January 27th 2010

© Zhang Jun/Xinhua/Photoshot

supported initiatives or the president vetoes congressional acts.

In both chambers, much of the work of formulating and drafting new laws is done within standing committees. There are 19 such committees in the House and 16 in the Senate. Normally a representative serves on two committees, a senator on three or four.

HOW A BILL BECOMES LAW

Any interested person or group, whether within or outside the political system, may draft a bill and seek the support of a US senator or representative to introduce it for congressional consideration. Of the many bills proposed annually, only a handful become law. Throughout the legislative process described below, a corps of lobbyists is generally operating behind the scenes to persuade legislators to protect the interests of their clients.

Each bill begins its journey when it is introduced on the floor of either the House or the Senate chamber; in many cases a similar proposal is introduced simultaneously in both houses. The chamber's parliamentarian then assigns it to an appropriate **standing committee** for consideration, and if deemed worthwhile, the proposal is normally referred to a subcommittee for further study. The **subcommittee** holds hearings eliciting the opinions of experts and interested parties. Such hearings,

especially in the House, are generally open to the public. The subcommittee must then "mark up" the bill, or rework the language and intent of various sections in light of the conclusions drawn from hearings. The marked-up bill then passes back to the full standing committee, which after further study either rejects the bill or "reports" it—that is, recommends its passage to the chamber. In the House, reported bills are then submitted to the Rules Committee before returning to the chamber. In the Senate, the leadership determines the course of action on each piece of legislation.

Having received committee approval, the bill is placed on the chamber's calendar, and at the scheduled time, it is debated, amended and put to a vote. At this point, a bill that has been introduced in only one chamber is sent to the other chamber, where the legislative process begins anew. If the bill has been introduced simultaneously in the Senate and the House and passed by both, the two versions are then referred to a **conference committee**, composed of members from both chambers who meet to resolve differences. The compromise version is then sent back to both the House and Senate, which separately vote on identical versions of the bill. After passage in both houses, the approved legislation next proceeds to the president, who may sign it into law or exercise his **veto** power by returning the bill to Congress unsigned, with a statement of his objections. Congress may override a presidential veto with a two-thirds majority vote in both chambers. The president has a third option: he can register his disapproval without a veto by retaining the unsigned bill, and after 10 days, it automatically becomes law, provided Congress is in session. If Congress is adjourned at that time, the president's failure to sign constitutes a "pocket veto," and the bill dies.

THE EXECUTIVE BRANCH

The president and vice president are the only elected officials of the branch's four million employees (including armed forces personnel). Presidential elections are held every four years, and a president may serve a maximum of two four-year terms, as stipulated by the 22nd Amendment (1951) to the Constitution. The Speaker of the House follows the vice president in the line of succession.

The Constitution also requires that a presidential candidate be at least 35 years old, be born in the US and live in the US for 14 years prior to running for office. Presidential candidates choose their running mates. In the event of the president's resignation, impeachment, incapacitation or death, the vice president assumes the presidency. According to the the 12th Amendment "no person constitutionally ineligible to the office of President shall be eligible to that of Vice-President of the United States" meaning the vice presidential candidate must also be at least 35 years old, be born in the US and live in the US for 14 years prior to running for office.

The president serves as commander-in-chief of the Armed Forces, with ultimate control over the nation's defense. However, as required by the Constitution and the War Powers Act of 1973, a protracted military action must be approved by Congress, which solely holds the power to declare war. In addition the president serves as the nation's chief executive. In this capacity he appoints all ambassadors, ministers, consuls and cabinet-level positions and approves the appointments of many policy-making personnel within the Executive branch. Whenever a vacancy

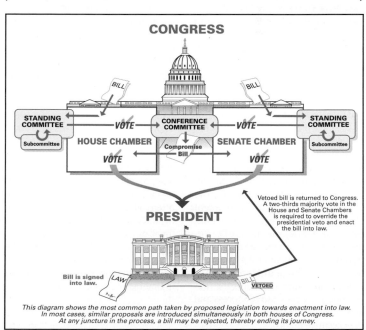

This diagram shows the most common path taken by proposed legislation towards enactment into law. In most cases, similar proposals are introduced simultaneously in both houses of Congress. At any juncture in the process, a bill may be rejected, thereby ending its journey.

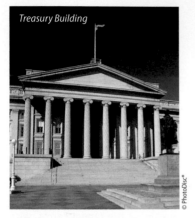

Treasury Building

© PhotoDisc®

occurs on the Supreme Court or among other federal judges, the president makes new appointments (which is subject to Senate approval). Through such appointments the president exerts an influence that may last far beyond his or her own tenure. The president can grant pardons and reprieves to those convicted of crimes against the government. Finally, the president, through his veto power, is instrumental in the law-making process.

The Executive branch comprises the **Executive Office of the President**— independent federal agencies, and all 15 **cabinet departments** (State, Treasury, Defense, Justice, Interior, Agriculture, Commerce, Labor, Health and Human Services, Homeland Security, Education, Transportation, Housing and Urban Development, Energy, and Veteran Affairs). The "secretary," or head, of each department advises the president.

The Executive Office of the President includes the White House staff and several departments that assist and advise the president including the Department of Justice, the Department of State, the Department of Commerce, Department of Defense, and the Department of Health and Human Services. A powerful component of the Executive Office is the **Office of Management and Budget,** which prepares the federal budget, works with Congress and acts as an organizational overseer for the Executive branch.

Crucial government responsibilities are executed by federal agencies chartered by Congress and overseen by the president, such as the Central Intelligence Agency, the Federal Deposit Insurance Corporation, the National Endowment for the Arts, the Environmental Protection Agency, and the Social Security Administration.

THE JUDICIAL BRANCH

The smallest branch, the Judiciary interprets the law. It is composed of three levels: **US District Courts** (94), **US Courts of Appeals** (13) and the **US Supreme Court**. Judges at all levels are appointed for life to by the president and must be confirmed by the Senate.

Federal cases may be civil or criminal in nature while criminal cases must concern a violation of federal law. For a civil case to be heard in federal court, it must involve one of the following criteria: a federal statute, a constitutional issue or litigants from different states in a case involving more than $75,000.

Normally federal cases are first filed and tried at the district level, though they may begin in special federal courts, such as the US Claims Court or Tax Court. Once a decision has been handed down in a district court, parties who feel the court wrongly applied the law may then file for an appeal.

The final court of review, the Supreme Court, is made up of eight associate justices and a chief justice. This body hears only about two percent of the some 10,000 petitions it receives each term. The court tends to focus on cases that question the constitutionality of existing laws or that challenge lower court interpretations of federal laws. Decisions handed down by the Supreme Court, often called the "high court" or by acronym SCOTUS, set the legal precedents for all other courts.

The law dictates that the term of the court begin on the first Monday in October and continue until the first Monday in October of the next year.

History

The history of the capital city is one of setbacks: delayed site selection, sluggish lot sales, L'Enfant's dismissal, Britain's torching of the White House, the Washington Canal boondoggle, Alexandria's retrocession, and the Civil War, to name a few. Compromise, self-interest or forbearance has always prevailed in this epicenter of politics and power. The new millennium is witnessing a boom in construction, the reversal of the city's population decline, and the addition of cultural and recreational venues.

200 YEARS OF GROWTH
SELECTING A SITE

After the Revolutionary War the delegates of the newly formed government expressed interest in designating a federal district to be the seat of power for the new country. A number of existing cities, including New York and Philadelphia, vied to be selected, offering money and land as incentives. Rivalry between the northern and southern states concerning the site of the new capital was resolved through a political compromise: In exchange for agreeing to locate the city in the "southern" precinct, the northern states would be relieved of the heavy debts they had incurred during the Revolution.

In July 1790 Congress passed the Residence Act empowering President George Washington to select a site for the new federal district. Ultimately Washington designated a tract on the Potomac River in the vicinity of Georgetown, though he left its exact boundaries and size undefined. Washington was well acquainted with this area, as his own plantation, Mount Vernon, was 16 miles down the Potomac, and he believed that the site had great commercial potential as a port if it were linked by canal to the productive lands of the Western frontier. To facilitate its development, Washington convinced major landholders in the area to give portions of their land to the new capital.

L'ENFANT'S "CITY OF MAGNIFICENT DISTANCES"

In 1789, even before Congress voted to create a federal district, the French Maj. **Pierre Charles L'Enfant** (1754-1825) expressed to President Washington his eagerness to draw up the plans for the new capital. Trained at the Royal Academy of Painting and Sculpture in Paris, L'Enfant arrived in the US in 1777 at the age of 22 and fought under General Washington in the American Revolution. After the war L'Enfant established himself in American social circles and enjoyed a fine reputation as a designer and architect, particularly for his work in remodeling Federal Hall in New York City. Impressed with L'Enfant's ideas, and realizing that there were few trained engineers from which to choose, Washington appointed him to design the city and its public buildings.

Following his appointment by Washington, L'Enfant traveled to Georgetown, arriving in March 1791. He had in hand a city layout sketched by Thomas Jefferson, who, along with Washington, was instrumental in fostering the early development of the federal city. L'Enfant immediately began reconnoitering the area, which at that time had been settled by several landowners and contained three settlements: the well-established Georgetown and the fledgling towns of Carrollsburg (adjacent to present-day Fort Lesley J. McNair) and Hamburg (now the site of the State Department Building in Foggy Bottom).

One of L'Enfant's first decisions was to situate the future "Congress house" on Jenkins Hill, which had a commanding view of the Potomac River. Along this east-west axis, L'Enfant planned a 400ft-wide "Grand Avenue" (now the Mall) to be lined by foreign ministries and cultural institutions. The avenue would culminate in an equestrian statue of George Washington, connected on a north-south axis with the "president's house." This mansion in turn would be linked back to the Capitol via a mile-long commercial corridor (present-day Pennsylvania Avenue). Tiber Creek, a tributary of the Potomac situated south of this projected corridor, would be transformed into a city canal that would run along the northern side of the Grand Avenue, turning south at the foot of Jenkins Hill before emptying into the eastern branch. The watercourse was to be decorative as well as functional, punctuated by reflecting pools and fountains.

L'Enfant laid out the remainder of the city in a grid pattern of streets intersected by broad diagonal avenues at "round-points," each intended to serve as the focus of a neighborhood area. In emphasizing monumental buildings, grand perspectives, gracious circles, wide avenues and expansive views, the Frenchman was influenced by the Baroque notions of urban planning then prevalent in Europe. L'Enfant's widely dispersed, multicentered city, which later earned the sobriquet "the City of Magnificent Distances," anticipated a population of approximately 800,000 people and extended north to the present Florida Avenue escarpment, encompassing an estimated 6,000 acres.

DREAMS AND REALITIES

Once Washington had approved the expanded city plan, L'Enfant directed his energies toward implementing his grand scheme. Refusing to divert his attention to practicalities, L'Enfant was seen as uncooperative and peremptory by the city surveyor, **Andrew Ellicott**, by Jefferson and by the three city commissioners appointed by Washington to oversee the capital's development.

In September 1791 the commissioners named the new diamond-shaped federal district the "Territory of Columbia" (the current designation, "District of Columbia," came into use in the 19C). Ten miles long on each side, the territory encompassed the County of Alexandria on the Virginia shore of the Potomac and portions of Maryland on the northern shore. The commissioners named the capital itself the City of Washington and stipulated that its street grid be designated by numbers and letters.

To generate revenue for public works and buildings, the commissioners held an auction of lots in October 1791, but only 35 parcels in the as-yet-undeveloped city were sold. Before long, a series of conflicts arose between L'Enfant and the commissioners. Finally, in February 1792, unable to defend the designer's recalcitrance any longer, Washington dismissed him. Gathering up most of his plans and drawings, L'Enfant left the town he had conceptualized. Thirty-three years later the talented Frenchman died penniless and forgotten in nearby Maryland, having never received just compensation or recognition during his lifetime. (In 1909 L'Enfant's remains were transferred to Arlington National Cemetery. The L'Enfant Plan of 1791, restored in 1991, is now in the custody of the Library of Congress.)

Andrew Ellicott took over where L'Enfant left off, reconstructing the Frenchman's original plan from preparatory sketches. Ellicott recruited the gifted, self-taught mathematician Benjamin Banneker, a free black, to assist with the surveying, and proceeded to lay out streets and avenues. On instructions from Jefferson and Washington, Ellicott named the latter after states of the Union.

During the same period, competitions were held to design the president's house and a home for Congress, but even after architects were chosen, work proceeded slowly because the lot sales needed to finance construction continued to lag. A syndicate of private financiers was formed in the late 1790s to act as a real-estate development company for Washington, but the syndicate's bankruptcy in 1797 curtailed further growth. In addition to the lack of an economic base, the city suffered from a critical shortage of stonemasons and other skilled laborers.

"CITY OF MAGNIFICENT INTENTIONS"

When Congress and President John Adams relocated from Philadelphia to Washington in November 1800, they found the skeleton of the nascent city etched into the wilderness. Both the Capitol and White House were incomplete; Pennsylvania Avenue was a

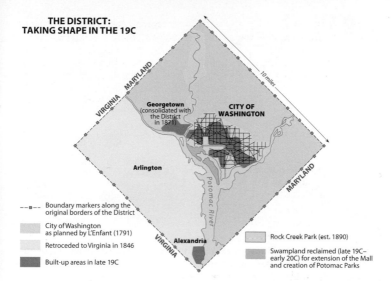

**THE DISTRICT:
TAKING SHAPE IN THE 19C**

Georgetown (consolidated with the District in 1871)

CITY OF WASHINGTON

VIRGINIA MARYLAND

10 miles

Arlington

Potomac River

MARYLAND

VIRGINIA

Alexandria

- – ∎ – Boundary markers along the original borders of the District

City of Washington as planned by L'Enfant (1791)

Retroceded to Virginia in 1846

Built-up areas in late 19C

Rock Creek Park (est. 1890)

Swampland reclaimed (late 19C–early 20C) for extension of the Mall and creation of Potomac Parks

rutted, marshy thoroughfare; and the town was bereft of finesse or comfort. In August 1814 the fledgling capital suffered a major setback when the British invaded the town and set fire to the Capitol, the White House and other public buildings.

After the war a contingent of federal officials, despairing that the town would ever become a capital, lobbied to desert Washington and move the federal government to a more established city. A group of local entrepreneurs put up their own funds as loans for rebuilding, thereby persuading the lawmakers to remain in Washington. Congress appropriated additional monies to repair the damaged Capitol and Executive Mansion, and development continued as before, slowly but a little more surely.

In 1815 the Washington Canal opened along Pennsylvania Avenue. Unfortunately, the canal provided neither the decorative element intended by L'Enfant nor the commercial boon that had been hoped for by George Washington and others. In 1835 the Baltimore and Ohio Railroad reached Washington, signaling the age of rail transport and the doom of the canal trade so necessary to the prosperity of Alexandria and Georgetown. Alexandrians, feeling they had suffered economically and politically by their integration into the federal district,

petitioned for retrocession to Virginia. Their petition was granted in 1846.

In spite of numerous setbacks, by the mid-19C Washington was on its way to becoming a city, and its prevailing Neoclassical flavor had been established, thanks to such monumental structures as the Old City Hall, the Treasury Building and the Old Patent Office Building. Impressive Federal-style residences were also scattered throughout the burgeoning city. Washington had newspapers, theaters and, if not a rich, at least a respectable cultural life.

In 1850 President Millard Fillmore commissioned **Andrew Jackson Downing** to devise a major landscape plan for Washington's central quarters, particularly Lafayette Square and the present-day Mall. Although Downing's plans were never funded, they represented an early and instrumental effort to unify the green spaces of the "monumental city." In 1855 the newly created Smithsonian Institution opened its brick Castle on the Mall.

During the Civil War, development in Washington came to a halt as the city turned its attention to national and local defense. A ring of forts was built along the Potomac, and several of the city's grand public structures became hospitals for the Union wounded.

Pennsylvania Avenue late 19th century

©The Print Collector / age fotostock

The brief period of territorial government that began in 1871 was dominated by **Alexander "Boss" Shepherd**, the driving force behind a citywide public works program that resulted in the development of such outlying areas as Dupont Circle; the alteration of street levels to improve drainage; the paving over of the old, unsanitary canal; and the planting of thousands of trees. Shepherd's grand plan also bankrupted the city, which, as always, relied on federal coffers for support. A disgruntled Congress revoked territorial government and returned the city to district status in 1874. In 1871 Washington was significantly enlarged by the incorporation of Georgetown. As the century drew to a close, railroad, streetcar and trolley lines led to the growth in nearby Virginia and Maryland of suburban communities that were linked economically and culturally to the city.

"THE CITY BEAUTIFUL"

In 1901 the US Senate appointed the four-member **McMillan Commission** to recommend an overall building and landscape plan for the Mall area, which was then an unsightly hodgepodge. The commission's report, inspired by L'Enfant's original plan, established an 800ft greensward for the Mall and extended it west and south along the reclaimed Potomac flats, where the grand monuments to Lincoln and Jefferson were subsequently positioned.

To oversee all future planning for and building in the capital, the Commission of Fine Arts was created in 1910.

In the same year, the Height of Buildings Act stipulated that no structures exceed 15 stories, thus ensuring that Washington would remain a horizontal and spacious city. Another law, the Public Buildings Act of 1926, resulted in the construction of a number of the city's monumental Classical Revival buildings, including those on the Federal Triangle and the structures housing the National Archives and the Supreme Court.

During the first half of the 20C, Washington's population increased from 278,000 to 800,000. The two world wars and the 1930s Works Progress Administration attracted an influx of workers to the city and its suburbs. To meet the administrative needs of the war efforts, a number of temporary buildings were constructed in the Mall area. In the postwar decades, Washington became a decentralized city with a decaying central core and an ever-increasing dependence on the automobile. While a system of expressways was built around the periphery of the District, traffic remained a critical problem. To alleviate congestion, a subway system, the Metrorail, began operations in 1976 and has since continually expanded its intercity and suburban service. The system's efficiency and elegant, albeit stark, design by the architect Harry Weese has won national acclaim.

THE CONTEMPORARY CITY

In the 1960s and 70s, tax laws favored the demolition of the city's old structures, and many charming architectural features were removed forever from the cityscape. At the same time, however, an awareness of historic preservation was burgeoning. The Kennedy administration (1961-63) began efforts to rejuvenate and restore historic Pennsylvania Avenue. In 1978 the city passed the Historic Landmark and Historic District Protection Act, which set guidelines for the designation and protection of historic structures and districts. By the 1980s the growing awareness of Washington's architectural heritage was reflected in commercial, as well as public, endeavors. Old buildings were renovated rather than demolished, new buildings were designed to interface with traditional architecture and the resuscitation of historic Downtown was well under way.

In addition to this architectural awareness, increasing focus was placed on developing and maintaining the parks and green spaces for which the city is famous. During her tenure as First Lady, **Ladybird Johnson** was instrumental in a city beautification process that led to the landscaping of park areas and public squares. In the late 1960s and 70s, the National Capital Planning Commission instituted long-range plans that strove to achieve an integrated look for the city and its natural areas. The commission's Extending the Legacy Plan (1997) and the National Capital Framework Plan (2006) are further attempts to develop and maximize the city's physical assets over time. The District's public parkland, some 7,000 acres that include the elm-lined lawns of the Mall and the hilly, forested terrain of Rock Creek Park, is administered and maintained by the National Park Service.

TIME LINE
THE COLONIAL PERIOD

1608	Capt. John Smith sails up the Potomac.
1662	The first land patent on the future site of the District is granted.
1749	Alexandria is laid out.
1751	Georgetown is established.
1763	The French and Indian War ends, affirming British supremacy in eastern North America.
1775–83	The American Revolution takes place.
1776	The Continental Congress sign the *Declaration of Independence* in Philadelphia.
1783	Britain recognizes the independence of the 13 colonies.
1788	Maryland cedes territory on the Potomac for the establishment of a federal city.
1789	The US Constitution is ratified. New York is designated capital. George Washington is elected first US president.
1790	The nation's capital is moved to Philadelphia. Congress passes the Residence Act, giving George Washington the power to choose the site for the new capital and 10 years to create a federal city.

BUILDING A CAPITAL

1791	President Washington selects a site for the federal district and authorizes Pierre Charles L'Enfant to draft city plans. Congress appoints three commissioners, who name the 10sq mi diamond-shaped area the Territory of Columbia (later known as the District of Columbia) and the capital the City of Washington.
1792	L'Enfant is dismissed by President Washington. The cornerstone is laid for the White House.
1793	The cornerstone is laid for the Capitol.

1800 President John Adams is the first occupant of the White House.
Congress convenes for the first time in the unfinished Capitol building.

1801 Thomas Jefferson is the first president to be inaugurated in Washington.

1802 Under congressional jurisdiction, the City of Washington is chartered.
The first district government buildings are erected.
City population: 3,000.

1808 Construction begins on the Washington Canal along present-day Constitution Avenue.

1812 War of 1812 begins. The US declares war on Britain.

1814 The British invade Washington and burn the Capitol, the White House and other public buildings. Washington banks offer $500,000 in loans to help rebuild the city and to quell a movement to abandon the capital.

1815 President James Madison signs the Treaty of Ghent, ending the War of 1812.

A CENTURY OF GROWTH

1824 Citywide celebrations take place on the occasion of the second visit of the Marquis de Lafayette, America's Revolutionary ally.

1832 A severe cholera epidemic sweeps the city.

1835 The Baltimore and Ohio Railroad reaches the District, initiating the eventual decline of canal traffic through Georgetown and Washington.

1836 Construction of the Treasury and Patent Office buildings gets under way.

1846 Congress establishes the Smithsonian Institution.

District territory south of the Potomac is retroceded to Virginia, reducing the District by one-third of its original size.

1850 Chesapeake and Ohio Canal is completed.

1855 The Castle, the Smithsonian's first building, opens on the Mall.

1861 Beginning of the Civil War. Many public buildings in the District become hospitals and barracks for Union soldiers. Forts are erected around the city's southern edge.

1862 Congress grants compensatory emancipation of all slaves in the District.

1863 President Abraham Lincoln issues the Emancipation Proclamation.

1864 Confederate Gen. Jubal Early is repulsed at nearby Fort Stevens, saving the capital from capture by the South.

1865 End of the Civil War. Gen. Robert E. Lee surrenders to Gen. Ulysses S. Grant at Appomattox. President Lincoln is assassinated five days later at Ford's Theatre.

1867 DC citizens are granted suffrage. Howard University, the capital's first black university, is chartered by Congress.

1871 DC population doubles largely due to the influx of former slaves.
Georgetown is incorporated with Washington.

1871–74 An act of Congress establishes a brief period of territorial government for the District.
Alexander "Boss" Shepherd begins a citywide public works project that results in a beautified but near-bankrupt city.

1874	The city's first art museum, the Corcoran Gallery of Art, opens on Pennsylvania Ave.
1880s	Establishment of streetcar lines leads to the growth of outlying areas.
1884	The Washington Monument, begun in 1848, is completed.
1897	The first Library of Congress building opens.

"THE CITY BEAUTIFUL"

1900	DC celebrates its centennial.
1901	The McMillan Commission is established to beautify the Mall.
1908	Union Station is completed.
1914	The Lincoln Memorial is begun in the reclaimed West Potomac Park.
1917	US enters World War I. Washington experiences a wartime boom. Rows of temporary war buildings, or "tempos," are erected around the Mall.
1918	Armistice ends World War I. DC population has risen to nearly 440,000.
1926	National Capital Park and Planning Commission is established. The Public Buildings Act leads to construction of many federal edifices.
1931–32	Hunger marchers demonstrate in Washington.
1941	US enters World War II. DC experiences another wartime boom. The National Gallery of Art opens on the Mall.
1945	World War II ends in victory for the US and Allied forces.
1950–53	Korean War takes place. DC population peaks at 800,000.
1961	John F. Kennedy is inaugurated 35th US president and appoints a committee to study the rejuvenation of Pennsylvania Ave.

	Congress ratifies the 23rd Amendment to the Constitution, giving District residents the right to vote in presidential elections.
1963	Martin Luther King Jr. leads 200,000 in the March on Washington for Jobs and Freedom. King delivers his "I Have a Dream" speech from the Lincoln Memorial. President Kennedy is assassinated.
Late 60s	Racial riots erupt in the capital. Areas of the city are looted and burned.
Early 70s	Anti-Vietnam War demonstrations are staged on the Mall. District residents are allowed to elect one nonvoting delegate to the House of Representatives.

TOWARD THE 21C

1973	Congress passes the Home Rule Act, establishing self-government for DC. US troops are withdrawn from Vietnam.
1974	President Richard Nixon resigns in the wake of the Watergate scandal.
1976	US bicentennial celebrations. Metrorail, the city's first subway system, begins operations. The Cooperative Use Act is passed, allowing commercial activities in federal buildings and encouraging restoration of historic structures.
1979	Farmers' Tractorcade invades DC. Pope John Paul II delivers a mass on the Mall.
1982	The Washington Convention Center opens, spurring downtown development.
1983	The renovated Old Post Office opens.

1987 The Smithsonian Quadrangle opens.

1990 The Washington National Cathedral, begun in 1907, is completed.

1993 The US Holocaust Memorial Museum and the Smithsonian Institution's National Postal Museum open.

The Vietnam Women's Memorial is dedicated.

Bill proposing DC statehood defeated.

1995 Million Man March.

Korean War Veterans Memorial is dedicated.

1996 Last Washington Redskins football game is played in RFK Stadium.

1997 Memorial to President Franklin D. Roosevelt opens, dedicated by President Bill Clinton.

1998 National Airport named in honor of President Ronald Reagan. President Bill Clinton impeached by the House of Representatives and acquitted by the Senate.

THE NEW MILLENNIUM

2000 After weeks of recounts and lawsuits, the winner of the presidential election is decided by the Supreme

Presidential inauguration January 2009

© Lisa Quiñones/UPPA/Photoshot

Court giving the victory to George W. Bush.

2001 As part of the worst terrorist attack in US history, the Pentagon suffers severe damage, resulting in 184 fatalities.

2003 The new Steven F. Udvar-Hazy Center opens near Dulles International Airport.

2004 Ronald Reagan, the 40th US president, dies. Following a funeral service at the Washington National Cathedral an interment ceremony is held at the Ronald Reagan Presidential Library in California.

The National World War II Memorial opens.

2005 The Washington Nationals return professional baseball to DC after a 34-year hiatus.

2006 The Smithsonian American Art Museum and the National Portrait Gallery reopen after a six-year renovation.

2008 New Washington Nationals baseball stadium opens.

2008 Barack Obama, a senator from Illinois, is elected the 44th US president, the first African-American ever to hold the office.

2009 Some 1.5 million people flood the Mall to watch Barack Obama be sworn in as US president, making the event the most attended one in DC history.

2010 Record-setting snow storms shut down the city, including the federal government.

2012 The Trust for the National Mall announces winners of the first design contest to transform the Mall into a world-class urban park.

2013 A new 2.5mi DC streetcar line is scheduled to begin service along H Street in the summer of 2013.

Architecture

Conceived as a national showplace, Washington, DC embodies the spirit of American idealism in its Neoclassical monuments and grand museums. From its inception Washington has attracted the talents of nationally prominent architects whose skills and vision are reflected in the city's many historic buildings. Because of the dominance of the Neoclassical style within the city and the strict building codes that set a 15-story height limit, modern Washington never developed as a center of innovative, high-rise architecture. Designed as a showcase for the new democracy, it remains in appearance a city of government, featuring massive, columned buildings adorned with allegorical motifs that recall the democratic and aesthetic ideals of ancient Greece and Rome. The District inventory of historic sites currently lists some 396 buildings, parks and historic districts, including lesser-known treasures such as the Classical Revival-style Embassy Gulf Service Station, a less prominent but enduring symbol of the capital.

The Octagon

R. Corbel/MICHELIN

of the successful English architects the **Adam brothers** was seen in the work of colonial designers who adapted the Adam style to an American idiom that became known as **Federal** architecture. This style relies on symmetry and decorative elegance, often integrating such adornments as delicate columns, rosettes, urns and swags. The circular and oval-shaped rooms that characterize this style were used to great effect in The Octagon and Tudor Place, both private residences designed by **Dr. William Thornton** (1759-1828), the first architect of the Capitol. Many of the late-18C and early-19C row houses in Georgetown and Old Town Alexandria also exemplify the Federal style.

18C

Washington preserves few vestiges from the 18C, since the city's foundation dates back to the 1790s. During the colonial period, the **Georgian** style, so named because it was popular in England under kings George I-IV (1714-1830), predominated in the design of brick and stone plantations and manor houses in nearby Virginia and Maryland. Existing examples of this style, which is typified by porticoes, cornices, quoins (prominent corner masonry) and hipped roofs, include Carlyle House, and Gunston Hall in Virginia.

In Georgetown the simple Old Stone House is one of the few extant buildings that reflect colonial vernacular architecture prior to the Revolution. Following independence, the influence

19C

In America, as in Europe, the 19C gave rise to an eclectic mix of revival styles. In Washington, however, the prevailing taste for Neoclassical style frequently led to criticism of buildings that broke with this tradition. Some fine 19C structures that did not adhere to classical principles, such as the Old Post Office, the Old Executive Office Building and the Pension Building, were little appreciated, neglected and even threatened with demolition.

The **Greek Revival** style, modeled on the Doric temple, gained prominence in the 1800s under the talented hands of **Benjamin H. Latrobe** (1764-1820), who modified the original White House design and was responsible for many small architectural gems, such as Decatur House and St. John's Church. Another proponent of this style, **Robert Mills** (1781-1855) created the Treasury Build-

Old Post Office

R. Corbel/MICHELIN

ing, the Old Patent Office Building and the original design of the Washington Monument. By mid century a few architects began experimenting with the **Romanesque Revival** style, as exemplified in the turrets and battlemented cornices of the Smithsonian Castle, designed by **James Renwick** (1818-95). In the 1870s and 80s, Henry Hobson Richardson (1838-86) modified this approach into the popular Richardsonian Romanesque. Distinctive for its massive stone constructions that feature arched windows, doorways and turrets, this style can be found in the Old Post Office and in private residences in the Northwest quadrant, such as the Heurich Mansion.

The **Italianate**, a simpler residential style, can be seen in several of the 19C brick row houses in Georgetown, the Dupont Circle area and Foggy Bottom. One of many versions of what is popularly called Victorian architecture, the Italianate employs overhanging cornices, decorative brackets, bow windows and porches.

The **Second Empire** style, a mid-19C French innovation, first made its appearance in America in the early 1860s, with the building that now houses the Renwick Gallery. Named after its architect, James Renwick, this building features the characteristic Second Empire mansard roof—a dual-pitched roof pierced with dormer windows on the steep lower slope. During the Grant administration (1869-77), the style became so prevalent that it was known as the

General Grant style. The massive Old Executive Office Building is one of the nation's finest examples. At the turn of the century, the exuberant **Beaux-Arts** style dominated the new buildings. Developed in France's famous École des Beaux-Arts, where many prominent American architects studied, this style was typified by a monumentality that reflected the optimistic spirit of the nation in the late 19C and early 20C. Its eclecticism combines classical elements with elaborate detailing, seen in public buildings like Union Station by **Daniel H. Burnham** (1846-1912) and the Library of Congress. In residential architecture, Waddy B. Wood and Jules Henri de Sibour designed a number of the palatial homes along Embassy Row in the Beaux-Arts manner.

Library of Congress

R. Corbel/MICHELIN

20C

In the 1920s Beaux-Arts enthusiasm gradually became restrained, evolving into the more formal **Classical Revival** architecture that again dominated Washington from the 1920s through World War II. The Federal Triangle complex, built in the 1930s, includes seven buildings designed in the Classical Revival style by seven different architects, one of whom was **John Russell Pope** (1874-1937). The most prolific proponent of this style, Pope is responsible for the National Gallery of Art, the National Archives and the Jefferson Memorial. Sweeping staircases, pedimented porticoes, domes, and unadorned surfaces are all hallmarks of Pope's edifices.

Post-World War II Modernism had little impact on Washington architecture. Rather than producing innovative designs, the 1950s, 60s and 70s saw the loss of many fine 19C structures, as boxlike office buildings proliferated throughout the city. It was during this uninspired period that the Kennedy Center and the National Geographic Society building, both by **Edward Durell Stone**, were erected.

National Archives

Washington does, however, possess a few exceptional examples of **modern architecture**: Dulles international Airport (1962, **Eero Saarinen**), the Brazilian Embassy (1971, **Olavo Redig de Campos**), the Martin Luther King Memorial Library (1972, **Mies van der Rohe**), and the East Building of the National Gallery of Art (1978, **I.M. Pei**).

In recent years the currents of **post-Modernism** have resurrected the use of columns, arches and other embellishments that had been banished during the Modernist period. Washington Harbour, designed by Arthur Cotton Moore, embodies the extravagances of the 1980s, while a more restrained and academic approach can be seen in the newer structures along the Pennsylvania Avenue corridor. The Market Square complex (between 6th and 7th Sts.) by Hartman-Cox exemplifies this trend. A decidedly post-Modern influence is apparent in the architecture of the US Holocaust Memorial Museum (James Freed), which opened in 1993.

The Ronald Reagan Building and International Trade Center opened in 1998 completing the Federal Triangle Project (Pei Cobb Freed & Partners).

21C

A flurry of embassy construction in a mix of architectural styles ushered in the new millennium in DC. The Nigerian embassy (2002, Shalom Baranes Associates), located in the International Center is a modernist mix of glass and stone. Overlooking the Potomac in Georgetown, the Swedish embassy (2006, Wingårdh Arkitektkontor AB) inhabits a simple, yet striking five-story geometric construction of glass windows framed in layers of blond wood and stone. The most ambitious chancery in Washington to date is the 350,000sq ft Embassy

of the People's Republic of China, that opened in 2008 near International Drive. The massive glass and limestone complex takes up nearly an entire city block and was designed by the two sons of renowned Chinese-American architect I.M. Pei. The majority of the construction was completed by hundreds of Chinese workers who were flown in for the project and lived in a nearby hotel and specially designed barracks.

Robust **modernism** coupled with historic preservation was the formula for the renovation of the 800 block of F Street NW, which houses the International Spy Museum (2002, Shalom Baranes Associates). Sleek new high-rise office towers and condominiums are dotting the landscape with a modernist aesthetic: examples include BBGM's condominium building (2005) in brick and precast concrete at 12th and K streets NW; the bay-windowed, brick-paneled Rutherford condominiums (2005, Eric Colbert and Assocs.); and the glass and steel 1875 Pennsylvania Avenue office building (2006, Baranes Associates). In 2003 the city witnessed the opening of the more than 2-milion-square-foot Walter E. Washington Convention Center (Thompson, Ventulett, Stainback & Associates) downtown.

The Newseum/Freedom Forum (Polshek Partnership Architects) is a 250,000-square-foot contemporary glass-and-steel building at the intersection of Pennsylvania Avenue and 6th Street, N.W. A 74-foot-high marble engraving of the First Amendment is among the building's many design highlights. The museum opened in April 2008, five years after the project's 2003 groundbreaking. In addition to the Newseum, the building includes more than 140,000 sq ft of residential apartments.

Cultural Scene

Rich in cultural offerings, the capital is truly an international city, with a world-class performing arts complex, fine restaurants, shops and art galleries, and a mixed population of foreign nationals.

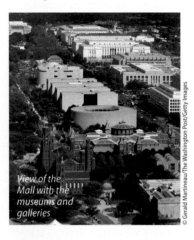

View of the Mall with the museums and galleries

© Gerald Martineau/The Washington Post/Getty Images

MUSEUMS

Founded in 1846 through a bequest to the US from an English scientist named James Smithson, the **Smithsonian Institution** now constitutes the largest complex of museums in the world. Of its 17 museums and galleries in Washington, DC, 10 are located on the Mall. (Although loosely affiliated with the Smithsonian, the National Gallery of Art is an independent institution.) The Smithsonian's National Zoological Park and five of its six other museums are also located in Washington.

The collections of the Smithsonian contain some 140 million objects, including cultural and scientific artifacts and artworks ranging from the prehistoric to the contemporary. Among them are revered relics that define the country's heritage: the Star Spangled Banner, the Wright Brothers' *1903 Flyer*, Dorothy's ruby slippers, Woody Guthrie's "This Land is Your Land" and the entire Folkways Records collection. The institution also maintains six special facilities supporting work in the arts and sciences and sponsors public lectures, concerts, classes, festivals and tours.

In addition to the Smithsonian attractions, the capital boasts several fine privately owned museums created through the generosity of prominent Washington collectors. Foremost among these institutions are the Corcoran Gallery of Art, the Phillips Collection, Hillwood and Dumbarton Oaks. The area has preserved many historic house museums that offer visitors glimpses into the capital's illustrious past. The federal city also abounds in exemplary public buildings, many of which are open to the public. A visit to such sights as the Capitol, Supreme Court, FBI or the

Smithsonian Institution

Mall Museums

+ Arthur M. Sackler Gallery
+ Arts and Industries Building
+ Freer Gallery of Art
+ Hirshhorn Museum and Sculpture Garden
+ National Air and Space Museum
+ National Museum of African Art
+ National Museum of American History
+ National Museum of Natural History
+ National Museum of the American Indian
+ Smithsonian Institution Building: *(The Castle)*

Off the Mall

+ Anacostia Museum
+ National Portrait Gallery
+ National Postal Museum
+ National Zoological Park
+ Renwick Gallery
+ Smithsonian American Art Museum Steven F. Udvar-Hazy Center

New York City
+ Cooper-Hewitt National Design Museum *(See THE GREEN GUIDE New York City)*

Monumental Sculpture in the Capital

The following is a selection of noteworthy works of modern sculpture adorning the public spaces of Washington, DC (℘ *see also Memorials and National Gallery of Art Sculpture Garden*):

Mountains and Clouds by Alexander Calder. Atrium of the Hart Senate Office Building, Constitution Ave. and 2nd St. NE.

Mobile (untitled) by Alexander Calder. Atrium of the National Gallery's East Building.

The Gwenfritz by Alexander Calder. Constitution Ave. and 14th St. NW on the grounds of the National Museum of American History.

The Spiral by Alexander Calder. Courtyard of the Old Patent Office Building.

Infinity by José de Rivera. Outside the Mall entrance of the National Museum of American History.

The Awakening by J. Seward Johnson. National Harbor.

The plaza and the sculpture garden of the Hirshhorn Museum provide an open-air showcase for works by prominent modern artists such as Rodin, Matisse, Calder, Moore, Maillol and Smith, as well as pieces by contemporary sculptors.

Bureau of Engraving and Printing can provide a unique learning experience in the workings of the US government. Throughout the year the area's cultural and educational institutions—both public and private—sponsor an impressive schedule of (usually free) exhibits, lectures and concerts catering to a wide range of tastes and interests.

PERFORMING ARTS

℘ *For addresses, telephone numbers and other practical information, consult Your Stay in Washington, DC.* With the opening of the John F. Kennedy Center for the Performing Arts in 1971, Washington finally began to attract an increasing number of world-class performers. Housing multiple theaters and the resident National Symphony Orchestra, the center offers drama, concerts, family and dance performances. The American Film Institute (AFI) Silver Theatre and Cultural Center in downtown Silver Spring, Maryland, offers a regular schedule of movie showings, film festivals and special events. The well-respected Arena Stage complex, entering its sixth decade, anchors the city's diverse and thriving theater community.

The Studio Theatre produces contemporary works on its four stages, while Shakespeare is the house playwright at the Folger Theatre. Touring Broadway musicals stop at the newly renovated Warner Theatre and the historic National Theatre, established on Pennsylvania Avenue in 1835.

The National Park Service maintains two theaters: the historic Ford's Theatre located downtown and the acclaimed Wolf Trap Farm for the Performing Arts, an outdoor summer theater in the nearby Virginia suburbs, which features renowned dance troupes, musicians and musicals.

John F. Kennedy Center for the Performing Arts

©Zain Deane/Michelin

Multilevel view, National Museum of African Art
©Gwen Cannon/Michelin

The city's high eastern ground, Capitol Hill is crowned by massive stone buildings serving the Legislative and Judicial branches of the federal government. Beyond them stretch the Hill's residential streets, neighborhoods of 19C row houses that reflect a true cross section of Washington's population.

Highlights

1 The impressive architecture of **The Capitol Building** (p71-73)

2 Exhibitions of rare collections at the **Library of Congress** (p77)

3 Taking a tour of the **Supreme Court** (p81)

4 Discover Elizabethan England at **The Folger's Shakespeare Library** (p81)

5 Lunch in the delightful surrounds of **Union Station** (p84)

Info: Capitol Hill Business Improvement District *(Union Station, bus level; ☎202-842-3333; www.capitolhillbid.org)*. Identified by the gold star on their blue shirt, roving "ambassadors" on foot and bicycles answer visitors' questions and provide directions free-of-charge.

P Parking: Union Station's multilevel garage *(open 24hrs/day; $7-$22)*.

Seat of Government

In 1791 when Pierre Charles L'Enfant chose this hilltop (then called Jenkins Hill) as Congress' future home, he expected the city's residential core to develop on its east flank.

The establishment of the Navy Yard and the **Marine Barracks** (8th and Eye Sts. SE) in the early 19C encouraged the growth of neighborhoods from the Capitol to the river. After the War of 1812, the area grew steadily and by the end of the 19C, the Hill became a middle-class enclave.

Federal Building Boom

At the turn of the 19C, the Beaux-Arts Library of Congress was erected. Later, Union Station and the City Post Office, both designed by Daniel H. Burnham, were built at the northern foot of Capitol Hill. In the 1930s the Folger Shakespeare Library, the John Adams Annex of the Library of Congress and the Supreme Court building went up. Meanwhile, the Senate erected three office buildings northeast of the Capitol: the **Russell Building** (1909, Carrère and Hastings), the **Dirksen Building** (1958) and the **Hart Building** (1982). Similarly, the House raised three buildings on the south side: the **Cannon Building** (1908, Carrère and Hastings), the **Longworth Building** (1933) and the **Rayburn Building** (1965). In 1980 the Library of Congress opened its third building, The James Madison Memorial Building. The modern structure also serves as a memorial to the fourth president.

Revitalized Neighborhood

The social composition of Capitol Hill's residential streets fluctuated in the 20C. In mid-century its middle-class population slowly moved out and low-income families began to occupy the old, often run-down row houses. The streets between the Capitol and Lincoln Park underwent renovation as professionals bought up the 19C homes here. Since the 1970s the Hill's residents have gained a reputation as civic activists capable of preventing development that would alter the area's residential feel. Today, **Eastern Market**, on the 200 block of 7th Street SE, is a nucleus for commerce. Independence Avenue, another commercial corridor, serves the Capitol's legislators. The latest landmark, the **Japanese American Memorial,** is located in the triangular park at Louisiana and New Jersey avenues and D Street, NW.

The Capitol★★★

Ⓜ *Capitol South or Union Station*
Floor plan pp 74-75

The grand Capitol building, with its cast-iron dome topped by the Statue of Freedom, is the city's most prominent landmark. This massive symbol of democracy in progress has housed the United States Congress since 1800.

A BIT OF HISTORY
Early Construction

L'Enfant chose Jenkins Hill as the site for the Capitol in 1791. He himself was called upon to design the Capitol and other public buildings, but he was dismissed in 1792 before realizing a single project. President Washington and Secretary of State Jefferson elicited architectural plans for the Capitol by holding a public competition, but the entries proved so uninspiring that **Dr. William Thornton**, a respected amateur architect, was allowed to submit a drawing five months late. His entry called for a stone structure modeled after the Pantheon in Rome. The design met with immediate approval, winning Thornton $500 and a city lot.

🛈 **Info:** The Capitol Visitor Center; 📞202-226-8000; www.visitthecapitol.gov.

◗ **Location:** Main entrance to the U.S. Capitol is through the underground Vistor Center beneath the Capitol's East Front Plaza at First St. and East Capitol St.

🅿 **Parking:** Street parking is difficult to find; there are parking lots at Union Station and on North Capitol St. (mulitlevel lot; $6-$19.) Enter lot from H St., NF

⊘ **Don't Miss:** The view of the Mall from the Capitol steps.

🕓 **Timing:** The Capitol is accessible by ticketed guided tour only; Visitor Center exhibits require no ticket. Visitation is heaviest in spring.

♿ **Also See:** The US Botanic Garden, Bartholdi Fountain.

On 18 September 1793, Washington presided over the laying of the cornerstone. A lack of skilled workers, tools and supplies in the then virtually nonexistent

U.S. Capitol dome
©Zain Deane/Michelin

city hampered construction, as did a lack of funds. The revenue from the sale of city lots was expected to finance building costs, but few people were attracted by the high prices and rudimentary conditions. By 1800, however, Congress was able to leave the temporary capital of Philadelphia and move to the nascent federal city. On 22 November 1800 President John Adams addressed the first joint session of Congress in the completed north wing (the original Senate wing) of the new Capitol.

Professional rivalry among the various architects working on the Capitol (including James Hoban, designer of the White House) led to Thornton's resignation. In 1803 British architect **Benjamin Henry Latrobe** was appointed surveyor of public buildings, and by 1807 he had completed the south wing (the original House wing). The two wings were linked by a wooden walkway crossing the present site of the rotunda. Latrobe began renovating and improving the north wing and submitted revised plans for the Capitol exterior that included a colonnaded central section.

Conflagration and Restoration

The War of 1812 saw the only enemy attack on the Capitol. In August 1814 the British set fire to it, gutting the interior. A providential downpour prevented total ruin, but when Congress returned in the fall, many members advocated abandoning the building and the city and finding a new home for the federal government. To discourage such a desertion, a group of private citizens had a temporary brick structure erected for Congress on the site where the Supreme Court now stands.

From 1815 to 1817 Latrobe worked at restoring the Capitol's interior, adding low domes over the building's two original wings and redesigning the House chamber (now Statuary Hall) into its semicircular shape of today. Among the decorative elements are the tobacco fronds and ears of corn that top the columns lining the House chamber. Though the building's grace was admired, the cavernous space produced echoes. Red draperies were hung behind the gallery to help muffle sounds.

When Latrobe resigned because of a clash with the commissioner of public buildings, Boston architect **Charles Bulfinch** took over and Congress was able to again meet in the Capitol in December 1819. Bulfinch served as the official architect of the Capitol until 1829. During his tenure he completed the building more or less according to Thornton's original plans, substituting a copper-sheathed wooden dome for the stone vault designed by Thornton.

Civil War Years

Legislature in the early 19C grew rapidly, keeping pace with the nation it represented. By 1850 Congress comprised 62 senators and 232 representatives. Spurred on by Sen. Jefferson Davis, who later became president of the Confederacy, Congress appropriated $100,000 for two new wings to house the cramped Senate and House. A contest was held, but as no clear winner emerged, a composite design based on several entries was favored, and **Thomas U. Walter** from Philadelphia was asked to draw up plans. Thomas Crawford designed the statue topping the new dome. His bronze **Freedom** is outfitted with flowing robes and an eagle's-head helmet. With civil strife in the air, construction began. When war finally did come, Congress was not in session, and the War Department quartered troops in the Capitol for several months. Soldiers called it the "Big Tent," and Army bakers built enormous ovens in the basement committee rooms, producing enough bread to feed troops bivouacked around the city. A year later the Capitol served briefly as a hospital for the wounded. Throughout the war, construction on the Capitol proceeded. Walter's enlarged dome, designed to replace the now disproportionately small dome built by Bulfinch, was made of cast iron and weighed almost nine million pounds. By 1863 the dome, considered a marvel of 19C engineering, was ready for Crawford's crowning statue. The two new wings were completed in 1867.

CONSTRUCTION OF THE CAPITOL

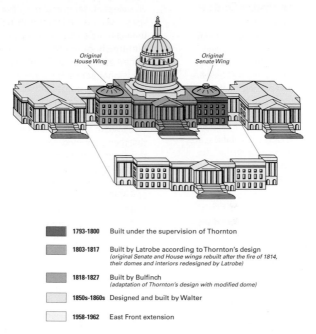

■	**1793-1800**	Built under the supervision of Thornton
■	**1803-1817**	Built by Latrobe according to Thornton's design *(original Senate and House wings rebuilt after the fire of 1814, their domes and interiors redesigned by Latrobe)*
■	**1818-1827**	Built by Bulfinch *(adaptation of Thornton's design with modified dome)*
□	**1850s-1860s**	Designed and built by Walter
□	**1958-1962**	East Front extension

Expansion

The nation's foremost landscape architect, **Frederick Law Olmsted**, was appointed in 1874 to lay out the grounds. Olmsted's landscaping reflects his propensity for natural sweeps of lawn and trees. His addition of the broad plaza on the east and the marble stairway and terraces on the west facilitated the creation of much-needed office space in the building's lower levels.

For the next 75 years, interior changes such as electrification (1897), fireproofing and improved plumbing continued. Under Elliott Wood's term as architect of the Capitol (1902-23), a fourth floor was added, and the Latrobe domes were rebuilt in fireproof cast iron. By the late 1950s Congress had again outgrown the Capitol. To provide more space the central section of the east facade was extended 32½ft *(see drawing)*. The new marble front was designed as an exact copy of the original sandstone facade so as not to alter the essential appearance of this national landmark (the columns of the original facade are conserved at the National Arboretum).

VISIT

Visit by guided 1hr tour only, *year-round Mon–Sat 8:50am–3:20pm. Closed Jan 1, Inauguration Day, Thanksgiving Day, Dec 25. Visitors may book tours in advance through their Congressional offices or online. Limited number of same-day tickets are given out throughout the day at the Visitor Center at 1st St and E. Capitol St. ✕⟁ ☎ 202-226-8000. www.visitthecapitol.gov. Tours begin in the Visitor Center. Recorded and online information includes a list of prohibited items. Be prepared to pass through metal detectors and/or have personal effects searched.*

Main Floor
The Rotunda

On the east side of the rotunda, the eight-paneled, 10-ton bronze **Columbus doors** depict in high relief scenes from Christopher Columbus' life. Of the eight large paintings around the room, the four on the east side show early events in American history, such as the *Embarkation of the Pilgrims at Delft Haven, Holland* by Robert Weir, dated

New Visitor Center

Since its December 2008 opening, the new Visitor Center has seen more than 7 million people enter the Capitol through its doors. Built below an existing parking lot, the 580,000sq ft Capitol Visitor Center occupies three levels below ground and includes a 550-seat cafeteria, exhibit space, gift shop, orientation theaters, ATM machines, pay phones and restrooms.

1843 **(1)**. The ornate Capitol **dome**★★— 180ft high and 98ft across—soars above rich artwork relating to the history of the country. The allegorical fresco in the eye of the dome, entitled the *Apotheosis of Washington*, was painted by Italian-born **Constantino Brumidi**, who had done restoration work in the Vatican. Brumidi worked on the Capitol from 1855 to 1880 and executed so many of its frescoes that he is often referred to as its "Michelangelo."

The grisaille frieze circling the base of the dome (total length of frieze: 300ft) records over 400 years of American history, from the landing of Columbus to the birth of aviation. Brumidi began the frescos when he was 72, but completed only six panels before he fell off the scaffolding, dangling for 15min before he was rescued. He died of poor health in February 1880. Filippo Costaggini carried on the work, but when he left in 1889, a 31ft gap remained in the frieze. Not until 1953 was the work completed by the American artist Allyn Cox.

The four paintings on the west side, all by John Trumbull, portray important moments of the Revolution, including the *Surrender of Cornwallis at Yorktown* (early 19C) **(2)**. Statues of American leaders from Washington **(3)** and Jefferson **(4)** to Martin Luther King Jr. **(5)**, encircle the room. During the Capitol's long history, such popular national figures as Abraham Lincoln and John F. Kennedy have lain in state here.

Statuary Hall

This elegant, semicircular, half-domed space was restored for the 1976 Bicentennial to its architectural appearance (unfurnished) of 1857, when it functioned as the House Chamber. A congressional act of 1864 allowed each state to place statues of two of its distinguished citizens in the Capitol.

Until the 1930s these statues were all displayed in Statuary Hall. It was feared that their combined weight might cause the floor to collapse, so some were moved. Notable among the 38 still in the room are the statues of Robert E. Lee of Virginia **(6)**, 19C social reformer Frances Willard of Illinois **(7)**, 18C missionary pioneer Padre Junípero Serra of California **(8)** and King Kamehameha of Hawaii **(9)**. The room's acoustics amplify the words spoken within.

Old Senate Chamber

Also restored for the Bicentennial, this room maintains the general appearance and several of the furnishings it had during the period the Senate occupied it (1810-14, 1819-59). Note the gilt shield and eagle over the vice president's desk and the porthole portrait of George Washington (1823, Rembrandt Peale). From 1860 to 1935, the chamber housed the Supreme Court.

Visiting the Offices of Your Senators or Representative

Offices are located in six buildings accessible from the Capitol via the basement-level subway: Russell, Dirksen and Hart Bldgs. (Senate); Cannon, Longworth and Rayburn Bldgs. (House). For assistance in locating offices, call ℘202-224-3121 or inquire at the Senate and House Appointment Desks *(ground floor)*. For an appointment with your senator or representative, write in advance.

Viewing a Session of Congress

(3rd floor galleries)

Passes to view a House or Senate session must be obtained at the office of your senator or representative *(above)*. Certain committee sessions are also open to the public. Consult the *Washington Post* or

☎ 202-224-3121 for the recess schedule and the day's agenda. International visitors: Apply to the Senate and House Appointment Desks *(ground floor)*.

Ground Floor
Crypt
Forty Doric columns ring the low-ceilinged crypt directly below the rotunda. Original plans called for the body of Washington to be enshrined in a vault below the crypt, but his relatives insisted that Mount Vernon be his final resting place. The crypt features displays on the history of the Capitol. The compelling sculpture of Lincoln's head **(10)** was done by Gutzon Borglum, who carved Mount Rushmore. He left off the statue's left ear as a symbol of Lincoln's unfinished life. A compass stone embedded in the floor **(11)** marks the zero point from which the city's four quadrants emanate.

▷ *Continue to the Senate wing.*

Old Supreme Court Chamber
An intimate chamber with red carpeting and green-topped desks, this room housed the Supreme Court from 1810 to 1860, except during the reconstruction period after the War of 1812. Note the original 19C furnishings and the room's vaulting, designed by Latrobe. Here, the Marshall Court heard cases that influenced the nation's development.

Brumidi Corridors
The arched ceilings and walls of these two intersecting corridors are embellished with Brumidi's murals. Long interested in ornithology, Brumidi included some 350 birds in his design. Interspersed among the murals are works of later painters, such as Allyn Cox's mural of the 1969 moon landing.

▷ *Return to the crypt and continue to the House wing.*

A number of the state statues originally destined for Statuary Hall now stand in the **Hall of Columns**. Paralleling this hall is the **Hall of Capitols**, which is decorated with murals by Allyn Cox.

Third Floor(Gallery Level)
House and Senate Chambers
♿*See Viewing a Session of Congress.*
The east stairway in the House wing (⊶ *not open to the public when the House is in session*) leads to the third-floor visitors' gallery for the House Chamber.
The Scene of the Signing of the Constitution of the United States (1940) by Howard Chandler Christy hangs on the second-floor landing. The **House Chamber** is dominated by a broad podium facing the seats of the 435 members of the House (Democrats are to the right of the presiding Speaker of the House, Republicans to the left). Beside the podium hangs a full-length portrait of *George Washington* (1834) by John Vanderlyn, and to the right, a portrait of Washington's Revolutionary compatriot *General Lafayette* (1824) by Ary Scheffer.
A third-floor hallway extends along the east face of the Capitol to the Senate wing. Round windows and the stone of the building's original facade (prior to the late-1950s extension) are visible along the interior wall of this hall.
The **Senate Chamber** is more soberly appointed than the House Chamber. The only works of art on display are the busts of early vice presidents. When the Senate is in session, the vice president (in his absence, the president pro tempore), flanked by the secretary of the Senate, the sergeant at arms and various clerks, presides from behind the veined marble podium. The 100 senators are seated at dark mahogany desks (Democrats on the right, Republicans on the left). A desk filled with candy for the senators sits in the back row on the Republican side. Senator George Murphy of California started this sweet tradition in 1965. Note on the second-floor landing of the east stairway in the Senate wing W.H. Powell's monumental painting *The Battle of Lake Erie* (1873). Upon leaving the Capitol, stroll around the **west terrace**, where you can admire a sweeping **view**★★ across the Mall to the Washington Monument.

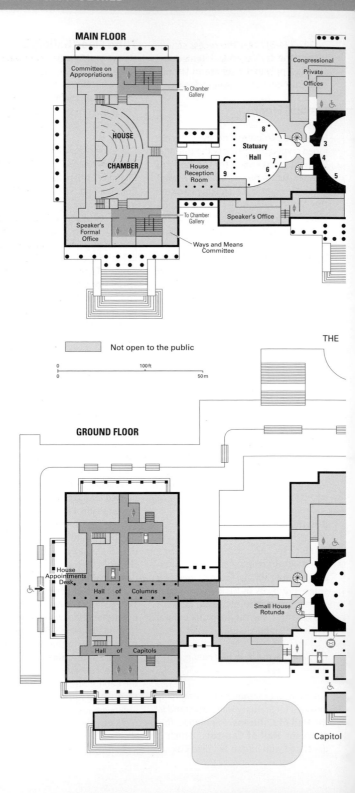

MAIN FLOOR

Committee on Appropriations

To Chamber Gallery

HOUSE CHAMBER

Statuary Hall

House Reception Room

Congressional Private Offices

8

3

7

4

9

6

5

To Chamber Gallery

Speaker's Office

Speaker's Formal Office

Ways and Means Committee

Not open to the public

0   100 ft
0   50 m

THE

GROUND FLOOR

House Appointments Desk

Hall   of   Columns

Hall   of   Capitols

Small House Rotunda

Capitol

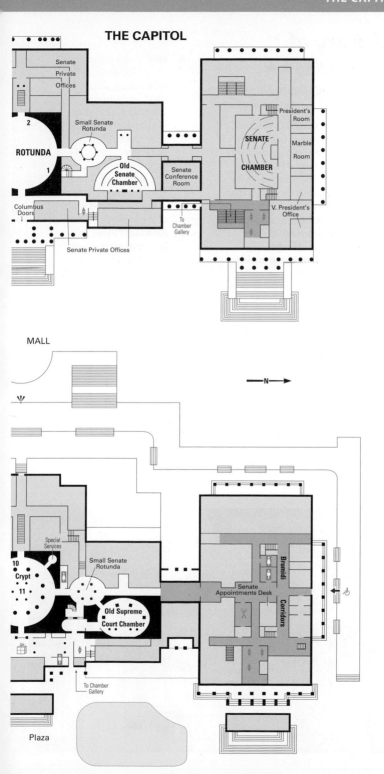

THE CAPITOL

Senate Private Offices

2

ROTUNDA

1

Small Senate Rotunda

Old Senate Chamber

Senate Conference Room

President's Room

Marble Room

SENATE CHAMBER

V. President's Office

Columbus Doors

To Chamber Gallery

Senate Private Offices

MALL

N→

Special Services

Small Senate Rotunda

10 Crypt

11

Old Supreme Court Chamber

Senate Appointments Desk

Brumidi Corridors

To Chamber Gallery

Plaza

Library of Congress★★

Ⓜ *Capitol South or Union Station*

A renowned Beaux-Arts landmark, the original Library of Congress is reputedly Washington's most richly ornamented building. The largest library in existence, it retains in its ever-growing collections more than 33 million books, as well as historical treasures. It functions as a reference library, open to anyone 18 years or older pursuing research. The general public is welcome to visit the complex.

A BIT OF HISTORY
Congress' Library

In 1800, while still convening in Philadelphia, Congress appropriated $5,000 for the establishment of a library for its own use. Originally the library was housed in the Capitol for the convenience of the legislators. When the library's 3,000 volumes were destroyed in the Capitol fire of 1814, Thomas Jefferson offered his extensive personal library to Congress, which purchased the 6,487 volumes for $23,950. The collection was shipped in 10 horse-drawn wagons from Monticello, Jefferson's Virginia estate, to the

🛈 **Info:** Visitor information 📞202-707-8000; general information 📞202-707-5000; www.loc.gov. The visitor center is on the ground floor of the Jefferson Building.

◖ **Location:** 1st St. and Independence Ave. SE. The Jefferson Building, the main building, lies just east of the Capitol and south of the Supreme Court.

🅿 **Parking:** Parking lots lie within about a half mile at Union Station and N. Capitol St.; public transportation is handier.

☺ **Don't Miss:** The view of the Main Reading Room from the visitors' gallery.

Capitol. Unfortunately, another fire in 1851 destroyed two-thirds of the existing library collection. Congress immediately appropriated funds to replenish the holdings and to build a new, multi-tiered library along the west side of the Capitol. In honor of the library's Bicentennial in 2000, an effort was begun to reconstitute the lost volumes as a gift to the nation.

Great Hall, Thomas Jefferson Building

Carol Highsmith/Library of Congress

A Library for the People

Though intended to serve only members of Congress and Supreme Court justices, the library was gradually opened to other governmental and diplomatic officials. In 1864 **Ainsworth Rand Spofford** was appointed librarian of Congress and began a process that changed the library into a public institution. To amass a more extensive collection, Spofford lobbied Congress to amend existing legislation so that the copyright for books, musical scores, maps and charts would be granted by the Library of Congress rather than the Department of Interior. This procedure ensured that newly published materials would find their way into the library's holdings, a practice that continues to this day.

In 1873 Congress approved a separate building for the library. In 1886 ground was broken, but the work progressed slowly, causing Congress to dismiss the building's principal architects, **John Smithmeyer** and **Paul Pelz**. They were replaced by Thomas Casey, the chief of Army engineers, and Bernard Green, a civilian engineer. Along with Casey's son Edward, Green planned the interior artwork and commissioned American artists to execute the decorative scheme, which blended mosaics, murals, marblework and sculptures. The library opened in 1897, under budget (total cost: $6.5 million) and ahead of schedule; it has functioned as the "national library of the United States" ever since.

In 1939 the library expanded to a second structure, the **John Adams Building** *(2nd St. SE, behind the main building)*, noteworthy for its Art Deco ornamentation. At that time the original building was designated the Thomas Jefferson Building. A third facility, the austere marble **James Madison Memorial Building** *(Independence Ave., between 1st and 2nd Sts. SE)*, was opened in 1980 and contains more than twice the floor space of either of the two older library structures. Its Memorial Hall *(left side of the lobby)* is dominated by a seated statue of James Madison, the fourth US president.

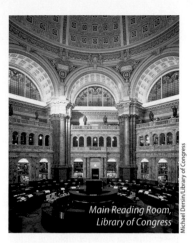

Main Reading Room, Library of Congress

Michael Dersin/Library of Congress

Holdings

The library retains more than 145 million items that fill the equivalent of some 745 miles of shelves. These include more than 63 million manuscripts; 5.3 million maps and atlases; 6 million musical items, such as scores, instruments and correspondence among musicians; 12.5 million photos; and 33 million books. The library acquires new holdings at the rate of 10,000 items a day. Foremost among the valuable works of art owned by the Library of Congress are two mid-15C masterpieces: the manuscript Giant Bible of Mainz and a Gutenberg Bible. American artifacts include Jefferson's rough draft of the *Declaration of Independence* and President Lincoln's handwritten drafts of the *Emancipation Proclamation* and the *Gettysburg Address*. The library's renowned music division contains a collection of Stradivarius violins and original scores by Brahms, Beethoven and other composers.

VISIT

🕐*Jefferson Building open year-round Mon–Sat 8:30am–4:30pm. Adams and Memorial Buildings 8:30am; closing hours vary.* 🕐*Closed major holidays.* 🔍*Guided tours (1hr) of the Jefferson Building Mon–Sat 10:30am, 11:30am, 1:30pm, 2:30pm &, 3:30pm (Mon–Fri only). On Sat & federal holidays 1st tour 9:30 am.* ☎*202-707-8000. www.loc.gov. Tour tickets (free) may be required; inquire at the visitor center.*

An orientation video *(12min)* is shown every 20min on the ground floor of the Jefferson Building in the visitor center. The Jefferson Building contains changing exhibitions and installations that celebrate the library's special collections. In the past, rare library materials such as George Washington's first inaugural address and Frank Lloyd Wright's architectural drawings have been exhibited. A copy of the *Handbook of the New Library of Congress*, which describes the library's history and architecture, may be purchased from the shop in the Jefferson Building or the Madison Building. A cafeteria is located in the Madison Building on the 6th floor *(open to the public 9am–10:30am, 12:30pm–3pm)*; a snack bar is located on the basement level.

For current visitor information or assistance in using the research facilities, consult the touch-screen terminals located in the visitor center.

The library offers a regular series of concerts and features public lectures and poetry readings, as well as showings of old films in its Pickford Theater, located in the Madison Building. For schedules, consult the touch screens at the visitor center in the Jefferson Building. For concert information, call ℰ 202-707-5502.

Thomas Jefferson Building

🕐 *Open year-round Mon–Sat 8:30am–4:30pm.* 🕐 *Closed major holidays.*
🔊 *Guided tours (1hr) available.*
♿ ℰ *202-707-8000. www.loc.gov.*
This Beaux-Arts showplace occupies a full block across from the Capitol on 1st Street SE. At street level the exuberant **Neptune Fountain** by Roland Hinton Perry depicts the sea god and his cavorting entourage.

Exterior

The building's central section is vaulted by a massive green copper dome surmounted by a lantern that supports the symbolic "torch of learning" *(step back from the facade across 1st St. to view)*. The intricate entrance stairway, replete with side flights, ornamented stone balustrades and candelabras, provides a ceremonial access to the edifice.

The granite facade, which resembles the 19C Paris Opera House, features a second-story portico of paired Corinthian columns and massive quoins, or cornerstones. Busts depicting famous men of letters are framed in the oculi, or round openings, that punctuate the portico.

Interior★★

Murals, sculptures, detailed mosaics, marble columns and floors, and vaulted corridors make the two-story **Great Hall** one of the most impressive spaces in the city. The hall's vestibule is especially noteworthy for the gold leaf adorning its ceiling, while blue and amber stained-glass skylights punctuate the vaulting of the hall proper. At the rear of the hall stand glass cases containing a Gutenberg Bible and the Giant Bible of Mainz, which is one of the last hand-illuminated manuscript versions of the Bible. A grand staircase sculpted with elaborate bas-relief cherubs leads to the second-story colonnade, where a visitors' gallery overlooks the Main Reading Room.

Occupying the vast rotunda under the library dome (height: 160ft from floor to lantern), the **Main Reading Room** is ringed by colossal Corinthian columns and arched windows, embellished with stained-glass state seals and eagles.

In the lantern of the coffered dome is an allegorical mural entitled *Human Understanding*. The eight 11ft stone statues between the arches symbolize such subjects as commerce, law, poetry and science. Sixteen bronze statues along the balustrade of the galleries represent pivotal figures in the development of civilization. Rotating items from the library's permanent Americana *(southwest galleries)* and international collections *(northwest galleries)* are on view.

Two rooms can be viewed by a special in-depth tour: the **Librarian's Room**, located at the east end of the Great Hall's north corridor; and the **Members of Congress Room**, a special reading room used today by members of the US Congress.

Supreme Court★★

Ⓜ *Capitol South or Union Station*

Positioned directly across the street from the Capitol, this white marble monument to the supremacy of law houses the highest court in the land. Within its walls the third branch of government exercises its mandate to protect and interpret the spirit of the US Constitution.

A BIT OF HISTORY
A Constitutional Basis

Article III of the US Constitution, ratified in 1788, called for a "supreme Court" of the land to act as a final arbiter of law and as a counterbalance to the other two branches of government (Executive and Legislative).

The first US Supreme Court convened in 1790 at the Royal Exchange Building in the temporary capital of New York City. During the first three years, the Court, as a body, had little work. However, the individual justices were kept busy riding circuits, as they were required to do until 1891, hearing cases in their districts. Because of the difficulty of travel at the end of the 18C, many justices served only a few years.

One of the earliest judicial precedents was set in 1793 when President Washington asked the Court to advise him on questions of international law. Under its

ℹ **Info:** Sessions are open to the public on a first-come, first-served basis. The daily schedule of Court hearings is posted a month in advance on the website. When the Court is not in session, lectures on the Supreme Court are held in the courtroom on the half hour 9:30am–3:30pm. A film (24min) about the Court is shown continuously in the theater at the end of the hall to the right of the Marshall statue.

▶ **Location:** 1st and E. Capitol Sts. NE.

🏛 **Don't Miss:** The Great Hall.

first chief justice, John Jay, it declined, explaining that in view of the Constitution's requirement of separation of powers, the Judicial branch had no place advising the Executive branch.

To jurists, the fourth chief justice, **John Marshall** (1755-1835), is the "Great Chief Justice." Appointed by President Adams in 1801, Marshall served until his death in 1835. During his long tenure he firmly established the fledgling Court as the supreme authority over the law of the land. Among the many important cases the Marshall Court ruled on, *Marbury v. Madison* (1803) set a critical precedent.

Supreme Court

© Gary Blakeley/Bigstockphoto.com

The Supreme Court Justices

♦ Chief Justice:
John G. Roberts Jr. *(Bush, 2005)*
♦ Associate Justices:
Antonin Scalia *(Reagan, 1986)*
Anthony M. Kennedy *(Reagan, 1988)*
Stephen Breyer *(Clinton, 1994)*
Clarence Thomas *(Bush, 1991)*
Ruth Bader Ginsburg *(Clinton, 1993)*
Samuel Alito Jr. *(Bush, 2006)*
Sonia Sotomayor *(Obama, 2009)*
Elena Kagan *(Obama, nominated May 2010)*

(Nominating president and year judicial oath taken are noted.)

In this case the Supreme Court affirmed its power to declare an act of Congress unconstitutional. Other important decisions reached under Marshall, in such cases as *McCulloch v. Maryland, Cohens v. Virginia* and *Gibbons v. Ogden*, reaffirmed the power of the Union and its authority over state laws.

A Body of Controversy

"We are very quiet here, but it is the quiet of a storm center," explained Justice Oliver Wendell Holmes Jr., who served from 1902 to 1932. Throughout its history the Court has been involved in controversy, sometimes settling it, at other times kindling it. In 1857 the Court handed down perhaps its most infamous decision, when, under Chief Justice Taney, it heard the case of a slave named Dred Scott. The Court's ruling—that Congress had no authority to limit the expansion of slavery—helped bring on the Civil War and badly damaged public respect for the Court.

A Home of Its Own

In its early years the Court had no regular meeting place, convening in various public buildings in New York City, then Philadelphia. In 1800 it moved to the new federal city and occupied different rooms in the Capitol, including the room now known as the Old Supreme Court Chamber. After the British burned the Capitol in 1814, the Court met in a number of temporary locations, including a private home and a tavern. When the Capitol was repaired, the Court returned to the Old Supreme Court Chamber, which it occupied from 1819 to 1860. It then moved upstairs to the Old Senate Chamber, which remained its home for 75 years.

William Howard Taft (1857-1930), the 10th chief justice (1921-30) and the only US president to serve on the Court, convinced Congress in 1928 to allocate funds for a building to house the Court. "The Republic endures and this is the symbol of its faith," Chief Justice Charles Evans Hughes decalred during the laying of the cornerstone for the Supreme Court Building on October 13, 1932. Three years later In October 1935, the present marble edifice was completed at a cost of $9,650,000, which was less than had been budgeted for the project. Upon completion of the building, $94,000 was actually returned to the US Treasury.

Precedent-setting cases heard in the courtroom of the current building include *Brown v. Board of Education*, which established school integration nationwide; *Engel v. Vitale*, outlawing school prayer; and the consitutionality of the 2000 presidential election.

The Court at Work

Woodrow Wilson called the Supreme Court "a kind of Constitutional Convention in continuous session." As the highest court in the country, it is the court of last appeal. The chief justice and associate justices are appointed by the president, with Senate approval, as vacancies occur. Only death, voluntary retirement or resignation, or congressional impeachment can remove a sitting justice.

Congress, not the Constitution, sets the number of justices on the Court. In the Court's first century, that number changed six times. Now, based on the Judiciary Act of 1869, it is set at nine.

The Court's term begins on the first Monday in October. From October through April the Court hears oral arguments on cases. Of the 7,000-plus requests for review it receives annually, the Court hears about 100 cases per term. It typically sits two weeks a month, Monday to Wednesday (10am–3pm) with a lunch recess (noon–1pm). Most case arguments are limited to an hour; 30 minutes for each side.

The rest of the week, the justices review arguments and consider requests for future reviews. From mid-May through June the Court convenes on Mondays (10am) to deliver its opinions.

VISIT

🕐 *Open year-round Mon–Fri 9am–4:30pm.* 🚫 *Closed major holidays.* ✕ ♿ 🖊 *202-479-3030. www.supremecourt.gov.*
A new entrance sees visitors enter on the ground floor. Outside, an oval plaza fronts the cross-shaped building of gleaming white marble, designed by Cass Gilbert. Flanking a broad staircase that leads to a colonnade of 32 Corinthian columns are two massive allegori-

cal figures. Sculpted by James Fraser, they represent the Contemplation of Justice *(left)* and the Authority of Law *(right)*. Carved under the bas-relief in the pediment are the words "Equal Justice Under Law."

A wide columned hall, adorned with a coffered 44ft-high ceiling and busts of chief justices, leads from the entrance to the **courtroom**. Here the justices sit on a raised bench positioned in front of 4 of the 24 massive veined columns that ring the 82ft-by-91ft chamber. The justices' places are ordered by their seniority, with the chief justice taking the center position.

The ground floor features changing exhibits on the history and function of the Supreme Court. Dominating the main hall on this level is a massive **statue of John Marshall**, depicting him in a relaxed seated pose that suggests his renowned affability and lack of pretense.

Folger Shakespeare Library★

Ⓜ *Capitol South or Union Station*

The world's largest collection of Shakespeare's works is conserved behind this Art Deco exterior. Renowned as a research institution, the Folger also encourages a larger public appreciation of the traditions of Elizabethan England and the Renaissance through its program of exhibits, concerts, readings and theatrical performances.

A BIT OF HISTORY
The Folger Bequest

The son of a Martha's Vineyard schoolmaster, Henry Clay Folger became a lifetime devotee of Shakespeare while attending Amherst College. There, in 1879, inspired by a lecture given by

▷ **Location:** 201 E. Capitol St. SE. By Metro walk from the Capitol South station (Blue and Orange lines) and by Bus: 30, 32, 34, 35, 36, 96, or 97 lines.

👥 **Kids:** Shakespeare 's Birthday Open House in April.

🕐 **Timing:** Allow 2 hrs.

👓 **Don't Miss:** The Seven Ages of Man stained-glass window in the Old Reading Room.

the aging Ralph Waldo Emerson, Folger bought a volume of Shakespeare's complete works.

Ten years later he made his first serious Shakespeare acquisition: a 1685 Fourth Folio edition purchased at an auction for $107.50. At the time, his finances were such that he was forced to request 30 days to raise the money. Through the years, however, his fortunes steadily

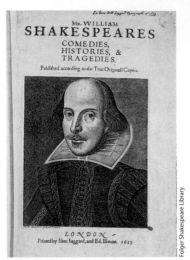

Title Page of 1623 First Folio

Folger Shakespeare Library

The Building—Paul Cret incorporated classical elements in this simple Art Deco marble facade. Nine long rectangular windows covered in a geometrical grill-work are offset by bas-relief underpanels depicting scenes from Shakespeare's plays. Chiseled into the facade, above the windows, are quotes about the Bard, and above the two entrances appear the masks of Tragedy and Comedy. Along the 2nd Street side of the building is a marble statue of the character Puck from *A Midsummer Night's Dream,* inscribed with his famous quote "Lord, what fools these mortals be."

VISIT

Open year-round Mon–Sat 10am–5pm, Sun noon–5pm. Closed major holidays. Guided tours (1hr) Mon–Fri 11am & 3pm, Sat 11am & 1pm, Sun 1pm). Research facilities are not open to the general public. 202-544-4600. www.folger.edu.

The 190ft-long **Great Hall**, with oak paneling and a barrel-vaulted ceiling, features changing exhibits based on the library's collection. The east end of the building houses a reproduction of an **Elizabethan theater**. The Folger Consort, a resident chamber music ensemble, performs in the theater and in the Great Hall. The library also sponsors poetry and fiction readings and an annual Emily Dickinson Birthday Tribute Reading. Outside, the small Elizabethan garden features plants well known in Shakespeare's day and eight large sculptors of famous characters from his plays. *(guided tours available Apr–Oct the third Sat of the month 10am and 11am).*

increased, and he eventually became chairman of the board of the Standard Oil Co. of New York.

His wife and co-collector, Emily Jordan, was a teacher and student of literature. She was particularly interested in acquiring different copies of the 1623 First Folio, the first collected edition of Shakespeare's plays. In the 1920s the Folgers, who lived in New York state, began searching for a site to establish a research library. They chose DC, and in 1930 the cornerstone was laid. Folger himself did not live to see the 1932 opening of the building that housed the 75,000 books, manuscripts, prints and engravings he and his wife had collected. Mrs. Folger continued to be active with the library until her death in 1936. The ashes of both are interred in the library.

The Library's Holdings

The Folger now owns more than 300,000 books and manuscripts relating to the Renaissance period in England and other European countries. About a third of its holdings are considered rare, the most valuable being the only known copy of Shakespeare's early play *Titus Andronicus*. It was discovered in a cottage in Sweden and purchased for $10,000 by the Folgers in 1905.

The library holds 79 of the 240 first editions of the collected works of Shakespeare that are known to exist (Japan's Meisei University, the next-largest owner of first editions, owns only eight). The library also owns theatrical memorabilia from 18C and 19C Shakespearean productions.

National Postal Museum★

Ⓜ *Union Station*

Occupying part of the ground floor of the stately Beaux-Arts **City Post Office Building** next to Union Station, this Smithsonian Institution museum houses the world's largest philatelic collection and chronicles America's mail service from colonial times to the present.

A BIT OF HISTORY

A gift of Confederate postage stamps in 1886 initiated the Smithsonian's philatelic collection. By 1908 the growing assemblage was housed in the Arts and Industries Building; in 1964 it was moved to the National Museum of American History. The landmark City Post Office Building (1914, Daniel H. Burnham) was chosen as the site for a new museum, a joint project of the US Postal Service and the Smithsonian. It opened in 1993 and includes the museum, a research library, theater and stamp shop.

The 16-million-item collection includes historic postal artifacts, personal letters and photographs, in addition to rare stamps and premier covers.

VISIT

≗ ⓞ*Open year-round daily 10am– 5:30pm.* ⓞ*Closed Dec 25.* ☜*Guided tours (30min) daily 11am & 1pm based on docent availability.* ⓰ ℘*202-633-5555. www.postalmuseum.si.edu.*

The lobby of the building, with its 40ft-high coffered ceiling, Ionic columns and marble floors, provides a grand passageway to the exhibit area *(located on the lower level)*, which is entered through a polished bronze and stainless steel **escalator arcade**. Three vintage mail planes, suspended from the ceiling, dominate the 90ft glass **atrium** gallery, where a walk-through railroad car with mail sorting bins, a Concord-style mail coach and a 1931 Model A Ford are also on view. The **Stamps and Stories** gallery contains changing selections of philatelic rarities from the collec-

▷ **Location:** *2* Massachusetts Ave. NE. Across the street from the top of the escalator on the Massachusetts Ave exit at the Union Station (Red line) Metro station.

ℙ **Parking:** Park at the garage attached to Union Station ($6-$19).

≗ **Kids:** The Souvenir Postcard Machine & The Stamp Gallery.

tion, such as the first prepaid stamps (1840), called "penny blues." Other galleries showcase little-known pockets of postal history like the annual Duck Stamp contest that since 1934 has raised $500 million for US waterfowl. Related activities like letter writing and envelope manufacturing are also explored. A number of interactive videos, including an electronic souvenir postcard kiosk, encourage visitor participation.

PIMCO founder and avid stamp collector William H. Gross has donated $10 million to create a new 12,000sq ft gallery that is scheduled to open in the fall of 2013.

Atrium Gallery, National Postal Museum

©Peter Wrenn/Michelin

Union Station

© John Kuo/Bigstockphoto.com

Union Station★

Ⓜ *Union Station*

Located north of the Capitol, this monumental granite building has long served as the hub of the city's rail travel. It is a formidable embodiment of the oft-quoted premise of its architect **Daniel H. Burnham:** "Make no little plans." More than 70,000 people pass through the station per day.

A BIT OF HISTORY

When the first trains pulled into the terminal in 1907, it was the largest train station in the world, measuring 760ft by 344ft (completed in 1908). Burnham designed the station with the colossal columns, arches and statues that characterize the Beaux-Arts style. For half a century Union Station served as the city's main point of arrival.

With the demise of rail travel in the 1950s and 60s, the station deteriorated. A renovation done in the 1970s met with much criticism, and an entirely new revamping was begun in 1986. The restoration project was completed in 1988 for $160 million. In addition to being the city's main railway terminal, the station also houses scores of shops, restaurants and a food court.

▷ **Location:** 50 Massachusetts Ave. NE. The Metro's Red line stops underneath Union Station. Amtrak, MARC and VRE trains also stop here. Lockers on-site, and baggage storage at Gate A 6am–10pm (prices vary by size and length of storage).

Ⓟ **Parking:** A five-level paid lot sits behind the station; enter on H St. NW.

VISIT

🕐*Public areas open daily year-round.* ✕♿Ⓟ 🕿*202-289-1908. www.union stationdc.com.*

A fountained plaza featuring a statue of Columbus and the Freedom Bell (a replica of the Liberty Bell) fronts the station, whose triple-arched, colonnaded entrance is modeled after Rome's Arch of Constantine. The Baths of Diocletian, served as the inspiration for the station's cavernous main hall. A vaulted ceiling with gilded octagonal coffers soars 96ft, and 36 statues of Roman legionnaires look down from the second-story balcony rimming the hall.

Sewall-Belmont House

Ⓜ *Union Station or Capitol South*

Reputedly one of the oldest buildings on Capitol Hill, this gracious house was erected in 1799 by Robert Sewall. The residence remained in the Sewall family for 123 years and served as one of Washington's first social centers. Among its noted tenants was Albert Gallatin, secretary of the Treasury under presidents Jefferson and Madison. According to certain sources, Gallatin worked out the financial arrangements for the Louisiana Purchase on the premises. Over the years the house has undergone major exterior and interior alteration. In 1929 the building was purchased by the National Woman's Party, and has been their headquarters ever since.

VISIT

🕐*Open year-round Wed–Sun noon–5pm (by appointment only Jan–Feb).* 🕐*Closed major holidays.* 💲*$5 donation requested.* 📞*202-546-1210. www.sewallbelmont.org.*

Designated a National Historic Site, the Sewall-Belmont House serves as the headquarters of the National Woman's

▶ **Location:** 144 Constitution Ave. NE, next to the Hart Senate Office building. Walking distance from Union Station (Red Line) and Capitol South (Blue and Orange Lines) Metro stations.

🕐 **Timing:** About 45 min.

😊 **Don't Miss:** The desk where Susan B. Anthony wrote the 19th Amendment & The Nina Evans Allender Cartoons.

Party (now solely an educational organization). It was the home of Alice Paul (1885-1977), the party's founder.

Inside, exhibits commemorate the women's movement with portraits and busts of the suffragists—those who fought for passage of the 19th Amendment (1920) granting women the right to vote. Highlights include the museum's digital collection of more than 5,000 vintage prints and photographs, political drawings by prominent cartoonists including Nina Allender, scrapbooks and other unique artifacts.

Sewall-Belmont House & Museum

©Sewall-Belmont House & Museuma

THE MALL★★★

The Mall serves as the cultural heart of the capital and a political forum for the nation. Its imposing buildings and broad vistas underscore Washington's reputation as "the City Beautiful." The nation's revered memorials and a number of excellent national museums welcome the public free of charge.

Highlights

1 The Albert Einstein Planetarium at **The National Air and Space Museum** (p92)

2 Viewing masterpieces at **The National Gallery of Art** (p98-107)

3 Climbing the steps of the **Lincoln Memorial** (p138)

4 Visiting the **Jefferson Memorial** in cherry blossom season (p133)

5 The stunning view from atop the **Washington Monument** (p141)

A Bit of History
"A Vast Esplanade"

The city's designer, Pierre Charles L'Enfant, envisioned the Mall as a grand avenue extending from Jenkins Hill to the current site of the Washington Monument. In 1848 ground was broken for the Washington Monument and, a year later, for the Smithsonian Castle, paving the way for a growing institutional presence on the Mall.

After a severe flood in 1881, Congress appropriated funds for draining the Potomac flats south and west of the Mall. By the turn of the 19C, 621 acres had been reclaimed for the creation of Potomac Park. The Tidal Basin was formed to ensure a flow of fresh water through the Washington Channel.

Early-20C Development

The McMillan Commission, appointed in 1901 to assess the future development of the city, called for transforming the Mall into a broad, tree-lined promenade. The commission succeeded in negotiating the transfer of the railroad facilities to the newly proposed Union Station (1903). In 1917, to accommodate wartime exigencies, barrackslike wooden structures known as "tempos" were

Info: The Castle, on the Mall; ℘202-633-1000; www.si.edu.

Location: The rectangular Mall stretches more than 2mi from the Capitol to the Lincoln Memorial between Constitution Ave. on the north and Independence Ave. on the south (⌚ see *Visiting the Mall opposite*). The Smithsonian Information Center in the Castle is a great place to get an overview of the attractions on the Mall. Due to the proximity of the Mall museums to one another, touring the area on foot is recommended.

Parking: Street parking is allowed, but spaces tend to be filled immediately after 10am, especially during the peak tourist season. There are lots several blocks away in the downtown area, but public transportation is easiest.

Don't Miss: Sweeping views of the Mall, monuments and the Potomac River from the Lincoln Memorial.

Timing: Distances are long and museums are large; focus on one major museum in the morning and another in the afternoon.

Kids: National Air and Space Museum, National Museum of Natural History and National Museum of American History are the big three.

constructed on the Mall. In 1923 the Smithsonian opened the Freer Gallery of Art on the south side of the Mall, and in 1941 the National Gallery of Art rose on the north side of the Mall, near the new National Archives. The southwestern portion of the general Mall area was extended in the late 1930s when the Jefferson Memorial was built on the shores of the Tidal Basin.

A Dream Realized

Following World War II, gardens, monuments and museums gradually replaced the unsightly tempos. Since the mid-1960s the Smithsonian has added six museums, and the National Gallery of Art has constructed its widely acclaimed East Building. The **National Museum of the American Indian** opened on the Mall in 2004. In 2006 the Smithsonian Institute announced plans for its newest museum on the Mall, the **National Museum of African American History and Culture**, devoted solely to African-American art, history and culture. Construction is slated for completion in 2015. The first of several projects of a $700 million plan to transform the Mall into a world-class urban park is scheduled for completion in 2016. Projects include gardens, recreational facilities and landscaping.

Traditionally a rallying point for political demonstrations, the Mall also hosts major national events, such as the annual Independence Day celebration on the Fourth of July.

Visiting the Mall
Orientation

Known as the **East Mall**, the mile-long, tree-lined esplanade extending from the foot of Capitol Hill to 15th Street contains one of the world's densest concentrations of museums. The dominating presence here is the Smithsonian Institution, which operates nine museums on the Mall proper. The building on Jefferson Drive known as the Castle houses the Smithsonian Information Center. Comprising two structures, the independently administered National Gallery of Art dominates the northeast corner of the Mall. The eastern end of the Mall is anchored by the Capitol Reflecting Pool. On the south side of the Reflecting Pool is a memorial to President Garfield, and on the north side there is an allegorical memorial to Peace.

Stretching from 15th Street to the Potomac River is the **West Mall**, home to the nation's best-known memorials. The monolithic Washington Monument is aligned on a north-south axis with the circular Jefferson Memorial, which overlooks the Tidal Basin. West of the Washington Monument stands Lincoln Memorial. South of it, the panhandle between the Potomac and the Tidal Basin serves as the setting for West Potomac Park.

In early July the Smithsonian holds its annual Festival of American Folklife. From Memorial Day to Labor Day, concerts are presented by military bands and other musical groups several times weekly in the Sylvan Theatre, an outdoor stage situated to the south of the Washington Monument (*see Calendar of Events*).

Helpful Hints

When entering museums, be prepared to pass through metal detectors and/or have your personal effects searched. All museums and historic sites on the Mall are free of charge. Smithsonian sights are open daily *(except Dec 25)* 10am–5:30pm *(The Castle opens at 8:30am)*. Several Metro stations serve the Mall. **ANC Tours, Big Bus Tours** and **Old Town Trolley** offer transportation to several sights on the Mall (*see Planning Your Trip*).

The information center inside the Smithsonian Castle is a good first stop; staff are on hand to answer questions. You can also pick up event schedules at Smithsonian museums. Cafes and cafeterias are located in many of the museums *(indicated by the ✕ symbol in the sight descriptions that follow)*. Lines can be very long, so eating an early or late lunch is suggested. Street vendors along Independence Avenue sell hot dogs, soft drinks and snacks. On the Mall there are a number of pleasant spots to enjoy a picnic.

National Air and Space Museum★★★

Independence Ave. at 6th St. SW

Ⓜ *L'Enfant Plaza*

Floor plan pp 90-91

This fascinating museum, commemorating man's aeronautical and astronautical achievements, welcomes more than nine million visitors annually, making it one of Washington's and the world's most popular museums.

A BIT OF HISTORY

In the Vanguard of Flight

In 1861. the Smithsonian's first secretary, Joseph Henry, encouraged Thaddeus Lowe's balloon experiments, resulting in President Lincoln's decision to use balloons in the Civil War. Fifteen years later kites brought from China for the Philadelphia Centennial Exposition were given to the Smithsonian and became the cornerstone of the collection, which evolved into the museum.

The appointment in 1887 of **Samuel Pierpont Langley** (1834-1906) as the third secretary of the Smithsonian was

▷ **Location:** The museum encompasses an entire block on the south side of the Mall, opposite the National Gallery of Art.

🅿 **Parking:** With limited street parking, the most practical transportation is the Metro.

⊕ **Don't Miss:** The Milestones of Flight gallery.

🕐 **Timing:** Spend a full morning or afternoon here; if you're short on time, study the floor plan in this guide to pinpoint your interests. There is a cafe inside *(first floor, east end);* vending carts are outside.

👥 **Kids:** Pretty much all the exhibits, but a Flight Simulator ride is among the most popular.

a key factor in the development of flight in the US. Langley had gained renown as an astronomer, inventor, writer and researcher. In 1896 his Aerodrome No. 5 proved that sustained mechanical flight with a device heavier than air was feasible. He prepared the way for manned flight and what he forecast as "the great universal highway overhead."

In the 20C the idea for a museum dedicated to the history of flight evolved from the concern that the aircraft used by the US Air Force in World War II would be relegated to the scrap heap. With congressional support a conservation program was conceived, and in 1946 the National Air Museum was established by law. In 1966 the museum's scope was enlarged to include space flight.

Companion facility to the Mall museum, the Steven F. Udvar-Hazy Center that sits adjacent to Dulles International Airport in Virginia, 26mi west of Washington, DC. Udvar-Hazy Center opened in 2003 and provides enough space for the Smithsonian to display the thousands of aviation and space artifacts that cannot be exhibited on the National Mall.

How Things Fly exhibit

©Zain Deane/Michelin

The Wright Brothers

A helicopter toy given as a present to young Wilbur (1867-1912) and Orville (1871-1948) Wright in 1878 sparked a passion for flight that remained with the brothers throughout their lives. As adults the self-taught engineers were among many in the US and abroad dedicated to making manned flight a reality. Drawing heavily from the experiences of Otto Lilienthal and other predecessors, they developed the 1903 *Wright Flyer*, an aircraft controlled by "wing warping," or changing the shapes of the wing tips to deflect the air.

Orville and Wilbur Wright

Courtesy of National Air and Space Museum, Smithsonian Institution

On December 17, 1903, in Kitty Hawk, North Carolina, their efforts succeeded. The longest of their four flights that day was 852ft in 59 seconds, after which a sudden gust of wind smashed the craft. There was little publicity about the brothers' breakthrough until 1905, but they patented their discovery and went on to build an airplane factory in Dayton, Ohio.

The Mall Building

Designed by the St. Louis-based architect Gyo Obata, the building opened in 1976 as part of the nation's bicentennial celebration. The unadorned structure, measuring 635ft by 225ft and reaching nearly 83ft in height, comprises four massive rectangles connected by three glass "hyphens." Faced with Tennessee marble, the structure contains 23 galleries, a theater, a planetarium, museum stores and a research library *(open by appointment only)*. A glass annex housing a dining facility was added to the east end in the late 1980s.

The Collections

The museum possesses hundreds of aircraft and spacecraft, including manned vehicles, rockets, launching devices, space probes and satellites. As the museum has rights to all flown manned spacecraft from the US, its holdings constitute the most comprehensive collection of its kind in the world.

Authenticity is the keynote of the National Air Space and Museum; nearly all the aircraft and most of the spacecraft in the galleries are genuine. As many spacecraft cannot be recovered once launched, the museum displays either the backup vehicle, a test vehicle, or a replica made from authentic hardware, as similar to the original as possible. Labels next to the exhibits specifically note such distinctions.

FLIGHT TIME LINE
Beginnings

early 16C Leonardo da Vinci studies bird flight and draws plans for flying devices—precursors of the airplane, helicopter and parachute.

1783 First manned balloon flight by the Montgolfier brothers in Paris.

1793 George Washington witnesses first US balloon flight in Philadelphia.

1861-65 Observation balloons are used in the Civil War.

1891-96 Otto Lilienthal makes 2,000 glides in weight-controlled monoplanes.

1896 The first successful engine-driven craft flight by Langley's Aerodrome No. 5 in Washington, DC.

20C Innovations

1903 In Kitty Hawk, North Carolina, the Wright brothers successfully perform the first manned motorized flight in their 1903 *Flyer*.

1909 Louis Bleriot crosses the English Channel in 36 minutes, flying a Type XI monoplane.

c.1910 Glenn H. Curtiss develops the first seaplanes, which are used subsequently by the US Navy.

1911 G.P. Rodgers makes the first coast-to-coast flight aboard the *Wright EX Vin Fiz*.

1918 Scheduled airmail service begins with a route between New York City and Washington, DC via Philadelphia.

1920 Beginning of regular passenger flights in Europe.

1923 The first nonstop coast-to-coast flight in the Dutch-built Fokker T-2.

1924 First round-the-world flight by two US Army Douglas World Cruisers.

1926 The first liquid propellant rocket is developed.

1927 Charles Lindbergh makes the first solo nonstop crossing of the Atlantic in the *Spirit of St. Louis*, covering 3,610 miles in 33 1/2hrs.

1932 Amelia Earhart is the first woman to make a solo nonstop transatlantic flight.

1944 The Germans begin launching the V-2, the world's first long-range ballistic missile.

1947 Air Force pilot Charles E. "Chuck" Yeager flies the Bell X-1 Glamorous Glennis faster than the speed of sound.

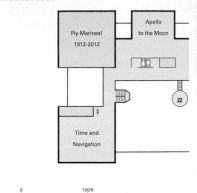

SECOND FLOOR

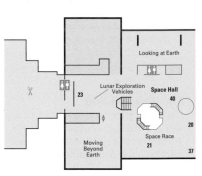

FIRST FLOOR

The Space Age

1957 The Soviets launch *Sputnik 1*, the first artificial satellite.

1958 The Boeing 707, the first US jet, begins commercial service. The National Aeronautics and Space Administration (NASA) is created.

1962 In *Friendship 7* John Glenn is the first American to orbit the earth.

1965 Traveling aboard the *Gemini 4* capsule, Edward White is the first American to walk in space.

1969 Astronauts fly *Apollo 11* to the moon and walk on its surface.

1970 Beginning of regular commercial service of the supersonic Concorde.

NATIONAL AIR AND SPACE MUSEUM

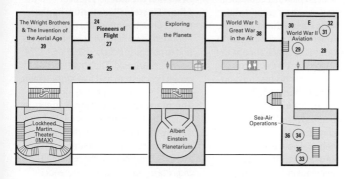

⑨ Suspended artifacts

1973-74	The manned space missions of the Skylab orbital workshop conduct experiments and gather valuable data. *Pioneer 10* is the first spacecraft to reach Jupiter.
1977	*Voyager 1* and *Voyager 2* are launched to photograph outer planets.
1979	*Voyager 1* and *Voyager 2* reach Jupiter.
1981	*Voyager 2* reaches Saturn. Space shuttle *Columbia* is launched.
1986	*Voyager 2* reaches Uranus.
1989	*Galileo* space probe is launched toward Jupiter.
1990	*Magellan* space probe begins mapping the surface of Venus. Hubble Space Telescope is launched into orbit.

1991	First close-up views of an asteroid obtained by *Galileo* probe.
1993	The longest space-shuttle mission (14 days) to date is completed.
1996	US space shuttle *Atlantis* and Russian Mir space station form largest structure ever assembled in space. Astronaut Shannon Lucid remains in space for 188 days, longer than any American. The longest flight in space-shuttle history is achieved by *Columbia* (US)—a record 17 days, 15 hours, 54 minutes.
1997	The Pathfinder mission lands on Mars. *Sojourner*, the first robotic rover, successfuly collects and

transmits data concerning the red planet's geological and chemical composition.

1998 John Glenn, the first American to orbit the earth, returns to space aboard the space shuttle *Discovery*, 36 years after his first mission aboard *Friendship 7*.

A new era in space flight begins with the initial construction of the International Space Station, the largest scientific cooperative endeavor in history.

2001 Astronomers discover the first distant multiplanet system in which the planets have orbits similar to those in our own solar system.

2004 Twin Mars Exploration Rovers touch down on opposite sides of the red planet. Sent as robotic geologists to analyze rocks and soil on Mars, the rovers will relay photographs back to earth.

2006 The first samples from a comet (Wild 2) are returned to earth by NASA's Stardust spacecraft.

2007 In June the Space Shuttle *Atlantis* completes its mission to prepare the International Space Station for expansion.

2009 Museum marks the 40th anniversary of the moon landing with special programs and exhibits.

2011 US Space Shuttle program is formally ended.

2012 First private rocket is launched in US, by SpaceX.

VISIT
♿☺🕐Open year-round daily 10am–5:30pm (hours extended in spring/summer). 🕐Closed Dec 25. 👥Guided tours (1hr 15min) daily 10:30am & 1pm. Self-guided cell phone tours on ☎202-747-3405. ✂☎202-633-1000. http://.airandspace.si.edu.

You can buy tickets *($9)* for the **Lockheed Martin IMAX® Theater** and the **Albert Einstein Planetarium** by phone, online or at the museum. *(For recorded information on films and screening times and to purchase tickets ☎866-868-7774; www.si.edu/imax).* The theater's IMAX® projection system and five-story screen create the illusion of being airborne. The **planetarium** presents shows in which the heavens are simulated on a 77ft overhead dome and discoveries of past centuries are re-created.
⌖Circled numbers on the floor plan indicate artifacts that are suspended from the ceiling.

First Floor

On the west wall of the lobby, **Earth Flight Environment (A)**, a mural by Eric Sloane depicts an ever-changing sky. On the east wall, Robert McCall's **The Space Mural—A Cosmic View (B)** represents the artist's vision of the universe.

Milestones of Flight

In the large hall that occupies the central part of the building, several epoch-making airplanes and spacecraft are displayed. Among the highlights are Charles Lindbergh's Ryan NYP *Spirit of St. Louis* **(1)**, Chuck Yeager's Bell X-1 *Glamorous Glennis* **(2)**, John Glenn's *Friendship 7* **(3)** and *Apollo 11* **(4)**. The exhibit also features the rocket-powered X-15 NASA **(5)** that set unofficial speed and altitude records of 4,520mph (Mach 6.7) and 354,200ft (over 67mi), as well as a replica of the Soviet satellite *Sputnik* **(6)**, a surprisingly small (22.8in) polished sphere with four rod-shaped antennae. The Breitling Orbiter 3 **(7)** is the aircraft used in the first nonstop flight around the world. Visitors can touch a four-billion-year-old basalt moon rock **(8)** retrieved by the crew of *Apollo 17* in 1972.

America By Air

Colorful aircraft fill this hall, illustrating the key stages of air transport. The sporty Pitcairn Mailwing **(9)** was designed to carry small loads for early mail routes in the eastern US. The all-metal Ford Tri-Motor **(10)** was a noisy but comfort-

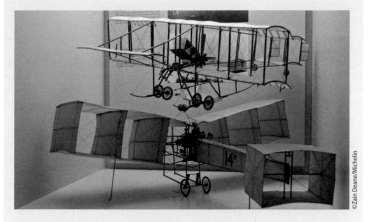

©Zain Deane/Michelin

The Physics of Flight

Flying is all about pressure and wing shape. To fly, an aircraft generates an upward force known as **lift**. To take off, lift must be greater than the aircraft's weight. An aircraft's **wings** are designed to be **curved** so that the air pressure at the top of the wing is different from the air pressure at the bottom of the wing. When the engines push the aircraft forward, air passes over the wings in such a way that a smaller pressure pushes down on the top of the wing and a higher pressure pushes up under the wing. This difference in pressure causes **lift**. The air coming off the wing is deflected downwards and the wing gets pushed upward. By varying this pressure difference, the pilot controls the altitude of the aircraft.

A pilot controls the amount of lift in two ways: by varying both the speed of the plane and the angle that the wing makes in relation to the plane's forward direction. In doing this, the pilot can make the aircraft climb, descend or fly level. Increasing speed increases lift. Increasing angle also increases lift. This is why the angle of the wing is so important. Varying the angle of the wing to the oncoming air changes the wing shape (and as such an airplane can fly upside down). Parts of the wing, such as flaps located in the back of the wing, can also be deflected to change the wing shape.

You might notice that at slower speeds, such as during climb or descent, the angle of the entire aircraft is high. The pilot is using angle to compensate for the lower speed. This allows the pilot to climb or descend at a controlled and desirable rate so as not to upset the passengers or to damage the aircraft.

able means of transport until the mid-1930s. Still used for passenger and cargo transport, the DC-3 **(11)**, inaugurated in 1935, supplanted Ford's "Tin Goose" as the airlines' favorite workhorse. Boeing's 247-D **(12)** led the familiar series whose later models, the Stratoliners, could cruise above turbulence on long flights. In the **At the Controls** gallery, test your skills in a flight simulator that lets you pick a SpaceWalk, Cosmic Coaster, F-18 or Wings experience (☞$7-$8).

The **Golden Age of Flight** celebrates the history of aviation between the two world wars. Highlights in this gallery include the Curtiss Robin **(13)** known as "Ole Miss," which achieved a world record of 27 days of sustained flight using air-to-air refueling, and a Hughes H-1 racer **(14)**, designed and flown by Howard Hughes, who set a world-record flight speed of 352mph in 1935. In **Jet Aviation**, the mural **(D)** spanning the length of the wall depicts 27 planes, from the Heinkel HE (1939) to the Concorde (1971) and the Airbus Industry A300B (1972). Opposite the mural are three jet fighters: a Messerschmitt Me262 **(15)**, a

Lockheed XP-80 **(16)** and a McDonnell FH-1 Phantom **(17)**. **Early Flight** displays craft in a facsimile of a 1913 indoor aeronautical exhibition. Among other planes located in this gallery are a glider (1894) designed by Lilienthal, the Wright 1909 Military Flyer **(18)**, which was the world's first military airplane, and a Bleriot Type XI monoplane **(19)**.

How Things Fly includes exhibits on gravity and air, stability and control, and other principles of flight. Visitors can man the controls of a Cessna 150, compare the heat resistance of materials, and interact with other exhibits. Live demonstrations by museum staff are held in the small amphitheater.
The development of aerial photography and its applications is presented in **Looking at Earth**. A Lockheed U-2 is on display, along with screens that show the Earth as the astronauts see it from the Space Station, some 200 miles away.

Space Hall
Large rockets, guided missiles and manned spacecraft are featured in the exhibit entitled **Space Race**. On display is the infamous V-2 rocket **(40)** as well as a replica of the Hubble Space Telescope **(37)**, a model of the *Columbia* space shuttle **(20)** and the *Apollo-Soyuz* spacecraft **(21)**, which was used for a joint docking-in-space experiment with the Russians in 1975. Visitors can walk through the Skylab Orbital Workshop **(22)** *(accessible from the 2nd floor)*.
The **Moving Beyond Space** gallery is a new exhibit showcasing space flight since the 1970s, including displays about the Space Shuttle and the International Space Station, and the Moon and Mars programs. Head for the large, wrap-around screen to pinpoint your home in the Google Earth booth.
The adjacent area is occupied by **Lunar Exploration Vehicles**, largely unmanned lunar probes that photographed the moon's surface. Although the *Apollo* lunar module **(23)** was never sent into space, it was nevertheless used for ground testing.

Second Floor
Pioneers of Flight
This open gallery houses planes that made historic flights. Among the artifacts displayed is Galbraith Perry Rodgers' *Wright EX Vin Fiz* **(24)**, named after a grape drink his sponsor was making at the time. This plane was the first to succeed in a coast-to-coast flight. Rodgers crossed the continent from 17 September to 5 November 1911, covering 4,321 miles in 82 hours with an average speed of 52mph. The Fokker T-2 **(25)**, built in the Netherlands and modified in the US, was the first to fly nonstop coast-to-coast. In 1923 this plane, manned by two pilots, flew almost 27 hours at an average speed of 92mph. The Douglas World Cruiser Chicago **(26)** was one of two biplanes to fly around the world, logging 27,553 miles in 175 days in 1924.
Amelia Earhart (1898-1937), the legendary aviator who lost her life in the South Pacific while attempting an around-the-world flight, set two world records with her Lockheed Vega 5B **(27)** in 1932. In May of that year, Earhart became the first woman to fly alone nonstop across the Atlantic, covering a total of 2,026 miles in less than 15 hours.
A replica of the *Voyager 1* probe is the main attraction of **Exploring the Planets**, which presents an introduction to the solar system.
Great War in the Air contrasts the realities of World War I with the war's romantic legacy, perpetuated in the films of Hollywood. Among aircraft on view is a 1918 German Fokker D VII **(38)**. Some of the airplanes that determined the fate of nations can be viewed in **World War II Aviation**. Displays here include a Messerschmitt Bf 109 **(28)**, a Mitsubishi Zero **(29)**, a Supermarine Spitfire **(30)**, a Macchi MC.202 **(31)** and a North American P-51D Mustang **(32)**. The mural **(E)** was executed by Keith Ferris in 1976.
Sea-Air Operations reproduces an aircraft-carrier hangar deck. Featured aircraft include the Boeing F4B-4 **(33)**, the Douglas SBD-6 Dauntless dive-bomber **(34)**, the Douglas A-4C Skyhawk **(35)** and the Grumman F4F Wildcat **(36)**.

The Wright Brothers and the Invention of the Aerial Age delves into the lives and achievements of the famous duo. The centerpiece display is their *1903 Flyer* (**39**), resting on the floor. The story of US manned spaceflight programs 1957-1980—from Project Mercury to Apollo 17—is retold in **Apollo to the Moon**.

Lunar samples are displayed along with space suits and lunar surface equipment such as a prototype of *Apollo 15's* Lunar Rover. **Beyond the Limits: Flight Enters the Computer Age** explores flight in the computer age. Here visitors find the Cray Serial 14 supercomputer used from 1978 to 1986 at the National Center for Atmospheric Research. Rotating works in **Flight and the Arts** feature interpretations of flight-related themes.

STEVEN F. UDVAR-HAZY CENTER★★

Occupying 175 acres near Dulles International Airport in Virginia, this $311-million repository for aircraft and spacecraft (2003) consists of a 10-story-tall aviation hangar three football fields long, the James S. McDonnell Space Hangar, and the Donald D. Engen Observation Tower. The center's major benefactor (and a pilot), Steven Udvar-Hazy arrived in the US from Hungary at age 12. In 1973 he started a commercial-aircraft leasing business that became the world's top company of its kind. He donated $65 million to the Smithsonian Institution toward the construction of this facility.

VISIT

14390 Air and Space Museum Pkwy., Chantilly, VA. From downtown, drive west on I-66 to Rte. 28 North (Exit 53B); continue 5mi north on Rte. 28 and exit at Air and Space Museum Parkway; follow the signs. ◷*Open year-round daily 10am–5:30pm (hours extended in spring/summer).* ◷*Closed Dec 25.* ♿✕🅿 (◉*$15*) ✆*703-572-4118.* *http://airandspace.si.edu/udvarhazy.*

At the Engen Observation Tower, watch planes take off and land at nearby Dulles Airport, and see exhibits on air-traffic control and airport equipment.

Stop at the IMAX® Theater for a schedule of films (◉*$9; films last about 45min*).

In the **Aviation Hangar**, aircraft on display include the Lockheed SR-71 Blackbird, the world's fasted jet-propelled aircraft (speeds of over 2,100mph). The Boeing B-29 Superfortress, the Enola Gay, dropped the first atomic bomb, on Hiroshima, Japan, during World War II. Military and commercial aircraft include the supersonic Concorde.

👁 *Access the elevated walkway for a bird's-eye view of the artifacts.* In the **Space Hangar**, the Space Shuttle *Enterprise* served as an atmospheric test vehicle (the *Enterprise* never flew in space).

Aviation Hanger, Steven F. Udvar-Hazy Center

©Cynthia Ochterbeck/Michelin

National Gallery of Art★★★

Ⓜ Archives
floor plan pp 102-103

The National Gallery's world-class collection of masterpieces traces the development of Western art from the Middle Ages to the present. The West Building concentrates on European works from the 13C through the early 20C. Its contemporary counterpart, the East Building, highlights works of modern artists.

A BIT OF HISTORY
One Man's Dream

The financier, industrialist and statesman **Andrew Mellon** (1855-1937) was the impetus behind the National Gallery of Art. Mellon began collecting art in the 1870s, traveling to Europe with his friend Henry Clay Frick, benefactor of the famed Frick Collection, for the purpose of acquiring 17C and 18C paintings. In the late 1920s, while serving as secretary of the Treasury, Mellon conceived of endowing a national gallery of art. From that time until his death in 1937, he became one of the world's foremost collectors of art. His intent was to amass

▷ **Location:** Madison Dr. between 3rd and 7th Sts. NW. Situated on the northeast corner of the Mall, the National Gallery is housed in the Beaux Arts-style West Building and the modernist East Building, the latter containing 20C works. Begin in the art information room of the West Building for an overview.

Ⓟ **Parking:** There are a limited number of parking lots within a few blocks to the north.

🅐 **Don't Miss:** West Building: Leonardo's *Ginevra de' Benci*, Bernardino Luini's *Fresco Cycle*, several Rembrandts. East Building: architecture, early Picassos.

🕐 **Timing:** Allow 2hrs for a tour of the West Building's highlights, or an in-depth look at a few galleries; allow 1hr for the East Building. *🌀 See Visiting the Museum opposite.*

masterpieces that would show the development of Western art from the 13C through the 19C. Among his acquisi-

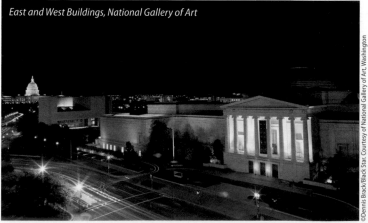

East and West Buildings, National Gallery of Art

©Dennis Brack/Black Star. Courtesy of National Gallery of Art, Washington

Tips for Your Visit

The main entrance is located at the top of the steps on the Mall side between 4th and 7th streets. Wheelchair access is via the entrance at 6th Street. A free checkroom is located to the right of the main entrance, beyond the Founders' Room. The **information room** is to the left. The main floor of the West Building houses 13-19C European paintings and sculpture, and American art. Sculpture and decorative arts, prints and drawings, and temporary exhibits are presented on the ground floor. Artworks are displayed, for the most part, in chronological order by school.

We suggest you begin your visit at the information room. Here you may obtain a list of current exhibitions, a schedule of docent-led tours and notices of temporary exhibits, lectures and special events. **Touch-screen monitors** allow visitors to research artists and hundreds of works from the permanent collection. Along with historical commentary and analysis, this system provides the viewing status and location of specific works in the gallery. The free audio **Director's Tour** covers highlights of the permanent collection. A free **Children's Tour** of the permanent collection is available (recommended for ages 7–12). All audio tours can be rented in the West Building Mall entrance.

tions were 21 works from the Hermitage museum in Leningrad. They included paintings by such masters as van Eyck, Raphael, Titian and Rembrandt.

In 1937 Congress granted a charter to the new National Gallery of Art and pledged funds to support it. The stately building erected on the Mall was a gift from Mellon to the American people. Further, Mellon left the museum an endowment: 126 paintings and a collection of fine 15-16C Italian sculpture. The National Gallery's original building (the West Building) opened to the public in 1941.

Other Benefactors

Following Mellon's lead, other major American collectors have contributed to the gallery. Many of these collectors were able to assemble private collections rich in the works of Old Masters and Impressionists. Joseph Widener offered the renowned Widener family collection of painting, sculpture and decorative arts to the National Gallery in the 1930s. Samuel Kress, a self-made business magnate, already had plans drawn up for a museum in New York City to house his Italian paintings and sculptures when he was persuaded in 1939 to donate his collection to the uncompleted National Gallery.

Works by French Impressionists and post-Impressionists were donated by financier Chester Dale. Lessing J. Rosenwald left the gallery 22,000 prints and drawings, and Edgar William Garbisch and his wife, Bernice Chrysler Garbisch, gave a collection of 18C and 19C American naive paintings. More than 1,300 donors have contributed works of art to the National Gallery. Donations from Andrew Mellon's son, Paul, and his wife account for some 900 works of art, including those by Bonnard, Degas, Gauguin, Picasso and other masters.

A New Building

In only 30 years the expanding collections had outgrown the original building. **Paul Mellon** (1907-99), Ailsa Mellon Bruce and the Andrew Mellon Foundation funded the construction of a second building on the Mall just east of the original one. The $95 million East Building opened in 1978, establishing the National Gallery's reputation as a vital center for the presentation and appreciation of modern art.

The Collections

Some 116,000 paintings, sculpture, decorative arts, drawings, prints and photographs trace the development of Western art from the Middle Ages to the present. About 2,000 of these objects are on display at any given time. The Italian works constitute one of the finest collections of its kind in the world. The gallery's *Ginevra de' Benci* represents the only portrait by Leonardo da Vinci in the Western Hemisphere. Federal funds support museum operations and maintenance. However, all of its acquisitions are made through private means.

VISIT
WEST BUILDING
🕐*Open year-round Mon–Sat 10am– 5pm, Sun 11am–6pm.* 🕐*Closed 1 Jan & Dec 25.* 🚶*Guided tours available.* ✕👤 ☎*202-737-4215. www.nga.gov.* 🏛*Collection highlights are listed. Some works of art mentioned may not be on view. Check the museum's website or terminals in the information room to find out the status of specific works.*
The Garden Café *(ground floor)* and Cascade Café *(concourse)* provide food service and a pleasant break.
The capital's leading proponent of Classical Revival architecture, John Russell Pope designed this formidable domed structure. The West Building's appeal derives from the seven shades of glowing pink Tennessee marble incorporated in the facade. Its sober exterior is adorned only by simple blind windows and pilasters. Ionic porticoes highlight the north and south sides. The 785ft-

Madonna and Child *(c.1330) by Giotto*

Samuel H. Kress Collection, National Gallery of Art, Washington

long edifice ranks as one of the world's largest marble structures.

Main Floor
🏛*Some main-floor galleries may be closed; stop by the information room to verify the location of works mentioned below.*
Flanking the entrance hall on the Mall side are the art information room *(left)*, and the **Founders' Room** *(right)*, a lounge where portraits of major founding benefactors are prominently displayed. The hall leads to the **Rotunda**, where greenblack Tuscan marble columns surround a fountain whose centerpiece is a statue of Mercury. The broad sculpture halls of the building's two wings extend from the rotunda past the galleries, culminating in garden courts. The **East Sculpture Hall** features classically inspired marble statuary from the 17-19C, while works in bronze, including a selection of Italian busts, are displayed in the **West Sculpture Hall.**

13-15C Italian Painting
Representing the evolution of Western painting from 1200 to the early 1500s, this section begins with the stylized Byzantine iconography that developed in Constantinople, capital of the Eastern Roman Empire and cradle of the Orthodox faith. The **icons**, or devotional images, are painted in egg tempera on wooden panels and enhanced with gold leaf. The Byzantine tradition transplanted in Italy gave rise to a more natural style. The Sienese school, whose most influential master was Duccio di Buoninsegna (1255-1318), is particularly well represented in the collection. In the late 13C, Florentine artists, notably Giotto (c.1266-c.1337), developed a realistic rendering of space that ushered in the Italian Renaissance. Gradually, the strict iconography was replaced with secular portraiture and more sensual paintings that depicted Biblical scenes. In the quattrocento (15C), Florentine artists like Fra Filippo Lippi and Botticelli looked to classical antiquity for its scientific notions of anatomy and perspective.

- *Madonna and Child*
  Giotto c. 1330
- *The Adoration of the Magi*
  Fra Angelico and Fra Filippo
  Lippi c.1445
- *Ginevra de' Benci*
  da Vinci c.1474
- *Giuliano de' Medici*
  Botticelli c.1478

Italian Sculpture and Furniture

The marble, bronze, wood, porphyry, and painted terra-cotta sculpture (13-16C) displayed here closely follows the evolution in Italian painting: the earlier pieces depict religious themes, while in later works, portrait busts, particularly of prominent Florentines, begin to appear. The Italian Cabinet Galleries *(25-27)* were designed to evoke the interior of an Italian Renaissance palace or villa. They contain 40 items from the gallery's permanent collection. A fresco cycle by Bernardino Luini (c.1480-1532) is showcased in Gallery 26. Small paintings provide a lustrous backdrop for bronze statuettes, glassware and porcelain.

- *Lorenzo de' Medici*
  Verrocchio and Benintendi c.1478/1521

16C Italian Painting

The Renaissance that began in 15C Florence spread to northern Italy, in part through the works of Andrea Mantegna (1431-1506). His bold lines and sense of perspective influenced artists in Ferrara and Venice. Another very different innovation in Venetian art of the 15C came from Giorgione (c.1478-1510), whose delicate use of color gave this period its characteristic style. Giorgione's teacher, Giovanni Bellini (c.1427-1516), preferred the three-quarter portrait to the traditional Renaissance profile, thus allowing more expression of emotion and character. The High Renaissance of the early 16C, the cinquecento, attained an unparalleled level of delicacy and grace, enhanced by the manipulation of light and shadow as expressed in the art of such masters as Leonardo da Vinci (1452-1519) and Raphael (1483-1520). Titian (c.1490-1576), the prolific master

whose outstanding talent was sought after by the leading European rulers of the day, dominated the 16C. Tintoretto (1518-94) carried innovations of his predecessors further with his own impressionistic, emotionally charged paintings. The allegorical representation of religious figures and classical gods and goddesses against a pastoral setting became the predominant subject of northern Italian art, with sensuality and color as its hallmarks.

- *The Small Cowper Madonna*
  Raphael c.1505
- *The Alba Madonna*
  Raphael c.1510
- *The Adoration of the Shepherds*
  Giorgione c.1510
- *The Feast of the Gods*
  Bellini and Titian c.1514/1529
- *The Conversion of Saint Paul*
  Tintoretto c.1545
- *Doge Andrea Gritti*
  Titian c.1548
- *Venus with a Mirror*
  Titian c.1555

17-18C Italian Painting

Marked by the creative vision of Annibale Carracci (1560-1609), 17C Bologna was the birthplace of the exuberant art of the Baroque, which had its greatest flowering in papal Rome. In the next century, Giovanni Battista Tiepolo (1696-1770) refined the Baroque's expansiveness into a lighter and more decorative style *(Gallery 32)*.

Tiepolo's frescoes adorned ceilings throughout Europe, but his genius marked the end of Italian dominance in art. Thereafter, the main innovations in art came from new centers in northern Europe. Also popular in 18C Italy were detailed cityscapes and architectural representations, such as those of Canaletto and Panini, that reflected fashionable interests in the grand tour of Italian antiquities.

Featured in gallery 36 are works by French artists Nicholas Poussin and Claude Lorrain, both of whom lived and painted in Rome.

- *River Landscape*
  Carracci c.1590

♦ *The Porta Portello, Padua*
Canaletto c.1741
♦ *Wealth and Benefits of the Spanish Monarchy under Charles III*
Tiepolo c.1762

Spanish Painting

Restraint characterizes the work of most Spanish artists during the 16C, with the notable exception of El Greco (1541-1614). Born on the island of Crete and trained in Venice, El Greco is nonetheless considered a Spanish artist, whose elongated shapes and religious fervor distinguish his unique style.

The preeminent 17C Spanish artist Diego Velázquez (1599-1660) obtained in his later works "impressionistic" effects of color and light that foreshadow 19C stylistic trends. A court painter, Velázquez was renowned for his portraits of the Spanish royal family.

In the 18C, Francisco de Goya (1746-1828) *(Gallery 52)* was Madrid's most fashionable portraitist. His early works reflect the lighthearted Rococo spirit of the period, while his more probing later portraits anticipate the psychological Expressionism of the 20C.

Gallery 38 is devoted to 14C and 15C sculpture and painting from the Netherlands and Germany.

♦ *Laocoön*
El Greco c.1614
♦ *The Needlewoman*
Velázquez c.1650
♦ *Two Women at a Window*
Murillo c.1660
♦ *Thérèse Louise de Sureda*
Goya c.1804

German Painting

Albrecht Dürer (1471-1528), the preeminent German artist of the late 15C and early 16C, has been called the "Leonardo of the North." Renowned throughout Europe, Dürer was recognized as a master printmaker as well as an outstanding painter. Dürer's contemporary, Matthias Grünewald (c.1475-1528), was a matchless interpreter of religious intensity, while Lucas Cranach the Elder (1472-1553) was known for both his religious works and his portraits. Hans Holbein the Younger (c.1498-1543) relocated to

England and became a court painter to King Henry VIII. The artist was admired for his ability to convey a sense of nobility in the royalty he painted.

♦ *The Small Crucifixion*
Grünewald c.1520
♦ *Portrait of a Clergyman*
Dürer 1516
♦ *Edward VI as a Child*
Holbein c.1538

Netherlandish Painting

Present-day Belgium, Holland, Luxembourg and even portions of France composed the Netherlands at the end of the Middle Ages. The wealthy regions of the Low Countries were a magnet for talented painters. During the 15C Flanders, in what is now part of Belgium, was a leading artistic center, thanks largely to Jan van Eyck (c.1390-1441). A technical virtuoso, van Eyck mastered the representation of interior space and, more importantly, is credited with having revolutionized painting by employing oil, as opposed to tempera, as the medium. This innovation, which allowed more subtlety in brushwork, attracted artists from throughout Europe to Flanders, among them Hans Memling (d.1494), whose delicate and serene paintings enjoyed great popularity. Rogier van der Weyden (c.1400-64), another Netherlandish master, achieved a virtuosity of brushstroke that influenced generations. François Clouet (c.1522-72) descended from a family of Flemish painters who lived in France. A celebrated court painter, Clouet is credited with popularizing bathing portraits.

♦ *The Annunciation*
van Eyck c.1436
♦ *Portrait of a Lady*
van der Weyden c.1460
♦ *A Lady in Her Bath*
François Clouet c.1571

Dutch and Flemish Painting

The robust vitality of Peter Paul Rubens (1577-1640) dominates the 17C Flemish Baroque. An artist of great versatility, Rubens enjoyed international renown for his allegories and portraits. His student Anthony Van Dyck (1599-1641) became one of Europe's most celebrated portrait painters (Galleries 42 and 43).

Among the numerous painters of the varied styles and genres developed in 17C Holland, Rembrandt van Rijn (1606-69) stands out as the abiding genius of this time (gallery 48). His mastery of chiaroscuro—the subtle play of light and shadow—influenced art for two centuries. The Mill, considered one of Rembrandt's finest landscapes, profoundly affected the work of 19C British artists such as J.M.W. Turner and Sir Joshua Reynolds. Rembrandt's deeply psychological approach to portraiture takes the inventiveness of a slightly earlier Dutch artist, Frans Hals (c.1583-1666), a step further. Employing lively brushwork, Hals had broken with the staid portraiture of the past to show his sitters with striking informality.

Johannes Vermeer (1632-75), another Dutch genius, used light and space in such a way that his scenes of the upper middle classes are infused with an ethereal quality. The numerous still lifes, landscapes and genre paintings that were produced by Dutch artists in the 17C often had allegorical meaning underlying their apparent realism.

- ◆ Daniel in the Lions' Den
  Rubens c.1615
- ◆ Willem Coymans
  Hals 1645
- ◆ The Mill
  Rembrandt c.1650
- ◆ Self-Portrait
  Rembrandt 1659
- ◆ Woman Holding a Balance
  Vermeer c.1664

17-18C French Painting

During the reign of Louis XIV, the French Academy controlled all aspects of cultural life, and traditions of classicism prevailed in art. The most noted proponent of classicism, Nicolas Poussin (1594-1665) (Gallery 36), worked much of his life in Italy yet strongly influenced French art. His works depict harmoniously composed subjects set against an Arcadian backdrop. Claude Lorrain (1600-82) (Gallery 36), who also worked in Rome, shared Poussin's love of landscape but gave it a nostalgic interpretation. Louis Le Nain (1593-1648) and his two brothers (Gallery 37) concentrated on realistic genre paintings.

By the early 18C, Paris had become the cultural hub of Europe, and the French Rococo style was the fashion. This florid style is best exemplified in the work of Antoine Watteau (1684-1721), who created whimsically poetic images that emphasize color and depict the sophisticated manners of 18C French society. Later, François Boucher (1703-70) introduced new sensuous pastoral reveries, while Boucher's student Jean-Honoré Fragonard (1732-1806) focused on French subjects, representing them in quick, colorful brushstrokes. Portraits by Elisabeth Vigée-Lebrun (1755-1842) (Gallery 56), painter and confidante to Marie Antoinette, reflect her close ties to aristocratic French society. Traditional classicism persisted, however, in the works of Jacques-Louis David (1748-1825) and Jean-Auguste-Dominique Ingres (1780-1867).

- ◆ Italian Comedians
  Watteau c.1720
- ◆ Madame Bergeret
  Boucher 1746
- ◆ A Young Girl Reading
  Fragonard c.1776

19C French Painting

In the early 19C the French Academy sanctioned the classicism of David and Ingres, but artists such as Eugène Delacroix (1798-1863) and Jean-Baptiste-Camille Corot (1796-1875) rebelled against such conventions, painting romantic landscapes in their own idiom. Gustave Courbet (1819-77), Honoré Daumier (1808-79) and Edouard Manet (1832-83) discarded romanticism in favor of an unsentimental realism that depicted everyday scenes. A group of young painters inspired by Manet's example broke from the state-sponsored Salon exhibitions in 1874 to show their works independently. Known as the **Impressionists** because of their unprecedented exploration of atmo-

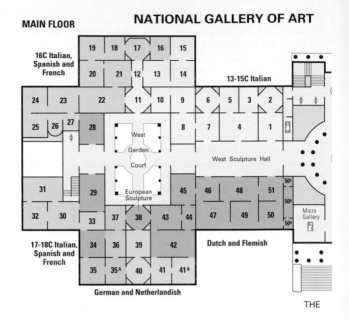

MAIN FLOOR

NATIONAL GALLERY OF ART

16C Italian, Spanish and French

13-15C Italian

West Garden Court

European Sculpture

West Sculpture Hall

Micro Gallery

17-18C Italian, Spanish and French

Dutch and Flemish

German and Netherlandish

THE

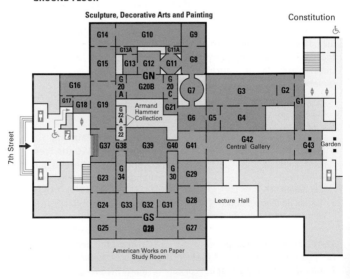

GROUND FLOOR

Sculpture, Decorative Arts and Painting

Constitution

Armand Hammer Collection

Central Gallery

Garden

Lecture Hall

7th Street

American Works on Paper Study Room

spheric light and color in natural landscapes and figure painting, the group was informally led by Claude Monet (1840-1926) and Pierre-Auguste Renoir (1841-1919). Edgar Degas (1834-1917) and Henri de Toulouse-Lautrec (1864-1901) depicted contemporary Parisian nightlife. Paul Gauguin (1848-1903), Paul Cézanne (1839-1906) and Dutch-born Vincent van Gogh (1853-90) developed a highly personal style of modern art. American-born Mary Cassatt (1844-1926), known for her depictions of women and children, painted in Paris

West Building

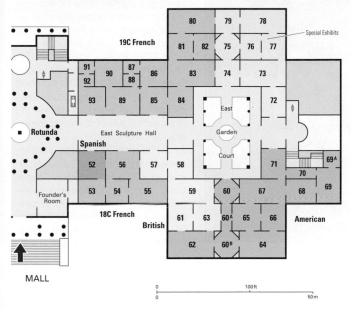

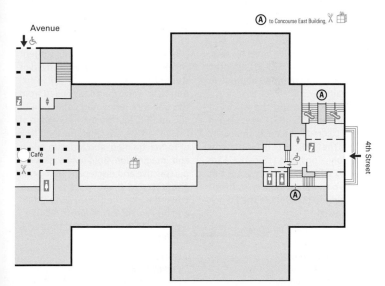

and exhibited with the Impressionists.

- *Madame Moitessier* (Ingres 1851)
- *Agostina* (Corot c.1866)
- *The Artist's Father* (Cézanne 1866)
- *The Railway* (Manet 1873)
- *Woman with a Parasol – Madame Monet and Her Son* (Monet 1875)

- *A Girl with a Watering Can* (Renoir 1876)
- *Self-Portrait* (van Gogh 1889)
- *Quadrille at the Moulin Rouge* (Toulouse-Lautrec 1892)
- *Fatata te Miti* (Gauguin 1892)
- *The Boating Party* (Cassatt c.1894)
- *Four Dancers* (Degas c.1899)

Self-Portrait *(1889) by Paul Gauguin*

Chester Dale Collection, National Gallery of Art, Washington

British Painting

British painting first achieved a distinctive voice in the mid-18C with William Hogarth (1697-1764), whose works depicted the London middle classes. Later in the century Thomas Gainsborough (1727-88) created his romantic portraits of English nobility, while his rival, Sir Joshua Reynolds (1723-92), adopted the formal grandeur of the Baroque in his portraiture.

In landscape painting the works of J.M.W. Turner (1775-1851), executed in swirls of colored light, are dramatically charged. The landscapes of his contemporary John Constable (1776-1837) are executed with scientific realism but convey a pastoral tranquillity. Both artists influenced the work of the French Impressionists.

- *A Scene from The Beggar's Opera*
  Hogarth 1729
- *Lady Caroline Howard*
  Reynolds 1778
- *Miss Juliana Willoughby*
  Romney 1783
- *Mrs. Richard Brinsley Sheridan*
  Gainsborough 1787
- *Wivenhoe Park, Essex*
  Constable 1816
- *Keelmen Heaving in Coals by Moonlight*
  Turner 1835

American Painting and Sculpture

Like British painting of the 18C and early 19C, American art focuses on portraiture in the grand manner. Eminent artists of this period include Benjamin West (1738-1820), Thomas Sully (1783-1872), Charles Willson Peale (1741-1827), John Singleton Copley (1738-1815) and Gilbert Stuart (1755-1828), who was sometimes called the "court portraitist to the young Republic" because of his many paintings of early leaders.

By the mid-19C, landscape painting emerged as the dominant force in American art, with painters such as Thomas Cole (1801-48) and Frederic Edwin Church (1826-1900) depicting the awe-inspiring natural wonders of the New World, while the paintings of George Caitlin capture the world of Native Americans in the early 19C West. Highly personal expression, as evidenced in the works of Winslow Homer (1836-1910) and the mystical paintings of Albert Pinkham Ryder (1847-1917), followed later in the century. European influences are seen in the works of James McNeill Whistler (1834-1903), Thomas Eakins (1844-1916) and John Singer Sargent (1856-1925), all of whom either lived or studied abroad.

American naïve paintings culled from the gallery's renowned collection of 18C and 19C folk art are the creation of "naïve" artists, so-called for their lack of formal training, abound with talent and imagination. Bold colors, skewed perspective and discrepancies in scale characterize these works, such as Edward Hick's *The Cornell Farm* (1848) and his *Peaceable Kingdom* (c.1834). Galleries 72-79 are devoted to special exhibits.

- *Watson and the Shark*
  Copley 1778
- *The Skater*
  Stuart 1782
- *Benjamin and Eleanor Ridgely Laming* Peale 1788
- *Autumn–On the Hudson River*
  Cropsey 1860
- *The White Girl*
  Whistler 1862
- *Breezing Up*

Homer 1876
* *Siegfried and the Rhine Maidens*
  Ryder 1891
* *Shaw Memorial*
  Augustus Saint-Gaudens 1900
* *Repose*
  Sargent 1911
  Allies Day
  Childe Hassam 1917

Ground Floor

🐧 *Some ground-floor galleries may be temporarily closed; check the information room terminals or the gallery's website to verify the location of works mentioned below.*

Sculpture and Decorative Arts

Small sculpture and medals in the collection date from the 15C to the early 18C. Marble busts and statuary, primarily French and Italian, date from the 17C and 18C. Works, mainly terra-cotta or marble, of 18C French sculptors such as Clodion and Houdon and 19C-20C sculpture by Degas, Rodin, Bartholdi and other masters complete the collection. Of special interest are Degas' *Dressed Ballet Dancer* (colored plaster, modeled 1881) and Rodin's *The Thinker* (bronze, 1880). Also note the miniature bronze busts by Honoré Daumier.

Decorative arts in the collection include 15C and 16C Flemish and 18C French tapestries, as well as Italian Renaissance and 18C French Rococo furnishings. Small ecclesiastical artworks, such as enamels and stained glass, of the Middle Ages

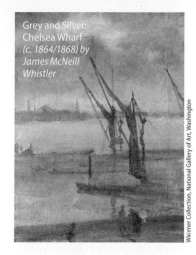

Grey and Silver: Chelsea Wharf (c. 1864/1868) by James McNeill Whistler

Wiener Collection, National Gallery of Art, Washington

and Renaissance, include a 12C bejeweled chalice of sardonyx and silver gilt.

Prints, Drawings and Photographs

The National Gallery owns some 100,000 American and European works on paper and vellum, the vast majority of which were acquired in the postwar period. The **Armand Hammer collection** of drawings spans five centuries and includes the works of da Vinci, Michelangelo, Manet, Degas and Cézanne.

EAST BUILDING

🕐 *Open year-round Mon–Sat 10am– 5pm, Sun 11am–6pm.* 🕐 *Closed 1 Jan & Dec 25.* 🔊 *Introductory guided tours (50min) available.* ✕ ♿ 𝄢202- 737-4215. www.nga.gov. Inquire at the*

East Building

©Brigitta L.House/Michelin

information desk inside the gallery for current exhibits.

The East Building houses the gallery's growing collection of Modern and Contemporary art, as well as a selection of small-format 19C French paintings.

The main entrance to the East Building is on 4th Street, across the plaza from the West Building. An underground concourse connects the two structures. Wheelchair access is to the left of the 4th Street entrance steps. All five levels of the East Building feature rotating exhibits drawn from the National Gallery's permanent collection of late-19C and 20C art. Works are not necessarily arranged in chronological order. The East Building's open interior space is easily adapted to changing exhibits; major traveling exhibits from all artistic periods are mounted here.

Begin your visit at the ground-level art information desk, where you may obtain notices of current exhibitions and events as well as the day's schedule of guided tours.

The Architecture – Generally considered Washington's most impressive example of modern architecture, the massive marble **building**★★ by **I. M. Pei** stresses line and angle over adornment. Pei's task was threefold: to design a structure that would showcase modern art, to harmonize with the West Building and to be monumental enough to anchor the northeast corner of the Mall. Given a trapezoidal lot formed by the intersections of Pennsylvania Avenue and the National Mall with 3rd and 4th streets, Pei chose a trapezoid formed of two distinct triangles. The northern isosceles triangle houses gallery space; the southern right triangle contains administrative and research facilities. Polygonal towers top the points of the isosceles triangle; each tower rises 108ft high, one foot less than the height of the West Building. The structure's marble veneer, which came from the same Tennessee quarries as that of the West Building, is currently being reinstalled with new supports, owning to structural problems. The work will be complete in 2014.

The 4th Street **plaza**, which fronts the East Building and links it visually to the West Building, is dominated by seven glass tetrahedrons, three-sided shapes that also serve as skylights for the underground concourse connecting the buildings. A fountain flows down a *chadar*, or water slide, that can be seen from inside the concourse.

The Art – The gallery's stated goal is to "present the great European and American movements and masters of the century rather than to speculate on new trends." Works are displayed in large, fluid spaces throughout the building. Represented in the collection

Alexander Calder, Untitled, 1976

©Lee Ewing, 2005; National Gallery of Art, Washington

are the creations of such 20C artists as Wassily Kandinsky, Henri Matisse, Constantin Brancusi, Pablo Picasso, Georgia O'Keeffe, Georges Braque, Joan Miró, Anselm Kiefer, Alberto Giacometti, Mark Rothko and Arshile Gorky.

Henry Moore's monumental bronze sculpture *Knife Edge Mirror Two Piece*, situated outside the main entrance, softens the building's exterior angles.

A skylit atrium opens from the low-ceilinged lobby of the ground level and is dominated by an immense red, blue and black mobile by Alexander Calder, specially commissioned for this space. Another commissioned work, a sculpture titled *National Gallery Ledge Piece*, by Anthony Caro, is displayed over the door to the administrative wing *(located near the escalator)*.

On the opposite side of the building, outside the wall of windows, is a new sculpture installation, Andy Goldsworthy's *Roof* (2005). Created specifically for this site, nine domes of stacked slate crowd the outdoor courtyard. The view from the mezzanine reveals a hole in each dome, suggestive of a beehive.

Two intimate ground-floor galleries feature rotating exhibits of smaller works, including American art, as well as French paintings from the collections of Ailsa Mellon Bruce and Mr. and Mrs. Paul Mellon. Works by Degas, Bonnard, Renoir, Vuillard, Manet, Morisot and other masters line the walls of these galleries.

Mezzanine galleries are generally devoted to large traveling exhibits from all periods. Primarily reserved for European paintings and sculpture, the upper-level galleries feature 20C artists such as Dubuffet, Derain, Mondrian, Picabia, Picasso, Miró, Gris, Brancusi, Modigliani, Giacometti, Magritte, Soutine and Gorky. The intimate tower gallery exhibits the museum's collection of **paper cutouts** by Matisse *(may be viewed Mon–Sat 10am-3pm, Sun 11am–3pm)*. The concourse galleries showcase predominantly American late-20C art, including works by Barnett Newman, Clyfford Still, Robert Motherwell, Andy Warhol, Agnes Martin, Louise Bourgeois, Roy Lichtenstein and Ellsworth Kelly.

SCULPTURE GARDEN

On the Mall between 7th and 9th Sts. (across from the 7th Street entrance to the West Building). ⏰*Open year-round Mon–Sat 10am–5pm, Sun 11am–6pm (extended hours in summer).* ⤙*Guided tours (50min) Apr–Jun & Sept–Oct Fri 12:30pm, Sat 1:30pm from the cafe.* ⏰*Closed 1 Jan & Dec 25.* ✕ ♿ ✆*202-737-4215. www.nga.gov.*

Opened in 1999, this spacious 6-acre garden displays more than a dozen major works from the National Gallery's collection of 20C sculpture. Richly landscaped with magnolia, oak, dogwood, maple, cypress and other trees, the grounds also feature flowerbeds and winding paths. In winter, the garden's central reflecting pool is used as an ice-skating rink. The benches surrounding the fountain were carved from the same pink Tennessee marble as the East and West buildings. The Pavilion Cafe makes a pleasant spot to enjoy a cold drink or light meal outdoors or inside.

Besides providing an outdoor escape from museum crowds, the space also presents a who's who in contemporary sculpture: Louise Bourgeois, Claes Oldenburg, Coosje van Bruggen and Roy Lichtenstein are just a few of the masters whose works are on display here.

Typewriter Eraser, Scale X, *1999 by C. Oldenburg and C. van Bruggen*

©Gwen Cannon/Michelin

Arthur M. Sackler Gallery★★

Ⓜ *Smithsonian or L'Enfant Plaza*

The Sackler Gallery is dedicated to the study and exhibition of the arts of Asia past and present. Highlights include Chinese jades, ancient Near Eastern gold and silverwork and 11-19C Islamic manuscripts. An underground gallery links the Sackler to the Freer Gallery.

A BIT OF HISTORY

The core of the museum's holdings was donated to the Smithsonian Institution in 1982 by **Dr. Arthur M. Sackler** (1913-87), a New York psychiatrist, medical researcher and publisher. Sackler began acquiring Asian art in the 1950s to supplement his collection of Western art. He was the main benefactor of Harvard University's Arthur M. Sackler Museum, and he contributed generously to the Eastern art holdings of the Metropolitan Museum of Art (*THE GREEN GUIDE New York City*).

VISIT

Open year-round daily 10am–5:30pm. Closed Dec 25. Guided tours most days check at information desk for times. *202-633-1000. www.asia.si.edu.*

Chinese Collections

Ancient Chinese culture centered largely around agriculture, and the attributes of nature became a powerful force in their religion. Clouds, rain, wind and stars appear frequently as symbolic ornamentation on vessels and objects, which the Chinese used presumably to deflect evil spirits and to invoke the protection of particular deities.

Jade Collection

The mountains of the Chinese provinces contained rich veins of nephrite jade, a gemstone so prized by the Chinese

Location: The Smithsonian Quadrangle at 1050 Independence Ave. SW.

Timing: Allow at least an hour for the Sackler Gallery.

Don't Miss: Xu Bing's suspended sculpture *Monkeys Grasping for the Moon*, which was created especially for the Sackler. The extensive Chinese jade collection that dates as far back as 3500 BC.

that they link it with the five cardinal virtues of charity, modesty, courage, justice and wisdom. The Sackler's jade collection of some 450 objects dates from about 3000 BC. Artifacts from the Neolithic period include axe blades (c.3000 BC) mostly used as ceremonial burial objects. The jades of the Shang dynasty (1700 BC) were used for ceremonial functions.

Chinese Bronzes

The gallery's bronzes date from the Shang through the Han dynasties (1700 BC-AD 220). Many of the vessels and objects are inscribed, providing a wealth of information about this period, which has long remained obscure to historians.

Ancient Near Eastern Gold and Silver

The civilizations that developed in ancient Iran, Anatolia (present-day Turkey) and the region around the Caucasus Mountains are credited with introducing metalwork as early as 7000 BC.

Over the ensuing millennia, the craftspeople of these regions produced exquisite objects in copper, silver, gold and lead. Many of the gold and silver vessels and ornaments in the collection are gilded or inlaid with niello (an enamel-like alloy) and date from 3000 BC to 8C AD. These objects offer glimpses of often sumptuous court life in the nations that developed in the Tigris-Euphrates Valley.

Freer Gallery of Art★★

Ⓜ *Smithsonian*

The Smithsonian's first museum on the Mall devoted exclusively to art, the Freer Gallery possesses an outstanding Asian collection and one of the world's largest collections of works by James McNeill Whistler (1834-1903).

A BIT OF HISTORY

The Connoisseur

A successful railroad car manufacturer, Charles L. Freer (1854-1919) became, like Arthur Sackler, a keen collector of Asian art. From his first purchase in 1887 of a Japanese fan, he gradually amassed thousands of objects, many of which were acquired during his trips to Japan, India and China. In 1887 he also bought several Whistler prints, his initial acquisition of works by the artist who would become his good friend. Retiring at age 45, Freer became a full-time collector and world traveler, expanding both his Asian and American holdings. In 1904 he revealed plans to bequeath a significant portion of his collections to the Smithsonian Institution and to finance the construction of a building to house the art. At his death his bequest totaled some 9,000 works. Today the museum's Asian properties have grown far beyond that. (Freer stipulated that his American collection not be expanded).

The Building

After the announcement of his gift, Freer embarked on a search for a suitable building design, visiting American and European museums to gather ideas as to gallery size, ventilation and lighting. In 1912 he hired New York architect Charles A. Platt, who employed Neoclassical symmetry in the marble and granite Renaissance-style structure that is built, as Freer had specified, around a central courtyard. The building's two entrances on Jefferson Drive and Independence Avenue are distinguished by triple arches. The arch motif is repeated in the bronze-framed Palladian windows and glass doors surrounding the 60sq-ft fountained courtyard, which is faced with white Tennessee marble. The stone balustrade of the exterior parapet appears again above the courtyard's arches. The museum was officially opened in 1923. After extensive renovation, begun in 1988, the museum reopened in 1993 with galleries on the first level and study rooms, an auditorium, a conference room and a gallery shop on the lower levels. An underground exhibition gallery connects the Freer and the Sackler Gallery.

▷ **Location:** Jefferson Dr. at 12th St. SW. Just a few steps from the Smithsonian Metro station (Blue and Orange lines).

🅿 **Parking:** Very limited street parking.

🕐 **Timing:** Allow at least an hour.

🎭 **Don't Miss:** The ornate Peacock Room decorated by James McNeill Whistler.

VISIT

🕐*Open year-round daily 10am–5:30pm.* 🕐*Closed Dec 25.* 👣*Guided tours available except Wed and federal holidays.* ♿ 📞*202-633-1000. www.asia.si.edu. A floor plan can be obtained from the information desk.*

Asian Collection

Highlights of the Chinese holdings include ornamental implements of the emperors of the Ming (1368-1644) and Qing (1644-1911) dynasties; 15C blue-and-white porcelain bowls from the imperial workshop in Jingdezhen in southeast China; and bronzes, jades and lacquerware from the Ancient Chinese collection, which dates from 3500 BC to the first century AD. Traditional Japanese painting and calligraphy can be seen on hanging scrolls (ink and color on silk or paper); 15-19C *byobu*, or folding screens; late-16-19C porcelain pieces

Peacock Room (1876-77) by James McNeill Whistler

©Freer | Sackler Galleries

and lacquered wooden boxes; and 13-17C stone and earthenware tea bowls. Korean ceramics from the 10C to the 14C, Indian 16-19C court paintings and Islamic manuscripts are also here.

American Collection

Paintings by prominent American artists include Whistler's *Caprice in Purple and Gold: The Golden Screen* (1864) and John Singer Sargent's *Breakfast in the Loggia* (1910). Of special interest are Whistler's *Notes*, miniature oils depicting Chelsea shops and English landscapes c.1882; and *Nocturnes*, dramatic paintings of the Thames River at night, inspired by

Detail of Hanging Scroll (1847) by Katsushika Hokusai

©Freer | Sackler Galleries

Japanese prints. Full of light and grace are his *Six Projects* of the late 1860s—varied compositions of figures against the sea *(all six paintings may not be on view)*. Oil portraits and landscapes by Abbott Henry Thayer, Thomas Dewing's paintings of women in fields, and Dwight Tryon's large landscapes adorn other American art galleries.

Permanently installed in Gallery 12 is the **Peacock Room**★, Whistler's only extant interior design (1876-77). Freer purchased the room in 1904 from a London art dealer; prior to the museum's opening, it was transferred from his Detroit home to the premises. Asked by English shipping tycoon Frederick Leyland to redecorate portions of his 20ft-by-32ft London dining room, the artist began what evolved into a major (ostensibly unauthorized) overhaul. The result was a highly original, gilded setting for Leyland's blue-and-white Chinese porcelain collection. Intricate paintings of golden peacocks and peacock motifs embellish the walls, shutters and ceiling. Dominating the mantel is Whistler's painting *The Princess from the Land of Porcelain*, which Leyland had purchased. In the mural depicting two fighting peacocks *(south wall)*, the artist immortalized his dispute with Leyland over payment for his interior work. The porcelain pieces on view are similar to those in Leyland's collection and were acquired for the room's 1993 restoration.

Hirshhorn Museum and Sculpture Garden★★

Ⓜ *L'Enfant Plaza or Smithsonian*

An unmistakable architectural statement on the Mall, this cylindrical building houses one of the finest collections of modern art in the country. Its sculpture holdings, ranging from the realistic to the monumental and abstract, make up the world's most comprehensive collection of 20C works in that medium.

▷ **Location:** Independence Ave. at 7th St. SW. A short walk from the L'Enfant Plaza Metro station (Green, Yellow, Orange & Blue) lines

Kids: The ArtLab for Teens workshops (preregistration required).

🕒 **Timing:** Allow at least 2 hours for the museum and the sculpture garden.

Don't Miss: Friday gallery talks at 12:30 pm.

A BIT OF HISTORY

The Benefactor

Born in Latvia on the eastern coast of the Baltic Sea, **Joseph Hirshhorn** (1899-1981) immigrated to Brooklyn with his widowed mother and 10 siblings when he was six years old. At age 13 he left school to help support his family, and at 18 he was a broker on Wall Street. He eventually became a wealthy financier and uranium magnate.

Hirshhorn traced his first interest in art to a series of paintings by Salon masters he saw reproduced in an insurance calendar. His early collecting followed in that vein but by the late 1930s his tastes had turned to the works of French Impressionists and post-Impressionists. That interest also passed, as he increasingly focused his collecting on contemporary American and European painting and on modern sculpture from around the world.

In 1962, with the first major public exhibition of his art treasures at the Solomon R. Guggenheim Museum in New York, his collection drew international attention. Representatives from several foreign countries approached Hirshhorn, offering to establish museums for the collection in their respective countries. However, in the mid-1960s, President Lyndon Johnson and Smithsonian secretary S. Dillon Ripley convinced Hirshhorn to donate his collection to the Smithsonian. In 1966 Congress established the Hirshhorn Museum and Sculpture Garden, to which the benefactor contributed more than 6,000 works. He continued to be an avid collector until his death in 1981. At that time, he bequeathed another 6,000 works to the museum.

A "Doughnut" on the Mall

Almost every new addition to the Mall has met with a certain degree of controversy, but the so-called "doughnut" by architect **Gordon Bunshaft** incited harsh criticism, since it was the first unabashedly modern building erected on the prestigious national showplace. Dillon Ripley said of Bunshaft's design, "If it were not controversial in almost every way, it would hardly qualify as a place to house contemporary art." Elevated on four piers, the drum-shaped, unadorned concrete building wraps around a fountain plaza that extends beneath the raised building, serving almost as a first floor.

The Collection

Some 5,000 paintings, 3,000 pieces of sculpture and mixed media and 4,000 works on paper compose the collection, roughly five percent of which is on view at any one time. The core collection is continually being refined and updated by an active acquisition program.

Hirshhorn Museum
and Sculpture Garden

©Gwen Cannon/Michelin

VISIT

🕐 *Museum open year-round daily 10am–5:30pm. Plaza open 7:30am - 5:30 pm & Sculpture garden open 7:30am-dusk.* 🕐 *Closed Dec 25.*
🚶 *Guided tours (30min) available daily from noon-4pm; inquire at information desk. Interpretive Guides also walk around the galleries to answer questions and discuss exhibitions.*
✕*(outdoors)* ♿ ✆ *202-633-1000.*
www.hirshhorn.si.edu.

Paintings

The paintings in the collection are organized chronologically, beginning with early-20C American works on the third floor. Among the artists featured here are such renowned painters as George Bellows and John Sloan, adherents of the Ashcan school; and prominent 20C artists Edward Hopper, Marsden Hartley, Max Weber, Stuart Davis and Georgia O'Keeffe, among others.

The third-floor galleries devoted to European and American modernism feature paintings and three-dimensional works by Constantin Brancusi, Alberto Giacometti, Jean Arp, Joan Miró, Isamu Noguchi, Jean Dubuffet, Francis Bacon, Willem de Kooning, Mark Rothko, and Richard Diebenkorn and others.

Also on this floor is a gallery titled **Directions**, devoted to rotating exhibits that highlight the work of emerging contemporary artists.

The second-floor galleries are reserved for major special exhibits and a variety of small, changing exhibits of art from the permanent collection.

Contemporary art and recent acquisitions are housed on the underground level. Also staged here is the **Black Box** series, a new media installation that changes every three months and showcases emerging artists .

Sculpture Ambulatories

On the second and third floors, continuous galleries following the interior circumference of the building and feature small sculptural works. The display begins on the second floor with such 19C European artists as Maillol, Rodin, Degas and Renoir. The Hirshhorn's collection of sculptures by **Henri Matisse** is particularly rich.

The third-floor ambulatory is devoted to 20C sculpture by masters like Pablo Picasso, Willem de Kooning, Alberto Giacometti and Alexander Archipenko. The Hirshhorn owns one of the country's most extensive collections of works by **Henry Moore** (1898-1986), with some 60 sculptures and 20 works on paper. Special exhibitions are also mounted on the second floor.

Outdoor Sculpture

The **plaza** on which the building stands is a showplace for monumental contemporary sculpture, including works by Alexander Calder, Claes Oldenburg, Tony Cragg and Juan Muñoz.

Smaller figurative works are featured in the sunken and walled **Sculpture Garden** *(across Jefferson Dr.)*. Prominent among these are the works of Rodin, including his monumental *Burghers of Calais*, and Maillol. Also on display are sculptures by Gaston Lachaise and Henry Moore, as well as a series of rare relief plaques by Matisse *(Backs)*.

The Hirshhorn recently acquired a new work by **Yoko Ono** titled *Wish Tree for Washington D.C.* (2007). A gift to the museum by the artist, the white-flowering Japanese dogwood is the only wish tree of 10 created for the Cherry Blossom Festival that will remain in the capital as a permanent installation.

National Archives★★

M Archives or Federal Triangle

This imposing Classical Revival "temple" just off the Mall holds the nation's documentary treasures, including the Declaration of Independence, the Constitution, and the Bill of Rights.

A BIT OF HISTORY

Strongbox for the Nation

Completed in 1937, the National Archives filled a pressing need for a central repository of official and historical records. Before its establishment, each department of the federal government stored its own archival material. Important documents were frequently lost or damaged due to haphazard treatment. In 1921 a fire destroyed all of the 1890 census records. That loss, coupled with the Public Building Act of 1926, finally precipitated plans to construct a fireproof federal archives building. Today the National Archives and Records Administration, as it is officially designated, safeguards billions of paper documents, millions of photographs, and hundreds of thousands of video, film and sound recordings. The collection includes such varied items as let-

▷ **Location:** Constitution Ave. between 7th and 9th Sts. NW. The Archives/Navy Memorial Metro station (Yellow & Green lines) is across Pennsylvania Ave. from the Archives building

◷ **Timing:** Allow 90 min. inside and an hour or more to enter if you don't have timed entry tickets.

☺ **Don't Miss:** The Charters of Freedom.

ters from private individuals to US presidents, Commodore Matthew Perry's journals from his historic 19C mission to Japan and Mathew Brady's Civil War photographs.

The Building

The massive rectangular limestone building, designed by John Russell Pope, fills an entire city block. Corinthian colonnades embellish its four facades, and elaborate bas-relief pediments top the entrance porticoes on the north and south sides of the building.

Inside, a sweeping staircase leads visitors up to the entrance of the National Archives' **rotunda**. Popularly known as "the Shrine," the cavernous, 75ft-high, half-domed space with its coffered ceil-

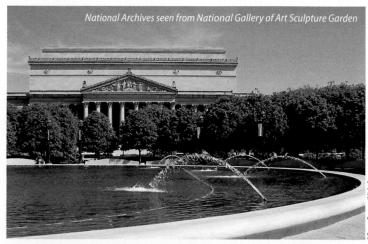

National Archives seen from National Gallery of Art Sculpture Garden

©Gwen Cannon/Michelin

Textual Records Stacks

© Earl McDonald/National Archives

ing inspires reverence. It is here that the nation's most revered documents are enshrined. The Public Vaults, an interactive exhibit, allows visitors to access the Archives' stacks.

VISIT
The Rotunda
Enter from Constitution Ave.
Open Labor Day-mid-Mar daily 10am–5:30pm, rest of year til 7pm. Closed Thanksgiving Day & Dec 25. Guided tour (1hr) tickets & timed-entry tickets may be purchased ($1.50) online or by phone: 877-444-6777. 866-272-6272. www.archives.gov.
On view are the country's esteemed documents known as the **Charters of Freedom**★★★: the **Declaration of Independence**, all four pages of the **Constitution**, and the **Bill of Rights**. These six fragile pieces of parchment are sealed in specially designed argon-filled cases of titanium and aluminum.

Other cases display historical documents relating to the charters. Two 34ft-long murals, painted in the 1930s by Barry Faulkner, adorn the walls on either side of the dais. The left mural, *The Declaration of Independence,* is Faulkner's fictitious depiction of Thomas Jefferson presenting a draft of the Declaration to John Hancock as the Continental Congress looks on. *The Constitution*, on the right, shows another imagined scene of James Madison offering the final document to George Washington.

Research Facilities
Enter from Pennsylvania Ave.
Open year-round Wed–Fri 9am–9pm & Mon, Tue & Sat 9am–5pm. Closed federal holidays. Must be 14 years of age or older and present photo ID to enter facility. 866-272-6272.
The National Archives functions as a major source of historical material for researchers from the US and abroad. The ornately paneled **Central Research Room** *(2nd floor)* serves visitors engaged in scholarly research. Among the holdings are the papers of the Continental Congress, court and congressional records, historical correspondence and records of federal agencies deemed to be of "enduring value."

The **Microfilm Research Room** *(ground floor)* serves persons engaged in genealogical research. It contains such materials as census, military service and pension records and ship passenger arrival lists. Pamphlets and staff offer instruction on how to trace family histories.

As of 1978 certain presidential papers were declared federal property and came under archival jurisdiction. Most are housed in separate presidential libraries administered by the National Archives. The **Nixon Watergate tapes**, kept in an archives facility in College Park, Maryland, are accessible to the public (*shuttle buses leave every hour on the hour 8am–5pm*).

National Museum of African Art★★

Ⓜ *Smithsonian or L'Enfant Plaza*

Originally located in a row of Capitol Hill town houses, the National Museum of African Art today occupies more spacious quarters in the underground Smithsonian Quadrangle complex. Devoted to the research, acquisition and display of traditional African arts, especially those of the sub-Saharan regions, the museum possesses a permanent collection of more than 7,000 items.

VISIT

ⓒ*Open year-round daily 10am–5:30pm.* ⓒ*Closed Dec 25.* ♿ ℘*202-633-4600. www.nmafa.si.edu. Obtain a floor plan from the information desk.* Ⓐ*Only a small selection of the collection is exhibited at any particular time.*

Collection Highlights

Pieces in bronze, copper, wood, ivory and fiber are exhibited on a rotating basis. The sculptures, utilitarian objects, architectural elements, decorative arts and textiles on display are organized by regions, thereby emphasizing how geography determines the selection of materials, as well as form and style.

The museum's collection of **Royal Benin Art** from the historic West African kingdom of Benin (present-day Nigeria) includes several cast-copper alloy sculptures on permanent display. The ceremonial figures, heads, pendants and plaques were created between the 15C and 19C and reveal the elaborate rituals and ornate regalia of the Benin *oba* (king) and his entourage.

Note especially the figure of an *oba* (19C); his regalia symbolizes his role as a divine ruler. A 16-17C carved ivory spoon, produced specifically for export, illustrates foreign influences Benin art style.

◗ **Location:** The Smithsonian Quadrangle at 950 Independence Ave. SW. The main entrance is located in the Enid Haupt Garden on Independence Ave. By Metro: Smithsonian station (Blue and Orange lines or the L'Enfant Plaza Station (all lines except Red) and take the Maryland Ave exit.

⊘ **Don't Miss:** The Walt Disney-Tishman African Art Collection

Items on display show the tremendous variety of shapes, proportions and designs present in African sculpture. The permanent collection includes a number of **ritual objects** that are believed to be conduits of communication with spirits. Medicinal figurines, arranged in a Chokwe fiber divination basket, play a significant role in the healing process.

©Franko Khoury/National Museum of African Art/Smithsonian Institution

Toussaint Louverture et la vieille esclave *(1989), Ousmane Sow 1935, Dakar, Senegal, Mixed media*

115

Finely sculpted Sherbo Bullom stone figures, like the ones seen here, are still used by the Mende people of the Guinea coast to assure a good harvest. An Igala shrine figure was part of an altar created as an intermediary space between the spiritual and physical worlds.

Recent Acquisition

The museum's most significant recent acquisition is the 525-object **Walt Disney-Tishman African Art Collection**, a gift from the Walt Disney World Co. Predominately masks and figures from west and central Africa, the collection was started by Paul and Ruth Tishman, in 1959. They sold their holdings to the Disney Company in 1984 in anticipation of its permanent display at Epcot; however, the collection was reserved for exhibit loans instead. Pieces on view at the museum include an exquisitely carved, late-15C ivory hunting horn from Sierra Leone; a late-19C to early 20C wooden door of the Tsogo peoples, Gabon; and an early 20C crown made of cloth, glass beads, iron and plant fiber from the Yoruba people in Nigeria.

National Museum of American History★★

Ⓜ *Federal Triangle or Smithsonian*

The repository for such popular national icons as the Star-Spangled Banner, the boxing robe of Rocky Balboa and the First Ladies' gowns, this unique museum captures the essence of America by presenting the objects and ideas that have figured prominently in the nation's material and social development.

- ▷ **Location:** Constitution Ave. between 12th and 14th Sts. NW. The museum stands just east of the Washington Monument on the north side of the Mall.
- Ⓟ **Parking:** Downtown lots are blocks away; public transportation is preferable.
- **Don't Miss:** The Star-Spangled Banner, the First Ladies' and the American Presidency exhibits. See the website for ongoing renovation information.
- Ⓛ **Timing:** Plan to spend at least 2 hours here. Check online for the museum's occasional late opening hours.
- **Kids:** The Gunboat is popular with children.

A BIT OF HISTORY

Totaling more than 3 million objects (only a small percentage of which are on view at any one time), the museum's collections trace their origins to 1858, when the models from the US Patent Office were transferred to the Smithsonian Institution. Beginning in 1881, selections from this collection were exhibited in the Arts and Industries Building. To provide adequate space for the rapidly expanding collection of diverse artifacts illustrating America's scientific, cultural, political and technological achievements, the current marble structure was opened in 1964 as the National Museum of History and Technology. Renamed the National Museum of American History in 1980, this institution has committed itself to presenting issue-oriented exhibits that explore key events and social phenomena in American culture.

For two years the museum was closed for extensive renovation, reopening in 2008. In 2012 it began a major overhaul of the west wing: some exhibits there will be closed (*check the museum's*

NATIONAL MUSEUM OF AMERICAN HISTORY

THIRD FLOOR WEST
Entertainment, Sports, and Music

THIRD FLOOR EAST
American Wars and Politics

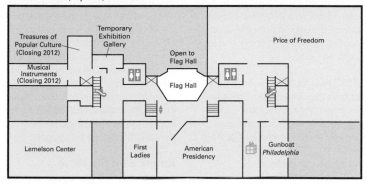

SECOND FLOOR WEST
American Lives

SECOND FLOOR EAST
American Ideals

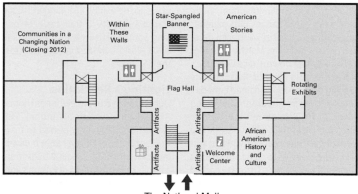

The National Mall

FIRST FLOOR WEST
Science and Innovation

Constitution Avenue

FIRST FLOOR EAST
Transportation and Technology

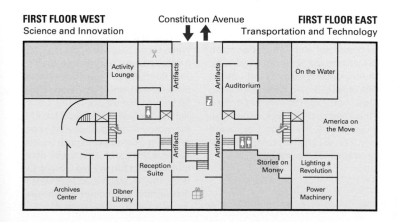

website for current floor-plan status and details of the ongoing renovation).

New exhibits will center on themes of American democracy and innovation; a third-floor Music Hall will provide a state-of-the-art venue for the Smithsonian Chamber Music Society and Jazzworks Orchestra.

VISIT HIGHLIGHTS

👥 *Enter the museum from Constitution Ave or from the National Mall.*
🕙 *Open daily 10am–5:30pm (hours extended in spring/summer).* 🕙 *Closed Dec 25.* ✖ ♿ ✆ *202-633-1000.* http://americanhistory.si.edu.

First Ladies

Be they silk, velvet, beaded or lace, the First Lady inaugural ball gowns remain among the most visited displays in the entire Museum of American History. The "First Ladies at the Smithsonian" *(third floor, west)* exhibit spans two galleries and features a total of 24 special occasion dresses including Martha Washington's silk taffeta gown, Grace Coolidge's black-and-gold metallic flapper-style evening dress and Jacqueline Kennedy's pale yellow one-shouldered evening gown. In 1912 Helen Taft started the custom of First Ladies donating clothing worn on historic occasions with the gift of the dress she wore to her husband's inaugural ball in 1909. The gift sparked the Smithsonian to mount its first-ever exhibit devoted to the First Ladies and the exhibit has taken several different forms since that time. In March 2009, First Lady Michelle Obama continued the 100-year-old tradition when she presented the white-silk chiffon gown she wore to the 2009 inaugural balls. The one-shouldered dress embellished with organza flowers now stands in the center of the exhibit's second gallery. Other items on display include portraits, shoes, jewelry, White House china and even a set of Christmas cards designed by Jacqueline Kennedy.

Treasures of Popular Culture

🖐 *Objects in this national treasures display rotate frequently.*

Young visitors, along with the young-at-heart visitors, may feel transported over the rainbow when they catch a glimpse of Dorothy's ruby slippers in the pop culture gallery *(third floor, west)*. Along with the famous red shoes worn by Judy Garland in the classic film *The Wizard of Oz*, other items in this small, but fun display include Mr. Rogers' red cardigan, Archie Bunker's threadbare armchair, and Jim Henson's Kermit the frog puppet.

America on the Move

If it rolls, drives or has wheels, chances are it's represented here. The Museum's 26,000-sq ft hall traces the history of American transportation from the railroad to the street car to the modern automobile. More than 300 objects make up the exhibit including a Chicago Transit Authority "L" train car, a 92-foot-long Southern Railway locomotive and a 903 Winton, the first car driven across the US.

Lighting a Revolution

Lighting a Revolution celebrates Thomas Alva Edison's historic inventions. This exhibition originally opened to mark the centennial of Edison's light bulb and includes one of the original bulbs from a public demonstration of Edison's light in Menlo Park during Christmas week, 1879. His less famous inventions such as the electric marshmallow toaster are also here.

Landmark Objects

When the museum re-opened in 2008 it installed two "landmark objects" on each floor (one at the entrance to each wing) to help highlight the theme of that section of the museum.

Among the landmark objects found at the museum are a portion of the once segregated Greensboro Lunch Counter that was the site of famous civil rights protests, Clara Barton's Red Cross Ambulance, the telescope used by America's first woman astronomer, Horatio Gre-

Facts about the Flag

The Star-Spangled Banner now resides in a new state-of-the art, environmentally-controlled chamber.

Size 30ft by 34ft (originally 30ft by 42ft).

Design Fifteen hand-sewn white cotton five-pointed stars (approximately 24in wide) on blue field of English wool bunting. 15 handsewn stripes (8 red, 7 white, approximately 24in wide) of wool bunting.

Weight 40-50 pounds.

Crafted by Mrs. Mary Pickersgill of Baltimore.

Date July–August 1813.

Features The red "V" is of unknown origin and date. The irregular "fly edge" has resulted from the flag's snapping in the wind and from the cutting of pieces during the 1800s.

Star-Spangled Banner Gallery

Courtesy of Smithsonian's National Museum of American History

enough's George Washington sculpture and a Dumbo car from Disneyland.

American Presidency★

This popular exhibition traces the history and culture of the presidency. Hundreds of objects are exhibited including a dispatch case used by George Washington during the Revolutionary War, a microphone used by Franklin D. Roosevelt for his fireside chats and the portable lap desk on which Thomas Jefferson wrote the *Declaration of Independence*.

Note some of the quirkier items in the collection: John Quincy Adams' chess set, Abe Lincoln's top hat, Warren Harding's silk pajamas, Teddy Roosevelt's chaps, and Bill Clinton's saxophone. The collection also has a significant online component which can be visited at http://americanhistory.si.edu/presidency/home.html.

Star-Spangled Banner★

The state-of-the-art, environmentally-controlled chamber *(second floor, center)* allows visitors to view the enormous flag (originally 30ft by 42ft) that was "still there" on the morning of 14 September 1814, after the British bombardment of Fort McHenry in Baltimore during the War of 1812. In British custody during the attack, Francis Scott Key saw this flag still waving at dawn and penned the lyrics that was later set to music and, in 1931, proclaimed the US national anthem. Photography is not allowed in this exhibit.

National Museum of Natural History★★

Ⓜ *Smithsonian floor plan opposite*

This museum, part of the Smithsonian Institution, ranks as one of the most visited museums in the world. Two floors of exhibits and two large-format cinemas explore life on earth through clues nature has left behind—among them dinosaur skeletons, prehistoric fossils and gemstones, as well as artifacts of human cultures.

A BIT OF HISTORY

Soon after the completion of the Arts and Industries Building (1881), more space was needed to accommodate the rapidly expanding Smithsonian collections.

In 1903 Congress authorized the construction of the Smithsonian's third building, today known as the National Museum of Natural History. Designed by Hornblower and Marshall in the Classical Revival style, the original four-story granite structure faced with a seven-column entrance portico was completed in 1910. Its octagonal rotunda is 80ft in diameter and rises to a height of 124.15ft. The addition of the six-story east and west wings in 1963 and 1965 brought the building's footprint up to 16 acres. Today the museum encompasses 300,000sq ft of exhibit space and two large-format theaters, conserves 126 million specimens and provides laboratory facilities for 500 geologists, zoologists, botanists, anthropologists and paleontologists.

The vast **Ocean Hall** on the first floor allows visitors to explore Earth's final frontier—the ocean.

◐ **Location:** Constitution Ave. at 10th St. NW. The museum is located in the north center of the Mall.

🅿 **Parking:** Downtown lots are several blocks away; public transportation is preferable.

🏛 **Don't Miss:** The Gem and Mineral collection.

🕓 **Timing:** Go first to the theater box office if you plan to see an IMAX show *(about 40min)*. Allow 2-3hrs to visit the museum. Take a break in the Atrium Café *(ground floor),* Fossil Café *(first floor)* or Café Natural.

👫 **Kids:** Insect Zoo, Giant Squid exhibit.

Science on a Sphere, Sant Ocean Hall

©Chip Clark, Smithsonian Institution

NATIONAL MUSEUM OF NATURAL HISTORY

SECOND FLOOR

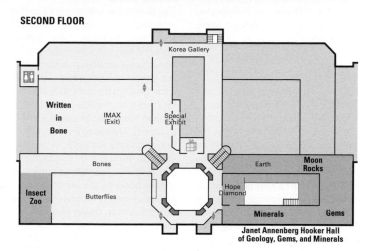

FIRST FLOOR

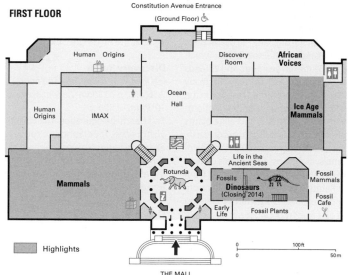

THE MALL

Highlights

VISIT

👥 Enter from the Mall (Madison Dr.).
🕐 Open year-round daily 10am–5:30pm
(extended hours in spring/summer).
🕐 Closed Dec 25. ✕ ♿ ✆ 202-633-1000.
www.mnh.si.edu.

Theater

Box offices for the Samuel C. Johnson IMAX® theater are locaated at the rear of the rotunda, near the Constitution Avenue entrance. Shows last about 40min. Tickets may be purchased

online, by phone or at the museum.
✆ *866-868-7774; www.si.edu/imax.*

🕐 *Some exhibits listed below may be temporarily relocated or not on view.*

First Floor

The rotunda is dominated by a 13ft-tall
African bush elephant, which weighed
nearly 12 tons at its death in 1955 at the
age of 50. Surrounding exhibits describe
the sights and sounds of the savanna,
home to creatures ranging from tiny

dung beetles to giant elephants like this one. It is also a popular meeting spot for groups and families touring the museum.

Dinosaurs

Closing spring 2014 for renovation.
"Hatcher," a **triceratops** skeleton, was created by 3-D computer modeling technology, which allowed scientists to show the 65- to 70-million-year-old dinosaur in a natural pose. The original skeleton was discovered in Wyoming by bone collector John Bell Hatcher in 1891. Shown doing battle with **Tyrannosaurus rex**, Hatcher is also kept company by a 90ft **Diplodocus skeleton**, a life-size model of a **pterosaur** and a **Stegosaurus stenops**.

Fossil Galleries

Encircling galleries describe the parade of life from the big bang 4.6 billion years ago through the Cenozoic era, which began 65 million years ago and extends through the present. Evidence for many of the theories presented here lies in the fossil record. Stone imprints of micro-organisms and stubby shoreline plants chart the first four billion years on earth, after which emerged a wild panoply of animals. In the Fossil Mammals gallery, a re-created 5ft **eryops** skeleton from the Permian era, a 50-million-year-old rhinocerous-like **uintatheres** skeleton and a large array of Oligocene mammals, including a **mesohippus** (tiny horse), are on view. The giant sea turtle and the massive mosasaur are highlights in the **Ancient Seas** gallery.

Ice Age

A brief presentation of glacial history precedes this display of fossilized mammal skeletons from the Pleistocene epoch, also known as the Ice Age. The woolly mammoth and the mastodon are both "cousins" of the elephant. The saber-toothed cat was recovered from Los Angeles' La Brea tar pits, where it met its sticky end along with more than one million other animals.

African Voices

This large-scale exhibit uses film clips, recorded narratives, poetry excerpts and music, along with 400 artifacts from the museum's permanent collection, to explore African history. Starting from the west entrance, a path leads through the millennia, as human life takes form, the Nile cultures rise and fall, and tribal cultures spread across the continent, producing a wealth of traditions and arts. An *aqals*, or Somalian portable house, is on display, as is a stunning 8ft-tall antelope mask made of corn husks by the Chewa people of Malawi. Exhibits on more recent history tell African stories of survival and protest: the slave revolts of the 1800s; the 1960s independence movements in Congo, Nigeria, Senegal and Kenya; the successful fight against apartheid in South Africa; and the ongoing struggle against the AIDS epidemic.

Discovery Room

🕑*Open year-round Tue–Thu noon–2:30pm, Fri 10:30am-2:30pm, weekends 10:30am–3:30pm.*
This hands-on educational exhibit offers visitors the opportunity to touch and examine various objects and artifacts (fossils, minerals, and animals both living and preserved) that are representative of those found in the museum.

Ocean Hall

The 23,000ft Ocean Hall focuses on the ocean as a global system and how it influences life on Earth. It's hard to miss the 45ft-long whale model hanging from the ceiling. The replica is based on an actual North Atlantic whale named Phoenix who scientists have been tracking since her birth in 1987. Other highlights include a giant squid exhibit and a 1,500-gallon aquarium with a live coral reef.

Mammals

In the Kenneth E. Behring Family Hall of Mammals, tall glass panels and cases offers the visitor an overview of the mammal class in all its diversity. Along with more familiar animals, the exhibit includes specimens of such exotic creatures as the jaguar, kinkajou, tapir, dingo, African civet, okapi and Chinese pangolin. Lifelike settings illustrate habitats and survival mechanisms (such as food gathering, migration and defense strategies) that either led these mammals to their present stage of development or caused them to perish. Mock thunder and lightning add a sense of realism.

Second Floor
Geology Hall
The **gem and mineral collection** ★★★ is housed in the Janet Annenberg Hooker Hall of Geology, Gems and Minerals. The largest blue diamond in the world at 45.5 carats, the legendary **Hope Diamond**, greets visitors. The 330-carat **Star of Asia** Sapphire from Sri Lanka and the 138.7-carat **Rosser Reeves Ruby** are among the finest in the collection. Set in a brooch containing 138 diamonds is the 75-carat **Hooker Emerald.** A flawless 127.88in Burma **quartz ball** and a headlight-size **golden topaz** from Brazil, the largest cut gemstone in the world at 22,892.5 carats, highlight the array. **Diamonds** on view show a remarkable range of sizes and colors, from the 253.7-carat **Oppenheimer Diamond**, which is uncut and unpolished, to the 2.9-carat pink beauty from Tanzania.

Smithsonite, or zinc carbonate, first identified by James Smithson, founder of the Smithsonian is also on view here. Actual crystal pockets and ore veins are re-created in the **mine gallery**, and how earthquakes, mountain chains and volcanoes result from the movement of the earth's plates is illustrated in **plate tectonics.** The **Earth, Moon, Meteorites** exhibit features a collection of meteorites of various origins from the moon to Mars to asteroids as well as the story of Earth's own geologic past. Moon rocks brought back to earth by astronauts on *Apollo* flights are also on view.

Insect Zoo
The arthropod group comprises 90 percent of animal life on earth. Many insects in the O. Orkin Insect Zoo exemplify the adaptations that have enabled arthropods to survive for 475 million years. Most are housed in low cases that make it easy for young children to peak in. Volunteers often walk around the exhibit holding the creatures allowing visitors to touch the bugs or ask questions.

An ant farm forms a complete, small-scale society, and a beehive is equipped with an exit tube to the outdoors, allowing inhabitants to forage for food. *Tarantula feedings Tue–Fri 10:30am, 11:30am & 1:30pm.*

Butterfly Pavilion
$6 (free Tue). Capacity is limited: avoid waiting in line by obtaining a timed ticket (daily every 15min beginning at 10:15am with last entry at 5pm); timed tickets can be reserved online or by calling 202-633-4629. A service fee is added to all orders.

Visitors can get an up-close look at the colorful winged creatures as they stroll among butterflies and exotic plants in the enclosed Butterfly Pavilion. Only 40 people can be accommodated in the pavilion at once, so advanced reservations are strongly encouraged for this popular attraction.

Korea Gallery
Korea's long history and remarkable culture are portrayed in this permanent exhibit. Topics covered include the family, the writing system, natural and constructed landscapes, and visual arts. Paintings, sculpture, ceramics, textiles and other works on display span the 6C BC to the present.

Butterfly Garden
Outside, on the 9th Street side, between the museum and the National Gallery of Art's Sculpture Garden. Same hours as the museum.

The separate Smithsonian Butterfly Garden features four separate habitats—wetlands, woods, meadow and urban—to demonstrate the natural partners of butterflies. Host plants for different species are labeled, and informative panels illustrate how visitors can make their own gardens bee- and butterfly-friendly.

National Museum of the American Indian★★

Ⓜ *Federal Center*

Opened in September 2004, the National Museum of the American Indian (NMAI) is the first national museum dedicated to Native Americans and the first new museum on the Mall since 1987. Fifteen years in creation, the museum holds 825,000 objects that represent more than 1,000 indigenous cultures spanning some 10,000 years of North, South, and Central American history.

A BIT OF HISTORY

The museum's holdings grew from the comprehensive collection of wealthy New York banker George Gustav Heye (1874–1957), which he amassed over a 45-year period. Heye was a member of the American Anthropological Association and the American Museum of Natural History; he was also a life fellow of the American Geographical Society, a fellow of the American Association for the Advancement of Science, and an honorary fellow of the Royal Anthropological

▷ **Location:** 4th St. and Independence Ave. SW. Obtain a floor plan from the information desk as you enter.

⊘ **Don't Miss:** An opportunity to try indigenous food in the Mitsitam Cafe.

🕔 **Timing:** Allow at least 90min for a visit if you eat in the cafe.

Institute. His collection first opened to the public in 1922 in New York's Museum of the American Indian. Among NMAI's treasures are Northwestern wood carvings and masks, Plains Indians clothes and feather bonnets, Southwestern pottery and basketry, Costa Rican ceramics, Maya jade objects, and Andean gold. Some 8,000 objects are on display at any given time.

VISIT

🕔*Open year-round daily 10am–5:30pm.* 🕔*Closed Dec 25.* ⤚*Highlight tours (45min) daily 1:30pm.* ℘*202-633-1000.* *http://nmai.si.edu/home.*

Exterior

A curving golden-hued limestone exterior, suggesting a Native American cliff dwelling, stands in contrast to sur-

National Museum of the American Indian

©Zain Deane/Michelin

rounding Classical-style buildings. The 4.25-acre site includes wetlands and 40 boulders, enhancing the museum's emphasis on the human connection to the natural world. The building intentionally is aligned perfectly to the cardinal directions and the center point of the Capitol dome, and filled with details, colors, and textures that reflect the Native universe.

Interior

Inside, a prism window reflects sunlight into a 120-foot-high atrium, and a wall of video screens welcomes visitors in 150 native languages, indicating the vitality and diversity of Indian culture.

Major exhibits focus on such topics as native cosmologies, history from Indian points of view, and the lifestyles of Indians in this century.

Our Universes

The Our Universes focuses on philosophies related to the nature of the universe and to the relationship between humans and the natural world. The exhibition introduces visitors to indigenous peoples from across the Western Hemisphere. The community galleries feature eight cultural philosophies and are designed to reflect each community's interpretation of the order of the world. The eight communities represented here are the Pueblo of Santa Clara (Española, New Mexico), Anishinaabe (Hollow Water and Sagkeeng Bands, Manitoba, Canada), Lakota (Pine Ridge Reservation, South Dakota), Quechua (Communidad de Phaqchanta, Cusco, Peru), Hupa (Hoopa Valley, California), Q'eq'chi' Maya (Cobán, Guatemala), Mapuche (Temuco, Chile), and Yup'ik (Yukon-Kuskokwim Delta, Alaska).

Our Peoples

The Our Peoples exhibition was conceived as a way for Native peoples to share their own stories and help correct the many inaccuracies and over simplifications that have been drawn about them over time.

The thread of Our Peoples focuses on the last 500 years of Native history and

Native Lunch

The museum's **Mitsitam Cafe** continues the aboriginal theme with native cuisines from various regions. Indigenous, and often organic, ingredients are used where possible. Diners can try cedar-planked, fire-roasted salmon; chicken tamales wrapped in corn husks; pinto bean and corn enchiladas; or grilled bison steaks. For a drink, try the hibiscus flower, chipotle and lime aqua fresca and for dessert the cinnamon fry bread. "Mitsitam" is Piscataway for "let's eat."

shows the long-lasting impact of the arrival of newcomers in the Western Hemisphere. Nearly every Native community wrestled with deadly new diseases and weaponry, the weakening of traditional spirituality, and the seizure of homelands by invading governments. But the story shown here is not just about destruction. It is also about how Native people intentionally and strategically kept their cultures alive.

Several tribes like the Seminole Tribe of Florida and the Blackfeet Nation in Montana have already shared their stories in this gallery and over time more tribes will share their tales as part of this ever-evolving permanent exhibit.

Our Lives

The Our Lives exhibit explores contemporary life in eight native communities ranging from the Igloolik of Canada to the Pamunkey of Virginia. Stories show how native languages, arts and culture have been kept alive in modern times. Native dress, baskets and artifacts, displayed in glass cases (3rd and 4th levels), can be researched on interactive touch screens in front of the cases.

A demonstration area in the atrium offers an opportunity to see native arts in action; the construction of an Inuit kayak or a Pueblo necklace, for example, gives context to the exhibits in the museum.

US Botanic Garden★★

Ⓜ *Federal Center*

Situated at the foot of Capitol Hill, this conservatory serves as the nation's living plant museum and provides a pleasant respite from the activity of the Mall.

A BIT OF HISTORY

This federally owned institution was chartered by Congress in 1818. The first greenhouse was established in 1842 to conserve the collection of exotic specimens brought from the South Seas by a team of US explorers. Originally located on the premises of the Patent Office Building, the collection was transferred to the Mall in 1850. The present conservatory, built in 1931, completed a four-year renovation in 2001. The garden features a skillful blend of two building types traditionally used for storing and displaying plants: the 19C iron and glass greenhouse and the stone orangerie of French palace gardens, with its full-length arched windows.

VISIT

Mall entrance on Maryland Ave.
🕙*Open year-round daily 10am–5pm.*
🚆*Tour schedule online. Self-guided cell phone tours on* ☎*202-730-9303.*
♿ ☎*202-225-8333. www.usbg.gov.*

US Botanic Garden

©United States Botanic Garden

▶ **Location:** 1st St. SW. The Conservatory's main entrance is located at 100 Maryland Ave, SW and the National Garden is adjacent to the Conservatory. Get off at the Federal Center SW Metro station (Orange or Blue lines.)

👪**Kids:** Winter holiday model train display

👁 **Don't Miss:** The orchid collection.

The garden court, the setting for seasonal floral exhibits, leads into a large glass pavilion with towering subtropical plants. The two smaller pavilions flanking this central space house flowering orchids, medicinal plants, desert flora, and a collection of cycad trees similar to those that grew on the planet 200 million years ago.

Hawaii, the newest permanent exhibit, brings the colorful blooms of the Aloha State to the nation's capital. The display includes rare and endangered plants from the 50th state, as well as a lava flow waterfall, and other typically Hawaiian land features.

Another permanent exhibit, Plants in Culture, explores the role of plantlife in everything from therapy to music to language.

The park, situated across Independence Avenue, blooms with a rainbow of seasonal flowering plants that provide the backdrop for the cast-iron **Bartholdi Fountain**, executed by Frédéric-Auguste Bartholdi (1834-1904), sculptor of the Statue of Liberty. Bartholdi originally created the fountain for the 1876 International Centennial Exhibition in Philadelphia. The fountain was then purchased for $6,000 (half of its value) by the US government at the suggestion of Frederick Law Olmsted, the landscape architect of the Capitol Grounds. It was moved to Washington in 1877 and placed at the base of Capitol Hill near the center line of the Mall, on what was then the Botanic Garden grounds.

US Holocaust Memorial Museum★★

Ⓜ *Smithsonian*

A deeply moving, wholly absorbing history lesson awaits visitors to this large museum-research complex, conceived "to commemorate the dead and to educate the living." Occupying nearly 2 acres of land, just off the Mall, the striking edifice houses a compelling permanent exhibit that focuses on the Nazi extermination of millions of Jews and others during World War II.

A BIT OF HISTORY
The Museum Takes Shape

In 1980 Congress chartered the United States Holocaust Memorial Council—the museum's governing body—and the federal government donated a museum site just south of the Washington Monument. Soon thereafter, the council began fund-raising and artifacts-collecting efforts. In 1986 the New York firm of I.M. Pei & Partners was chosen, with James Freed as principal architect, to design an appropriate structure. Construction began on the $90-million building in 1989, and the museum formally opened in 1993.

An Unconventional Building

Given the museum's highly charged subject matter, the challenge to design a suitable structure, able to match its powerful message with dignity and sensitivity, was immense. The main five-story brick and limestone building is a post-Modern "penitentiary," with its series of "watchtowers" lining the north and south walls. The exposed metal beams, railings and metal-framed glass doors of the building's 7,500sq ft glass-roofed central atrium, the **Hall of Witness**, amplify the feeling of imprisonment. The contrasting hexagonal, 6,000sq ft beige limestone annex *(located on the west side)* houses, on the second floor, the 60ft-high **Hall of Remembrance**,

> **Location:** South of Independence Ave. between 14th St. and Raoul Wallenberg Pl. SW. The permanent exhibit covers three floors. Visitors take an elevator to the 4th floor and walk down through the exhibits to the 2nd floor.

🅿 **Parking:** There's a parking garage at 12th and C St., SW, east of the museum *($4/hr)*; hourly metered parking along Independence Ave. is 3 to 5 blocks away.

🕐 **Timing:** Allow 2.5hrs.

👫 **Kids:** "Daniel's Story: Remember the Children" designed for young visitors aged 8 and older as an alternative to the permanent exhibit.

an unadorned, natural-light-filled space provided for quiet contemplation. Four nonrepresentational works by prominent artists were commissioned for the museum: wall art by Ellsworth Kelly and Sol LeWitt graces transition rooms between the floors of the permanent exhibit; Richard Serra's steel monolith anchors the atrium's lower staircase; and Joel Shapiro's monumental sculpture fronts the west entrance.

VISIT

🕐*Open year-round daily 10am–5:20pm (hours extended in spring).* 🚫*Closed Yom Kippur & Dec 25. Free timed-entry passes, from the box office, required for the permanent exhibit Mar-Aug (arrive early for same-day passes); advance passes obtainable online or ☏877-80-USHMM) carry a service charge.* ✕♿ ☏*202-488-0400. www.ushmm.org.* 👫 *Daniel's Story: Remember the Children exhibit is for young visitors, in lieu of the permanent exhibit.*

Before entering the elevator, visitors are given a keepsake photo identification card containing the background and fate of a Holocaust victim.

In the darkened surroundings of the fourth floor are photographs, archival films and artifacts in the exhibit entitled **Nazi Assault 1933-1939**. Informative panels begin the tragic story of the calculated deprivation of the property, human rights, dignity and eventually the lives of nearly six million European Jews, and some five million others, including three million Soviet POWs, as well as Slavs (Czechs, Poles and Russians), Gypsies, communists, homosexuals, Jehovah's Witnesses and people with disabilities. The exhibit is augmented by documentaries, newspaper headlines, vintage newsreels, documents, letters and architectural casts. Two small theaters offer continuous showings of films on anti-Semitism *(14min)* and on the Nazi regime's rise to power *(13min)*.

Ghetto and concentration camp life is evoked in **Final Solution: 1940-1944** on the third floor. Personal articles, food and work implements are interspersed with an actual railcar, that visitors can walk through, and a scale model of a gas chamber. Especially sensitive topics are presented discreetly, for optional viewing, by way of sunken video monitors. In **Voices of Auschwitz** visitors can listen to survivors' stories.

In **Aftermath 1945 to the Present** on the final floor of the permanent exhibit, the valor and success of various rescue and resistance efforts are hailed. Here, resistance fighters' weapons and hundreds of photos of rescuers, prison martyrs and survivors are on view, as are photos of "death" marches. Shown continuously is film footage recording the liberating armies' arrival at the camps, and the Nuremberg trials. A display is devoted to Raoul Wallenberg, the Swedish diplomat stationed in Budapest who led the War Refuge Board's mission to save Hungarian Jews. Near the exit a small, open theater presents filmed interviews with Holocaust survivors.

Bureau of Engraving and Printing ★

M *Smithsonian*

This nondescript 20C building at the foot of the 14th Street Bridge calls itself, justifiably, "the nation's money factory." Here, paper currency and many of the official documents issued by the US government are produced.

- **Location:** 14th and C Sts. SW. Smithsonian Metro station (Blue or Orange lines).
- **Parking:** Extremely limited metered street parking.
- **Timing:** The tour takes 40 minutes. Arrive at the ticket kiosk early as tickets are popular and distributed on a first-come first-serve basis.

A BIT OF HISTORY
Early Exchange

The most widely circulated currency during the colonial period was the Spanish *peso de 8 reales*, or "piece of eight." During the Revolution the hoarding of *reales* and other coins led to a shortage and consequently to the Continental Congress' issue of its own currency. Under the Articles of Confederation enacted after the war, the dollar was adopted as the unit of currency, but paper money was not issued until 1861 when non-interest bearing "demand notes" were first issued by the US government as an emergency measure to help pay Civil War costs.

Growth of the Bureau

Functioning as a division within the Treasury Department, the Bureau initially consisted of four women and two men who, working in the basement of the Treasury Building, sealed and separated notes printed by private companies. By 1878 it was responsible for all currency printing. The green ink, chosen for these bills because of its resistance to physical and chemical change, earned the notes the name "greenbacks." In 1880, the bureau moved into its own building and in 1914 moved to its current building. In 1938 the annex building was constructed across 14th Street where engraving facilities are now housed. (⚊ *not open to the public*). The total floor space of the bureau is 30 acres.

VISIT

Visit by guided tour (50min) only, late Mar–Aug Mon–Fri 9am–11am, 12:15pm–7pm (rest of Mar 9am–2pm). Rest of the year Mon–Fri 9am–10:45am, 12:30pm–2pm. ◷*Closed Jan 1, Dec 25 & federal holidays. Same-day free tickets from kiosk (open 8am) on west side (R. Wallenberg Pl.) are required Mar–Aug.*

Best to pick up tickets before 9am in peak season, 11:30am other times. Congressional visits available (see Planning Your Trip). 🚻 ☎202-874-2330. www.moneyfactory.gov.

The entrance hall contains displays and a film *(7min)*. The remainder of the tour leads past four processing rooms. In the first room, $20, $50 and $100 bills undergo the coloring process. In the second room, bills are printed by a process called intaglio printing, whereby impressions are made by pressing inked engravers' plates into the currency fabric, a blend of 75 percent cotton and 25 percent linen. In the third area, sheets are trimmed and examined for imperfections. Any defective sheets are shredded. The fourth room is devoted to printing Treasury seals and serial numbers on the bills. After this final printing the bills are cut, stacked and banded in preparation for their dispersal to the Federal Reserve banks throughout the country. The tour ends in the exhibit hall.

Smithsonian Quadrangle★

Ⓜ *Smithsonian or L'Enfant Plaza*

▷ **Location:** Independence Ave. between 9th and 12th Sts. SW. A short walk from the Mall exit of the Smithsonian Metro station. (Blue or Orange lines).

Topped by a street-level garden, this underground complex occupies a prime site in the shadow of the Castle building. Opened in 1987, the quadrangle comprises two Smithsonian museums—the National Museum of African Art and the Arthur M. Sackler Gallery—and an education center, the S. Dillon Ripley Center.

A BIT OF HISTORY

The Smithsonian Quadrangle is the brainchild of S. Dillon Ripley, secretary of the Smithsonian from 1964 to 1984. During his tenure, Arthur Sackler pledged a portion of his Asian artifacts to the Smithsonian, but the institution lacked space for their display. Ripley also had to find a larger facility for the Museum of African Art (see entry heading). He spearheaded a project for an "international center of advanced study."

In 1982 Congress appropriated $36.5 million (about half the total cost) for the project. In 1983, construction began on the site bordered by the Castle, the Freer Gallery and the Arts and Industries Building. More than 90 percent of the Quadrangle is underground.

VISIT

Enid A. Haupt Garden

◷*Open year-round daily dawn–dusk.* ◷*Closed Dec 25.* *Guided tours May–Sept. Wed 1pm.* 🚻 ☎202-633-1000. www.gardens.si.edu.

This 4-acre garden, named for its New York benefactor, is a haven of antique benches, urn planters and 19C-style lampposts. The centerpiece is the ornamental parterre, adorned with seasonal plantings. The iron and red-sandstone gate opening onto Independence Avenue is based on designs by James Renwick, architect of the Castle.

On either side of the gate stand entrance pavilions to the two underground museums. Behind the Sackler Gallery (*see entry heading*) pavilion is an intimate garden with a circle-in-square fountain, based on the Temple of Heaven in Beijing, and two 9ft pink granite "moon gates." Adjacent to the Museum of African Art pavilion are fountains and canals terminating in a *chadar*, or water wall, inspired by the Alhambra gardens in Granada, Spain.

Concourse

3rd underground level; accessible through the street-level kiosk situated between the Freer Gallery and the Castle. ◷*Open year-round daily 10am–5:30pm.* ◷*Closed Dec 25.* ☏*202-633-1000. www.si.edu.*

Visitors enter the glass-enclosed kiosk and descend one floor down a circular staircase, flooded with light from above. An escalator ride completes the descent to the third-level Ripley Center, where a passageway leads to an open concourse complete with trees and a fountain. A trompe-l'œil mural by Richard Haas dominates the eastern wall. Classrooms and offices line both sides of this airy concourse.

Arts and Industries Building

Ⓜ *Smithsonian or L'Enfant Plaza*

This 19C brick and Ohio sandstone building has long served the Smithsonian Institution as a storehouse for various collections and as a showcase for art, history, science and culture.

○━*The building is currently closed for renovation.* ♿ ☏*202-357-2700. www.si.edu.*

Location: Jefferson Dr. at 9th St. SW. Walk from the Mall exit of the Smithsonian Metro station. (Blue or Orange lines).

Timing: Currently closed in preparation for renovation, check before you visit.

Kids: A ride on the carousel located on the Mall outside of the Arts and Industries Building.

A BIT OF HISTORY

In 1876 the US celebrated its centennial by hosting the nation's first world's fair, known as the International Exhibition, in Philadelphia. When it ended, 60 freight cars full of centennial exhibits were shipped to the Smithsonian. Congress authorized the construction of a national museum, now called the Arts and Industries Building, on the Mall.

Adolph Cluss designed the elaborate structure with four turreted wings radiating from a skylit fountained rotunda. Completed in 1881, the museum was the setting for President Garfield's inaugural ball.

A restoration undertaken for the 1976 Bicentennial celebration returned the building to its former glory. In more recent years the building began showing signs of deterioration. The building is currently closed in preparation for another much-needed renovation.

The Castle

Ⓜ *Smithsonian*

The turreted red sandstone "castle" on the Mall has become the symbol of the Smithsonian Institution. The building functions as a visitor information center providing orientation to the Smithsonian's many museums and to other Washington sights.

◯ **Location:** Smithsonian Institution Building. Jefferson Dr. at 10th St. SW. Smithsonian Metro station. (Blue or Orange lines).

🅿 **Parking:** Very limited metered street parking in the area.

👥 **Kids:** The Children's Room on the first floor.

👁 **Don't Miss:** The crypt tomb of James Smithson.

A BIT OF HISTORY
The Gift of an Englishman

The Smithsonian Institution is the brainchild of an Englishman who never visited America: **James Smithson** (1765-1829), an enlightened thinker and prominent Oxford scientist.

As the illegitimate son of Elizabeth Macie and Hugh Smithson, the first duke of Northumberland, James Smithson spent the first 34 years of his life as James Macie. Eventually the British Crown granted his petition to bear the Smithson name.

Smithson wished to acknowledge blood ties before all else, and he left his wealth to his only surviving relative, a nephew. When the nephew died in 1835 without descendants, he left his remaining money to the US, "to found at Washington, under the name of the Smithsonian Institution, an Establishment for the increase and diffusion of knowledge."

A National Institution

Thanks primarily to the efforts of John Quincy Adams, Congress passed a bill establishing the Smithsonian Institution in 1846. The bill called for the formation of a board of regents including the chief justice of the Supreme Court, the vice president, members of both houses of Congress and private citizens. Smithson's assets were worth about $515,000 at the time.

In 1846, Congress appointed American physicist Joseph Henry as the Smithsonian Institution's first secretary. During his controversial 32-year tenure, Henry insisted on focusing the institution's role on scientific research rather than on museum development.

It was Henry's assistant secretary and successor, the biologist Spencer Fullerton Baird, who developed the Smithsonian as a federal institution of public exhibitions. Today it is the largest museum complex in the world.

Renwick's "Castle"

The Smithsonian's first building, an example of Romanesque Revival architecture, was designed by **James Renwick** in the late 1840s and completed in 1855.

VISIT

🕐*Open year-round daily 8:30am– 5:30pm.* 🚫*Closed Dec 25.* *Guided tours (1hr) Mon & Fri 9:30am, Sat 9:30am & 10:30am, Sun 10:30am.* ♿ ✆ *202-633-1000. www.si.edu.*

The Castle's **information center** features interactive touch screens and wall maps, as well as three-dimensional maps and an orientation film *(20min)* that summarizes each Smithsonian Institution museum. Staff members are on hand to answer visitors' questions.

A crypt containing the body of James Smithson was moved here in 1904 and lies in the north foyer. Located at the south entrance, the **Children's Room**, commissioned in 1899 by Smithsonian secretary Samuel Pierpont Langley, contains the original ceiling mural depicting a vine-covered arbor.

The Castle also houses administrative offices.

The Memorials★★★

Offset by the graceful Tidal Basin and Potomac River, the landscaping in the West Mall lends grandeur and contemplative beauty to the memorials to past US presidents Washington, Jefferson and Lincoln. Skillfully positioned at major focal points of the city's monumental axes, these three memorials command striking vistas that further enhance their tremendous emotional impact. By contrast, the design of recent memorials often seeks to blend in with the existing landscape, making more subtle yet equally powerful statements.

A BIT OF HISTORY

The National Park Service administers the National Mall and Memorial Parks: the sweep of national parkland that stretches from the Capitol building to the Potomac River, including the memorials. The centerpiece of **West Potomac Park** is the **Reflecting Pool**, which stretches 350ft in front of the Lincoln Memorial. Created in the 1970s, **Constitution Gardens**, 45 acres of landscaped grounds borders the pool to the north. The small island in the pond is the setting for the semicircular memorial to the signers of the *Declaration of Independence*, which was dedicated in 1984. Discreetly positioned in the northwest corner of the gardens is "the Wall," a simple but revered black granite monument to US soldiers killed or remain missing in Vietnam. A classically inspired memorial (1924) to DC veterans graces the Reflecting Pool's south side. The Korean War Veterans Memorial, also south of the Reflecting Pool, was dedicated in 1995, and the Franklin D. Roosevelt Memorial in 1997. Two memorials, one to Virginia statesman George Mason and the other to World War II veterans, were added in recent years. The latest monument, honoring Dr. Martin Luther King, Jr., was erected in 2011 on the Tidal Basin's shoreline.

Encircling the Tidal Basin are the city's famous **Japanese cherry trees**★★ (in bloom late March or early April), a gift from the mayor of Tokyo to the city in 1912. In 1958 the Japanese presented DC with a 17C granite lantern and a stone pagoda. Both can be found on west bank of the Tidal Basin.

East Potomac Park, the peninsula projecting southeast from the Tidal Basin, is also bordered by cherry trees.

JEFFERSON MEMORIAL★★★
South bank of Tidal Basin.

In a peaceful shaded spot on the south shore of the Tidal Basin, the nation's third president is commemorated with a 20C adaptation of the ancient Roman Pantheon. Inscribed on its marble walls are Jefferson's own writings concerning the role of government in safeguarding human liberties.

- 🛈 **Info:** National Park Service; 202-426-6841; www.nps.gov.
- ▶ **Location:** The memorials lie in the western part of the Mall (west of 15th Street) and around the Tidal Basin. In this chapter, they are described in alphabetical order. Use the Map of Principal Sights to orient yourself.
- 🅿 **Parking:** There is street parking along Ohio Dr. along the Potomac.
- 👁 **Don't Miss:** The memorials at night, aglow with lighting.
- 🕐 **Timing:** The memorials must be seen on foot: group them into two or three at one visit; then take a meal break or save some for another day. The park is open 24 hours a day. Park rangers are on duty to answer questions 9am to 11:30pm every day.

The Man

Statesman, architect, musician, inventor, horticulturalist, philosopher and president, **Thomas Jefferson** (1743-1826) was one of the country's greatest geniuses. He brought his talents to bear on many of the issues facing the new nation, helping to formulate its system of government, assisting in the planning of its capital city and developing such fundamental principles as public education and religious freedom. In 1962 President Kennedy paid Jefferson a lasting homage when he greeted a group of Nobel Prize winners by saying that they were "the most extraordinary collection of talent, of human knowledge, that has ever gathered together at the White House—with the possible exception of when Thomas Jefferson dined alone."

Early Years

Born into a well-respected Virginia family, Jefferson spent his boyhood on the edge of what was then the Western frontier, in Albemarle County. His father, Peter, was a civil engineer and prominent local figure, serving as a justice of the peace, a colonel of the local militia and a member of the House of Burgesses. While a student at the College of William and Mary in Williamsburg, Virginia, young Tom turned his prodigious intellect to the study of the natural sciences, the arts and especially law, which he believed shaped the social and political conditions of man.

After studying law for five years with the famous Virginia jurist George Wythe, Jefferson practiced on his own for another seven years. In 1769 he was elected to the House of Burgesses and, while serving, participated in the colonists' protests against British taxation. In 1774 he was elected to the first Continental Congress in Philadelphia. At the second Continental Congress a year later, he was appointed to a five-man committee charged with drafting a statement to the British Crown that justified the colonists' stand on independence. Noted for his eloquent writings, Jefferson was encouraged by his fellow committee members to draft the document himself. On July 4, 1776, his *Declaration of Independence* was signed by the Continental Congress.

Serving the New Nation

In 1790 President Washington appointed Jefferson as the first secretary of State. Along with Washington, he was a major force behind implementing plans for the new federal city. It was also at this time that he became embroiled in his historic conflict with secretary of Treasury Alexander Hamilton. Their strident opposition to one another's views on the power of state versus federal governments under the Constitution led to the formation of a two-party political system. From 1797 to 1801 Jefferson served as vice president under John Adams before becoming the third US president, as well as the first to be inaugurated in Washington. During his two terms in office (1801-09), the US negotiated the Louisiana Purchase, effectively doubling the size of the country and strengthening its position in the international arena. The accession of this vast territory, which included lands west of the Mississippi purchased from France for $27,267,622, led to the country's westward expansion. Jefferson's administration also sponsored the Lewis and Clark expedition, which explored and charted this new land.

The Final Years

In 1809 Jefferson retired to his beloved Monticello, the domed plantation house he had designed in his elegant brand of Neoclassicism, outside Charlottesville, Virginia. Here, he pursued his long-cherished dream of founding an institution of public education. Jefferson personally conceived both the architecture and the educational approach for the University of Virginia in Charlottesville, which opened in 1825. On 4 July 1826—the 50th anniversary of the signing of the *Declaration of Independence*—Thomas Jefferson died at Monticello.

Jefferson Memorial in spring

© Robert Goldberg / iStockphoto.com

A Controversial Monument

In 1934 Congress enacted a resolution authorizing this memorial, which became the last in the city's triumvirate of presidential monuments along with those honoring Lincoln and Washington. From the beginning, the project was beset by controversy. John Russell Pope, the designer of numerous federal buildings in the capital city, planned the structure as an adaptation of the Pantheon in Rome, in deference to Jefferson's love of classical architecture. Critics demanded that a more contemporary architectural plan be used or that a utilitarian building, such as a national auditorium or stadium, be built instead of a monument. Ultimately Pope's design, though scaled down to half its initial size, triumphed.

The site lies on an axis with the White House, thus creating a monumental north-south perspective consistent with the spirit of L'Enfant's original plan for the city.

VISIT

⏱ *Open year-round 24hrs daily.*
💬 *Intrepretive tours daily 10am–10pm on the even hours. Visitor facilities open year-round daily 8am–11:30pm.*
🚫*Closed Dec 25.* ♿ 🅿 ☎ *202-426-6841. www.nps.gov/thje.*

The wide, paved plaza in front of the monument along the Tidal Basin offers a sweeping **view** of the capital's famous cherry trees, which bloom around late March and early April. Stairs lead from the plaza to the monument's entrance portico, which supports a sculpted marble pediment depicting Jefferson surrounded by the four other members of the committee chosen to draft the *Declaration of Independence* (from left to right: Benjamin Franklin, John Adams, Jefferson, Roger Sherman and Robert Livingston).

Encircled by an Ionic colonnade, the open-air interior of the monument is dominated by a 19ft bronze **statue** of Jefferson by Rudulph Evans. Standing on a 6ft pedestal, the likeness of a middle-aged Jefferson, in knee breeches and a fur-collared coat, clutches a rolled parchment on which the *Declaration of Independence* is written. The four wall panels surrounding the statue are inscribed with Jefferson's writings, including portions of the *Declaration of Independence*, admonitions against slavery, and statements promoting religious freedom in government.

Situated near the Tidal Basin's inlet bridge, southwest of the Jefferson Memorial, the **George Mason Memorial Garden** commemorates the author of the first document in America to call for freedom of the press, religious tolerance, and other rights that citizens take for granted today. George Mason (1725-92) wrote the *Virginia Declaration of Rights* in 1776, and refused to put his name to the Constitution because it did not contain a Bill of Rights—a document added, largely due to his steadfast urging, in 1791. The memorial garden features a bronze statue of Mason seated beneath an arbor and flanked by stone walls inscribed with his words. A project of the regents of Gunston Hall Plantation, the garden was completed in 2002.

FRANKLIN DELANO ROOSEVELT MEMORIAL★★★

Tidal Basin, west of the Jefferson Memorial.

Situated on 7.5 acres bordering the Tidal Basin, this memorial to the nation's 32nd president combines sculpture, water and natural landscape to forge a dramatic setting for recounting the lifetime events and terms of office of **Franklin D. Roosevelt** (1882-1945).

In 1955 Congress authorized a commission to oversee the construction of a memorial to Roosevelt. The present site in West Potomac Park was set aside in 1959. After years of rejecting design submissions, the Commission of Fine Arts approved a design by Lawrence Halprin in 1978. In the 1980s Congress authorized construction and partial funding. The groundbreaking ceremony was held in September 1991, followed by a fund-raising drive to raise an additional $10 million from private sources for construction, which began in the fall of 1994. The memorial opened to the public in May 1997.

VISIT

◕Open year-round 24hrs daily.
◕Closed Dec 25. ⟜Intrepretive tours daily 10am–10pm on the even hours.
♿ ☏202-426-6841. www.nps.gov/fdrm.
Ornamental plantings, trees, waterfalls and quiet pools lend a sense of tranquility and seclusion to this expansive memorial. Four outdoor galleries constructed of red South Dakota granite contain sculptured figures and cascading water walls designed to symbolize each of FDR's terms as president (1933-45). The First-Term Room (1933-37) symbolizes the dedication of the president and his determination to overcome the nation's economic problems with optimism and courage. A country in the depths of the Great Depression is represented in the Second-Term Room (1937-41). World War II's devastation

is symbolized by strategically placed, rough-hewn granite blocks in the Third-Term Room (1941-45). In the Fourth-Term Room (1945), a bronze bas-relief, *Funeral Cortege*, depicts the president's death, while a statue of Eleanor Roosevelt honors and commemorates her role as First Lady, champion for human rights, and first delegate to the United Nations.

President Bill Clinton dedicated an addition to the memorial in January 2001. A bronze statue, sculpted by Robert Graham and sited at the memorial's entrance, depicts FDR sitting in the wheelchair he designed and used daily after his crippling bout of polio in 1921. While the depiction of FDR in his wheelchair was met with great controversy, it was decided that the statue's demeanor emphasizes his indomitable spirit.

MARTIN LUTHER KING, JR. MEMORIAL★★★

Tidal Basin, Independence Ave. at W. Basin Dr.

This dramatic most recent addition to the Tidal Basin shoreline centers on the white granite **Stone of Hope**, featuring an image of the African-American pastor, activist and Nobel Laureate, whose courageous inspiration was the driving force behind the 1960s civil rights movement. Dedicated in 2011 by

Martin Luther King, Jr. Memorial

©Gwen Cannon/Michelin

President Barack Obama, the memorial rises on the west bank of the Tidal Basin in a direct line between the Jefferson Memorial and the Lincoln Memorial, where King delivered his historic "I Have a Dream" speech during the 1963 protest March on Washington.

The idea for the memorial was conceived in the mid-1980s by the Alpha Phi Alpha Fraternity, of which King was a member while working on his doctoral degree in theology at Boston University. In 1998 Congress authorized the fraternity to establish the Martin Luther King, Jr., National Memorial Project Foundation. Its efforts, along with other private and governmental support, led, after some controversy, to the designation of the current four-acre site on the west bank of the Tidal Basin. The street address of the $120million-dollar memorial—1964 Independence Avenue—is an intentional reference to the year the Civil Rights Act championed by King was enacted.

VISIT

🕐 *Open year-round 24hrs daily.*
🕐 *Closed Dec 25.* 🔊 *Interpretive tours 10am–10pm on the even hrs.* ♿ ☎ *202-426-6841. www.nps.gov/mlkm.*

King's own words provide the symbolic underpinnings for the memorial, and his promise in the 1963 speech, "out of a mountain of despair, a stone of hope" is echoed in the design. Approaching the memorial from Independence Avenue, visitors walk through a polished opening where a piece is missing from the otherwise rough-hewn Mountain of Despair. That piece, seemingly thrust toward the horizon, rises beyond as the Stone of Hope. Its far side features a 30ft relief of King, arms folded, contemplatively staring out over the Tidal Basin and the cherry trees rimming it. The stone is incised with two of his quotations: the "out of a mountain of despair…" quote, and "I was a drum major for peace, justice and righteousness." The later is a paraphrase of King's exact words and has aroused much controversy. Ways to correct it are now being considered. Backdropping the image of King and extending on either side of the Mountain of Despair are two low, polished granite inscription walls incised with 14 quotes from famous King speeches given during the civil rights struggle, including an address he delivered during the 1955 Montgomery, Alabama, bus boycott that propelled him to a leadership position in the movement. A number of the quotations are from 1967, the year before King's death. On April 4, 1968, as he left his Memphis, Tennessee, hotel room, the 39-year-old King was assassinated by lone gunman and fugitive, James Earl Ray. Named in tribute to Dr. King, the third Monday in

Korean War Veterans Memorial

National Park Service

January is today a federal holiday, first celebrated in 1986.

KOREAN WAR VETERANS MEMORIAL★★★

Independence Ave. at French Dr. SW.
Located southeast of the Lincoln Memorial, this compelling ensemble of statues, freestanding wall and circular pool honors the members of the US armed forces who served in the Korean War (1950-53). The $18 million memorial was funded by private contributions and dedicated in 1995 by President Bill Clinton and Kim Young Sam, president of the Republic of Korea at the time.

"The Forgotten War"

American veterans of the Cold War attached this sobriquet to a war they felt was overshadowed by the magnitude of World War II and the controversy of Vietnam. As memories of Korea faded from the national consciousness, veterans began pursuing a means to formally commemorate the war. In 1986 Congress authorized the American Battle Monuments Commission to oversee the design of a memorial, and in 1988 the current 2-acre site on the Mall was approved. A team of architects from Pennsylvania State University won the design competition in 1989 but withdrew from the project when reviewing agencies requested alterations. Washington, DC firm Cooper-Lecky Architects completed the project. The human figures were sculpted by Frank Gaylord and the granite "mural" was crafted by Louis Nelson. At the groundbreaking ceremony in 1992, President George Bush stated that the memorial's realization would assure that "no American will ever forget the test of freedom" faced by US troops. Of the 1.5 million Americans serving in the Korean War, more than 54,000 died, over 110,000 were captured or wounded and some 8,000 were declared missing.

VISIT

Open year-round 24hrs daily. Closed Dec 25. Intrepretive tours daily 10am–10pm on the even hours. 202-426-6841. www.nps.gov/kowa.

Nineteen larger-than-life stainless-steel statues (each about 7ft tall) of men wearing combat rain gear stand in patrol formation within a triangular plot of junipers. One side of this "field" is lined with a 164ft-long wall of polished black granite, etched with the faces of more than 2,500 servicemen and women. The wall recalls the neighboring Vietnam Memorial, but it provides no written identification of those who lost their lives in the war. Mounted in the granite apex, an American flag stands guard over the dedicatory inscription: "Our nation honors her sons and daughters who answered the call to defend a country they never knew and a people they never met." A circular pool behind the flagpole is interrupted by a lower, separate wall bearing the words "Freedom is not free." Etched on the rim of the pool, the statistics of the war's toll bear witness to this poignant summary.

LINCOLN MEMORIAL★★★

The Mall at 23rd St. NW.
From this stately memorial the famous marble likeness of a seated, brooding Lincoln stares across the Reflecting Pool to the Washington Monument and to the Capitol beyond. On the southwest side of the monument, Arlington Memorial Bridge serves as a symbolic link between Lincoln and the South's great hero, Robert E. Lee, whose home,

Lincoln Memorial

©PhotoDisc

Arlington House, overlooks the monument from the Virginia bluffs.

Preserver of the Union

Born in Kentucky in 1809 to a poor farming family, **Abraham Lincoln** (1809-65) was a self-educated, self-made man who became the country's 16th president and perhaps its most admired political hero. He is remembered by an affectionate public as "Honest Abe," the down-home, commonsensical statesman; as the Great Emancipator who ultimately freed the country of slavery; and as the president who fought a protracted civil war in order to keep the nation intact. Catapulted from state politics to the presidency, Lincoln was faced with a nation in turmoil even before he took the oath of office in March 1861. South Carolina, knowing Lincoln to be an opponent of slavery, seceded from the Union shortly after he was elected. Other southern states quickly followed suit. The month after Lincoln's inauguration, Confederate and Union troops exchanged fire at Fort Sumter, South Carolina. For the next four years, Lincoln waged a war to bring the Southern states back into the Union.

In 1863 he issued his renowned **Emancipation Proclamation**, decreeing that slaves in the Confederate states would thereafter be free. Though this was more a symbolic gesture than a real reversal of slavery nationwide, it helped set the stage for the eventual passage in 1865 of the 13th Amendment to the Constitution, which did in fact abolish slavery.

In April of 1865, at the start of Lincoln's second term, Robert E. Lee surrendered to Ulysses S. Grant at Appomattox, Virginia. With the long war over, the president turned his thoughts to the reconstruction of the South, but his plans of reconciliation were never realized.

On April 14, 1865—five days after Lee's surrender—he was shot at Ford's Theatre by the actor John Wilkes Booth. The following day, at age 56, President Abraham Lincoln died of his wound.

An Anchor for the Mall

A congressional commission was established two years after Lincoln's death to plan a monument in his memory. It was not until 1901 that the McMillan Commission, with the backing of the Commission of Fine Arts, endorsed a memorial at the western end of the recently extended Mall.

Inspired by Greek architecture, the monument's designer, Henry Bacon, produced his version of a Doric temple, reminiscent of the Parthenon in Athens. However, Bacon positioned the main entrance on the long side of the structure, overlooking the Mall. Work began on the memorial in 1914; it was dedicated in 1922 in a ceremony attended by Robert Todd Lincoln, the president's only surviving son.

A National Forum

Over the years this monument epitomizing Lincoln's ideals has served as the forum for public protests and demonstrations. The acclaimed black opera singer Marian Anderson gave a historic outdoor concert here in 1939, after being refused permission to perform at the DAR's Constitution Hall. It was here in 1963 that Martin Luther King Jr. inspired a crowd of 200,000 with his famous "I Have a Dream" oratory. During the Vietnam War, President Richard Nixon paid an unofficial late-night visit to the protesters gathered here.

VISIT

🕐 *Open year-round 24hrs daily. Visitor facilities open year-round daily 8am–11:30pm.* 🕐 *Closed Dec 25.*
🐾 *Intrepretive tours daily 10am–10pm on the even hours.* ♿ ✆ *202-426-6841. www.nps.gov/linc.*

Reproduced on copper pennies and $5 bills, the facade of this building is easily identifiable. Thirty-six Doric columns form a continuous colonnade ringing the edifice and symbolize the states in the Union at the time of Lincoln's death. The names of the 36 states are inscribed in the entablature above the columns. The parapet crowning the structure is adorned with a frieze sculpted with bas-relief swags and bearing the names of the 48 states that existed at the time the monument was completed.

Lincoln's craggy aspect comes into view as you ascend the long flight of marble stairs of the memorial. **Daniel Chester French** collaborated with Bacon to create a statue of Lincoln that would harmonize with the architecture. French's powerful marble **statue**★★★, 19ft high, depicts a contemplative Lincoln and captures the force of the man himself. The right wall is inscribed with Lincoln's second inaugural address and a mural by Jules Guerin, allegorically portraying the freeing of slaves. The Gettysburg Address (1863), the celebrated oratory that begins with the oft-quoted words "Four score and seven years ago," is chiseled into the left wall and topped by a similar Guerin mural showing the unity of the North and South.

The monument steps afford a **view**★★ of the Mall from the Reflecting Pool to the Washington Monument.

NATIONAL WORLD WAR II MEMORIAL★★★

The Mall at 17th St. NW. Ⓜ *Smithsonian.* The **National World War II Memorial** was dedicated on Memorial Day 2004. Encompassing 7.4 acres, it pays homage to the more than 400,000 Americans who lost their lives in what has been called the most devastating war in history. It also stands as a testament to all those who served in the American Armed Forces as well as those who contributed to the wartime effort at home.

In 1993 President Bill Clinton signed an act authorizing the establishment of the memorial; $195 million was received in private donations and $16 million from government sources. A symbolic groundbreaking took place on Veterans Day, 11 November 2000, and construction began in September 2001. Though its location has been hotly contested by those who believe it mars the open spaces and vistas of the Mall, the memorial itself is not under debate. Architect Friedrich St. Florian's design maintains 70 percent of the area as a parklike setting of water, grass and trees, with the remaining 30 percent as hard surface.

A War of World Proportions

The Second World War (1939-45) was fought on all but one of the seven continents and involved most of the world's powerful nations. Some 50 million people were killed, millions wounded and millions left homeless. In this global conflict, the Axis powers of Germany, Italy and Japan confronted the Allied Forces of Great Britain, France, the Soviet Union, China and a number of smaller nations, joined in 1941 by the United States. By September 1945, the last surrender was signed; the Allies were finally victorious.

World War II Memorial

©Gwen Cannon/Michelin

VISIT

Open year-round 24hrs daily.
*Closed Dec 25. Intrepretive tours
daily 10am–10pm on the even hours.*
202-426-6841. www.nps.gov/nwwm.
At the 17th Street entrance to the memorial, a low-lying granite block, aligned with the Lincoln Memorial, is inscribed with a dedicatory message to "those 20C Americans" who struggled and sacrificed to preserve liberty. Bas-relief sculptures depicting wartime activities line the sidewalks leading down to an oval-shaped plaza. Larger than a football field, the plaza features a central pool graced with fountains. Flanking the plaza on the north and south, identical arched pavilions symbolize the Atlantic and Pacific theaters of the war. Each bearing a bronze wreath, 56 pillars representing US states and territories line the ends of the plaza. Backdropped by the Reflecting Pool, a Freedom Wall bears 4,000 gold stars, each star symbolic of 100 American war-related deaths.

VIETNAM VETERANS MEMORIAL★★★

Constitution Gardens at Constitution Ave. and 22nd St. NW.
Though it was conceived in controversy, this long, solemn black wall has become one of the nation's most cherished and moving memorials.
Tucked away in the sylvan setting of Constitution Gardens, it bears the names of all those killed or missing in the Vietnam War.

"Serenity, Without Conflict"

The impetus for this monument came from a small group of Vietnam veterans living in the capital. Troubled by the public's indifference toward those Americans who served in the Southeast Asian conflict, they formed the Vietnam Veterans Memorial Fund in 1979, soliciting congressional support and contributions from individuals and corporate donors. In July 1980, President Jimmy Carter signed a joint congressional resolution authorizing the placement of the monument on a 2-acre plot in Constitution Gardens just northeast of the Lincoln Memorial.
The fund then held a national design competition for the memorial and appointed an eight-member jury of internationally-known artists and designers to judge the entries. Among the criteria was that it make no political statement about the Vietnam War. The competition attracted 1,421 entries.
The winning design was submitted by **Maya Ying Lin**, a 21-year-old architectural student at Yale University. Lin's wall was conceived as a symbol of healing.

The Wall

Begun in March 1982, the monument, known as "the Wall," was completed and dedicated by November of the same year. Its abstract simplicity aroused controversy, and in an attempt to quell the dissatisfaction, a realistic sculpture by Frederick Hart was added nearby in 1984. The life-size work, portraying three young soldiers of different ethnic origins, is intended to commemorate all US military men who served in the conflict.
However, the Wall quickly became accepted as the moving shrine it was intended to be, a place of healing where family and friends could touch the names of loved ones lost in battle.

Vietnam Veterans Memorial

Courtesy National Park Service

VISIT

Open year-round 24hrs daily.
Closed Dec 25. *Intrepretive tours*
daily 10am–10pm on the even hours.
202-426-6841. www.nps.gov/vive.
Directories specifying the memorial
panels on which names appear are
located at the approaches to the Wall.
Inset in a low hill, the memorial is actually two triangular walls that join at a 125° angle, with their ends pointing toward the Washington Monument and the Lincoln Memorial. Composed of granite from Bangalore, India, they are intended to reflect the surroundings in their polished surface. The memorial extends 493.5ft in length and rises to a height of 10ft at its apex. The names of the more than 58,000 men and women incised in the Wall are arranged chronologically, beginning with the first casualty in 1959 and ending with the last in 1975 (more than 200 names were added in 1996).

Those who died in the war are indicated by a diamond; those missing or imprisoned are denoted by a cross.

A grove of trees just south of the Wall is the site of the **Vietnam Women's Memorial.** Dedicated in 1993, it features a bronze statue (1992, Glenna Goodacre) nearly 7ft high depicting three military women tending a wounded male soldier. It stands as a memorial to the more than 265,000 women who served in the US armed forces in Vietnam.

WASHINGTON MONUMENT★★★

The Mall at 15th St. NW.
Ⓜ Smithsonian.
Currently closed for repair; scheduled to reopen in 2013.
The capital's most conspicuous landmark, and the world's tallest freestanding stone structure, this austere white marble obelisk rises from the middle of the Mall. Though it took nearly four decades to complete, the monument, ringed by US flags, stands as a commanding memorial to the man who was "first in the hearts of his countrymen," and as an indelible symbol of the city that bears his name.

Military Commander

Soldier, statesman and leader, **George Washington** (1732-99) began his long service to this country while in his early 20s, distinguishing himself as a commander during the French and Indian War in the 1750s. Following the war, Washington served as a loyal British member of the Virginia House of Burgesses in Williamsburg, Virginia. However, as tension over British taxation grew among the colonists, Washington became increasingly disenchanted with the mother country. In 1774 he served as one of seven Virginia delegates to the Continental Congress in Philadelphia. A year later, at the second Continental Congress, he was unanimously elected head of the Continental Army.

For eight years Washington spearheaded the fight against Britain, frequently keeping the war effort alive through the strength of his own convictions. In addition to battling the superior forces of the British, Washington had to contend with poorly trained troops, as well as a Congress reluctant to provide necessary funds or moral support. After countless setbacks and lost battles, the Continentals, thanks to Washington's military brilliance and the help of French allies, won a decisive victory against Lord Cornwallis' troops on 19 October 1781, at Yorktown, Virginia.

Father of the Nation

For six years, from 1783 to 1789, Washington enjoyed a respite from public life at his plantation, Mount Vernon, near

Washington Monument Statistics	
Height	555ft 5 1/8in
Weight	90,854 tons
Thickness at base	15ft
Thickness at top	18in
Width at base	55ft 1 1/2in
Width at top	34ft 5 1/2in
Depth of foundation	36ft 10in
Cost	$1,187,710

Washington Monument

Gwen Cannon/MICHELIN

A Monument to the Man

In 1783 the Continental Congress passed a resolution to erect an equestrian statue honoring the hero of the Revolution. Lack of funds delayed the project for decades. Finally, in 1833, a group of prominent citizens formed the Washington National Monument Society. Having raised $28,000 by 1836, the group held a contest to choose a design for the monument. The well-respected architect **Robert Mills** won. The cornerstone was laid 4 July 1848.

Progress was slow due to insufficient funding. Work ceased when the funds finally ran dry in 1853, leaving the monument a truncated 152ft shaft that languished in neglect for nearly 25 years, until President Ulysses S. Grant approved an act authorizing the federal government to complete the project. Dedicated on 21 February 1885, the monument opened to the public in 1888.

Alexandria, Virginia. But in 1787, when growing anarchy and lack of centralized government threatened the new confederation of states, he presided over the Constitutional Congress in Philadelphia. Judicious and nonpartisan, Washington served as a stabilizing force that allowed the contentious delegates to arrive at a mutually acceptable Constitution for the young Republic. Two years later, in 1789, the new electoral college unanimously voted Washington the first president of the nation. On 30 April 1789, he took the oath of office on the steps of Federal Hall in New York City. Faced with defining the presidency, Washington proceeded cautiously. He managed to keep the young country out of European wars, and to establish federal authority over individual states and presidential authority over issues of foreign policy. He argued (unsuccessfully) against the adoption of a partisan political system, and set a standard of ceremonial decorum for his office. He also approved and began construction of the new federal city that would bear his name. After eight years and two terms as president, he refused a third term, and in 1797 retired for a final time to Mount Vernon.

VISIT

🕐*Currently closed for repair due to damage from the August 2011 earthquake. Expected reopening in 2013. Normally open year-round daily 9am–5pm. Closed Jul 4 and Dec 25.*
&202-426-6841. www.nps.gov/wamo.
A state-of-the-art elevator makes a 70-second ascent from the ground to the observation room at the summit of the monument. Eight small windows afford the best **panorama**★★★ of the city. The south-facing windows overlook the Tidal Basin and the Jefferson Memorial; the western view highlights the Reflecting Pool and the Lincoln Memorial; the north faces the Ellipse and the White House; and the east overlooks the long stretch of Mall ending at the Capitol. Photographs above the windows reproduce the views and identify major landmarks for visitors.

☐ **a.** 🏰 *Luxury hotel ?*

☐ **b.** 😊 *"Bib Hotel": accommodation at moderate prices ?*

☐ **c.** 🛋 *Very quiet hotel ?*

Can't decide ?

Find out more with the Michelin Guide Collection!

- A collection of 13 titles
- 30 000 hotels around Europe
- 1 600 town plans
- The best addresses in every price category

  Discover the pleasure of travel with the Michelin Guides

Inspired by the stately presence of the Executive Mansion, this area maintains a decorous gentility, with manicured parks, elegant row houses and grandly conceived public structures.

Highlights

1 A guided group tour of **1600 Pennsylvania Avenue** (p145)

2 The stunning *Salon Doré* at the **Corcoran Gallery of Art** (p151)

3 The permanent collection at the **Renwick Gallery** (p155)

▷ **Location:** Area attractions form a horseshoe around the White House and Ellipse, with Lafayette park at the top. Make your first stop the White House Visitor Center.

🅿 **Parking:** Garages on New York and Pennsylvania Aves. and 17th and 18th Sts.

◉ **Don't Miss:** The view of the White House from Lafayette Park, pew 54 in St. John's Church, and the Corcoran and the Renwick galleries.

🕐 **Timing:** Allow 3hrs. The White House tour takes less than 1hr.

A Bit of History

Lafayette Square

In the early 19C, Jefferson ordered Pennsylvania Avenue extended in front of the still incomplete White House. The 7-acre plot to the north of it became a public park known as President's Square. In 1824 the park was renamed Lafayette Square to honor America's French ally in the Revolution, the Marquis de Lafayette. That same year **Blair House** *(no. 1651)* was built on Pennsylvania Avenue. Today it serves as an official guest house for dignitaries *(o—not open to the public)*. An equestrian statue of Andrew Jackson stands at the park's center; other statues are of foreign heroes of the American Revolution: Lafayette (1891, southeast corner); Jean-Baptiste Rochambeau (1902, southwest corner); Friedrich von Steuben (1910, northwest corner); and Thaddeus Kosciuszko (1910, northeast corner). Following the Civil War, the first landscaping of the park was carried out in keeping with an 1850s design prepared by Andrew Jackson Downing. Lafayette Square and the Ellipse *(below)* have been integrated into a **President's Park**, which includes plazas, walkways, and outdoor seating.

Grandiose Buildings

Though work began on the White House in 1792, the building evolved gradually. On its east side is the stately Treasury Building, completed in 1869. To the west is the colossal Old Executive Office Building, completed in 1881.

In the late 19C and early 20C, several dignified buildings went up on 17th Street south of the White House, including the Corcoran Gallery of Art, American Red Cross headquarters, and the Daughters of the American Revolution complex.

From "White Lot" to Ellipse

South of the White House, the expanse of ground called the **Ellipse** was once marshy lowland. During the Civil War, military livestock was enclosed here behind a whitewashed fence giving rise to the term "white lot." In the late 19C the area was reclaimed. At the corner of Constitution Avenue and 17th Street, a stone **lock keeper's house** stands as a reminder of the Washington Canal. Across the avenue, on either side of the Ellipse, are a pair of gatehouses that once stood on the Capitol grounds. In the mid-20C, the Ellipse became a ceremonial grounds for the White House. On its north side is the **Zero Milestone**, from which all distances in the city are computed. Also here is the **National Christmas Tree**, a blue spruce planted during Jimmy Carter's presidency.

White House★★★

🅼 *McPherson Square, Metro Center, or Federal Triangle*

For almost two centuries the White House has been the home of America's first families. More than just an official residence, the stately structure has become a universally recognized symbol of the US presidency. Today its public rooms house an exemplary collection of Americana, both furnishings and historic memorabilia, reflecting the tastes of the nation's leaders.

🅘 **Info:** White House Visitor Center; ✆ 202-456-7041; www.whitehouse.gov.

▷ **Location:** 1600 Pennsylvania Ave. NW. Stop first at the White House Visitor Center in the Commerce Building on Pennsylvania Ave. (👉 *see below*).

🅿 **Parking:** No street parking is available near the White House.

A BIT OF HISTORY
The President's Palace

L'Enfant had envisioned the "President's house" as a grand structure, five times its current size, but after the Frenchman's dismissal in 1792, a design competition for the official residence was held. The $500 prize went to **James Hoban**, a young Irish builder. His plan called for a three-story stone structure reminiscent of a Georgian manor, with a hipped roof surrounded by a balustrade. The main facade featured a columned portico with an eagle carved in the pediment.

The cornerstone was laid on October 13, 1792, but due to a lack of skilled labor and public funds, the work proceeded slowly. Faced with financial challenges, the city commissioners approached President Washington with a plan to reduce the mansion's dimensions. In October 1793 Washington compromised by agreeing to omit the third floor, and Hoban redrew plans for a two-story building. (It wasn't until 1927 that a third floor was added.)

First Occupants

The structure was not completed until November 1800. The second president, **John Adams** (1797-1801) became the first president to occupy the mansion. Though conditions in the still incomplete house were drafty and unpleasant, Adams nonetheless left a lasting benediction on it. After his first night there, he wrote, "May none but honest and wise men ever rule under this roof!"

White House

©PhotoDisc

Thomas Jefferson, the mansion's first long-term resident (1801-09), turned his architectural attentions to the design of the White House, as the whitewashed sandstone building had come to be known. Collaborating with his surveyor of public buildings, **Benjamin H. Latrobe**, Jefferson designed colonnaded wings on the east and west sides to house domestic and office spaces. Latrobe also replaced the mansion's heavy slate and mortar roof with a lighter one of steel.

Fire and Reconstruction

James Madison's stay in the Executive Mansion (1809-17) was marked by disaster. In August 1814, during the War of 1812, the British entered the city and set fire to several public buildings, including the White House. Thanks to the forethought of Dolley Madison, many important documents, as well as a Gilbert Stuart portrait of George Washington that now hangs in the East Room, were saved. Had a summer rain not put out the fire, the mansion might have burned to the ground. The city commissioners called on James Hoban to salvage the mansion; he demolished weakened stone walls and began rebuilding.

In 1818 President **James Monroe** was able to occupy the house. During his administration (1817-25) the south portico was added, and the French Empire pieces that remain at the core of the White House's historic furniture collection were acquired.

Throughout the 19C, architectural changes and redecorating occurred as funds were available. In order to customize the house to his own taste, a new president frequently resorted to raising funds by selling old furnishings at public auction. Congressional appropriations for the upkeep and refurbishing of the chief executive's home were generally dependent on the political and economic climate.

During the popular administration of **Andrew Jackson** (1829-37), for example, bountiful funds allowed for the purchase of new china and glassware,

the installation of indoor plumbing and the completion of the north portico. In other administrations, however, furnishings became seriously dilapidated. During **James Polk**'s tenure (1845-49), gas lights were added. **Chester A. Arthur** (1881-85) undertook a major refurnishing of the mansion in 1882. According to contemporary reports, he had 24 wagonloads of old furniture carted away for public auction. He then called on the celebrated New York designer Louis C. Tiffany to redecorate the interior. Electricity was installed in the building in 1891.

20C

In 1902 vast changes were again wrought on the mansion by **Theodore Roosevelt** (1901-09), who entrusted the prominent architectural firm McKim, Mead and White with large-scale renovation. The extensive greenhouses that had flanked the west and south sides of the house for decades were demolished. The west wing was added and an expansive carriage porch built on the east. The interior, whose old plumbing, wiring and flooring were in disrepair, was modernized. The Roosevelt renovation began restoring the White House to its original appearance—a process that has been continued by succeeding presidents. In 1942, while **Franklin D. Roosevelt** was in office (1933-45), the current east wing was built. Under Roosevelt's successor, **Harry S. Truman** (1945-53), another major structural renovation was undertaken to shore up and replace weakened flooring, walls and foundations. The second-story balcony was added to the south portico during the Truman presidency.

During her stay in the White House (1961-63), Jacqueline Kennedy began a campaign to acquire items of historic and artistic interest. Following her precedent, in 1964 President **Lyndon Johnson** (1963-69) established the Committee for the Preservation of the White House, which provided for a permanent curator. The curatorial staff today continues to expand and document the White House collection.

VISITING THE WHITE HOUSE

White House Visitor Center

Pennsylvania Ave. between 14th and 15th Sts. NW. ⊙Open year-round daily 7:30am–4pm. ⊙Closed 1 Jan, Thanksgiving Day & Dec 25. ♿ ℘202-456-7041. www.whitehouse.gov.

Housed in the spacious, ground-floor Baldridge Hall in the Commerce Building, the center has an information booth staffed by National Park Service rangers, displays and rest rooms. Pick up a map of the White House area.

White House Tours

✏Free timed tickets for self-guided tours must be requested from your member of Congress up to 6 months in advance (♿ see Congressional Visits). Foreign nationals should submit requests to their embassy in DC.
⊙Visit by advance reservation only Tue –Sat 7:30am–1pm (Thu til noon). ♿ ℘202-208-1631. www.whitehouse.gov. US citizens 15 years and older must present a government-issued photo ID; foreign visitors must show a valid passport. See the website for a list of items prohibited on the tour.
☎Phone the 24hr information line the morning of your visit to make sure the White House is open for tours ℘202-456-7041.

Set off by 18 acres of gardens, lawns and trees *(grounds not included on tour)*, the White House sports a balustraded roof, Ionic pilasters and windows with alternating rounded and triangular pediments on the rectangular facade of the main structure. The columned and balconied south portico extends out in an expansive bay overlooking the south lawn. The colonnade of the north portico facing Pennsylvania Avenue supports an unadorned pediment. Elaborate carvings grace the area above the fanlight of the entrance. Pavilions connect the one-story east and west wings to the main mansion. The west wing (⚬ *not open to the public*) houses the Cabinet Room, several staff and reception rooms, and the president's Oval Office, which opens onto the Rose Garden.

In the mansion, the ground-floor and first-floor rooms function as formal state reception areas, while the first family's private living quarters are located on the second and third floors.

Ground Floor

Visitors first enter a security building at 15th St. NW and Hamilton Pl.

In the paneled entrance hall of the east wing, portraits of First Ladies and presidents adorn the walls. A glassed colonnade overlooking the intimate **Jacqueline Kennedy Garden** displays exhibit panels explaining White House history. Portraits of recent First Ladies hang in an elegant vaulted marble corridor, and a large Sheraton breakfront holds presidential porcelains. The **library**, which opens off the hall's right side, is decorated in late Federal style and contains some 2,700 volumes. The **Vermeil Room**, directly across the hall, is so named for its collection of French and English gilded silver, or vermeil, dating from the 17C to the early 20C.

First Floor

The vast and ornate **East Room**, the setting for White House concerts, parties and official ceremonies, contains elaborate plaster ceiling decorations and entablatures, Bohemian cut-glass chandeliers and four marble mantels. Because it is used for a variety of purposes, the gold and white room is sparsely furnished. The legendary 1797 **portrait of George Washington** that Dolley Madison saved hangs here. The small drawing room off the East Room is known as the **Green Room**, owing to the color scheme it has retained since the days of President John Quincy Adams (1825-29). An intricately patterned Turkish Hereke carpet complements the room's green watered-silk wall coverings. On the dropleaf sofa table is the silver-plated coffee urn that John Adams called one of his "most prized possessions."

The French Empire furnishings in the elliptical **Blue Room** include seven of the original Bellange gilded armchairs ordered from Paris by James Monroe.

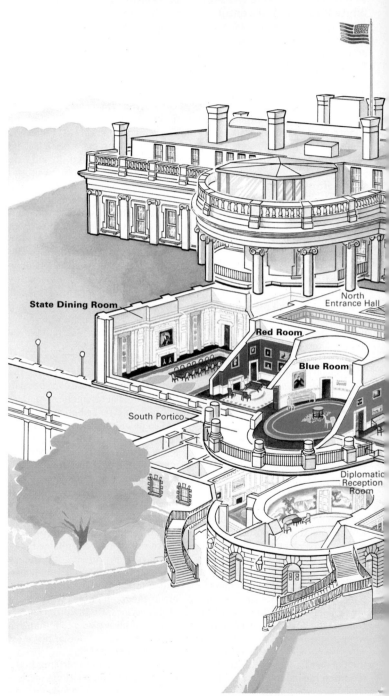

State Dining Room

North Entrance Hall

Red Room

Blue Room

South Portico

Diplomatic Reception Room

White House Receptions Rooms

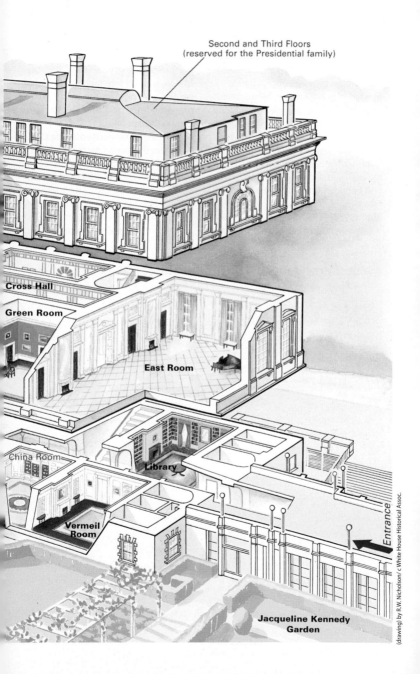

Second and Third Floors
(reserved for the Presidential family)

Cross Hall

Green Room

East Room

China Room

Library

Vermeil Room

Entrance

Jacqueline Kennedy Garden

(drawing) by R.W. Nicholson/ c White House Historical Assoc.

149

The gilded wood chandelier and Carrara marble mantel contain classical motifs mirrored in the wallpaper frieze that forms a border around the wainscoting and entablature. Portraits of the first presidents are among the paintings found here. The three long casement windows afford a striking **view** of the Washington Monument and the Jefferson Memorial beyond. From this standpoint visitors can easily discern the extent to which the Washington Monument is positioned off the axis linking the White House with the Jefferson Memorial. The small parlor known as the **Red Room** also contains French Empire-style furnishings including gilded chairs with red and gold damask. Displayed on the wall between the windows is a bust by Hiram Powers of President Martin Van Buren (1837-41). Above the fireplace hangs a painting of Van Buren's daughter-in-law and official hostess, Angelica. The bust is featured in the painting.

In the gold and white **State Dining Room**, the Neoclassical pilaster, wall paneling and ceiling molding are modeled on decor found in late-18C English estates. Gold upholstered Queen Anne-style chairs surround the long mahogany dining table. Over the mantel is the 1869 Abraham Lincoln portrait by George P.A. Healy. Marble-topped side tables with gilded eagle pedestals rim the room. When prepared for a state dinner, this room can seat 140 people.

Marble columns separate the long **Cross Hall** from the North Entrance Hall. Both halls are hung with portraits of recent presidents. The carpeted marble staircase, connecting the state rooms to the first family's private quarters, is frequently used by the president and First Lady for ceremonial entrances.

Presidents of the United States of America

George Washington	1789-1797	Benjamin Harrison	1889-1893
John Adams	1797-1801	William McKinley	1897-1901
Thomas Jefferson	1801-1809	Theodore Roosevelt	1901-1909
James Madison	1809-1817	William H. Taft	1909 1913
James Monroe	1817-1825	Woodrow Wilson	1913-1921
John Quincy Adams	1825-1829	Warren G. Harding	1921-1923
Andrew Jackson	1829-1837	Calvin Coolidge	1923-1929
Martin Van Buren	1837-1841	Herbert Hoover	1929-1933
William Henry Harrison	1841	Franklin D. Roosevelt	1933-1945
John Tyler	1841-1845	Harry S. Truman	1945-1953
James K. Polk	1845-1849	Dwight D. Eisenhower	1953-1961
Zachary Taylor	1849-1850	John F. Kennedy	1961-1963
Millard Fillmore	1850-1853	Lyndon B. Johnson	1963-1969
Franklin Pierce	1853-1857	Richard M. Nixon	1969-1974
James Buchanan	1857-1861	Gerald R. Ford	1974-1977
Abraham Lincoln	1861-1865	James Carter	1977-1981
Andrew Johnson	1865-1869	Ronald Reagan	1981-1989
Ulysses S. Grant	1869-1877	George H. Bush	1989-1993
Rutherford B. Hayes	1877-1881	William J. Clinton	1993-2000
James A. Garfield	1881	George W. Bush	2001-2009
Chester A. Arthur	1881-1885	Barack H. Obama	2009-
Grover Cleveland	1885-1889 1893-1897		

Corcoran Gallery of Art★★

Ⓜ *Farragut West or Farragut North*

In a city now dominated by federal museums, the Corcoran Gallery of Art can claim to be the capital's oldest institution and its most venerable private gallery. Although it houses a fine collection of European art, the Corcoran is primarily known as a showcase for 18th, 19th and 20th century American art. The gallery also pays particular attention to local artists.

A BIT OF HISTORY

A self-made man, self-educated connoisseur and philanthropist, **William Wilson Corcoran** (1798-1888) halted construction of a museum to house his private collection in 1861, when he left wartime Washington. His Southern sympathies had made him unwelcome. Upon his return in 1865, the building, now the Renwick Gallery, was completed and opened as one of the first major galleries of art in 1874.

In 1897 a larger building (Ernest Flagg) opened several blocks south to hold the expanded 700-work collection. Frank Lloyd Wright considered it "the best designed building in Washington."

VISIT

Ⓞ*Open year-round Fri-Sun & Wed 10am–5pm, Thu 10am–9pm.*
Ⓞ*Closed 1 Jan, Thanksgiving Day & Dec 25 & 3pm closing on Dec 24 and 31. Tickets can be purchased at the admission desk or by calling* ☏*202-397-7328. Free tours daily at noon & 7 pm on Thu and 3pm on weekends.* ☜*$10.* ✕&. ☏*202-639-1700. www.corcoran.org.* ☝*Exhibits change frequently, as do the specific locations of pieces of art within the museum.*

First Floor

One of the Corcoran Gallery's best-known works, Hiram Powers' nude sculpture **The Greek Slave** (1846)

▷ **Location:** 17th St. and New York Ave. NW. By Metro: Farragut West (Orange/Blue Line) Farragut North (Red Line). By Bus: 11Y, 32, 36, 42, G8, P17, P19, W13

ⓟ **Parking:** Metered street parking is available in the area from 9:30am to 4pm daily. It is free after 6:30 pm, and on Sundays and holidays.

♟ **Kids:** Family Workshops for kids aged 8-12 on select Saturdays *(see the website for details).*

☺ **Don't Miss:** Edward Hopper's *Ground Swell* and Gilbert Stuart's *George Washington* portrait.

(second floor) scandalized Victorian audiences when it was first shown in the Renwick Gallery. The white marble sculpture that shows a nude woman with her hands chained together, and its showing, represented the first life-size American sculpture depicting a fully nude human to go on public display. It was considered so risqué that the museum held separate viewing times for men and women and prohibited children from seeing it. In a gal-

Salon Doré

© Corcoran Gallery of Art

Detail of The Last of the Buffalo, *(1888), Albert Bierstadt, oil on canvas, 71 x 118 3/4 inches*

©Corcoran Gallery of Art, Washington, DC; Gift of Mary Stewart Bierstadt (Mrs. Albert Bierstadt)

lery off the far end of the south atrium, Rembrandt Peale's *Washington Before Yorktown* (1825) dominates an entire wall. The painting of the first president came from William Wilson Corcoran who counted several George Washington portraits among his collection.

Spend time in the regal **Salon Doré**, a gilded room paneled from floor to ceiling with Corinthian pilasters, trophy panels, garlands and large framed mirrors crafted by the Comte d'Orsay in the 18th century. This room was originally part of the hôtel de Clermont, an important private residence in Paris. The Salon Doré was bequeathed to the Corcoran by Senator William Clark of Montana. Appointed with gilded woodwork, the salon is considered one of the country's finest French-Rococo interiors. The impressive space is sometimes rented out for exclusive private gatherings.

Second Floor

Highlights include *The Old House of Representatives* (1822) by Samuel F.B. Morse, inventor of the Morse code. Before beginning the massive painting, which depicts the Seventeenth Congress preparing to debate the nation's Indian policy, Morse made small portrait sketches of more than 80 of the figures that ultimately appear on the completed painting. The portrait sketch of Joseph Gales, a reporter for the National Intelligencer, is one of only two that survive and is also on display in the gallery.

Frederic Edwin Church's **Niagara** (1857) can also be seen here. In the third gallery are Thomas Eakins' genre painting **Singing a Pathetic Song** and John Singer Sargent's painting of **Madame Edouard Pailleron** (1879). Sargent's **Oyster Gatherers of Cancale** (En route pour la peche) (1878) is also part of the Corcoran's permanent collection.

The works of John Sloan, Robert Henri and George Bellows reflect the **Ashcan school** of early-20C realism. *Into Bondage* by Aaron Douglas is part of the Tibbs collection of African-American art. The large oil painting depicts the forced removal of Africans to America.

It actually is one in a series of four Douglas, an African-American painter, muralist and printmaker, created for the Hall of Negro Life at the Texas Centennial Exposition in Dallas in 1936.

Daughters of the American Revolution ★

Ⓜ *Farragut West*

This stately complex occupies an entire city block and is reputedly the world's largest group of structures owned and maintained exclusively by women. The national headquarters of the Daughters of the American Revolution (DAR), it houses an extensive collection of genealogical materials and artifacts relating to the colonial and early Republic periods through the mid-19C.

A BIT OF HISTORY

The DAR was established in 1890 by a group of four women who were descended from Revolutionary War patriots. The non-profit, non-political organization has achieved a national reputation for perpetuating "the memory and spirit of the men and women who achieved American independence." Today it is supported by 165,000 members belonging to chapters throughout the US. The DAR accepts any woman, 18 years or older, regardless of her race, religion, or ethnic background, who can successfully prove lineal descent from a soldier of the American Revolution.

The Beaux-Arts edifice known as **Memorial Continental Hall** was designed at the turn of the 19C by Edward Pearce Casey, who also collaborated on the construction of the Library of Congress. Facing the Ellipse, the original entrance is dominated by a porte-cochere, or carriage entry, covered by a pedimented roof. The semicircular portico that rises from the balustraded terrace on the C Street side features 13 columns, representing the 13 colonies. In the 1920s, having outgrown its original building, the DAR commissioned John Russell Pope to design **Constitution Hall**, a colossal structure whose columned, pedimented entrance faces 18th Street. The building contains a U-shaped, 3,800-seat auditorium, where

▷ **Location:** 17th and D Sts. NW.

🅿 **Parking:** Some metered street parking. Also several paid garages on New York and Pennsylvania Aves. and on 17th and 18th Sts.

👪 **Kids:** Hands-on family fun programs every third Sat Sept–Jun. (Kids 7 and older.) Also, the toy collection.

😊 **Don't Miss:** Docent-led tours of the Period Rooms *(approx 45min)*.

the Daughters meet for their annual convention. In addition, the hall functions as a public auditorium where a variety of concerts and lectures are held. It is DC's largest concert hall.

VISIT

🕐 *Museum open year-round Mon–Fri 9:30am–4pm, Sat 9am–5pm. Period rooms open year-round Mon–Fri 10am–2:30pm, Sat 9am–4:30pm.* 🕐 *Closed major holidays and 1 week in late Jun or early Jul.* 🔊 *Guided tours Mon–Fri 10am–2:30pm, Sat 9am–4:30pm.* ♿ 📞 *202-628-1776. www.dar.org.*

Memorial Continental Hall houses more than 30 **period rooms** that depict scenes of early American life, including a colonial home, tavern, church and other historical interiors dating from the late 17C to the mid 19C. Of note are the Georgia Room, portraying the late-18C Peter Tondee Tavern in Savannah; the brick-floor Oklahoma kitchen; and the Virginia room, reproducing an 18C dining room.

The original meeting hall, an enormous room overhung by a vaulted skylight and elaborate Neoclassical trim, is now the DAR library, a repository of genealogical material. The **DAR Museum** displays ceramics, silver, glass and textiles. Additional pieces from the permanent collection of more than 30,000 objects are on view in changing exhibits. Unless it is reserved for DAR or other functions, Constitution Hall is visited on the tour.

Dwight D. Eisenhower Executive Office Building★

Ⓜ *Farragut West or Farragut North*

The massive granite pile that rises like a tiered wedding cake to the west of the White House is one of Washington's foremost architectural treasures. Having survived years of neglect, it has been restored to its former grandeur and houses several key government offices of the Executive branch.

Info: www.whitehouse.gov/about/eeobtour.

Location: 17th and G Sts. NW. The Dwight D. Eisenhower Executive Office Building is located right next to the West Wing. The building is ⛔ not open to the public, but its grand facade can be viewed from the street.

A BIT OF HISTORY
Second Empire Landmark

Built as headquarters for the departments of State, War, and Navy, this grand building (1888) symbolized the renewed vitality of the post-Civil War government. Its chief architect was Alfred Mullett. He opted for the French Second Empire style, following the example of the Corcoran Gallery (now the Renwick Gallery). Known as the General Grant style because of its popularity during the Grant administration (1869-77), this style is characterized by mansard roofing and prominent corner and central pavilions. With 900 exterior columns, 1,572 windows and nearly 2 miles of corridors, this lavish construction was Washington's largest office building and is considered among the finest surviving example of the Second Empire style.

A Threatened Monument

When the edifice was completed in 1888, the Second Empire style was no longer in fashion. The building was allowed to deteriorate, and demolition seemed inevitable.

In 1947 the Executive Office of the President appropriated the building as an annex to the adjacent White House (hence its name).

The Kennedy administration was instrumental in the building's rehabilitation. Among the most influential divisions of the Executive branch housed in the building today are the Office of Management and Budget, the National Security Council, and the Office of the Vice President.

Dwight D. Eisenhower Executive Office Building

©Gwen Cannon/Michelin

Renwick Gallery★

Ⓜ *Farragut West or Farragut North*

The earliest major example of the Second Empire style in America, and embodying Victorian tastes, this ornate brick building is home to the Smithsonian American Art Museum's American studio craft and contemporary decorative arts collection. Inside, its galleries highlight the best works of contemporary and traditional American craftsmanship. The Renwick Gallery reopened in 2006 following a six-year renovation.

A BIT OF HISTORY
The City's First Art Museum
In 1858 the wealthy financier William Wilson Corcoran commissioned one of the period's most influential architects, **James Renwick**, to design a building to house his private art collection. Impressed by the innovative contemporary architecture he had seen on a recent visit to Paris, Corcoran requested that Renwick adopt the fashionable Second Empire style.

In 1874 the Corcoran Gallery of Art, as the building was then called, opened as Washington's first art museum. By 1897 the collection had outgrown the original building and the museum moved down 17th Street to the building it occupies today.

Renewal and Rebirth
Sold to the government, the old building was used by the US Court of Claims until 1964, the year in which demolition was proposed. The successful campaign to preserve the threatened landmark was championed by the Kennedy and Johnson administrations. Renamed the Renwick Gallery in honor of the building's architect, it became part of the Smithsonian Institution in 1965. To return the structure to its original appearance, restoration architects used old drawings and the photographs of Mathew Brady.

> **Location:** Pennsylvania Ave. and 17th St. NW. Steps from the White House, the Renwick is best accessed by either the Farragut North (Red line) and Farragut West (Blue and Orange lines) Metro stations.
> **Don't Miss:** The **American crafts** collection, especially Albert Paley's metalwork entitled *Portal Gates*.

The refurbished Renwick opened as a department of the Smithsonian American Art Museum in 1972.

VISIT
Open year-round daily 10am–5:30pm. Closed Dec 25. ♿ ☎202-633-7970. www.americanart.si.edu.

Exterior
The brick facade is embellished with sandstone pilasters, vermiculated quoins, garlands and window trim. Filigreed ironwork caps the ridges of the building's mansard roof. On the long western facade, niches hold statues of Rubens and Murillo, replicas of two of the original eleven statues of artists that once adorned the facades.

The capitals of the two pilasters flanking the entrance feature sculpted tobacco fronds and ears of corn. Above the entrance bay is a medallion profile of Corcoran, inscribed with his motto: "Dedicated to Art."

Interior
A red-carpeted staircase leads from the entryway to the second-floor **Grand Salon**. Decorated in the style of a Victorian picture gallery, the 90ft-long room is furnished with red velvet poufs—circular settees—and brocade sofas and chairs. Paintings, hung in tiers, cover its raspberry walls from the wainscoting to the ceiling molding. In 2009 a new installation of 70 paintings from the Smithsonian American Art Museum's collection went on permanent display

Larry Fuente, Game Fish, 1988, Renwick Gallery

Photo by Tony Brown, imjination, 2011

in the salon. The installation features landscapes, portraits and allegorical works by 51 American artists from the 1840s to the 1930s. It's the first time in many years some of these works have been on display.

The **Octagon Room** *(directly opposite the Grand Salon)* showcases works by Winslow Homer, Albert Pinkham Ryder and Thomas Wilmer Dewing, also from the Smithsonian American Art Museum's permanent collection.

The galleries on both sides of the Octagon Room feature pieces from the Renwick Gallery's outstanding comprehensive collection of **American crafts**. Highlights include the elaborate metalwork of Albert Paley's *Portal Gates,* Larry Fuente's playful *Game Fish,* Wendell Castle's trompe-l'oeil *Ghost Clock,* Kim Schmahmann's elegant *Bureau of Bureaucracy* and Beth Lipman's tour-de-force glass sculpture, *Bancketje,* a 2007 acquisition.

Organization of American States

Ⓜ *Farragut West*

The Organization of American States headquarters is made up of five buildings all in the vicinity of each other: the Main Building (MNB), General Secretariat Building (GSB), Administration Building (ADM), Art Museum of the Americas and The Casita. Together the OAS serves as a forum for discussions and conferences affecting the political and economic climate of the Western Hemisphere. Conceived as a symbolic amalgam of North and South American architecture,

▷ **Location:** 17th St. and Constitution Ave. NW. On the corner of 18th St. & Virginia Ave, just past C Street. A six-block walk from the Farragut West Metro station (Blue/ Orange Lines).

the white marble main building has the gracious ambience of a Spanish Colonial villa.

A BIT OF HISTORY

Established in 1890 as the International Union of American Republics, this organization is the oldest such alliance of nations in the world. Created to engender peaceful relations and economic cooperation among the independent countries of the Americas, it has grown from 24 member nations to 35. The US was a charter member.

In the early 20C, Washington was chosen as the site for this headquarters building because it was the only city in which all member nations maintained permanent legations. Congress donated the tract of land, which then became international territory. In addition to housing the offices of the permanent staff, the building serves as headquarters of the General Secretariat, the 700-member body responsible for OAS administration and policy implementation.

VISIT

⏱Open year-round Mon–Fri 9am–5pm. ⏱Closed major holidays. ♿ 📞202-458-3000. www.oas.org.

Headquarters Building

For their innovative blending of classical elements and traditional Latin motifs, Paul Cret and Albert Kelsey won the architectural competition to design the structure. A plaza fronts the triple-entry arches, which are flanked by allegorical statues.

The lobby is dominated by the **tropical patio**, designed after a Spanish Colonial courtyard. A fountain occupies the center of the patio, whose lush vegetation includes the enormous "peace tree," a grafted fig and rubber tree planted at the building's dedication in 1910. The coats of arms of the member nations embellish the roofed overhang. A gallery behind the patio features changing exhibits, generally from the collection of the OAS museum (below). On the second floor the columned **Hall of the Americas** contains three Tiffany rock-crystal chandeliers and Tiffany stained-glass windows. The adjacent Old Council Room features bronze bas-relief friezes depicting scenes in the histories of the Americas.

Museum and Grounds

Behind the main building, the Aztec Gardens display contemporary and traditional sculpture. The stuccoed loggia fronting the garden pool is the rear of a building designed by Cret and Kelsey to serve as the residence of the OAS secretary-general.

In 1976 it was converted to the **Art Museum of the Americas** (⏱open year-round Tue–Sun 10am–5pm; ⏱closed major holidays; ☞group tours available Tue–Fri, reservations required; 📞202-458-3362; http://.museum.oas.org).

The museum rotates works of the modern Caribbean and Latin American artists represented in its permanent collection of some 700 pieces.

St. John's Church

Ⓜ **McPherson Square**

Occupying a prominent corner of Lafayette Square since 1815, this elegant structure is one of the most historic and prestigious churches in Washington. Since its inception, every chief executive has worshiped in this "church of Presidents" while in office.

▸ **Location:** Lafayette Square at 16th and H Sts. NW. By Metro: McPherson Square (Orange and Blue lines), Farragut North (Red Line), or Farragut West (Blue Line)

🅿 **Parking:** Free valet parking is available Sun mornings from 9:30am to 1:30pm for those attending services.

A BIT OF HISTORY

In the early 19C parishioners of the capital's only Episcopal church, Christ Church on Capitol Hill, began to consider creating a new parish in the area that was then developing around the White House. In 1815 **Benjamin H. Latrobe** was engaged to draft plans for the building. Latrobe's church took the shape of a Greek cross.

Throughout the church's history, its vestry has attempted to maintain the integrity of Latrobe's design even as the building has been expanded and altered. A pillared porch was added to the west side in 1822; thereafter this side replaced Latrobe's south entrance as the main entrance. The bell tower was also added at this time, and the west transept extended, changing the church's shape to a Latin cross.

In 1883 James Renwick oversaw further renovation to the church, including the addition of a Palladian window behind the altar and stained-glass windows designed by Madame Veuve Lorin, curator at Chartres Cathedral in France.

VISIT

🕐 *Open year-round Mon–Sat 9am–3pm, Sun 8am–3pm.* 🕐 *Closed major holidays.* ♿ 📞 *202-347-8766. www.stjohns-dc.org.*

Latrobe's graceful, saucered dome and lantern draw the eye to the midpoint of the low-ceilinged church. A brass plate on **pew 54** indicates the president's pew, where attending chief executives are seated. The kneeling stools in this and nearby pews are covered in needle-point patterns bearing the presidential seals and the names of presidents.

Adjoining the church on H Street is Ashburton House, a Federal-style structure (1836) that now functions as the parish house.

Treasury Building

Ⓜ *Metro Center*

Pictured on the back of the $10 bill, the stately Treasury Building, which flanks the executive mansion on the east, is the seat of government finances and a prominent architectural landmark in its own right.

A BIT OF HISTORY

Department of the Treasury

The Treasury was established in 1789 as a department of the Executive branch. The Postal Service, General Land Office (now the Department of the Interior), departments of Commerce and Labor, and the Coast Guard all initially began as arms of the Treasury.

Today the Treasury Building houses executive and support offices for the secretary of the Treasury. A number of bureaus administered by the department are housed elsewhere in the city. Among these are the Bureau of Engraving and

▶ **Location:** 15th St. and Pennsylvania Ave. NW. Visitors must enter through the south building entrance located at 15th St and Hamilton Pl, NW (Washington Monument side). Enter through the gate in the iron fence by pressing the call button for admittance.

🅿 **Parking:** Parking is very limited so take public transportation if possible.

Printing, where currency is printed; and the Internal Revenue Service.

The Building

One of the few official buildings completed when Congress moved to Washington in 1800, the first Treasury Building, designed by George Hadfield, was burned down during the British invasion of 1814. Its replacement, designed by James Hoban, was destroyed in a fire set by arsonists in 1833.

The current building was begun in 1836, with the construction of the T-shaped east wing, designed by **Robert Mills**. Mills employed brick vaulting to fireproof the interior and, in compliance with the wishes of Congress, used Aquia Creek sandstone, an ill-suited material that was also used in the construction of the White House and the Capitol.

In 1851, due to political wrangling, Mills was dismissed and eventually replaced by Thomas U. Walter, who modified Mills' E-shaped structure by adding a west wing that would enclose the E in a square and create two interior courtyards. The south, west and north additions took 14 years to complete and were supervised by a number of architects who added their own embellishments. The granite building (the Aquia Creek sandstone exterior and east colonnade were replaced in 1909) covers two blocks and reflects the Greek Revival style prevalent in the 1830s and 40s. The building's most distinctive feature is the Ionic colonnade of 30 monolithic columns, each 36ft high, that adorns the east facade. The south, north and west entrances are approached by wide plazas. The south plaza contains a statue of **Alexander Hamilton**, first secretary of the Treasury (1789-95), and the north plaza, one of Hamilton's successor, **Albert Gallatin** (1801-14). Both statues were designed by James Earle Fraser.

VISIT

Visit by guided tour (1hr) only on Sat mornings, by advance reservation through your senator or representative (see Congressional Visits). Use the south building entrance at 15th St. and Hamilton Pl. NW (Washington Monument side); enter through the gate in the iron fence by pressing the call button for admittance.

The hallways in the original T-shaped east wing were conceived by Mills with Doric columns and groin- and barrel-vaulted ceilings. The more elaborately ornamented hallways of the south, north and west wings exemplify the Greek Revival style. Cast-iron pilasters lining the hall feature eagles and a hand holding the Treasury key. Cast-iron balustrades adorn the circular staircases. The third-floor corridors serve as a portrait gallery hung with paintings of the secretaries of the Treasury, arranged in chronological order. The **Secretary's Conference and Reception Rooms** have been created to reflect the decor popular in the late 1860s through the 1880s. The conference room features a painting of George Washington attributed to portraitist Gilbert Stuart and one of Salmon Chase (Treasury secretary under Lincoln from 1861 to 1864) attributed to Thomas Sully.

The **Andrew Johnson Suite** has been restored to its appearance in 1865, when the suite served as the Executive Office for President Andrew Johnson following Lincoln's assassination. Johnson had his office in the Treasury building until Mrs. Lincoln vacated the White House. The walls and ceilings of the **Secretary Salmon Chase Suite** are decorated with stenciling, allegorical figures and gilt detailing.

The second floor holds the Treasurer's Office, where a cast-iron **vault wall**, designed by Isaiah Rogers in 1864, is visible. Incised with seals and medallions, the wall was obscured behind other vault extensions and forgotten about for 80 years. Its interior lining of steel balls, intended to prevent burglary, can now be viewed through a wall cutaway.

The north lobby, fronting Pennsylvania Avenue, opens onto the **Cash Room**★, designed by Alfred Mullett. The site of Ulysses S. Grant's inaugural reception in 1869, the impressive 72ft-by-32ft chamber features immense bronze chandeliers, a coffered ceiling, and walls and floors faced in seven different kinds of marble. A mezzanine with ornate pilasters and an elaborate bronze railing rims the room.

Intended to inspire public trust in paper money, which the government first issued in 1862, the Cash Room functioned to redeem government-issued certificates and to supply commercial banks with coins and currency. It ceased operations in 1976 and is now used for official functions.

Traditionally the commercial heart of Washington, Downtown reflects the flavor of the city's past and present. Large office buildings and retail complexes rise above 19C shop fronts, and the process of revitalization continues as new condominiums, restaurants, shops and attractions make the area their home.

Highlights

1 High-tech gadgets at the **International Spy Museum** (p162)

2 Viewing presidential portraits at the **National Portrait Gallery** (p163)

3 Stepping into the past at **Ford's Theater** (p166)

4 The Folk Arts collection at the **Smithsonian American Art Museum** (p170)

5 Stunning views from the **Old Post Office Tower** (p175)

A Bit of History

19C

Conceived by planner L'Enfant to link the White House and the Capitol, **Pennsylvania Avenue** was the capital's first major thoroughfare, and as such it gave rise to the city's commercial district.

In 1801 President Jefferson authorized the building of a central market on the avenue between 7th and 9th streets, and in 1807 construction began on the ill-fated Tiber Creek canal, which was eventually covered over in the 1870s.

For much of the 19C, Pennsylvania Avenue was lined with hotels, boardinghouses and theaters, in keeping with L'Enfant's intent that this be a thoroughfare "attractive to the learned and affording diversion to the idle."

Among the diversions were the **National Theatre**, an institution still in operation between 13th and 14th streets, and the **Willard Hotel** (◖ see Where to Stay), for decades Washington's premier hostelry. Established in the 1850s, the Willard has occupied several buildings on the same site. The present building (1901) was designed by H.J. Hardenberg, architect of Manhattan's celebrated Plaza Hotel.

ℹ Info: Downtown D.C. Business Improvement District; ☏202-638-3232; www.downtowndc.org. The district's roving "ambassadors," identified by red ball caps, are on hand to answer questions and give directions at no charge. Information kiosks are located Downtown as well.

▶ Location: Sights covered here lie east of the White House and north of the Mall, an area compact enough to be walkable.

🅿 Parking: Several lots are scattered throughout; many offer early-bird specials. The former Convention Center (9th St. NW between New York Ave. & H St.) has been converted to a 1000-space garage ($24 maximum weekdays; $12 weekends).

🕐 Timing: Allow 2 days to see the sights.

👥 Kids: The International Spy Museum, particularly the gift shop.

As the city grew, F Street became the site of major government buildings and fashionable residences. North-south growth occurred along 7th Street, where two- and three-story brick buildings housed shops and residences. In the 1830s 7th Street was chosen as the site for the Patent Office and became an enclave for German immigrants working in the dry-goods trade.

By the turn of the 19C, their businesses had made this street the commercial hub of Downtown.

Decline and Rebirth

During the first half of the 20C, Downtown continued to thrive, with major new development occurring in the land bordered by Pennsylvania and Constitution Avenues. Known as **Federal Triangle**, this cluster of Classical Revival government buildings was designed by a group of eminent architects working in collaboration.

After World War II, Downtown declined as it lost business to suburban malls. When John F. Kennedy's inaugural parade moved down Pennsylvania Avenue, the thoroughfare was described by one cabinet member as "a vast, unformed, cluttered expanse." A cabinet committee established by Kennedy in 1960 began a redevelopment process gradually revitalized the avenue. At the core of this rebirth was the renovation of the Old Post Office while other landmark construction includes the 53,879sq ft **Navy Memorial** dedicated in 1987. An international trade center, the 3 million sq ft **Ronald Reagan Building** (1997, Pei Cobb Freed & Partners, and Ellerbe Becket), houses federal offices and conference rooms, restaurants, exhibit space and the Washington, DC Visitor Information Center.

Mixed-use complexes such as Hartman-Cox's Market Square (1984), near the site of the old city market, have risen on Pennsylvania Avenue. The Lansburgh complex (7th, 8th and E Sts.), home of the **Shakespeare Theatre** (1992), was the result of the overhaul of several buildings. Both Market Square and the Lansburgh are part of booming **Pennsylvania Quarter** (more commonly called "Penn Quarter", the designation for the avenue's north side between 6th, 9th and E streets.

21C Growth

Today a refurbished Willard Hotel overlooks Pershing Park, a pleasant square with an outdoor cafe. Nearby **Freedom Plaza**, designed by the prestigious architectural group, Venturi, Rauch and Scott Brown, has a large-scale copy of **L'Enfant's city plan** incised in its pavement. Anchoring the northern portion of Downtown rises the massive **Washington Convention Center** (2003).

On G and 9th streets stands the **Martin Luther King Memorial Library** (1972), an austere building designed by Mies van der Rohe, one of the 20C's most influential architects.

Chinatown, a small stretch of restaurants and shops on H Street between 6th and 7th streets, is recognizable by its ornate Friendship Archway. Chinatown neighbors the **Verizon Center**, a 20,000-seat sports arena for the city's basketball and hockey teams. The old Atlas and Le Droit buildings on F Street, between 8th and 9th streets, were revitalized to house the **International Spy Museum** (2002). At Pennsylvania Ave. and 6th Street, the **Newseum** relocated from Arlington and opened in 2008 in a new seven-level, 215,000sq ft building. The international museum features a large "window on the world" overlooking Pennsylvania Avenue and the Mall, state-of-the-art broadcast studios and six levels of exhibits showcasing the news media past and present.

In 2008 **Madame Tussauds** opened its 27,000 sq ft wax museum in the former Woodward & Lothrop building *(10th and F Sts. NW)*. Inside find the likenesses of everyone from Michelle Obama to Angelina Jolie. A $2 million presidential gallery with wax figures of all 44 US presidents made its debut in late 2010.

Nearby, the 2007 opening of the Shakespeare Theatre Company's newly constructed 776-seat **Sidney Harman Hall** *(6th and F Sts. NW)* has allowed the center to expand its offerings.

Now world-class Shakespearean and Shakespearean-inspired productions grace the stages of both Sidney Harman Hall and the Lansburgh Theatre.

In early 2012 Ford's Theatre's new **Center for Education and Leadership** opened its doors to the public.

Penn Quarter is the site of a **farmers' market** every Thursday (Apr–Dec) from 3pm–7pm *(north end of 8th St., between D and E Sts.; ℘202-362-8889; www.fresh farmmarkets.org)*. Throughout the year, countless festivals and celebrations are held in Downtown.

International Spy Museum★★

Ⓜ *Gallery Place*

The late-19C exteriors of the renovated Atlas and Le Droit buildings disguise the sleek interior that now holds this intriguing, interactive museum. Opened in 2002, the museum gives visitors access to the largest and most fascinating collection of spying paraphernalia ever to be displayed in public.

Location: 9th and F Sts. NW. Self-guided tours move from the third floor to the first-floor.

Don't Miss: Spy gadgets like the lipstick pistols.

Timing: Allow 90min for the museum; 30min for gift shop.

Kids: The interactive code-breaking room.

VISIT

Open late Mar & May–early Sept daily 9am–7pm. Mid-Sept–mid-Dec daily 10am–6pm, with exceptions (check online before you visit). Rest of the year, check online. Closed Jan 1, Thanksgiving Day & Dec 25. $19.95. Advance tickets recommended. 202-393-7798. www.spymuseum.org. Visitors enter a high-tech security portal and take elevators to the third floor. There, visitors choose a "cover" identity from those on display, and in the Briefing Theater, view a film (*5min*) on the real world of spying. Then begins a self-guided tour of third- and first-floor exhibits. **School for Spies** features, among other gadgets, buttonhole cameras, lipstick pistols and equipment for listening in on bugged conversations. A fully equipped Aston Martin, boasting machine guns and rotating license plates, highlights the exhibit. **The Secret History of History** traces spying from George Washington's era to the beginnings of the Secret Service. Intelligence-gathering during World War II is depicted in **Spies Among Us**, highlighted by an interactive code-breaking room.

In **War of the Spies** (*1st floor*), visitors enter a replicated section of Berlin, complete with a cafe and a tunnel for eavesdropping on the Soviets. The exhibit showcases spy technology spawned during the Cold War, from shoe phones to satellites. Challenges confronting today's intelligence community are revealed in the final exhibit, **The 21st Century.**

National Portrait Gallery★★

Ⓜ *Gallery Place*

Sharing the interior of the Old Patent Office Building with the Smithsonian American Art Museum since 1968, this museum serves as the nation's family album. Modeled after its namesake in London, the National Portrait Gallery conserves some 19,400 paintings, sculptures, photographs, engravings and drawings of "men and women who have made significant contributions

Location: Old Patent Office Building 8th and F Sts. NW. The portrait gallery and the art museum are connected by hallway galleries.

Don't Miss: The presidential portraits (*2nd floor*)

Timing: Allow 2hrs, minimum.

to the history, development and culture of the people of the United States."

A BIT OF HISTORY
Home for the Arts
In the mid-1830s Congress authorized a "temple of the useful arts"—a patent office—to be constructed on this site. In 1836 construction began on the Greek Revival edifice designed by William Parker Elliott. The monumental stone **Old Patent Office Building**★★ features a pedimented Doric portico on each of its four sides and encloses a central courtyard. Robert Mills oversaw construction of the south wing (1840), whose golden sandstone contrasts with the granite of the rest of the building.

The War Years
During the Civil War, the building served as a hospital for Union soldiers. Clara Barton, a Patent Office copyist and founder of the Red Cross, ministered to the wounded, as did poet Walt Whitman, who read to them from his works. In 1865 Lincoln's second inaugural reception was held here. A benefit to raise funds for the families of Union soldiers, the gala took place in the 264ft-long, marble-pillared hall on the third floor of the east wing.

Structure Preserved
When completed in 1867, the building also housed, at various times, the Department of the Interior and the Civil Service Commission. In 1958 Congress saved the building from demolition and gave it to the Smithsonian Institution. In July 2006 the building reopened after a six-year overhaul, financed in part by a $45 million gift from the Donald W. Reynolds Foundation of Las Vegas. The museums are known, collectively, as the Donald W. Reynolds Center for American Art and Portraiture but their individual names remain the same.

As a result of the renovation, which included structural repairs and replacement of aging infrastructure, three floors are now exclusively devoted to exhibits. A new conservation center allows visitors to view the preservation process. Display space has been significantly expanded and a 346-seat auditorium has been added. The enclosed Kogod Courtyard with its elegant glass canopy (by architects Foster + Partners) was named one of the seven modern architectural wonders of the world by Condé Nast Traveler magazine.

VISIT
Open year-round daily 11:30am–7pm. Closed Dec 25. ✕ ♿ ✆202-633-8300. www.americanart.si.edu.

First Floor
To the right after entering from F Street. The ongoing special exhibit **Portaiture Now** features the art of portraiture and its many manifestations in 21C America. The long corridor along 7th Street presents a chronological overview of prominent people and events from 1600-1900 in **American Origins**. Included are portraits of Pocahontas, Ben Franklin, John Singleton Copyley (*Self-Portrait*, 1784), Seminola chief Osceola, Thomas Edison, Walt Whitman and Frederick Douglass. The end of the corridor is devoted to the **Civil War** period, where likenesses of Abraham Lincoln, Julia Ward Howe, abolitionist John Brown, generals Ulysses S. Grant and William Tecumseh Sherman, and other renowned figures are on view.

Mounted in the hallway leading to the G Street lobby is a selection of the museum's recent acquisitions.

Second Floor
The museum's series of **presidential portraits**, featuring representations in various media of those who have held the nation's highest office, occupy much of the second floor *(to the right of the landing)*; the highlights are Gilbert Stuart's full-length **Lansdowne portrait**★ of George Washington and his **Athenaeum Portraits** of George and Martha Washington. The Athenaeum portrait is the most widely known representation of the first president, since it served as the model for the portrait that appears on the $1 bill. Stuart's **Thomas Jefferson portrait** is also noteworthy. George P.A.Healy's oil painting depicts a pensive, seated Abraham Lincoln, and particularly moving is the facsimile of

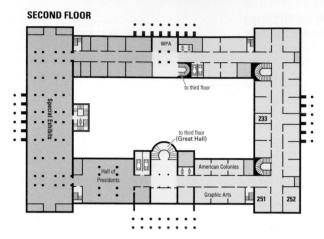

SECOND FLOOR

WPA

to third floor

to third floor
(Great Hall)

Special Exhibits

233

American Colonies

Hall of Presidents

Graphic Arts

251   252

**NATIONAL PORTRAIT GALLERY/
AMERICAN ART MUSEUM**

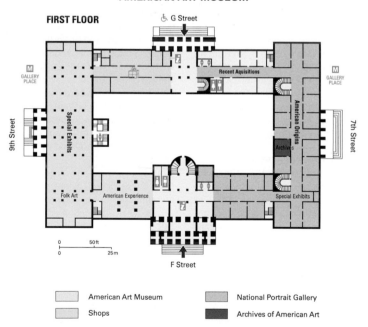

FIRST FLOOR

G Street

GALLERY PLACE

GALLERY PLACE

Recent Aquisitions

Special Exhibits

American Origins

9th Street

7th Street

Archives

Folk Art   American Experience

Special Exhibits

0   50 ft
0   25 m

F Street

	American Art Museum			National Portrait Gallery
	Shops			Archives of American Art

the museum's famous **"cracked plate" photograph of Abraham Lincoln** taken on 5 February 1865, just weeks before his assassination.

The remaining galleries are reserved for special exhibitions. An entire gallery *(opposite the G Street elevators)* is devoted to works by the noted sculptor **Jo Davidson** (1883-1952), who immor-

talized in bronze, stone or terra-cotta many prominent figures of his day including Gertrude Stein, Franklin D. Roosevelt and Fiorello La Guardia.

Third Floor

The entire south wing of the museum on this floor is occupied by the **Great Hall**, whose decor of multicolored Milton tiles,

164

carved ceiling medallions, and a yellow and blue central skylight reflects late-19C tastes. The frieze of six relief panels illustrating sources of technology speaks to the hall's originally designed to display miniature patent models.

The exhibit **20th-Century Americans** dominates both sides of the hall and features portraits of historical and contemporary Americans such as Rachael Carson, Jackson Pollock, James Baldwin, and Jonas Salk. In the section devoted to American Justice are likenesses of such human-rights advocates as Thurgood Marshall, César Chávez, Malcolm X, Shirley Chisholm and Christover Reeves. Mezzanines flank the long sides the hall. **BRAVO!** showcases portraits of performing arts greats including Marian Anderson, Benny Goodman, Elvis Presley, Joan Baez and Jerry Seinfeld.

Lined with paintings, photographs and hanging banners, **Champions** features well-known sports figures Arthur Ashe, Lance Armstrong, Muhammad Ali and many others.

Federal Bureau of Investigation★

Ⓜ *Federal Triangle*

Officially known as the J. Edgar Hoover FBI Building, this immense, fortress like structure bordering Pennsylvania Avenue houses the national headquarters of the Federal Bureau of Investigation (FBI).

A BIT OF HISTORY

An arm of the Justice Department, the FBI traces its beginnings to 1908, when a permanent investigative force of special agents was placed under the control of the attorney general. In 1935 this force was designated the Federal Bureau of Investigation and its powers broadened in an effort to combat rampant gangsterism. Under the 48-year leadership (1924-72) of director **J. Edgar Hoover,** the bureau became the supreme federal authority in matters of domestic crime. Begun in 1963, the headquarters building was completed 12 years later in 1975, at a cost of over $126 million.

Stanley Gladych's design exemplifies the New Brutalism school of architecture, which features exposed concrete and little embellishment. Covering a city block, the building wraps around an

◌ **Location:** E St. between 9th and 10th Sts. NW. The FBI is in walking distance to four Metro stations: Federal Triangle on the Orange/Blue lines; Gallery Place/Chinatown and Metro Center on the Red line; and Archives/Navy Memorial on the Yellow and Green lines.

◷ **Timing:** Tours are currently suspended due to renovations and security restrictions. Call ☏202-324-3000 or go online at www.fbi.gov to check the current status of tours.

interior courtyard. An exterior arcade along the perimeter is lined with rows of massive pillars. The building houses nearly 8,000 workers. In addition, the FBI maintains 56 field offices and more than 400 resident agencies, employing more than 12,000 agents. The Bureau also operates more than 60 international offices called "Legal Attaches" in U.S. embassies around the world.

In the past, tours showcased the laboratories where bullet, firearm and fiber analyses are conducted. A small exhibit hall contained displays on the history of the bureau.

Ford's Theatre and Petersen House★

Ⓜ *Metro Center*

In the heart of Downtown, amid a stretch of 19C structures, stands old Ford's Theatre, where Abraham Lincoln was shot by an assassin, and Petersen House, where he died of his wound.

A BIT OF HISTORY
A Tragic Gala

On the evening of 14 April 1865, President and Mrs. Lincoln attended a performance at Ford's Theatre. The capital was in a festive mood as, only five days before, Confederate Gen. Robert E. Lee had surrendered to Union Gen. Ulysses S. Grant at Appomattox, Virginia. Grant and his wife had, in fact, been in Washington on 14 April and were to have attended the theater with the Lincolns, but they made the decision to leave town earlier in the day. In their stead, Clara Harris, daughter of Sen. Ira Harris, and her fiancé, Maj. Henry Rathbone, attended. That night the theater was full of Washingtonians hoping for a glimpse of Grant, who had rarely visited the city. In preparation for the president's arrival, boxes no. 7 and no. 8 had been draped with flags and the partition between them removed to allow the presidential party more space. The Lincoln party was engrossed in the third act of the play when **John Wilkes Booth** silently entered the box and shot the president at close range. The bullet from the small, single-shot derringer entered behind Lincoln's left ear and lodged behind his right eye. Major Rathbone immediately tried to subdue the attacker, but Booth defended himself with a large knife, stabbing the major in the arm. Booth leaped over the balustrade of the box, but as he did so, his feet got tangled in the draped flags. He landed off balance on the stage 12ft below, breaking a small bone in his leg. Most accounts claim that Booth then stood and bran-

> **Location:** 10th St. between E and F Sts. NW. Two Metro stations are in walking distance to the theatre: Metro Center and Gallery Place (both on the Red line).
>
> 🅿 **Parking:** Limited paid street parking and garages.
>
> 🕐 **Timing:** Check the website for the daytime schedule in order to plan your visit. The schedule for the interpretive program *(either by the National Park or Ford's Theatre Society, approx 30mins)*, theater walk-through and museum entry varies.

dished his knife, declaring "Sic semper tyrannis!" ("Thus always with tyrants"). The audience, believing that Booth's appearance was part of the play, was slow to respond. In the theater alley Booth mounted a horse and escaped.

Lincoln's Final Hours

Three army surgeons in the theater audience immediately attended the stricken Lincoln. Recognizing the seriousness of the wound, they ordered him moved to the nearest bed; the president was carried across the street to a boarding house owned by a tailor named Petersen. He was laid in a first-floor back room then being rented by a young man in the Union Army. Due to Lincoln's height (6ft 4in), he had to be placed diagonally across the bed. As the night passed, Cabinet ministers, physicians and other prominent people gathered in the back parlor, while Mrs. Lincoln was consoled by friends in the front parlor. Lincoln never regained consciousness. At 7:22am the following morning, he died.

The Pursuit of the Assassin

John Wilkes Booth apparently sought to achieve lasting fame for himself by what he considered his "heroic" act on behalf of the Confederacy. Once he had inflicted the mortal wound, Booth made for the home of Dr. Samuel Mudd in the Maryland countryside. Mudd set his leg, and Booth continued his flight, accompanied by a fellow conspirator, David Herold. The two men crossed into Virginia and were apprehended on 26 April by a cavalry detachment in Port Royal, Virginia. Herold surrendered, but Booth refused, forcing his pursuers to set on fire the barn in which he was hiding. As the building burst into flames, he was fatally shot in the neck .

Ford's Theatre

©Jason Maehl/Bigstockphoto.com

FORD'S THEATRE

When John Ford opened the doors of this brick structure in 1863, it was one of the country's grandest theaters. Though its facade was adorned only with arched door bays, window trim, pilasters and an undecorated pediment, its interior was lavishly appointed. A cantilevered "dress circle," or balcony, flanked by private boxes, sloped toward the stage.

After Lincoln's assassination, the theater was ordered closed by the federal government. John Ford's announced intention to continue dramatic productions in the theater met with threats, so the War Department leased the building from Ford and began converting it into office space, purchasing it a year later for $100,000.

In 1893, 22 office workers were killed when the floors collapsed. Thereafter the building was used only for storage until 1932, when the government opened it as a museum dedicated to the 16th president. In the mid-1960s Congress authorized a restoration of the building to its 1865 appearance. Ford's Theatre reopened in 1968 as both a memorial and an active playhouse.

Visit

🕘 *Open year-round daily 9am–5pm.*
🕘 *Closed Dec 25.* 🎫*Timed entry tickets (free) required to enter theater, museum, and Petersen House. Tickets for www.fords.org. 📞202-426-6924. www.nps.gov/foth.* The theater and museum reopened in 2009 after the site underwent an extensive restoration and renovation that

upgraded the theater and its systems while preserving its historic integrity. The **box** where Lincoln sat is decorated as it was on the night of April 14, 1865, with Victorian period pieces, including the settee that had been specially placed there for the president. On the balcony level is an imposing **bronze head of Lincoln** by Carl Tolpo, which was presented to Ford's Theatre in 1965.

In the basement, the refurbished **Lincoln Museum** (🕘 *same hours as the theater*) displays such artifacts from the assassination as Booth's pistol and a replica of the coat Lincoln wore that night.

PETERSEN HOUSE

Across the street at 516 10th St. 🕘*Open year-round daily 9:30am–5:30pm.* 🕘*Closed Dec 25.* 📞*202-426-6924.* The simple three-story brick row house where Lincoln died on April 15, 1865, was built in 1850 by William Petersen, a German-born tailor. Its three first-floor rooms, a front and back parlor and bedroom, decorated in Victorian period furnishings, are open to the public and visitors learn more about the President's final hours.

Adjacent at no. 514, the new **Center for Education and Leadership** (2012) has exhibits on Lincoln's legacy and leadership qualities. A stack of books written about him towers 34ft.

National Museum of Women in the Arts★

Ⓜ *Metro Center*

Behind this Beaux-Arts exterior is the world's only major museum devoted exclusively to the works of women artists. The 4,000-piece permanent collection includes works from the 16C to the present, covering every medium from native American pottery to abstract sculpture.

A BIT OF HISTORY

Local philanthropists Wilhelmina and Wallace Holladay founded the museum in 1981 as a private institution "to encourage greater awareness of women in the arts." The Holladays donated their own collection to form the core of the museum's holdings, which today comprise works from more than 800 women artists.

A limestone and granite trapezoid, the edifice housing the museum was once a Masonic temple (Waddy B. Wood, 1908). It was designated a National Historic Landmark in the early 1980s.

The Shepherd David Triumphant *(1895) by Elizabeth Gardner Bouguereau (1837 - 1922)*

National Museum of Women in the Arts, D.C. / Gift of Wallace and Wilhelmina Holladay

▷ **Location:** 1250 New York Ave. and 13th St. NW. By Bus: Take routes 80, G8, S2, S4, X2, D6, D3, 68, D1 or 42 to the corner of H and 13th Sts, NW. By Metro: Take the Red, Blue or Orange line to Metro Center, use the 13th St. exit and walk two blocks north.

☺ **Don't Miss:** Mary Cassatt's painting *The Bath*.

In 1983 the newly founded museum purchased the building from the fraternal order of Masons and formally opened at this new location in 1987. An $8 million renovation transformed the interior into three levels of exhibit space, a library and research center and an auditorium, where public lectures, workshops, films and concerts are held. The Kasser Wing, which houses additional exhibit space, a conference room and an expanded museum shop, was completed in 1997.

VISIT

🕐 *Open year-round Mon–Sat 10am–5pm, Sun noon–5pm.* 🕐 *Closed Jan 1, Thanksgiving Day & Dec 25.* *$10. Free admission the first Sun of the month.* ✕ & 📞 *202-783-5000. www.nmwa.org.*

The main floor is dominated by the **Great Hall**, a two-story expanse of rose, white and gray Turkish marble (and faux marble) overhung by three crystal and gold-leaf chandeliers. The mezzanine level is rimmed with a heavy marble balustrade that extends along the twin staircases on opposite sides of the hall. The gilded lions' heads topping the columns and the ornate ceiling are the only features from the building's original interior. Light shines through the mezzanine's large arched windows.

Selected works from the museum's permanent collection are hung in the Great Hall and on the mezzanine on a rotating basis; the second floor is reserved for temporary exhibits.

The third-floor galleries, arranged chronologically, are devoted to works from the **permanent collection** (🛗 take elevator to 3rd floor). The earliest works (displayed in the 16-18C gallery) are primarily still lifes and portraits, characteristic of the subject matter of early women artists. The oldest work in the collection is the *Portrait of a Noblewoman* (c.1580) by Lavinia Fontana, a 16C Italian painter from Bologna considered to be the first professional woman artist. *Still Life of Fish and Cat* by Clara Peeters, a 17C Flemish artist, highlights her contributions to the development of that genre. Two still lifes of flowers are representative of the work of Rachel Ruysch, a 17C Dutch artist. This gallery also contains a portrait by Elisabeth Vigée-Lebrun (1755-1842), Marie Antoinette's favorite painter.

The 19C gallery displays works by the well-known animal portraitist Rosa Bonheur and *The Cage*, a still life by the famous French Impressionist Berthe Morisot, as well as the sculpture *Young Girl With a Sheaf* by Camille Claudel. Among the 19C American works are an early portrait by Cecilia Beaux, and *The Bath*, from a renowned series of graphics by Impressionist Mary Cassatt. Lilla Cabot Perry, who introduced the work of Monet to Americans, is represented by her *Lady with a Bowl of Violets* and *Lady in Evening Dress*.

The museum's notable collection of **19C sculpture** includes the works of Malvina Hoffman, Anna Vaughn Hyatt Huntington, Bessie Potter Vonnoh and Evelyn Beatrice Longman.

The 20C galleries feature paintings by Helen Frankenthaler, Elaine de Kooning, Lee Krasner and others. Mexican artist Frida Kahlo painted her *Self-Portrait Dedicated to Leon Trotsky*, as a gift for the Russian revolutionary leader and depicts the artist standing on a stage-like floor between a set of tied back curtains.

Smithsonian American Art Museum★

🅜 *Gallery Place*

Housed in the landmark Old Patent Office Building, this museum contains the country's oldest federal collections of art. Its holdings run the gamut of American art from early-18C portraiture and 19C landscapes to the free-form sculpture and large, abstract canvases of contemporary artists.

▷ **Location:** 🦽 See the National Portrait Gallery above.

🎨 **Don't Miss:** George Catlin Gallery and the Folk Art collection.

A BIT OF HISTORY

The museum traces its beginnings to the efforts of a Washingtonian named John Varden. In 1841 his collection of art, artifacts and natural history specimens was joined with that of the congressionally mandated National Institute. The combined collections were exhibited in the Patent Office Building.

In 1862 the collection was donated to the Smithsonian Institution, which exhibited selected pieces in several buildings in the city. In 1906 the collection was officially designated the National Gallery of Art, but it still had no permanent home. Even its title was short-lived, since the new museum being built on the Mall to house the Mellon Collection was officially named the National Gallery of Art in 1937.

The National Collection of Fine Arts, as it was then called, remained in the Museum of Natural History until 1968, when it was permanently installed in its original quarters—the Old Patent Office Building. Since then, the collection has increased fivefold and now includes more than 41,000 objects. It received its previous name, the National Museum of American Art (NMAA), in 1980, to reflect its mandate to display exclusively the works of US artists. In 2000 President Bill Clinton signed into law a bill renaming the museum the Smithsonian American Art Museum. In July 2006 the building was reopened after a six-year renovation. *For details, ☞ see the National Portrait Gallery.*

VISIT

ⓘ *Open year-round daily 11:30am–7pm.* ⓘ *Closed Dec 25.* ✕♿ ☎ *202-633-7970. www.americanart.si.edu.*

First Floor

The **American Experience** *(to the left of the F Street lobby)* showcases 19C landscape paintings as well as works by renowned 20C artists such as Hans Hoffman, Milton Avery, Joseph Stella, Richard Diebenkorn, Georgia O'Keeffe, Edward Hopper and the sculpture of Isamu Noguchi, among others.

Not to be missed in the **Folk Art** section is James Hampton's **Throne of the Third Heaven of the Nations' Millennium General Assembly**.

This three-dimensional work depicts the throne of God surrounded by altar-like pulpits and offertories. While employed as a Washington janitor from 1946 to 1960, Hampton created this work from discarded furniture, bottles and other items that he wrapped in aluminium and gold foil. Paintings, toys, quilts and sculpture from the museum's collection of 19C and 20C American folk art are also on view. The remainder of the corridor is reserved for special exhibits.

Second Floor

American art from colonial times through 1940 is exhibited on this floor *(to the left of the landing)*. The first three rooms on the right are reserved for changing displays of graphic arts. Opposite, the **American Colonies** includes works by artists Ralph Earl, Thomas Sully and John Trumbull. John Singleton Copley's portrait of *Mrs. George Watson* (1765) is especially noteworthy.

The two opposite rooms *(Galleries 251 and 252)* at the end of the 7th-Street Corridor showcase late 18C and early 19C furniture, such as a 1790 mahogany dining table. The **Early Republic** spotlights Albert Bierstadt's *Among the Sierra Nevada* (1868). **Western Art** includes sculpture such as *The Dying Tecumseh* by Ferdinand Pettrich (1856) and a gallery devoted to the early-19C paintings of American Indians by artist-anthropologist **George Catlin** (1796-1872). In the central hall, a standout is Eastman Johnson's *The Girl I Left Behind Me* (1875). Gallery 233 features black and white photos from the Civil War. Next door, floral still life and a portrait of *Elizabeth Winthrop Chanler* (1893) by John Singer Sargent are highlights. American **Impressionism** includes works by Childe Hassam, John Henry Twachtman (*Round Hill Road*, c.1900) and Mary Cassatt (*The Caress,* 1902).

Galleries at the end of the corridor display works by artists of the **Gilded Age**, such as John La Farge, Abbott Thayer, and Augustus Saint-Gaudens, whose bronze Adams Memorial sculpture dominates the hallway.

The spacious gallery devoted to Modernism highlights major schools and trends in mid-to-late-20C art.

In the center of the G Street corridor, art from the **WPA** (Works Progress Administration) includes works by Thomas Hart Benson and Morris Kantor's delightful *Baseball at Night* (1934).

Third Floor

Art Since 1945 and **Contemporary Art** feature works by Jesus Moroles, Chaim Gross and Paul Feeley. Don't miss the humorous *Any Questions* sculpture (1985) by William King.

Luce Foundation Center

Extending over three floors *(3rd, 3rd-floor mezzanine and 4th)*, this open storage displays some 3,500 works of American Art enclosed within glass partitions. In-depth information on individual objects is available from computer kiosks.

Newseum★

Ⓜ Archives-Navy Memorial-Penn Quarter

In today's age of 24/7 news coverage and point-and-click headlines, it seems fitting that a museum devoted to the Fourth Estate now occupies 250,000 square feet of Pennsylvania Avenue, between the White House and the Capitol. From recordings on ancient cuneiform tablets up to today's global digital media, the Newseum chronicles the news with depth and dazzle.

A BIT OF HISTORY

In its original incarnation, the Newseum sat over the river in Arlington and was a fraction of its current size. That version closed in 2002 after the Freedom Forum foundation purchased the land on Pennsylvania Avenue for $100 million. Six years later on April 11, 2008, the "new" Newseum opened to the public.

The Building

Sporting a 74ft-high Tennessee marble engraving of the First Amendment on the facade, the steel, stone and glass building houses 15 major galleries, 15 theaters, a food court and a Wolfgang Puck restaurant (👌 see EAT). On the Pennsylvania Avenue side, a huge glass facing offers a window into the 90ft-high atrium, and lets visitors appreciate

Location: 555 Pennsylvania Ave. NW at 6th St. By Metro: Archives-Navy Memorial-Penn Quarter.

Timing: Allow 2hrs to do justice to the exhibits. Take a break in the ground-level food court.

Don't Miss: The Berlin Wall, the view from the 6th floor, the museum shop.

the historic view of the city as they move up the museum's six levels.

VISIT

Open year-round daily 9am–5pm.
Closed Jan 1, Thanksgiving Day & Dec 25. $21.95. ✕ ♿ ☎ *888-639-7386. www.newseum.org.*

Near the entrance, the front pages of the day's national and international newspapers are enlarged and displayed. The selection is part of the larger exhibit (*Level 6*) that is updated every morning at 6am. See a short film in the Orientation Theater (*Concourse level*) as a preview of the museum's exhibits.

Highlights

Eight 12ft-high sections of the **Berlin Wall** stand in the gallery (*Concourse*) devoted to the media's role in the wall's history and ultimate fall. The fronts of

Newseum, Berlin Wall exhibit

©Gwen Cannon/Michelin

Newseum Statistics

Below are a few of the numbers boasted by the Newseum:

35,000 newspaper front pages

8,861 artifacts (including a letter dated 1416 and a 3000-year-old cuneiform brick from Sumeria).

3,800 graphic elements (such as cartoons, comics, etc.)

2,386 press passes

130 interactive stations

48 embedded 32-inch monitors

2 television studios

Try being a TV broadcaster in front of a live camera in the **Interactive Newsroom** (Level 2). See the World Press Freedom Map in **World News** (Level 3).

In the **9/11 Gallery** (Level 4), the September 11 exhibit shows how journalists in New York, Pennsylvania and at the Pentagon reported the deadly attacks. Front pages of newspapers from all 50 states, DC, plus 34 countries are on display as is a mangled piece of the antenna mast from the World Trade Center.

The **News History Gallery** (Level 5) has a collection of 30,000 historic newspapers. Among the highlights are Tim Russert's now-famous dry-erase board from the 2000 presidential election and the November 3, 1948 edition of the *Chicago Daily Tribune*, which proclaims, "Dewey Defeats Truman."

Don't miss the **Front Pages Gallery** (top floor) or the **view** of the Capitol and Pennsylvania Avenue from the **outdoor terrace** (top floor).

the sections that faced West Germany are covered in political graffiti. In stark contrast, the backs, which faced East Germany, were painted white so that attempting escapees could easily be seen by guards.

Crime and Punishment Museum

Ⓜ *Gallery Place*

This three-floor museum, opened in 2008, holds visitors' attention with its interactive tests of ability and absorbing exhibits on America's crime and detection.

VISIT

👤👤🕐*Open late May–Sept 4 Mon–Sat 9am–7pm (Fri–Sat til 8pm), Sun 10am–7pm. Rest of year, see website for hrs.* 🕐*Closed Thanksgiving Day, Dec 25.* 👓*$21.95 (discount online).* ♿ ✆*202-621-5550. www.crimemuseum.org.*

Pirates, Western outlaws, Bonnie and Clyde, 1920s mobsters, FBI's most wanted and today's white-collar thieves: you'll find traces of them here, along with torture devices from the Middle Ages; a Colonial-era pillory; firearms; Wild West-

▶ **Location:** 575 7th St. NW, between E and F Sts.

👤👤 **Kids:** Police Lineup and Fingerprint scanner.

🕐 **Timing:** Allow 1-2hrs, unless you are a history buff or amateur detective.

👁 **Don't Miss:** The Autopsy Room, Al Capone's prison cell, Crack-a-Safe, the Lie Detector, and the Firearms Simulator.

style OK Corral shooting range; police badges and a police motorcycle; replicas of a jail cell as well as Al Capone's stylish prison room; and a modern-day crime scene and labs C.S.I. style.

Learn about crime-solving devices and processes such as the lie detector test, footprint analysis, and booking procedure (including mug shots). Among the many hands-on exhibits, test your skills in the High-Speed Police Chase Simulator or the Firearms Training Simulator.

Marian Koshland Science Museum

Ⓜ *Judiciary Square*

This museum operates under the auspices of the National Academy of Sciences in Washington, DC, and seeks to "explore current scientific issues at the core of many of the nation's public policy decisions." Established by molecular biologist Daniel Koshland, the facility is named for his wife, Marian (1921-1997), also a molecular biologist, known for her immunology work.

VISIT

👥 🕐 *Open year-round Wed–Mon 10am–5pm.* 🕐 *Closed Thanksgiving Day, Dec 25 & Jan 1.* ⊜*$7.* ♿ 📞 *202-334-1201. www.koshland-science-museum.org.*

- ▷ **Location:** 6th and E Sts. NW. By Metro: A short walk from both the Gallery Place/Chinatown (Red, Green, & Yellow lines); and Judiciary Square station (Red line).
- 🅿 **Parking:** Limited.
- 👥 **Kids:** Museum is designed for children 13 and older.
- 🕐 **Timing:** Allow an hour.
- 🕊 **Don't Miss:**The interactive Lights at Night exhibit.

Exhibits are designed for visitors 13 years of age and older.
Interactive stations allow visitors to manipulate satellite images of earth's night time illuminations and view real-time DNA representations.
Other exhibits investigate the role of cows in climatic changes and the use of DNA fingerprinting for criminals.

National Aquarium

Ⓜ *Federal Triangle*

This small aquarium is the nation's oldest. Established in 1873 under the auspices of the Federal Fish Commission, it has occupied various locations, including ponds on the grounds of the Washington Monument. In 1932 the aquarium was moved to its present location in the basement of the Department of Commerce Building. Since 1982 the aquarium has functioned independently of the government as a private, nonprofit organization.

VISIT

👥 🕐 *Open year-round daily 9am–5pm (last admission 4:30pm), extended summer hours.* 🕐 *Closed Thanksgiving Day & Dec 25.* ⊜*$9.95. Animal feedings daily 2pm.* ♿ 📞 *202-482-2825.*

- ▷ **Location:** 14th St. and Constitution Ave. NW. A short walk from the The Federal Triangle Metro (blue & orange lines).
- 🅿 **Parking:** Very limited street parking and some paid parking structures nearby.
- 👥 **Kids:** Daily 2pm animal feedings.
- 🕐 **Timing:** About 45min.

www.nationalaquarium.com.
Exhibit renovations may be underway, but the aquarium remains open.

The aquarium houses some 200 species of aquatic life, including sea turtles, lemon sharks and piranhas.
Tanks are grouped to highlight the animals and habitats preserved and protected by the National Marine Sanctuaries Program.

National Building Museum

🅜 *Judiciary Square*

Formerly known as the Pension Building, the colossal brick edifice was long considered one of the capital's most monumental eyesores. Painstakingly refurbished, this example of 19C eclecticism now houses a museum devoted to America's achievements in the building arts.

▷ **Location:** 401 F St. NW. The museum is across the street from the Judiciary Sq Metro station (Red line).

👥 **Kids:** The Building Zone & family tours given by junior docents (ages 10-18).

🕐 **Timing:** Allow about 2 hrs to take a tour & experience the building and its exhibits.

👁 **Don't Miss:** Peering down at the Great Hall from the 4th floor.

A BIT OF HISTORY
"Meigs' Old Red Barn"

In the 1880s, US Army engineer Gen. **Montgomery Meigs** (1816-92) was commissioned to design a permanent workplace for the 1,500 employees of the Pension Bureau, the federal agency responsible for distributing government pensions. Nicknamed "Meigs' Old Red Barn," the **Pension Building**★ occupies an entire city block. The massive rectangular edifice stands almost 160ft tall. The exterior design, with its prominent overhanging cornice and three stories of pedimented and linteled windows, is a double-scale version of the Palazzo Farnese in Rome. The 3ft-high terra-cotta **frieze** around the entire structure was created by 19C sculptor Casper Buberl as a memorial to the Civil War Union dead. The oversized "palazzo" is crowned by a roof of intersecting gable-ended clerestories, designed to provide light within and to conserve heat in winter. Meigs incorporated a ventilation system that afforded a crosscurrent between the roof, windows and the openings below each window. The structure was made fireproof by the use of brick and metal. The Pension Bureau transferred to more spacious accommodations in the 1920s. In the 1950s demolition was considered, but the building's survival was ensured, thanks to its designation as a National Historic Landmark. The Pension Building is now the home of the National Building Museum (NBM), created in 1980 by congressional mandate to commemo-

rate American architecture. Since 1885 the Great Hall has been the setting of **inaugural balls** for 13 presidents.

VISIT

🕐*Open year-round Mon–Sat 10am–5pm, Sun 11am–5pm.* 🕐*Closed Jan 1, Thanksgiving Day & Dec 25.* 🎟*$8.* 👥*Guided tours (45min) daily 11:30 am, 12:30pm & 1:30pm. Family tours (30min) Sat 10:30am, 11am & Sun 1pm.* ✕&. 📞*202-272-2448.* *www.nbm.org.*

Measuring 116ft by 316ft, the vast interior court known as the **Great Hall** is punctuated by eight 75ft Corinthian columns made of brick and painted to resemble Siena marble. These colossal pieces of solid masonry support the central roof, through which light floods. The court is flanked by two stories of galleries lined with 72 Doric and 72 Ionic columns. The third-floor parapet is dotted with plaster replicas of terra-cotta urns originally designed for the building. In the cornice of the hall's central section high above the colossal columns, 244 niches (best seen from the upper floors) contain life-size busts symbolic of American builders and craftsmen. Deep-set brick stairways are covered by pure-lined barrel and groin vaulting. The exhibit Washington: Symbol and City *(1st floor),* featuring models of prominent monuments, offers an overview of the development of architecture in the nation's capital.

Old Post Office

Ⓜ *Federal Triangle*

Saved from the wrecker's ball at the eleventh hour, this rejuvenated Pennsylvania Avenue landmark has been converted into a "festival market" that attracts residents and tourists throughout the year.

A BIT OF HISTORY

Designed in the then-outmoded Richardsonian Romanesque style, the massive granite structure met with public disfavor after its completion in 1899. Built as the headquarters of the US Postal Service, the building greatly deteriorated in the decades following the postmaster general's 1934 move. In 1971 demolition was approved, but preservation groups saved the structure ultimately transforming it into a multi-functional complex.

VISIT

🕐*Tower open Memorial Day– Labor Day Mon–Sat 9am–7:45pm, Sun 10am–5:45pm; rest of the year Mon–Sat 9am–4:45pm, Sun noon–5:45pm.* 🕐*Closed Jan 1, Thanksgiving Day & Dec 25.* ✕ ♿ ✆*202-606-8691. www.oldpostofficedc.com.*

▶ **Location:** Pennsylvania Ave. and 12th St. NW. By Metrto: Walk from Metro Center (Red, Blue & Orange lines), Federal Triangle (Blue & Orange lines), Archives-Navy Memorial (Green & Yellow lines) stations.

🅿 **Parking:** Limited paid street and garage parking.

👪 **Kids:** Ice cream cones at Ben & Jerry's.

Interior

The central glass-roofed **courtyard** (160ft high) is surrounded by seven floors of offices. The first three levels host cafes, fast-food stands, souvenir shops and a stage for entertainment.

Tower

A glass elevator *(in the courtyard's north-west corner)* takes visitors to the top of the 315ft clock tower.

Near the summit are the **Congress bells**, which are played every Thursday night and on special occasions. The observation deck, the area's second-highest public vantage point offers a **view** of the surroundings.

Old Post Office

©Zain Deane/Michelin

FOGGY BOTTOM★★

Once industrialized riverfront, this bottomland lying west of the White House was transformed after World War II into an administrative quarter. Today it houses private institutions, government departments, a celebrated performing arts complex and the George Washington University campus in the middle of the city.

Highlights

1 Admiring the American decorative arts of the **Diplomatic Reception Rooms** (p177)

2 A jazz performance on the intimate Terrace Theater of the **Kennedy Center** (p180)

3 Learning about Federal-style architecture at **The Octagon** (p181)

A Bit of History
Breweries and Gasworks

In the early 19C a glassworks and brewery attracted Germans here, but the area called Foggy Bottom—because of the mists and smoke that rolled off the Potomac—developed slowly. In 1856 the Washington Gas Light Storage Facility was built here and became a major employer, particularly for the Irish immigrants who lived in Connaught Row, south of Virginia Avenue. While two breweries employed many of the German residents. The area's growing African-American population commissioned James Renwick to design **St. Mary's Episcopal Church**. Established in 1886, the Gothic Revival church is found at 728 23rd Street.

Transformation

In 1912 **George Washington University** opened in the neighborhood's northern end while the lowlands remained industrial with substandard housing. In 1947 the State Department moved into a large, new headquarters at 23rd and D streets. The century-old gas plant ceased operations and a new era began for Foggy Bottom.

In the 1950s the neighborhood shifted to middle-class professional. Office-residential buildings went up and in the 1960s the Potomac shoreline became the

Info: ☎202-661-7581; www.culturaltourismdc.org.

Location: This neighborhood lies west of the White House and south of Washington Circle, extending eastward from the Potomac River.

Parking: Garage parking at the Kennedy Center for patrons; limited metered spaces in the immediate area of the State Department.

Don't Miss: A free performance (daily 6pm) at the Kennedy Center's Millennium Stage.

Timing: Reserve your State Rooms visit 90 days in advance. Group the sights geographically, given the distances between them; and see Kennedy Center by attending a performance.

site of the **John F. Kennedy Center for the Performing Arts**. Beside it stands the exclusive **Watergate complex** of condominiums and shops. In the 1970s the complex gained notoriety as the site of the break-in that led to President Richard Nixon's resignation. Pleasant 19C row houses can still be found near the university (18th-25th Sts. and E-K Sts.). The **World Bank** (1818 H St.), the **Pan-American Health** and **WHO** (both at 523 23rd St.) operate their headquarters in the southern quarter. The north side of Constitution Avenue is lined with the **Department of the Interior** (1937), the **Federal Reserve** buildings (1937), the **American Pharmaceutical Assn.** (1934) and the **National Academy of Sciences** (1924), where a whimsical Albert Einstein memorial attracts curious passersby.

Diplomatic Reception Rooms★★

Ⓜ *Foggy Bottom*

Housed in an undistinguished 1960s government office building, these reception rooms have been transformed into architectural masterpieces of 18C interior design. They are furnished with one of the most impressive collections of American decorative arts in the country.

▷ **Location:** Department of State. 23rd St. between C and D Sts. NW. Take the Blue or Orange Metro Line to the Foggy Bottom station and walk 5 blocks south to the station

👥 **Kids:** Tours are not recommended for children younger than 12 years old.

🅿 **Parking:** There is very limited metered street parking.

A BIT OF HISTORY

When the State Department headquarters building opened in 1961, its eighth-floor rooms, used for official functions in honor of visiting dignitaries, were furnished in a stark, streamlined decor in keeping with the building's concrete and glass modernism. Before long, an effort called the **Americana Project**, under the direction of the Fine Arts Committee of the State Department, was begun to upgrade these reception areas.

Spearheaded by Clement E. Conger, then the department's deputy chief of protocol and curator of the White House, the project solicited private donors for contributions of funds and furnishings. Over the past decades, it has amassed a collection of **American decorative arts**★★ from the period 1725-1825 valued at approximately $90 million.

Edward Vason Jones, a Georgia architect, dedicated the last 15 years of his life to redesigning the rooms in the style of great 18C American manor houses. The ornately plastered ceilings, pilasters, paneling, entablatures and pediments complement the fine furnishings. Today the secretary of state, vice president and presidential cabinet members entertain world leaders and dignitaries in the regal rooms.

VISIT

🔊 Visit by guided tour (45min) only, by 90-day advance reservation via https://receptiontours.state.gov or a congressional office, year-round Mon–Fri 9:30am, 10:30am & 2:45pm. Photo ID required. 🕐Closed major holidays. ♿ ℘202-647-3241. https://diplomaticrooms.state.gov.

From the austere modernism of the building lobby, elevators ascend to the Edward Vason Jones Memorial Hall. Originally a nondescript elevator hall, it now serves as an elegant **foyer** appointed with marbleized pilasters and entablatures and rare King of Prussia gray marble floors.

The **Entrance Hall** contains the Chippendale furnishings, oriental rugs and English cut-glass chandeliers characteristic of the 18C American decor

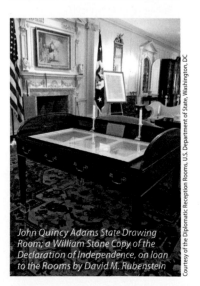

John Quincy Adams State Drawing Room; a William Stone Copy of the Declaration of Independence, on loan to the Rooms by David M. Rubenstein

Courtesy of the Diplomatic Reception Rooms, U.S. Department of State, Washington, DC

Painted History

The State Department's reception Rooms are famous for their historic furnishings but they also house an impressive collection of paintings. Keep an eye out for these pieces of painted American history: *View on the Kiskeminitas* by Joshua Shaw; *The Key House* by John Ross Key; *Spirit of '76* by Archibald McNeal Willard; *Boston Harbor* by Fitz Hugh Lane; and *The Flutist*, by an unknown artist.

seen throughout most of the reception rooms. The mahogany bombé secretary-bookcase in this hall is the oldest dated and signed piece of bombé furniture in North America. It was made by Benjamin Frothingham of Boston in 1753.

A short passageway opens onto the **Gallery**, a long, narrow room that was lightened and enlarged by adding Palladian windows at either end. Among the **Chippendale** and **Queen Anne furniture** is a bombé chest of drawers made in Boston about 1765 and considered one of the finest examples of its kind in the world. Also made in Boston about the same time, the mahogany secretary belonged to an 18C colonial shipping magnate of Massachusetts.

Two portraits by John Singleton Copley hang here. The five-part breakfront holds Chinese export porcelain in the Fitzhugh pattern. Ordered from England about 1800, the 65-piece set arrived in Philadelphia with an incorrect family monogram. It remained in its original shipping boxes until put on display here. In the large 18C-style **John Quincy Adams State Drawing Room**, guests are greeted by officials and other dignitaries in receiving lines. Wall paneling, door and window cornices, an elaborate mantelpiece and oriental rugs ornament this formal room. Portraits of Mr. and Mrs. John Quincy Adams hang on the walls. The original **portrait of John Jay** (1784) by Gilbert Stuart is considered the finest painting in the collection. The English Sheraton tambour,

or desk, where Jay signed the Treaty of Paris, Britain's formal acceptance of American Independence, is among the room's furnishings, as is the simple architectural desk on which Thomas Jefferson may have drafted the *Declaration of Independence*. The room also houses an oval oil on wood portrait of George Washington by American artist Charles Willson Peale. The story goes that Peale set up his easel alongside that of his 17-year-old son Rembrandt Peale and the two painted the founding father. It is the elder Peale's portrait that can be seen in the State Department.

The Neoclassical proportions and Doric entablature of the **Thomas Jefferson State Reception Room** reflect Jefferson's own architectural tastes. A copy of the David Anger statue of Jefferson that stands in the US Capitol occupies a pedimented niche at the end of the room. Several Jefferson portraits, including Thomas Sully's 1822 work, are on display. A fine pastel portrait of Benjamin Franklin by Jean-Baptiste Greuze also hangs here. The Savonnerie carpet is a reproduction of one originally made for the palace at Versailles.

The cavernous **Benjamin Franklin State Dining Room** was redesigned by John Blatteau and completed in 1985. Red-veined scagliola columns are set off by gilded capitals and entablatures. An 8,000-pound **Savonnerie** rug in rose and gold covers the floor, and eight cut-glass chandeliers flank a gilded Great Seal of the US in the ceiling. Above the mantel hangs Benjamin Franklin's favorite portrait of himself, painted by David Martin.

The elegant **Marta Washington Ladies Lounge** is adorned with a Ming-type Chinese rug from the late 1800s. Note the rare Massachusetts table with candle slides in front of the New York Settee. The matching Portsmouth high chest and dressing table and a Philadelphia Queen Anne Armchair help complete the room named for the country's very first, First Lady.

John F. Kennedy Center for the Performing Arts★★

Ⓜ *Foggy Bottom*

Its gleaming horizontal mass dominating Foggy Bottom's riverfront, the Kennedy Center today ranks as one of the country's leading cultural institutions. Designation as the capital's official memorial to the 35th president of the US has greatly contributed to the center's popularity as a tourist attraction.

- ▷ **Location:** New Hampshire Ave. at Rock Creek Parkway. Take the guided tour; it's free and lasts about 1hr.
- 🅿 **Parking:** The center's underground garage (*$20 if attending a performance*).
- 😊 **Don't Miss:** A performance here.
- 👤 **Kids:** A show in the Family Theater.

A BIT OF HISTORY
"A Living Memorial"
Although the idea of establishing a national cultural center in Washington dates back to the early days of the capital, it was only in 1958 that such an undertaking received congressional approval. In that year President Eisenhower signed the National Cultural Center Act authorizing the creation of a national showplace for the arts.

A prime Foggy Bottom site comprising just under 10 acres of government property was chosen for the facility's location, and architect Edward Durell Stone was commissioned to design the complex.

Due to a lack of sufficient private funds, the project lagged until early 1964, when Congress unanimously voted to designate the center as the capital's only monument to assassinated President John F. Kennedy. Unlike the other presidential memorials erected in Washington, the John F. Kennedy Center for the Performing Arts, as the complex was renamed, was to be "a living memorial." To hasten construction of the privately funded project, Congress appropriated $23 million in federal matching funds. The groundbreaking ceremony took place in December 1964. More than 40 foreign governments offered gifts—primarily works of art—to adorn the presidential memorial.

To mark the center's official opening on 8 September, 1971, the world premiere of Leonard Bernstein's *Mass* was performed in the Opera House.

The Kennedy Center launched their "Performing Arts for Everyone" initiative in 1997 which aims to expand the access to the performing arts to a wider audience through education and by making low- and no-cost tickets available for many performances.

Operation of the Center
Headed by a board of trustees appointed by the US president, the Kennedy Center operates as a nonprofit institution supported by private gifts and ticket sales.

Opera House

©Scott Suchman

As a presidential memorial, the building and its property (excluding theater and administrative facilities) are maintained by the National Park Service.

The complex houses six theaters with a total seating capacity of over 7,000, as well as an educational resource center. Home of the National Symphony Orchestra, the Kennedy Center also produces and presents jazz, pop, folk and world music. Alongside the musical offerings, the center schedules a wide spectrum of world-class entertainment in dance, multi-media performances and theater, including hit Broadway shows and the Royal Shakespeare Company.

VISIT

🕐 *Open year-round daily 10am–9pm.* 🚶 *Guided tours (1hr) Mon–Fri 10am– 4:30pm, Sat–Sun 10am–1pm.* 📞 *202- 416-8345 (to join a tour, go to Tour Office on Level A). Tickets must be purchased for most performances.* ✕ ♿ 🅿 📞 *202- 467-4600. www.kennedy-center.org.* 🚌 *Free shuttle to/from Foggy Bottom Metro station and Kennedy Center every 15min Mon–Sat 9:45am–midnight, Sun and holidays 11:45am–midnight.*

Exterior

The low rectangular structure (630ft by 300ft) is surrounded on all sides by a colonnade of metal piers supporting a roof terrace, above which rises the building's central section. Clad in white Carrara marble (a gift from Italy), the stark structure seems to echo the overall design of the Lincoln Memorial, situated just a half mile downstream.

Interior

The two principal entrances, situated on the east facade, lead to a pair of lofty galleries clearly designed to inspire awe. The dizzying effect experienced upon entering is created by the relative narrowness of these spaces.

The **Hall of States** (*north side*) displays flags of the 50 states, while the **Hall of Nations** (*south side*) is decked with flags of all foreign countries diplomatically accredited by the US. These parallel halls traverse the building's width, separating the three main auditoriums and ultimately connecting with the **Grand Foyer**, reputedly one of the largest rooms in the world (630ft long, 40ft wide, 60ft high). Occupying the entire length of the river facade, this awesome space is lined with 60ft-high mirrors (a gift from Belgium) that reflect the river terrace outside the foyer's floor-to-ceiling windows.

Eighteen Orrefors crystal chandeliers (donated by Sweden) illuminate the gigantic expanse. In the central section of the foyer, note the expressive bronze bust of President Kennedy by Robert Berks.

The foyer serves as a vestibule to the three main auditoriums: the **Opera House** (2,300 seats), flanked by the **Concert Hall** (2,442 seats) and the **Eisenhower Theater** (1,100 seats). Renowned for their excellent acoustics, these theaters contain gifts, in the form of stage curtains, chandeliers and artwork, from foreign countries that contributed to the project.

Occupying the former site of the American Film Institute Film Theater, the **Family Theater** (324 seats) made its debut in December 2005 and has been a hot ticket for DC families ever since. Incorporating state-of-the-art technology, the theater stages performances geared to the young like the 2010 Kennedy Center -commissioned musical based on the popular children's book *Knuffle Bunny*. (AFI moved to new facilities in Silver Spring, Maryland.)

The roof level (*accessible by elevators in the Hall of States and Hall of Nations*) houses two additional theaters, the educational resource center, restaurants and exhibit spaces.

A gift from Japan, the **Terrace Theater** (*off the north gallery*) was designed by noted architects Philip Johnson and John Burgee. This performance space is home to the popular Kennedy Center Jazz Club. *Shear Madness* has been playing in the **Theater Lab** (350 seats) for more than 20 years, making it the second longest running play in American theater (the first is the Boston production of the same show).

The Octagon★

Ⓜ *Farragut West*

One of Washington's earliest and finest residences, this many-sided architectural gem played a decided role in the history of the young Republic. Still retaining its Federal appearance, the Octagon houses period rooms and a gallery of exhibits organized under the auspices of the American Architectural Foundation, which administers the property and is working to restore it.

▷ **Location:** 1799 New York Ave. NW. Take the Metro to the Farragut West station (Blue & Orange lines) or Farragut North (Red line). By Bus: Take the 52, 80, 81 or S1.

🅿 **Parking:** Limited metered street parking and some paid garages.

🕐 **Timing:** Call ahead to arrange a tour and to check if the house is open.

A BIT OF HISTORY

Historical Role

In the 1790s, wealthy Virginia planter, Col. John Tayloe commissioned Dr. William Thornton to build a town house for him. Tayloe's lot was triangular. To harmonize the house with its setting, Thornton conceived a multisided structure. The Tayloes used it as their winter residence after its completion in 1801, entertaining the capital's most influential figures here.

During the 1814 burning of Washington by the British, the French Minister was in residence at the house, and at his request, the British spared the Octagon. The White House, however, was gutted by fire, and while it was being repaired, President Madison lived in the Octagon. During the Madisons' stay, peace was negotiated, ending the War of 1812. The Treaty of Ghent, signed by the British in Ghent, Belgium, on 24 December 1814, was brought to Washington and signed by James Madison at the Octagon, on 17 February 1815.

Decline and Revival

By the time of Mrs. Tayloe's death in 1855, the house had deteriorated. By the late 19C it had become an ill-kept tenement, but its architectural integrity attracted the **American Institute of Architects** (AIA). In 1902 the institute purchased the building, moved its headquarters here and began a meticulous restoration. In 1972 the AIA built the modern structure that wraps around the rear of the Octagon to house its offices, library facilities and bookstore. The courtyard that separates the buildings features a sculpture by James Rosati titled *Triple Arc 1* (1984).

VISIT

🕐*Open Jun–Aug Wed–Fri 1pm–4pm. Rest of the year Thu–Fri 1pm–4pm. The gift shop in the back of the museum is open during regular business hours.* 📞*202-626-7439. www.theoctagon.org.*

Though its name suggests eight sides, this brick structure is actually six-sided, with a rounded front pavilion that serves as an entrance foyer. The main hall is dominated by an oval staircase. Opening off the main hall are two large public

The Octagon

The American Institute of Architects

181

rooms, furnished in Federal style. The drawing and dining rooms are notable for their rare mantels of Coade stone, an artificial material produced in England until the mid-19C. In the symmetrical, Adam-style dining room hang portraits of Col. and Mrs. Tayloe by Gilbert Stuart. The circular study on the second floor is known as the **Treaty of Ghent Room**. President Madison signed the historic document at the round mahogany table in the center of the room. The two flanking rooms are devoted to changing exhibits on architecture.

The brick-floored basement houses a kitchen, servants' quarters and a wine cellar.

The Octagon's ever-expanding **Prints and Drawings Collection** has grown into an important repository of architectural records with more than 100,000 original architectural drawings, 30,000 historic photographs, scrapbooks, sketchbooks, manuscript material, and models. Among the gems of the collection are the drawings, correspondence and architectural records belonging to prominent 19C American Architect **Richard Morris Hunt**. Hunt holds the distinction of being the first American to complete the architecture program at the École des Beaux-Arts in Paris and was a founding member of the American Institute of Architects. Hunt designed the pedestal of the Statue of Liberty and the Metropolitan Museum of Art, Fifth Avenue.

White the Octagon is primarily known for its architectural collections and significance. it is also known for the ghost lore associated with it.

Many believe the historic house to be haunted and have claimed to see ghosts appear within its walls.

Among the spirits thought to inhabit the Octagon is that of former resident and First Lady Dolley Madison.

B'nai B'rith Klutznick National Jewish Museum

Ⓜ *Farragut North or Farragut West*

Sponsored by B'nai B'rith International, the world's oldest Jewish service organization, this small museum (seventh floor) houses a collection of Judaic ceremonial, folk and fine art.

VISIT

🕓 *Visit by advance reservation only.*
🚫 *Closed Jewish holidays and major holidays.* ♿ 📞 *202-857-6647.*
http://bnaibrith.org/prog_serv/ museum.cfm.

Changing exhibits from the permanent collection feature antique and contemporary ritual objects such as Sabbath candlesticks, spice boxes, torah scrolls, menorahs and Kiddush cups.

▷ **Location:** 2020 K St. NW. Walking distance from either the Farragut North Metro Station (Red line) or the Farragut West (Blue & Orange lines).

🅿 **Parking:** Limited metered street parking and several paid garages nearby.

🕓 **Timing:** Allow about 30 minutes for the tour.

The museum's collection also contains several original pieces by famous Jewish artists Marc Chagall, Ben Zion, Yosi Bergner, and Philip Ratner.

Photographic and other temporary exhibits sometimes go on display.

Department of the Interior Museum

Ⓜ *Farragut West*

This museum dating back to the 1930s, located in the Interior Department building (first floor), showcases the department's mission.

A BIT OF HISTORY

In 1849 Congress created the Department of the Interior to conserve and manage the country's natural resources, including public lands, mineral resources, forests and wildlife.

The department was also given the responsibility for American Indian reservations and the US island territories. Today, the department's principal bureaus are Reclamation, Indian Affairs, Land Management, Minerals Management, Surface Mining, US Geological Survey, US Fish and Wildlife, and National Park Service. In 1935 Secretary of the Interior Harold Ickes suggested that space for a museum be included in the Interior building, which was completed in 1936. Opened in 1938, the museum contained a gallery for every bureau to display its equipment, documents, maps, models, natural history specimens and other artifacts. The museum became such a popular attraction that opening hours had to be extended into the evening and maintained even during World War II.

VISIT

🕑*The Interior Museum is closed for renovation indefinitely.* ♿ ☎*202-208-4743. www.doi.gov/interiormuseum.*.
Seven bureaus have gallery space in the museum. The Bureau of Mines closed in 1996, but its exhibit continues to be on display.

Throughout the museum **dioramas** depict historic or characteristic scenes from the nation's past, such as the meeting of generals Washington and Lafayette at Morristown in 1780 and

> **Location:** Department of the Interior Building. C St. between 18th and 19th Sts. NW. By Metro: Exit the Farragut West (Blue or Orange line) on the 18th St side and walk 5 blocks south.
>
> 🅿 **Parking:** Some metered street parking nearby.
>
> **Don't Miss:** The Native American crafts and jewelry for sale in the gift shop.

a 19C Indian trading post in 1835. The dioramas, and the **metal cutouts** of the first two sections, were executed by artists in the 1930s.

The **Native American section**— featuring a canoe, pottery and baskets—presents only a small fraction of the department's extensive collection. In the passageway leading to the other exhibits hang four paintings by artist William H. Jackson depicting some of the earliest survey teams on assignment in the West during the second half of the 19C. Working from authentic period photographs, Jackson executed these paintings in 1938 when he was in his 90s. Surveying equipment used at the turn of the 19C, as well as facsimiles of early documents granting land to homesteaders and to military personnel, are found in the section devoted to the Bureau of Land Management.

Artifacts from various Pacific islands, such as Micronesia, the Marshall Islands and American Samoa include watercraft and a wooden Palauan storyboard.

During the renovation, the museum **shop** across the hall remains open. Here Native American arts, jewelry, baskets, pottery and other crafts are for sale (🕑*open year-round Mon–Fri 8:30am–4:30pm; third Sat of the month 10am–4pm; photo ID is required to enter the building where the shop is housed;* 🕑*closed federal holidays;* ♿ ☎*202-208-4056; www.indiancraftshop.com).*

One of Washington's most popular neighborhoods, Georgetown is a mix of fashionable nightspots, restaurants and shops surrounded by picturesque residential streets. Predating Washington itself, this historic quarter functions as a well-preserved village, bounded on the south by the Potomac and on the east by Rock Creek. Congressional representatives, foreign dignitaries and the capital's intelligentsia live in many of its impeccably restored late-18C and 19C row houses.

Highlights

1 Viewing the Potomac from **Washington Harbour** (p185)
2 Strolling along the historic **canal towpath** (p186)
3 Admiring elegant architecture on **N Street** (p187)
4 Peace and tranquility in the garden of **Dumbarton Oaks** (p188)

Info: Georgetown Visitor Center; 1057 Thomas Jefferson St. NW; ℘202-653-5190; www.nps.gov/choh/planyourvisit.georgetownvisitorcenter.htm. Open weekends only.

Location: In the northwest quadrant of Washington, DC. Wisconsin Ave. and M Street are Georgetown's main commercial thoroughfares. The neighborhood is located on the Potomac River waterfront.

Parking: Garages are scarce. There is no Metrorail service, so you may want to take the bus line (nos. 31, 32 and 36) that runs from Washington along M St. and Wisconsin Ave.

Timing: Allow a full day.

A Rock and a Knave

In 1703 Ninian Beall, a Scottish immigrant, patented a 795-acre tract on which most of present-day Georgetown now stands. Thirty years later George Gordon acquired an adjacent tract of land and established a tobacco inspection house on it. A small settlement of Scottish immigrants began to grow up here, and in 1751 the inhabitants petitioned the Maryland Provisional Assembly to establish a town.

The assembly agreed, appointing commissioners to negotiate the sale of lots on the lands of George Gordon and those of George Beall, who had inherited his father's holdings. To this day historians have not reached a consensus on the town's namesake—former owners George Gordon and George Beall or King George II.

The Golden Age

Positioned at the head of the Potomac, Georgetown thrived in the late 18C as a port of entry for foreign goods and as an exporter of products from the Ohio Valley in the West. Even during the Revolution the town prospered, as a base of supplies and munitions.

After the war, the town continued to thrive. Well established and respected, Georgetown was considered the "court end" of the still rough federal city. During this golden age, such grand manors as Evermay (1623 28th St.) and Tudor Place dotted the hills of upper Georgetown, and elegant Federal-style town houses lined its lower residential streets. In 1789 the country's first Catholic institution of higher learning, Georgetown College—now **Georgetown University**—was founded.

Decline and Rebirth

By the late 1820s Georgetown found itself being eclipsed by Washington. In 1828 construction on the Chesapeake and Ohio Canal, with its eastern terminus in Georgetown, was begun

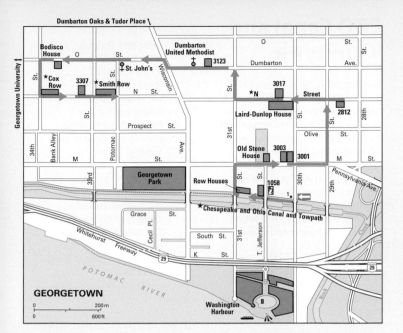

GEORGETOWN

```
0        200m
0        600ft
```

in an attempt to stimulate commerce and westward migration. As the canal was being built, so was the Baltimore and Ohio Railroad. Train travel slowly brought an end to barge transport. At the same time steam navigation, which required deeper ports than the town could provide, also grew in popularity. Georgetown's shipping business was doomed.

By mid-century, as the town continued its decline, residents began a movement to consolidate Georgetown and Washington, but those plans were waylaid by the Civil War. In 1871, with the war over, Georgetown was consolidated with the District of Columbia. Street names were changed to the letters and number system used in Washington.

From the late 19C through the first half of the 20C, Georgetown fell into decline. Though its great houses remained in the hands of the wealthy, many of its old row houses were divided into apartments and rooming houses. Only in the last 40 years has the neighborhood regained its prestige.

Under the Old Georgetown Act of 1950, the area was declared a National Historic District. Demolition, new construction and renovation are subject to review by the Commission of Fine Arts.

Today Georgetown's residential streets, with their carefully restored Federal-style and mid-19C houses, exude refinement. Georgetown's commercial district is concentrated around Wisconsin Avenue and M Street, which are lined with numerous restaurants and small trendy boutiques. **Georgetown Park**, an urban mall, sits at the intersection of these two streets. Anchoring the intersection of these two main thoroughfares is the golden dome of the former Riggs National Bank, a prominent Georgetown landmark. Along the canal and the waterfront, redevelopment has generally taken the form of large brick office complexes. An exception is the riverfront showcase **Washington Harbour** (1986), a glittery complex of condominiums, offices, shops and restaurants. Its elaborately terraced and fountained courtyard affords a pretty **view** down the Potomac.

The old **towpath** along the canal, saved through the efforts of conservationists, remains a quiet pedestrian walkway reminiscent of the town's historic past.

C&O Canal and Vicinity★★

Georgetown is the terminus for the old **Chesapeake and Ohio Canal**, which runs 185 miles through 75 lift locks to Cumberland, Maryland. In 1971 the entire canal was designated a National Historic Park. At lift lock no. 3, a **bust (1)** of Supreme Court Justice William O. Douglas commemorates his work in spearheading the movement to preserve the canal as a recreation area for local people and visitors.

🐾 WALKING TOUR

🖐 For local map see p185

▷ *1.5 miles. Begin at the corner of the towpath and 30th St. NW.*

At the intersection with Thomas Jefferson Street, the brick Federal structure (c.1810) at **no. 1058** originally housed the Potomac Masonic Lodge, whose early members were present at the laying of the Capitol's cornerstone.
The quaint **row houses** along the towpath were built after the Civil War as residences for artisans and laborers.

🛈 **Info:** 1057 Thomas Jefferson St. NW; 📞202-653-5190; www.nps.gov/choh.
▷ **Location:** See the local map in this chapter.
🅿 **Parking:** Nearby street parking is difficult to find.
🕐 **Timing:** Follow the walking tour (allow 45min) by beginning with a leisurely stroll along the canal. When you have completed the tour, be sure to stop for lunch or a snack at one of the many restaurants along M Street.
👁 **Don't Miss:** Cox Row and Smith Row.

▷ *Turn right on 31st St. and then right on M St., one of Georgetown's main thoroughfares.*

Old Stone House

3051 M St. 🕐*Open year-round daily noon–5pm.* 🚫*Closed major holidays.* 📞*202-895-6070. www.nps.gov/olst.*
The front of this two-story house, one of the oldest structures in Washing-

C & O Canal

©Zain Deane/Michelin

ton, was built by Christopher Layman around 1765. Since 1960 the National Park Service has maintained it as a visitor center and museum. Note the paneling in the dining room. A large garden in the rear offers a respite from the bustle of M Street.

▷ *Continue east on M St.*

The twin buildings at nos. 3037 and 3039 (known as the Nathan Loughborough houses) date from the turn of the 19C. The Junior League of Washington, a women's civic organization, restored them in 1963 and now uses them as its DC headquarters. The late-18C buildings at **nos. 3001** and **3003** were the home of Thomas Sim Lee, governor of Maryland and friend of George Washington. In 1951 the buildings were saved from demolition under the strictures of the Old Georgetown Act.

▷ *Turn left on 29th St., then right on N St.*

N Street★

This handsome street contains some of the finest Federal-style architecture in the city. The elegant brick residence at **no. 2812** was built in the early 19C.

▷ *Return to the corner of N and 29th Sts. and continue to 30th St.*

A bastion of Southern support during the Civil War, the **3000 block of N Street** boasts many of Georgetown's most distinguished town houses.
At the corner of N and 30th streets stands the **Laird-Dunlop House** (no. 3014), a brick building constructed in 1799 by John Laird, a wealthy tobacco merchant. Laird's daughter Barbara married James Dunlop, a law partner of Francis Scott Key, who penned *The Star-Spangled Banner*. In 1915 Abraham Lincoln's son Robert Todd, who had been a secretary of War and minister to Britain, bought the house from Dunlop heirs. He added the attached dwelling at no. 3018.

The large house across the street at **no. 3017** was built in the 1790s by Thomas Beall, descendant of one of the original Georgetown landowners. **Jacqueline Kennedy** briefly lived here in 1963, after President Kennedy's death. The dwelling at no. 3038, with its elegant doorway and shingled dormers, is a fine example of the smaller town houses built during the early 19C.

▷ *Turn right on 31st St. and left on Dumbarton Ave.*

Surrounded by a lush garden and a white picket fence, the imposing residence at **3123 Dumbarton Avenue** was built by Henry Foxall, a prominent Georgetown businessman. Dating back to the early 19C, the house is considered one of the area's most architecturally pristine structures. According to local legend it also houses a famous Georgetown ghost—a maiden lady who came to luncheon at the McKenneys' and never left.
The yellow-brick **Dumbarton United Methodist Church** *(no. 3133)* was constructed in 1849 in the Romanesque Revival style. During the Civil War the church was used as a hospital, and poet Walt Whitman, serving as a nurse, ministered to the Union wounded here. The current facade was added in 1894.

▷ *Continue across Wisconsin Ave. and turn left on O St.*

Note the remnants of the old trolley track embedded in this brick-paved street.

St. John's Church

3240 O St. ◷*Open year-round Mon–Thu 9am–4pm, Fri 9am–3pm, Sun 9am–noon.* ◷*Closed major holidays except Thanksgiving Day & Dec 25.* ♿ *☎202-338-1796. www.stjohnsgeorgetown.orgv.*
Built between 1796 and 1804, the interior walls of this Federal-style stucco structure make it the oldest Episcopal church in Georgetown. Thomas Jefferson donated money for its building, and Francis Scott Key served as one of its

Georgetown

©Zain Deane/Michelin

vestrymen. In 1831 the church was abandoned due to lack of funds. Financier and art patron William Wilson Corcoran purchased it as a philanthropic gesture in 1837 and gave it back to the church. The 3300 block of O Street has a typical Georgetown mix of Federal and late-19C structures.

Bodisco House

3322 O St. Built about 1815, the, porticoed Federal dwelling was home to Robert E. Lee's mother after she left Alexandria. The residence most renowned occupant was Baron Alexander de Bodisco, the Russian minister to the US in the mid-19C. At that time the structure housed the Russian legation. The 62-year-old baron married a 16-year-old Georgetown belle, Harriott Beall Williams. The couple threw lavish parties in the house that became a focal point of Georgetown society.

○ *Turn left on 34th St. and left again on N St.*

Cox Row★

This handsome group of five Federal houses (nos. 3339-3327), adorned with swags and high dormers, was built in 1805 by Col. John Cox. Georgetown's first mayor elected by popular vote, Cox held that office for 22 years (1823-45). No. 3339 was Cox's home for a time. In 1824 he entertained the Marquis de Lafayette in no. 3337.

Sen. **John F. Kennedy** purchased **no. 3307** in 1957 as a present for his wife. The Kennedys lived here until moving into the White House in 1961. This house and its twin at no. 3311 were built in 1811.

Like several Federal period Georgetown homes, the facade of the building at no. 3311 has been embellished with 19C Italianate detailing.

Smith Row★

An unbroken, manicured block of Federal row houses extends from no. 3267 to no. 3255. Their exteriors have been little altered since they were built by Clement and Walter Smith in 1815.

Dumbarton Oaks★★

Renowned for its outstanding collection of Byzantine and pre-Columbian art, this museum and research institution is situated on a 16-acre estate set on a ridge above Rock Creek Park. The harmonious ensemble of buildings is surrounded by beautiful gardens.

A BIT OF HISTORY
The Oaks

In 1800 and 1801 Sen. William Dorsey of Maryland purchased 22 acres on the northern edge of Georgetown, and constructed the brick Federal-style home still standing at Dumbarton. He and his family lived here for only a year before personal and financial problems forced Dorsey to sell. The property passed through a succession of prominent owners, among them Edward Linthicum, a self-made businessman who, in the 1860s, added substantial wings to the original structure and renamed it "The Oaks," because of the stand of white oaks surrounding it.

A Marriage of Taste and Wealth

In 1920 Robert and Mildred Bliss purchased the estate. The Blisses had known each other from adolescence, because their widowed parents had wed, making them stepbrother and stepsister. Cultured, widely traveled and independently wealthy, the Blisses transformed Dumbarton Oaks, as they renamed it, into an elegant "country house in the city." With the help of the architectural firm McKim, Mead and White, the interior was restructured and the exterior restored to its original Federal style. In 1929 a large music room was added. Beatrix Jones Farrand, a noted landscape architect, designed the extensive gardens.

Robert Bliss' career in the foreign service prevented the couple from living here until 1933. During their years abroad, they acquired Byzantine artifacts, and

> **Location:** 1703 32nd St. NW. To get to Dumbarton Oaks, take bus 31, 32 or 36, or bus D1 or D2 to Wisconsin Ave. and R St. and walk one block east on R St.
>
> **Parking:** Two-hour street parking near the museum on weekdays; unlimited street parking on Sun.
>
> **Don't Miss:** The gardens.

once settled at Dumbarton they continued collecting, amassing an extensive research library.

A west wing was added with two pavilions and an enclosed courtyard to function as a museum open to the public.

In 1940 the Blisses gave the house, grounds, their Byzantine collection, a library of some 14,000 volumes and an endowment to **Harvard University**, which maintains the estate. They also donated an adjacent 27-acre tract known as Dumbarton Oaks Park (*open year-round daily dawn–dusk*) to the National Park Service. In 1944 the famous **Dumbarton Oaks Conferences**, involving representatives from the US, the United Kingdom, China and the Soviet Union, were held at the Blisses' former home. The accords reached among the participants ultimately resulted in the creation of the United Nations.

MUSEUM

Museum open Tue Sun 2pm-5pm. Gardens open Tue Sun 2pm-6pm and close at 5pm Nov-Mar. Closed federal holidays (see opposite below). 202-339-6401. www.doaks.org.

Byzantine Collection★★

The collection comprises some 1,500 artifacts—all examples of the artistic production of the Byzantine empire, that held sway over the eastern Mediterranean region from the 4C to 15C. The collection of 12,000 Byzantine coins is one of the most extensive in the world. The columned interior courtyard is devoted to artifacts predating, or created on the periphery of, the Byzantine empire. Displays include late Roman and early Byzantine bas-reliefs, Roman glass and bronze (1-5C), textiles from Egypt and the eastern Mediterranean (6-12C) and a 6C Syrian floor mosaic. The adjacent gallery displays 6C ecclesiastical silver from the Sion Treasury, found in present-day Turkey, and Byzantine icons, lamps, liturgical vessels, crosses and enameled adornments.

Pre-Columbian Collection★

In 1962 Robert Bliss donated his pre-Columbian collection to Dumbarton Oaks, and commissioned architect **Philip Johnson** to design an addition to house it. Johnson's concept consists of eight circular, glass-walled pavilions built around a central fountain.

Arranged by cultures, the pavilions house Olmec figurines and masks *(Gallery II)*; Maya architectural reliefs and ceramics *(III-IV)*; stone yokes and axes from Veracruz *(V)*; gold jewelry from Central America *(VI)*; pottery, gold and tapestries from ancient Peruvian and Bolivian cultures *(VII)*; and Aztec carvings, frescoes, masks and vessels *(VIII)*.

Music Room★

This hall is dominated by a stone chimney piece from the Château de Thébon (16–17C) in France's Bordeaux region. The wooden ceiling beams are modeled on those in the 17C Château de Cheverny in the Loire Valley. Flemish and German tapestries hang on the walls, as does El Greco's *Visitation* (c.1610) *(left wall)*. The frescoes adorning the arched stair alcove *(far wall)* were painted by Allyn Cox, who executed many of the murals in the Capitol. During the Blisses' residency, a number of famous musicians performed here, including Ignace Paderewski, Nadia Boulanger and Igor Stravinsky, whose *Concerto in E-flat*, also known as the *Dumbarton Oaks Concerto*, was commissioned by the Blisses for their 30th anniversary.

A rotating selection of rare books from the permanent collection of the garden library is displayed in the hall to the right of the entrance pavilion. In 2008 both the house and the gardens underwent an extensive renovation and restoration programme.

GARDENS★★

Entrance at 31st and R Sts.
🕐*Open mid-Mar–Oct Tue–Sun 2pm–6pm. Rest of the year Tue–Sun 2pm–5pm.* 🚫*Closed major holidays and in inclement weather.* 💲*$8 (free Nov–early Mar).* 📞*202-339-6401. www.doaks.org.*
📖*In the flowering season, a map is available at the garden gate.*

A year after the Blisses purchased the 53-acre property, the couples hired famed landscape gardener Beatrix Jones Farrand (also Edith Wharton's niece) to design the gardens, beginning her almost 30 year relationship with the magnificent grounds and the family. Together with Mildred Bliss, Farrand planned every last detail of the garden from the benches to the floral borders to the decorative urns. Farrand designed broad terraces leading from the house to the lower garden, planted with flowering trees, shrubs and bulbs. The book Farrand wrote about the gardens is still referenced today by the groundskeepers and gardeners as a prized reference on keeping and preserving Dumbarton's treasured grounds.

Several elegant "garden rooms" function as extensions of the house itself. The grounds include 10 acres of formal terraces devoted to such plantings as rose and herb gardens. Paths lead to secluded fountains, pools, terraces and arbors, offset by flowering trees and shrubs. The centerpiece of the lovely **Pebble Garden**, added in the 1960s, is a shallow pool framed by Rococo borders of moss and paved with a mosaic of Mexican stones arranged to represent a wheat sheaf.

Tudor Place★

1644 31st St. NW

The landmark mansion and stately grounds of Tudor Place were home to the prominent Peter family for six generations. Today the estate functions as a house museum and a monument t o old Washington.

Location: To reach Tudor Place, take bus D1, D2 or D3 to 31st St.

Parking: Street parking is usually available.

A BIT OF HISTORY

Tudor Place was built as the home of Thomas Peter and his wife, Martha Custis Peter, the granddaughter of Martha Washington. In 1805, with the $8,000 inheritance Martha Peter received from her stepgrandfather, George Washington, the Peters purchased an 8-acre city block in Georgetown Heights. Dr. William Thornton, the first architect of the Capitol, designed the house. Thornton's project called for a two-story central structure to be joined to the preexisting east and west wings by means of one-story hyphens. The stuccoed brick mansion was finally completed in 1816.

At her death in 1854, Martha Peter left the estate to the youngest of the three Peter daughters, Britannia Wellington Peter Kennon, widowed after a year of marriage. During the Civil War, Britannia, a Southern sympathizer and relative of Robert E. Lee, allowed Union officers to stay at Tudor Place. 19C visitors include the Marquis de Lafayette, Andrew Jackson, Daniel Webster and John C.

Calhoun. The Tudor Place Foundation opened the house to the public in 1988.

VISIT

Mansion visit by guided tour (1hr) only, Feb–Dec hourly Tue–Sat 10am–3pm, Sun noon–3pm. $8. Grounds open Feb–Dec Mon–Sat 10am–4pm, Sun noon–4pm. $3. Closed major holidays. 202-965-0400. www.tudorplace.org.

The simple Federal-style north facade of the building fronts a boxwood-edged carriage drive. The centerpiece of the design is the circular south portico. The recessed semicircular wall of the portico projects into the interior, creating a convex glass wall in the central salon. A number of the furnishings come from Mount Vernon.

The 5 1/2 acres of **grounds** surrounding the house are devoted on the north side to more formal plantings, including a flower "knot," a circular garden and a bowling green. The south lawn slopes in a broad green expanse. Against the south facade of the house is a border of old roses, a few dating from Martha Custis Peter's time.

Tudor Place, South Facade

© Tudor Place Historic House and Gardens

Dumbarton House

This brick Federal-style house serves as a house museum and the headquarters of a national women's organization.

A BIT OF HISTORY

Built in the last years of the 18C, the house quickly passed through several owners until 1804, when it was purchased by Joseph Nourse, registrar of the US Treasury. In the early 20C, Georgian Revival quoins, balustrades and other embellishments were added, and in 1915 the house was moved 100 yards north to accommodate the eastward extension of Q Street.

After the move, the present east and west wings were added to the house. In 1928 the **National Society of the Colonial Dames of America**, a women's organization dedicated to historic preservation, bought the property and renamed it Dumbarton House, after the original Rock of Dumbarton tract that once included much of present-day Georgetown. With the consultation of the architectural preserver Fiske Kimball, the Dames had the house restored to its Federal appearance.

- ▷ **Location:** 2715 Q St. NW. Take the D-2 or D-6 busS or walk 6 blocks west from the Q Street exit of the Dupont Circle Metro stop.
- ⚇ **Kids:** Monthly family fun days.
- ◷ **Timing:** 45 min.
- ⊙ **Don't Miss:** The portrait of the Stoddert children.

VISIT

◷*Open year-round Tue–Sun 11am–3pm.* ☜*For guided tour, call 3 weekdays in advance.* ◷*Closed major holidays.* ✆*$5.* ♿▯ ✆*202-337-2288. www.dumbartonhouse.org.*

The exterior features a columned portico with a fanlight over the doorway and stone lintels above the windows. A sweeping staircase dominates the wide interior entrance hall, flanked by a formal library, a dining room, a music room and a parlor. The rooms, furnished in the Federal period, display china, crystal, quilts and clothing that belonged to Martha Washington and her granddaughter Eliza Custis Law. Also notable is a 1789 painting by Charles Willson Peale. It portrays the children of Benjamin Stoddert, first secretary of the US Navy,

Dumbarton House

© Dumbarton House

Dining Room Chamber

Dumbarton House

with a view of old Georgetown and the Potomac River in the background. The second floor contains four bedrooms, also furnished predominantly in the Fed-eral style. The Dumbarton House manu-script and document collection includes one of five original known copies of the Articles of Confederation.

Oak Hill Cemetery

One of the city's oldest cemeteries, Oak Hill occupies a wooded 25-acre tract of land along the west bank of Rock Creek.

A BIT OF HISTORY

William Wilson Corcoran, financier and founder of the Corcoran Gallery of Art, donated the original 15 acres of ground to the cemetery company, incorporated by Congress in 1849.

VISIT

Entrance at R and 30th Sts. ◷*Open year-round Mon–Fri 9am–4:30pm, Sun 1pm–4pm.* ◷*Closed major holidays and inclement weather.* ✆*202-337-2835. www.oakhillcemeterydc.org.* James Renwick, the architect of the Smithsonian Castle and the first Corco-ran Gallery (now the Renwick Gallery), designed the **Gothic Revival cha-**

▷ **Location:** 3001 R St. NW. To reach the cemetery, take bus 31, 32 or 36 to Wisconsin Ave. and R St. Walk east on R St. to 30th street.

◷ **Timing:** Leave at least an hour to walk some of the grounds.

⊙ **Don't Miss:** The Renwick Chapel and the Van Ness Mausoleum.

pel (1850) and the cast-iron gate that encloses the cemetery along R Street. Most graves date to the 19C. Corcoran's own grave is marked by a replica of a Doric temple, designed by 19C Capitol architect Thomas U. Walter. Among the many other prominent citizens buried here are John Howard Payne, composer of *Home, Sweet Home*; Dean Acheson, secretary of State under Truman; and relatives of George Washington.

193

ARLINGTON ACROSS THE RIVER★

Arlington is a mixture of high rises, middle-class neighborhoods and ethnic enclaves. Along its Potomac shoreline, a network of pleasant parkways, dotted with memorials and statues, connects Arlington to the capital.

Highlights

1 Changing of the Guard at the **Tomb of the Unknowns** (p196)

2 Paying your respects to John F. Kennedy at **Arlington National Cemetery** (p196)

3 Sweeping views of Washington, DC from **Arlington House** (p196)

4 The striking **Marine Corps War Memorial** (p200)

Info: A touch-screen visitors kiosk is available at the corner of N. Lynn and N. 19th Streets St.; ✆703-228-080; www.stayarlington.com.

Location: Arlington lies across the Potomac, west of The Mall.

Parking: Street parking and parking garages are available.

Timing: Allow 5hrs for Arlington sights if a tour of the Pentagon (1hr; two-week advance reservation required) is included in your itinerary.

The Beginnings

By the mid-17C, much of the present county had been claimed by absentee landholders. Chief among them were members of the Alexander family, after whom the town of Alexandria, established in 1748, is named. Throughout the colonial period and into the 19C, the Arlington region was bound, both administratively and economically, to Alexandria, which served as the urban focus for the small farms in the area.

Part of the Capital City

By a 1789 act of the Virginia General Assembly, land along the Potomac River was ceded for the new federal city. These former Virginia lands officially became the County of Alexandria of the District of Columbia. For the first half of the 19C, the current jurisdiction of Arlington was part of the capital. In 1846, disillusioned with their association with the nation's capital, the county's residents voted by public referendum to retrocede to Virginia.

War and Devastation

During the Civil War, Arlington's lands were occupied by Union forces guarding the southern flanks of the capital city against Confederate incursions. Robert E. Lee's own home, Arlington House, became the headquarters for various Union commanders.

After the war, Virginia's adoption of a new constitution added to the community's troubles. Under the 1870 law, cities with populations of 5,000 or more became independent units, separate from county jurisdictions leaving Arlington to fare on its own. It took 30 years to recover from the war, but business slowly returned. Between 1910 and 1920, Arlington's population grew by 60 percent, in large part due to an influx of workers in the World War I years. In 1920 the Virginia General Assembly recognized the county's growing prominence by changing its name from the County of Alexandria to Arlington County, named in honor of General Lee's Arlington home.

Arlington Today

In the last six decades, Arlington has continued its phenomenal growth, becoming a kind of suburb of DC. World War II saw federally funded housing for this white-collar work force sprout up in the southern part of the county, as did military buildings, including the Pentagon. More than 200,000 people now live in Arlington's 25.7sq mi.

Arlington National Cemetery★★

Ⓜ *Arlington Cemetery*

A sylvan retreat situated just minutes from the hubbub of the Mall, Arlington National Cemetery is the country's most revered burial ground and one of the capital's most poignant sights. This vast military cemetery, lined with endless rows of gleaming white headstones, contains the graves of a host of distinguished Americans.

A BIT OF HISTORY
A Vengeful Act

At the outbreak of the Civil War, Arlington House was established as the headquarters for the defense of Washington, and military installations were erected around the 1,100-acre estate. As much of the early fighting took place around the capital, the need for burial space soon became evident.

In 1864, Quartermaster-General of the Army Montgomery Meigs (the architect of the Pension Building), who was responsible for overseeing the appropriation of government land for military purposes, recommended that the grounds of Arlington House be used to inter war casualties. With the approval of secretary of War Edwin Stanton, 200 acres of the estate were designated as a burial ground and, on 13 May 1864, the first soldier was laid to rest there. Showing considerable vindictiveness toward Robert E. Lee, whom he viewed as a traitor, Meigs ensured that the first graves were situated in the immediate vicinity of the mansion as a deterrent to the return of the Lee family.

In 1883, following a Supreme Court decision that the Arlington estate should be returned to the Lees family, family members accepted $150,000 as compensation rather than demanding the restitution of the estate, which by that time contained the remains of some 16,000 war casualties.

▷ **Location:** The cemetery is located on the Arlington side of Memorial Bridge, about 3/4mi from the Lincoln Memorial. It is a short walk across Memorial Bridge. The cemetery has its own Metro stop on the Blue and Yellow lines, and is served by Metrobuses. It can be accessed by tour buses (☙*see Planning Your Trip*), such as **ANC Tours**, which operates within the cemetery, as well as **Big Bus Tours** and **Old Town Trolley**, both of which have an Arlington Cemetery stop.

🅿 **Parking:** Cross Memorial Bridge to the parking lot *(hourly charge)* situated adjacent to the visitor center.

◉ **Don't Miss:** Tomb of the Unknowns, Changing of the Guard, Arlington House.

🕐 **Timing:** The cemetery grounds can be explored on foot *(allow half a day and wear comfortable walking shoes)*. If you are pressed for time, ride the ANC Tour bus (☙*see above*), which makes stops at the most popular sights within the cemetery.

A National Shrine

Arlington became the official national cemetery of the US in 1883, the year of the Supreme Court decision.

The cemetery now comprises 612 acres and contains the graves of more than 300,000 military personnel, their dependents and others buried here. Among those laid to rest in the cemetery are veterans of every armed conflict in which the US has participated since the Revolutionary War.

Arlington National Cemetery

©Arlington National Cemetery

CEMETERY GROUNDS

🕐 *Open Apr–Sept daily 8am–7pm. Rest of the year daily 8am–5pm.* ♿ 🅿 🖉 *877-907-8585. www.arlington cemetery.org.* 🚗 *Car traffic is permitted only for disabled visitors and relatives of persons interred in the cemetery.*

The cemetery is situated on a tract of hilly terrain crisscrossed with meandering paved routes.

Situated at the entrance to the cemetery, the **Women in Military Service for America Memorial** is a testament to all US women who have served in the armed forces from the Revolutionary War to the present. Two US presidents are buried in Arlington Cemetery: President **William H. Taft** (1857-1930); and President **John F. Kennedy** (1917-63), whose simple grave is marked by an eternal flame. The grave of **Robert F. Kennedy** (1925-68), marked by a white cross, lies near to his older brother.

Designed by Carrère and Hastings, the 5,000-seat **Memorial Amphitheater** (1920) is used for special ceremonies such as Memorial Day and Veterans Day services. As the country's most prestigious burial ground, Arlington Cemetery has been chosen to house numerous **memorials** dedicated to special groups or particular events in the nation's history. Scattered throughout the cemetery, these memorials include group headstones, statues, plaques and even trees. Especially moving is the **Tomb of the Unknowns** *(located behind the Memorial Amphitheater)* containing the remains of soldiers from each of the two world wars and the Korean War.

The remains of these soldiers represent symbolically all the men and women who lost their lives in those conflicts as well as those who died in the Vietnam War. Not to be missed at the tomb is the **Changing of the Guard**, whereby visitors can witness the precision and skill of the military sentries (🕐 *Apr–Sept daily on the half-hour; rest of the year daily on the hour).*

The cemetery's most prominent memorial, Arlington House, occupies a hilltop site overlooking the cemetery.

ARLINGTON HOUSE/ THE ROBERT E. LEE MEMORIAL★

Surrounded by the white headstones of Arlington Cemetery, the dignified mansion that has been designated the official Robert E. Lee Memorial tops a high bluff overlooking Washington. Lee, hero of the Confederacy, called this his home for 30 years.

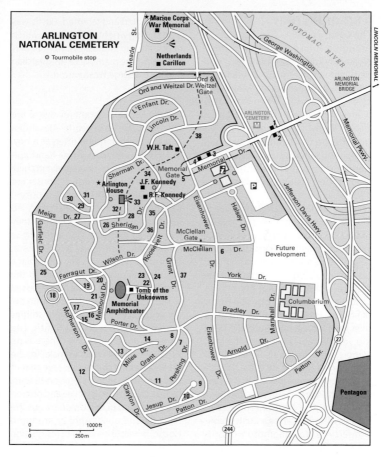

ARLINGTON NATIONAL CEMETERY

⊙ Tourmobile stop

1 Seabees Memorial
2 United Spanish War Veterans Memorial
3 Admiral Richard E. Byrd Memorial
4 101st Army Airborne Division Memorial
5 Women in Military Service for America Memorial
6 Memorial to service personnel killed in Beirut, 1983
7 *USS Serpens* Memorial
8 Mary Roberts Rinehart: mystery writer, war correspondent
9 William Jennings Bryan: Secretary of State
10 US Coast Guard Memorial
11 John P. Pershing: General of the Armies
12 Argonne Cross (dedicated to Americans killed in France during World War I)
13 Virgil Grissom and Roger Chaffee: *Apollo* I astronauts

14 Walter Reed: instrumental in combating yellow fever
15 Nurses Memorial
16 John Foster Dulles: Secretary of State
17 Rough Riders Memorial
18 Confederate Monument
19 *USS Maine* Memorial
20 Shuttle *Challenger* Astronauts Memorial
21 Memorial to service personnel killed in the attempt to rescue US hostages in Iran, 1980
22 Frank Reynolds: broadcast journalist
23 Joe Louis: heavyweight boxing champion
24 George C. Marshall: General, Secretary of State
25 James Parks: Arlington House slave
26 Claire L. Chennault: Commander of the World War II Flying Tigers
27 Montgomery Meigs: Quartermaster-General, engineer, architect

28 Johnny Clem: youngest soldier in the US Army
29 Lockerbie, Scotland, Pan Am 103 Memorial
30 Anita Newcomb McGee: first female Army surgeon
31 Tomb of the Unknown Dead of the War of 1812
32 Tomb of the Unknown Civil War Dead
33 Pierre Charles L'Enfant: planner of Washington DC
34 Oliver Wendell Holmes Jr.: Supreme Court Justice
35 Richard E. Byrd (grave): polar explorer
36 George Westinghouse: inventor
37 Dashiell Hammett: detective novelist
38 Medgar Evers: civil rights leader

A BIT OF HISTORY
The Custises
Arlington House, as the mansion is commonly known, was built by George Washington Parke Custis, whose father, John, was the son of Martha Washington by her first husband. When John Custis died during the Revolution, George and Eleanor (Nelly), the youngest of his four small children, were brought to Mount Vernon and raised by the Washingtons. George Custis spent his childhood among the Washingtons' illustrious circle of acquaintants.

Washington died in 1799 and Martha in 1802. Mount Vernon passed to Bushrod Washington, a nephew of George Washington, and the 21-year-old Custis moved to a 1,100-acre tract of land his father had left him across from the newly established federal city.

Custis began planning a mansion worthy of housing his Mount Vernon memorabilia. Architect George Hadfield's building, incorporating the lines of a Doric temple, was the area's first example of the Greek Revival style. By 1804 the south wing was completed. In the same year Custis married Mary Lee Fitzhugh. About this time he also renamed his estate Arlington, after a Custis family property in Northhampton County, Virginia. The mansion was completed in 1818.

Sophisticated and talented, Custis was a poet, playwright and painter. Much of his skill and enthusiasm went to perpetuating the memory of his guardian and idol, George Washington.

The Lees
Robert E. Lee, a distant relative of the Custises, grew up in nearby Alexandria and visited their home often as a boy. In 1831, he and Mary Anna Randolph Custis, the Custises' only surviving child, were married at Arlington House. For the next 30 years, the Lees were posted to various locations as Robert pursued his military career. During this time they considered Arlington House their true home and spent many winters here. Arlington House was the birthplace of six of the seven Lee children. At the Custises' death, title to the house passed to the Lees. In January 1861, fearing the consequences of mounting hostilities between the North and South, Lee wrote to a friend, saying "There is no sacrifice I am not ready to make for the preservation of the Union, save that of honour." Three months later, on 18 April, he was called to Blair House and offered the command of the Union troops. He refused, and on 20 April at Arlington House, he wrote his letter of resignation from the US Army. On 22 April he left Arlington House for Richmond, Virginia, where he accepted command of the Virginia forces. He would never return to his beloved home again.

Confiscation
In May 1861 Union troops crossed the river to Virginia and quickly made the strategically located Arlington House into the headquarters for the Army of the Potomac. Throughout the war the estate grounds were turned into fortifications, and ultimately into a national cemetery for the Civil War dead (Arlington National Cemetery).

In 1864 Arlington House was claimed by the federal government due to a dubious tax law that required Mrs. Lee to pay a $92 property tax in person. Mrs. Lee, in poor health, chose not to travel to Washington, sending a cousin instead. The

Arlington House in winter

©Arlington National Cemetery

government refused payment from the cousin, seized the property, and offered it up for public auction.

As no bidders came forth the government bought it for $26,800. After a legal battle that was decided by the Supreme Court, the Lees' eldest son, George Washington Custis Lee, won a suit for the return of the property. In 1883 Lee accepted the congressional appropriation of $150,000, based on the estate's market value, rather than reclaiming the land, which by then had the character of a cemetery. Congress designated the house a national memorial to Robert E. Lee in 1925, and the National Park Service began administering it in 1933.

VISIT

Open Apr–May daily 9:30am–5pm, Jun–Aug daily 9:30am–5:30pm, Sept–Mar daily 9:30am–4:30pm. Closed 1 Jan and Dec 25. 703-235-1530. www.nps.gov/arho.

The mansion commands a spectacular **view**★★ of Washington, with the Abraham Lincoln Memorial in the near distance and the city beyond it. The main facade, with eight large Doric columns supporting an unadorned pediment, provides a gracious entrance to the off-white stucco structure.

Interior

Off the entrance hall to the right is the family parlor, where the Lees were married. Over the simple mantel is a portrait of a young Mary Custis painted by Auguste Hervieu. Beyond the parlor is the artist's studio used by George W.P. Custis and for Mary Lee, who, like her father, was a painter. On an easel sits Custis' *Battle of Monmouth, New Jersey*, which once hung in the US Capitol.

On the lawn in front of Arlington House is the **tomb of Pierre L'Enfant**, whose remains were moved here in 1909.

A marble plaque incised with his original city plan for Washington commemorates his unique contribution. A small museum *(behind the house and to the north)* has exhibits highlighting Robert E. Lee's career.

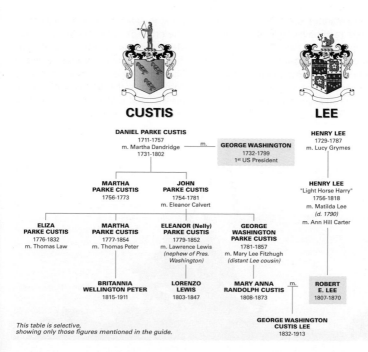

CUSTIS

DANIEL PARKE CUSTIS
1711-1757
m. Martha Dandridge
1731-1802 — m. — GEORGE WASHINGTON
1732-1799
1st US President

MARTHA PARKE CUSTIS
1756-1773

JOHN PARKE CUSTIS
1754-1781
m. Eleanor Calvert

ELIZA PARKE CUSTIS
1776-1832
m. Thomas Law

MARTHA PARKE CUSTIS
1777-1854
m. Thomas Peter

ELEANOR (Nelly) PARKE CUSTIS
1779-1852
m. Lawrence Lewis
(nephew of Pres. Washington)

GEORGE WASHINGTON PARKE CUSTIS
1781-1857
m. Mary Lee Fitzhugh
(distant Lee cousin)

BRITANNIA WELLINGTON PETER
1815-1911

LORENZO LEWIS
1803-1847

MARY ANNA RANDOLPH CUSTIS
1808-1873 — m. — ROBERT E. LEE
1807-1870

LEE

HENRY LEE
1729-1787
m. Lucy Grymes

HENRY LEE
"Light Horse Harry"
1756-1818
m. Matilda Lee
(d. 1790)
m. Ann Hill Carter

GEORGE WASHINGTON CUSTIS LEE
1832-1913

This table is selective, showing only those figures mentioned in the guide.

National Park Service; coats of arms redrawn by permission of Arlington House

Marine Corps War Memorial ★

Ⓜ *Arlington Cemetery or Rosslyn*

This striking sculpture, honoring all US Marines who have lost their lives in military duty, ranks as one of the nation's most famous war memorials. Its prominent location, across the Potomac in near-perfect alignment with the Mall's principal axis, visually links the memorial to the heart of Washington.

Location: Iwo Jima Memorial. Off N. Meade St. By car: Leave Washington via Memorial Bridge heading toward Rte. 50 West and follow signs to the memorial and Fort Meyer. To reach the memorial from the grounds of Arlington Cemetery, exit by the Ord and Weitzel Gate.

VISIT

⊙Open daily year-round 6am–midnight. The US Marine Corps Sunset Parade is held Tue evenings in summer. www.nps.gov/gwmp/marinecorpswarmemorial.htm.

The sculpture depicts six Americans raising the Stars and Stripes on Mount Suribachi in 1945 during the assault of the Japanese-controlled island of Iwo Jima (hence the memorial's popular nickname). The capture of this strategically located island is considered one of the Marines' greatest victories and marked a turning point in the American campaign in the Pacific.

Based on the Pulitzer Prize-winning war photograph by **Joseph Rosenthal**, the memorial was designed by Horace W. Peaslee and sculpted by Felix de Weldon. The work's poignancy is further intensified by the incessant waving of the US flag that rises from the bronze statue.

The nearby tower, known as the **Netherlands Carillon**, is a gift from the Dutch people in appreciation of American assistance during and after World War II. Reminiscent of the pure geometrical style of the 20C Dutch masters Rietveld and Mondrian, this lofty metal structure contains 50 bells. **Carillon concerts** are given here from May to September. *For concert information, ℘703-289-2552; www.nps.gov/gwmp/nethcarillon.htm.*

The grounds of the US Marine Corps Memorial and the Netherlands Carillon afford striking **vistas**★★ of the Mall area. The eye is drawn across the Potomac past the Lincoln Memorial and the Washington Monument to the dome of the Capitol in the distance.

Marine Corps War Memorial

© Sandra Henderson/Dreamstime.com

Pentagon

Ⓜ *Pentagon*

The heart of the American military establishment, this enormous pentagonal building houses the offices of the highest authorities of the armed services—the secretary of Defense and the joint chiefs of staff (Army, Navy, Air Force and Marines)—all of whom answer to the commander in chief, the president of the US.

A BIT OF HISTORY

Conceived during World War II, the Pentagon combined for the first time all of the branches of the Department of War, as it was then called, under one roof. Army engineers were given one weekend in July 1941 to design the building, which was to be situated on the Arlington shore of the Potomac. Since the lot was five-sided, they devised a pentagonal shape for the building. Though the new structure was not ultimately constructed on the original lot, the five-sided shape was retained.

Built of reinforced concrete faced with limestone, the five-story Pentagon was constructed in a relatively short 16 months and was completed on 15 January 1943. On 11 September 2001 the west wall of the Pentagon was struck by a hijacked commercial airliner resulting in the loss of 184 lives.

This event, coupled with the attack, on the same day, on New York City's World Trade Center, was the worst terrorist attack on US soil in the nation's history.

VISIT

Visit by guided group tour (1hr) only, by reservation Mon–Fri 9am–3pm. Tours (minimum 5 people) must be requested up to 90 days in advance online (choose Request a Tour from website below). Arrive 30 min before tour time to clear security. Check the website for the current list of items that are not allowed in the building. ⓧ *Closed major holidays.* ⊙ *Visitors must show a photo ID.* ♿ ✆ *703-697-1776. http://pentagon.osd.mil.*

▷ **Location:** I-395 at Washington Blvd. The Metro stop (Pentagon) is closer than parking (ꙮ *see below*) and walking to the Pentagon from the parking garage.

🅿 **Parking:** Park in the Fashion Centre at Pentagon City mall parking garage; then it's a 10min walk to the Pentagon.

Pentagon Profile

The Pentagon contains six and a half million sq ft, making it one of the world's largest single-structure office buildings. Its interior comprises five concentric circles that enclose a five-acre central courtyard. Each of its five sides is larger than the Capitol, and together they contain 17½ miles of corridors. Some 23,000 personnel, about half of whom are military, work here in round-the-clock shifts.

An introductory film *(12min)* explains the history of the construction of the Pentagon and its significance.

The remainder of the tour walks visitors through office corridors displaying military art (battle scenes, portraits of high-ranking officers) and the **Hall of Heroes**, where the names of those who have received the prestigious Congressional Medal of Honor are listed.

Tours also spend time on the west side of the building at the spot where American Airlines Flight 77 crashed into the Pentagon on 11 September. Tour guides then take groups inside the somber September 11th Memorial Chapel.

At the beginning of the 20C, this neighborhood was the preferred address of Washington's moneyed elite. Back in vogue, the Dupont Circle area today boasts many of the city's trendiest boutiques, galleries, restaurants and cafes.

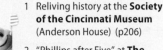

Highlights

1 Reliving history at the **Society of the Cincinnati Museum** (Anderson House) (p206)

2 "Phillips after Five" at **The Phillips Collection** (p208)

3 Checking out the temporary exhibits at the **National Geographic Museum** (p209)

Information: ℘202-661-7581; www.cultural tourismdc.org.

Location: Use the map and take the walking tour described herein.

Parking: Street parking may be available on the less busy side streets.

Timing: Allow 4hrs for the walk and the museum visits.

Kids: National Geographic Museum at Explorers Hall.

A Bit of History
Early Development

It was during the public works projects overseen by Alexander "Boss" Shepherd in the early 1870s that the Dupont Circle area developed. The improvements attracted a group of real estate investors including Sen. William Stewart of Nevada. In 1873 he began constructing an elaborate home between Massachusetts and Connecticut avenues. Stewart's Castle was an extravagant Second Empire estate, complete with a stable of thoroughbreds. The mansion was razed in 1901; a branch of Riggs Bank stood on the site from 1924 until 2005, when PNC acquired it.

In 1874 the British legation constructed an impressive Second Empire structure at N Street and Connecticut Avenue. The side streets in the area developed as a working-class neighborhood. During the 1890s the area become a "millionaires' colony." Typical of these millionaires was Levi Leiter, a Chicago department store magnate who in 1891 built a 55-room mansion on the circle.

In the early 20C, Massachusetts Avenue became a corridor of Beaux-Arts palaces. The Virginia architect Waddy B. Wood designed some 30 mansions in this area and in **Kalorama**, another prestigious neighborhood northwest of the Circle. As the mansions rose along the avenue, the working-class houses on the side streets gave way to stylish brick row houses. A number of foreign missions were also built in the area.

20C Vicissitudes

In the 1920s the character of Dupont Circle shifted toward the commercial; a number of the fine homes were torn down to build offices and stores. During the Great Depression the area lost its cachet as a neighborhood of the fabulously rich. By the 1950s private clubs and businesses moved into many of the mansions and the row houses were converted into boarding houses. During the 1960s student activists and "hippies" turned the area into a counterculture haven.

The Tax Reform Act of 1969 encouraged the demolition of old buildings and many of the surviving grand structures were lost. To counter the razing, citizen groups petitioned the city to provide legal protection for the Dupont Circle environs. In 1978 the streets around the circle and north to T Street were designated a historic district.

Now the neighborhood's renovated 19C row houses are once again home to professionals, and great efforts have been made to preserve the elegant old mansions that still grace Massachusetts Avenue.

Dupont Circle and Vicinity★

Ⓜ *Dupont Circle
Map below*

Situated at the junction of five thoroughfares—Massachusetts, Connecticut and New Hampshire avenues, and 19th and P streets— this bustling intersection has become a focal point of the city's Northwest quadrant. It is here that planner Pierre Charles L'Enfant's proposed arrangement of streets and avenues converging on a central green with a monument at its center can best be appreciated.

A BIT OF HISTORY

Originally known as Pacific Circle, it was renamed in 1884 to honor Rear Adm. Samuel F. Du Pont (1803-65), the Civil War hero who directed Union naval operations along the south Atlantic coast. A bronze statue of Du Pont stood in the center of the circle until 1921, when the hero's family transferred the memorial to Wilmington, Delaware. Shortly thereafter, the Du Ponts replaced the statue with the marble **fountain** that now occupies the center of the circle. Designed in 1921 by Daniel Chester French, sculptor of the statue of

- ▷ **Location:** Take the 19th St. exit at Dupont Circle Metro station.
- ▲▲ **Kids:** Mitchell Park, 1801 23rd St., NW.
- ◑ **Timing:** Allow at least a half day.
- ◉ **Don't Miss:** The Gandhi Statue at 21 and Q sts. NW.

Abraham Lincoln in the Lincoln Memorial, the fountain consists of a wide basin resting atop a central pillar adorned with figures symbolizing the sea, wind and stars—references to Samuel F. Du Pont's naval career.

During the 1960s and 70s, Dupont Circle gained prominence as a major gathering place for the counterculture and political activists. Today this busy urban park is frequented by a representative cross section of Washington's diverse residential population, making it one of the capital's best outdoor spots for people watching.

⌁⚫WALKING TOUR

▷ *1-1/3miles. Begin at the Circle. Then cross over to Massachusetts Ave. south of P St. on the east side of the Circle.*

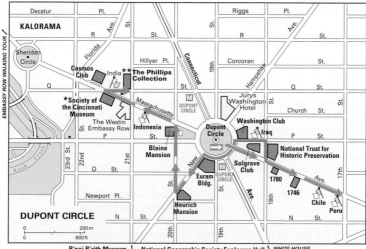

203

Sulgrave Club (Wadsworth House)

1801 Massachusetts Ave. NW.
www.sulgraveclub.org.
⊶Not open to the public.

This buff brick mansion was the residence of Herbert and Martha Wadsworth, from upstate New York.

Constructed around 1900 (architect unknown), this two-story structure is crowned by a roof balustrade and features a Palladian window above the principal entrance *(on Massachusetts Ave)*.

In 1918 Wadsworth donated his residence to the Red Cross, which occupied the mansion until 1932. It was then sold to a group of Washington women who established the Sulgrave Club, one of the city's private social clubs.

▷ *Continue on Massachusetts Ave. to the corner of 18th St.*

The 1700 block of Massachusetts Avenue contains four buildings by **Jules Henri de Sibour** (1872-1938), a French-born architect who trained at Yale and at the École des Beaux-Arts in Paris.

National Trust for Historic Preservation (McCormick Apartments)

785 Massachusetts Ave. NW.
◔The lobby is open to the public year-round Mon–Fri 9am–5pm. ◔Closed major holidays. ♿ ✆202-588-6000.
www.preservationnation.org.

Completed in 1917, the five-story edifice takes its name from the original owner, Stanley McCormick, son of Cyrus McCormick, inventor of the reaper and founder of the International Harvester Co.

The two principal facades are accented by a rusticated first story, bas-relief panels and a balcony with cast-iron railings. The steep mansard roof is lined with chimneys and pedimented dormers adorned with characteristic Beaux-Arts ornamentation.

The original interior reflected the fabulous lifestyle of the early-20C millionaires. Each floor held a single apartment (except the ground floor, which was divided into two) containing six bedrooms and measuring 11,000sq ft, with ceilings more than 14ft high.

Today the landmark building is the headquarters of the National Trust for Historic Preservation.

▷ *Continue east on Massachusetts Ave.*

Across the street stands **no. 1780**, built by de Sibour in 1922 for the Ingalls, another wealthy Washington family. The building was remodeled and is now occupied by Planned Parenthood.

The five-story limestone and brick mansion at **no. 1746** was commissioned in 1906 by Clarence Moore, a West Virginia tycoon who perished on the ill-fated *Titanic* (1912). The building housed the Canadian diplomatic mission from 1927 until 1988.

The brick and sandstone building (1889), now the **Chilean chancery** *(no. 1732)*, was constructed as a private residence by local architect Glenn Brown. It served as the headquarters of the Washington chapter of the Daughters of the American Revolution (DAR) from 1940 to 1973.

The dignified mansion at the corner of Massachusetts Avenue and 17th Street, now the **Peruvian embassy** *(no. 1700)*, was designed by de Sibour in 1910 for the widow of Beriah Wilkins, a congressman from Ohio and publisher of the *Washington Post*. Its imposing facade is reminiscent of a Renaissance palazzo.

▷ *Walk back up Massachusetts Ave. toward Dupont Circle, turn right on 18th St. and left on P St.*

On the corner of P and 18th streets, note the **Iraq Consulate** (*1801 P St.*), a tan brick structure with Richardsonian detailing. Completed in 1893, the building was designed by the architectural firm Hornblower and Marshall.

▷ *Continue on P St. to Dupont Circle.*

Washington Club (Patterson House)

15 Dupont Circle NW.
www.thewashingtonclub.com
⊶Not open to the public.

This ornate white marble and terra-cotta mansion, which resembles a Mannerist palazzo, was built in the early 20C by Stanford White of the New York firm McKim, Mead and White.

Commissioned by the Chicago socialite Mrs. Robert Patterson, this opulent residence was yet another setting for lavish entertaining in the capital. The Pattersons' daughter, Cissy (1884-1948), publisher of the *Washington Times-Herald*, assumed the role of the capital's premier hostess in the 1930s and early 40s.

During the renovation of the White House in the summer of 1927, Patterson House served as the temporary residence of President and Mrs. Coolidge. In the course of their stay, the Coolidges hosted the nation's hero, Charles Lindbergh, just back from his historic transatlantic flight.

The family's Washington residence was donated to the Red Cross after Cissy's death in 1948. Three years later the mansion was sold to the Washington Club, the elite women's organization that now occupies the building.

▷ *Walk clockwise along the circle.*

Note the **Euram Building** at 21 Dupont Circle. Designed in 1971 by the Washington architectural firm Hartman-Cox, this glass, brick and concrete office building enclosing a handsome courtyard is one of the capital's most innovative works of contemporary architecture.

▷ *Turn left on New Hampshire Ave. and continue one block to the intersection of New Hampshire Ave., 20th St. and Sunderland Pl.*

Heurich House Museum

1307 New Hampshire Ave. NW.
Mansion visit by guided tour (1hr) only, year-round Thu–Fri 11:30am & 1pm, Sat 11:30am, 1pm & 2:30pm. $5. Garden open Memorial Day–Labor Day Mon–Fri 10am–4pm. 202-429-1894. www.heurichhouse.org.
This landmark Richardsonian Romanesque building is one of the city's best-preserved house museums.

The imposing mansion (1894) was commissioned by Christian Heurich, the German-born founder of a brewery that stood on the present site of the Kennedy Center. The house remained in the Heurich family until 1956, when Heurich's descendants donated the building to the Columbia Historical Society (later renamed the Historical Society of Washington, DC), founded in 1894. The society maintained the property as its headquarters and a museum until 2003, when the society moved to Mount Vernon Square. Two of Christian Heurich's grandchildren established a foundation for the purchase of the mansion, and in fall 2003, Heurich House reopened to the public as a house museum.

▷ *Upon leaving the building, cross over to 20th St. and continue north to the corner of Massachusetts Ave.*

Blaine Mansion

2000 Massachusetts Ave. NW.
Not open to the public.
This severe brick edifice (1881) is Dupont Circle's oldest surviving mansion. It was built for **James G. Blaine** (1830-93), cofounder of the Republican Party. Displeased with the high maintenance costs, the Blaines leased it to Chicago real-estate baron Levi Leiter from 1883 until the early 1890s. Inventor George Westinghouse purchased the Blaine mansion in 1901 and lived there until his death in 1914.

▷ *Continue west on Massachusetts Ave.*

Washington Club

Indonesian Embassy (Walsh Mansion)

2020 Massachusetts Ave. NW.
Guided tours (15min) year-round Mon–Fri 9am–5pm. Closed Indonesian and major holidays. Phone before visiting. 202-775-5306. www.embassyofindonesia.org.

This turn-of-the-19C mansion was designed by Danish-born architect Henry Andersen for Thomas Walsh, an Irish immigrant who struck it rich in the Colorado goldfields.

The Walshes were prominent social figures, using their palatial home for lavish parties. At Mrs. Walsh's death in 1932, the house passed to her daughter Eva-lyn. Married to Edward Beale McLean, whose family owned the *Cincinnati Enquirer* and the *Washington Post*, Eva-lyn Walsh McLean was a Washington socialite and the last private owner of the celebrated Hope Diamond (*see National Museum of Natural History*). In 1951 she sold the home to the Indonesian government.

▷ *Continue west on Massachusetts Ave.*

Society of the Cincinnati Museum (Anderson House)★

2118 Massachusetts Ave. NW.
Open year-round Tue–Sat 1pm–4pm. Closed major holidays. Guided tours (1hr) available. 202-785-2040. http://.societyofthecincinnati.org.

This edifice serves as the headquarters of the Society of the Cincinnati and a house museum displaying its collection of Revolutionary artifacts.

The Society – George Washington was the first president-general of this patriotic organization, founded in 1783 by former officers of the Revolution. Named for a 5C Roman military hero and farmer, the society extols the ideal of the soldier returning to civilian life ,and spearheaded military pensions in America. Membership passes, by tradition and charter, through the line of eldest sons.

The Andersons – Larz Anderson, who had the 50-room house (1905, Little and Brown) built, was a member of the society. At her husband's death in 1937, Mrs. Anderson donated the house to the Society of the Cincinnati.

Visit

Arched carriage gates lead into a walled courtyard dominated by a rounded portico. Inside the front hall is a bust of Washington by Thomas Crawford, who designed the statue that tops the Capitol. The small room to the right is lined with late Renaissance choir stalls.

On the wall above is a frieze by Henry Siddons Mowbray that depicts awards. In the billiard room hang military portraits by Gilbert Stuart, John Trumbull and George Catlin.

The great stair hall contains cases with battle dioramas, French miniatures of soldiers and other memorabilia. *The Triumph of the Dogaressa Anna Maria Foscari* in the Year 1424, by José Villegas y Cordero, dominates the staircase landing. On the second floor, the reception room is notable for its Siena and white marble floor bearing the pattern of the Greek key. The allegorical wall and ceiling friezes were painted by Mowbray.

A Louis XV-style parlor displays jade trees from the Andersons' Ching dynasty collection. Among the furnishings in the adjoining English parlor are Hepplewhite pieces, English portraiture and Chinese porcelains from the 16C to the 19C. The long corridor contains Asian antiques and Italian paintings, while the formal dining room is decorated with early-17C Belgian tapestries.

This room opens onto a musicians' gallery, overlooking the grand **ballroom**. Over the ballroom mantel is a portrait of Gen. Henry Knox, considered the society's founder. A solarium overlooks a walled sculpture garden. The reflecting pool is faced by an 18C statue of a Japanese Buddha.

▷ *Cross Massachusetts Ave.*

Cosmos Club
(Townsend House)

2121 Massachusetts Ave. NW.
www.cosmosclub.org
☛ *Not open to the public.*

Set behind a landscaped entrance driveway, this limestone mansion is the headquarters of one of the country's most exclusive social clubs. In 1899 Richard Townsend, the president of the Erie and Pittsburgh Railroad, and his wife, Mary, heiress to the Pennsylvania Railroad fortune, commissioned Carrère and Hastings to design a palatial residence. The architects received strict instructions to integrate the site's preexisting brick house into their plan because Mrs. Townsend had been warned by a fortune-teller that calamity would strike if she moved into a brand-new house. Despite the precautions taken, Mr. Townsend died from a riding accident in 1902, a year after the house's completion. In accordance with the Townsends' request for a house in the style of the 18C Petit Trianon at Versailles, the architects designed a central facade composed of three bays separated by colossal pilasters and crowned by a roof balustrade. A mansard roof punctuated by dormer windows constitutes the fourth floor.

Mrs. Townsend gained fame among the capital's affluent circles for her extravagant entertaining. In the 1930s the mansion was home to the Townsends' daughter, Mathilde, and her second husband, Sumner B. Welles, undersecretary of State during most of the Roosevelt administration. The Welleses hosted President and Mrs. Roosevelt for several weeks in January 1933 before the first family moved to the White House. In 1950 the residence was purchased by the Cosmos Club, a social club founded in 1878 for men of distinction in the fields of science, literature and the fine arts. Inscribed in its prestigious register are the names of three US presidents and more than 80 Nobel and Pulitzer Prize recipients.

▷ *Continue one block east on Q St. to the corner of 21st St.*

The Phillips Collection★★

Ⓜ *Dupont Circle*

- ▷ **Location:** 1600 21st St. NW.
- 👥 **Kids:** The Children's Gallery
- 👁 **Don't Miss:** Renoir's *Luncheon of the Boating Party.*

The Phillips Collection, the nation's first museum of modern art, exhibits outstanding works by prominent American and European artists in an intimate setting and hosts a year-round schedule of music, gallery talks and films.

A BIT OF HISTORY
The Collector

The grandson of one of the cofounders of the Jones and Laughlin Steel Co., **Duncan Phillips** (1886-1966) developed an interest in art during his studies at Yale and in travels abroad. In 1908, Duncan and his brother, James, began expanding the small private collection that hung in the family's unpretentious brick and brownstone home built by the firm of Hornblower and Marshall in 1896. Following James' death in 1918—only 13 months after the death of his father—Duncan devoted himself to transforming the family's private collection into a public memorial to his beloved father and brother. In the fall of 1921, eight years before the founding of the Museum of Modern Art in New York City, the Phillips Memorial Art Gallery, occupying two rooms of the family home, opened to an appreciative public.

That same year Phillips married Marjorie Acker, a talented painter in her own right. During the 1920s they acquired many of the collection's most

Enjoying Luncheon of the Boating Party *(1881) by Pierre-Auguste Renoir*

©The Phillips Collection

provide space for the expanding collection. A new wing was added in 1960 (Goh Annex), and in 1961 the museum was renamed the Phillips Collection. The annex was expanded in 1989. In 2006, the Sant Building was completed, which allowed for more gallery space, an auditorium, and an expanded café and museum shop.

The Collection

Throughout his life Duncan Phillips eschewed the cold formality of the art establishment. He and his wife relied on their judgment and taste, rather than the advice of curators or art dealers. Phillips did not adhere to any one specific doctrine or school of art and largely avoided the avant-garde and cult movements of the day. While concentrating primarily on modern art, he frequently juxtaposed 19C and 20C works with Old Masters paintings to suggest sources from which modern artists might have sought inspiration. Phillips conceived his collection as "a museum of modern art and its sources."

famous paintings, including Renoir's *Luncheon of the Boating Party*, which was purchased for the record sum of $125,000 in 1923. By 1930 the collection had assumed its basic form, containing paintings by all the major French Impressionists, post-Impressionists and Cubists as well as outstanding works by several 17C and 18C masters, including Goya and El Greco. In 1931 Phillips and his family moved out of their home to

Most of the museum's more than 3,000 works, primarily from the 19C and 20C, were selected by Phillips and his wife. Artists represented in the collection include Daumier, Degas, Cézanne, Monet, Bonnard, van Gogh, Matisse, Klee and Picasso, along with noted American painters such as Ryder, Marin, Dove, O'Keeffe and Tack. The collection continues to expand with new acquisitions, including work by major living artists.

VISIT

🕐 *Open year-round Tue–Sat 10am–5pm (Thu til 8:30pm), Sun 11am–6pm.* 🕐 *Closed major holidays.* ⊛ *$12 weekends (weekdays by donation).* ✕&. ✆ *202-387-2151. www.phillips collection.org. On Thu evenings "Phillips after Five" features gallery talks, live music and other activities (admission charged). The Phillips also offers an array of public prgrams.*

To the right of the street-level entrance hovers the bas-relief of a bird in flight, based on a work by Georges Braque, one of Phillips' favorite painters.

The Migration Series, Jacob Lawrence

©The Phillips Collection, Washington, DC/ Max Hirshfeld

Paintings are hung in simply furnished rooms to create an informal domestic setting that Phillips considered conducive to the appreciation of art. The works, which are rotated frequently, are not arranged chronologically, but large-scale contemporary pieces are generally found in the ground-floor galleries. The house's largest room, the oak-paneled **Music Room** *(1st floor)*, which features raised plaster medallions on the ceiling, a dark oak staircase and molding in the foyer, showcases works from the permanent collection. Added to the house in 1907 as a recreation room, this space is the setting for Sunday concerts *(Oct– May 4pm)*.

The second floor of the house contains additional gallery space for the permanent collection. The Goh Annex *(floors G2 and G3)* is linked to the original building by two walkways. Among the works frequently displayed in the annex are paintings from the **Bonnard Collection**, reputed to be the country's largest collection of the French artist's paintings, and Swiss painter **Paul Klee** (1879-1940).

Also on exhibit in the annex *(floor G2)* is the museum's most renowned treasure: **Luncheon of the Boating Party** (1881) by Renoir.

In the Sant Building, a small gallery is exclusively devoted to four works by abstract expressionist **Mark Rothko** (1903-70), known for his hauntingly simple canvases of large expanses of color. The third-floor galleries are reserved for temporary exhibits.

Outside, off the cafe, the Hunter Courtyard is graced with sculptures by Ellsworth Kelly and Barbara Hepworth.

National Geographic Museum at Explorers Hall

Ⓜ *Farragut West or Farragut North*

The National Geographic Society's century-long support of explorers, archaeologists, oceanographers and other scientists is showcased in this museum. Housed in the society's three-building headquarters complex, the hall was opened in 1964. It occupies the ground floor of a 10-story marble and glass structure designed by Edward Durell Stone, architect of the Kennedy Center.

VISIT

👤Ⓞ*Open year-round daily 9am– 5pm.* Ⓞ*Closed Dec 25. Tickets (💳$8) required for special exhibits; purchase online, at the museum, or call ☎202-575-7700.* ♿. ☎*202-857-7588. www.ngmuseum.org.*

- ▷ **Location:** 17th and M Sts. NW.
- 👤 **Kids:** 3-D Mt Everest model & National Geographic Live! programs.
- Ⓞ **Timing:** Allow 45 min.
- ⊙ **Don't Miss:** The rotating photography exhibit.

The museum at Explorers Hall showcases 3-D models, from the National Geographic Society's permanent collection, of Mount Everest, the Grand Canyon and other regions. Interactive displays involve visitors in such topics as underwater exploration, dinosaurs and other aspects of natural history.

Changing exhibits on cultural, geographic or scientific topics, generally feature photographs and discoveries made by photographers and researchers who work for the country's National Geographic Society.

EMBASSY ROW

Embassy Row is the popular name of the two-mile portion of Massachusetts Avenue between Scott Circle and Observatory Circle where some 50 diplomatic missions are concentrated. The buildings housing the chanceries (the embassies proper) and the ambassadors' residences (which may be separate from the chanceries) are recognizable by the colorful flags or plaques that generally adorn their facades.

Highlights

1 The **Beaux-Arts Mansions** at 2305, 2311, and 2315 Massachusetts Avenue, NW (p213)

2 Marveling at the handmade works at the **Textile Museum** (p214)

3 A romantic sunset picnic by the **Spanish Steps** (p214)

A Bit of History

Massachusetts Avenue beyond 22nd Street developed as an extension of the Dupont Circle residential enclave. Overlooking Rock Creek Park, this area offered spacious, relatively inexpensive lots suited to the construction of the palatial residences fashionable before the advent of income tax. By 1915, the Sheridan Circle area was home to some of the capital's wealthiest residents. After the 1929 stock-market crash and Great Depression, formerly affluent residents were forced to set up households in more modest quarters. In 1931 the governments of Great Britain and Japan constructed new embassy compounds in the area. The two-mile stretch between Scott Circle and Observatory Circle soon supplanted the Meridian Hill district as the capital's premier diplomatic quarter.

In the construction boom that followed World War II, some of Embassy Row's buildings were sacrificed to make way for modern structures, but the avenue's upper portion (north of Florida Avenue) has conserved its elegant character.

In **Kalorama**, the residential neighborhood north of Florida Avenue between Massachusetts and Connecticut avenues, additional diplomatic missions

Info: ☏ 202-661-7581; www.culturaltourismdc.org.

Location: From 22nd Street to Observatory Circle is considered the most distinctive and elegant segment of Embassy Row. Use the map on page 210.

Parking: Street parking should be available on the less busy side streets.

Timing: Allow 2hrs for the walking tour and 2hrs for the museums. Embassies are usually open for official business or social functions only. Contact the individual embassy about possible tours open to the public.

have been established in reconverted upper-middle-class dwellings.

Beaux-Arts Architecture

The upper portion of Embassy Row preserves a concentration of residences designed in the Beaux-Arts style. Among the Washington-based architects who traveled to Europe to study this style were George Oakley Totten Jr. (1866-1939), Waddy B. Wood (1869-1944) and Nathan C. Wyeth (1870-1963).

The returning expatriates brought their knowledge and appreciation for the Beaux-Arts back home with them and incorporated in into their designs. As a result, the American edifices they built were characterized by symmetrical design, exuberant decorative details (swags, garlands, carved panels, ornamented keystones and brackets), a rusticated first floor generally with an entry canopy, and a mansard roof rising above a stone balustrade.

Embassy Row and Vicinity

Ⓜ *Dupont Circle*

It's best to visit this area on foot, particularly the most noteworthy portion of Embassy Row— Massachusetts Avenue between 22nd Street and Observatory Circle. Part of Massachusetts Avenue below 22nd Street is included on the Dupont Circle walking tour (👜 *see Dupont Circle chapter).* Unless otherwise specified, all sights described or mentioned on the tour are located on Massachusetts Avenue NW.

> **Location:** The stretch of Massachusetts Ave. NW between 22nd St. and Observatory Circle.
>
> **Kids:** The Textile Museum's Interactive Learning Center, and its Celebration of Textiles held every June.
>
> **Timing:** Allow at least 90 minutes to stroll along this architecturally rich section of the city.

🔍 WALKING TOUR

▷ *1mi (not including visits). Begin the tour at the corner of Massachusetts Ave. and 22nd St.*

2200 Block

This gently sloped portion of Massachusetts Avenue, flanked by attached town houses, provides entry to Sheridan Circle, situated on a rise to the northwest. The limestone mansion at no. 2200, which today houses the **embassy of Luxembourg**, was designed by Jules Henri de Sibour for Alexander Stewart (1829-1912), a lumber magnate and congressman from Wisconsin. Completed in 1909, the building incorporates characteristic Beaux-Arts features: symmetrical design, a rusticated first floor, arched windows, and a mansard roof rising above a stone balustrade.

The embassies of Togo and the Sudan are located at nos. 2208 and 2210 respectively. At **no. 2230** stands the smallest of the four Embassy Row residences built by George Oakley Totten Jr. Completed in 1907, this brick-faced row house was designed in the so-called Chateauesque manner—an eclectic style briefly in vogue around the turn of the 19C. Derived from large-scale 16C European estates, Chateauesque buildings are characterized by gabled dormers, steeply pitched hipped roofs

and balconies carved with reliefs or tracery. With elegant facades on both Massachusetts Avenue and Sheridan Circle, **no. 2234** was erected in 1909 as a private residence by William Cresson (1873-1932), an architect turned rancher, diplomat and law professor. Cresson's training at the École des Beaux-Arts is reflected in the building's overall design and ornamental details. Since 1949 the building has housed the embassy of Ireland. The freestanding structure across the avenue is the embassy of Greece.

Sheridan Circle

Originally called Decatur Circle in honor of the early-19C naval hero Stephen Decatur, the park was renamed in 1890 after Gen. Philip H. Sheridan (1831-88), leader of the Union cavalry. Dedicated in 1908, the bronze equestrian **statue** of Sheridan was designed by Gutzon Borglum, renowned for the colossal presidential heads at Mount Rushmore.

This tree-lined circle provides a graceful setting for the surrounding palatial mansions and town houses. At **no. 2301** the four-story mansion with a convex facade and Palladian arch is the Egyptian ambassador's residence.

Other embassy buildings facing the circle are the residence of the ambassador of the Philippines at **2253 R St.** and the embassy of Kenya *(2249 R St.)*.

▷ *Continue to the corner of 23rd St. and Sheridan Circle.*

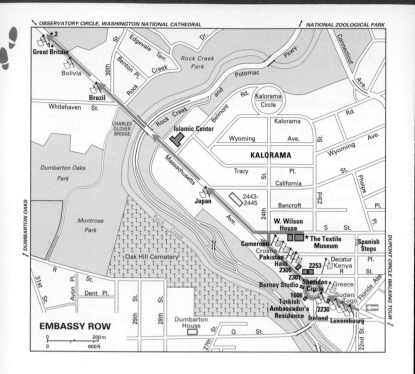

OBSERVATORY CIRCLE, WASHINGTON NATIONAL CATHEDRAL / NATIONAL ZOOLOGICAL PARK

Turkish Ambassador's Residence (Everett House)

1606 23rd St.

Designed by George Oakley Totten Jr., this grandiose structure (1915) was the home of Edward H. Everett, multimillionaire industrialist and inventor of the fluted soft-drink bottle cap.

The glass-covered carriage porch, the semicircular columned portico and the balustrade crowning the roof lend an air of opulence to the structure. Totten incorporated a colonnaded porch above the south wing.

The interior, richly appointed with carved wood paneling and inlaid floors, featured an indoor swimming pool and a ballroom with walls hung with gold-thread damask. Mrs. Everett, an opera singer, hosted a concert series featuring world-renowned divas and attended by Washington's cultural elite. Now located at no. 2525, the Turkish chancery occupied the mansion from 1936 to 1999. Today Everett House serves as the Turkish ambassador's residence.

▷ *Continue clockwise along the circle.*

Barney Studio House

2306 Massachusetts Ave.

⊶ *Not open to the public.*

Rather modest by Embassy Row standards, this town house on the southwestern rim of Sheridan Circle played a pivotal role in the cultural life of Washington in the early 20C.

Built about 1902 by Waddy B. Wood, the five-story structure, inspired by Spanish Colonial architecture (stucco facade, quatrefoil windows, curved parapet and red tile roof), was the home of Alice Pike Barney (1857-1931). Painter, playwright and trendsetter, Barney established her studio-home to serve as one of the capital's earliest private artistic centers. During her lifetime it provided the setting for much-needed cultural events. In 1960 her daughters donated the building to the Smithsonian Institution. It currently serves as the Embassy of Latvia.

▷ *Continue north on Massachusetts Ave. (right side).*

2300 Block

Occupying adjacent lots just steps from Sheridan Circle, the Beaux-Arts mansions at **nos. 2305** and **2311** were designed between 1909 and 1910 by architect Nathan Wyeth (who also drew up the plans for the Key Bridge linking Georgetown with Arlington). Sold to the Chilean government in 1923, no. 2305, with its gracefully curved central section and roof balustrades, is the ambassador's residence. No. 2311, faced with colossal Corinthian pilasters and surmounted by a steeply pitched mansard roof, was owned by the Nationalist government of China (Taiwan) from the 1940s to the 1970s; it was subsequently purchased by the government of Haiti.

Located on a prominent triangular lot on the corner of Massachusetts Avenue and Decatur Place, the mansion at **no. 2315** boldly completes this distinguished block. The stucco Beaux-Arts pile, built in 1909 for the Moran family by George Oakley Totten Jr., is dominated by an imposing round tower adorned with limestone and terra-cotta detailing—oval cartouches, swags and bas-relief decorative panels. It was occupied by the embassy of Pakistan until 2003.

No. 2315 Massachusetts Avenue

©R. Corbel/MICHELIN

◖ *Cross Decatur Pl. past the Croatian embassy (no. 2343) to the intersection of Massachusetts Ave. and 24th St.*

Embassy of Cameroon (Hauge Mansion)

This prominently situated limestone "chateau" (*No. 2349*) was the first of the four Embassy Row residences designed by George Oakley Totten Jr.

Christian Hauge, Norway's first minister to the US, commissioned the building to serve as both his private residence and his government's legation offices. In 1908, less than a year after the mansion's completion, Hauge died accidentally in Norway. Hauge's wife, Louise, a prominent East Coast socialite lived in the grand home for the next 19 years. Like the sumptuous Sheridan Circle mansion of the Everetts, Mrs. Hauge's residence was, according to a local newspaper, "the scene of much of Washington's most brilliant entertaining." After almost 40 years as the Czechoslovakian foreign mission, the mansion was sold to the Cameroon government in 1972.

The Hauge mansion is the city's finest example of the Chateauesque manner. Bolder in scale and design than the row house at 2230 Massachusetts Avenue that Totten designed around the same time, this freestanding structure is based on the 16C French chateau Azay-le-Rideau, in the Loire Valley. The mansion's outstanding architectural feature is the imposing rounded tower with its candlesnuffer roof.

◖ *Turn right on 24th St. and right again on S St.*

Woodrow Wilson House

2340 S St, NW ◖*Visit by guided tour (1hr) only, year-round Tue–Sun 10am–4pm.* ◷*Closed major holidays.* ◐*$10.* ♿ ☏*202-387-4062. www.woodrowwilsonhouse.org.*

The 28th president of the US chose this residence as his place of retirement upon completing his second term in the White House in 1921. The brick Georgian Revival town house was designed in 1915 by Waddy B. Wood.

The house has been converted into a **museum** that preserves the lifestyle of an upper-middle-class family in the 1920s and serves as a window on the family life of the president who led the US through World War I and into a position of world leadership.

◖ *Continue on S St.*

©Renée Comet/Textile Museum

Velvet yastık face, Bursa, 17th century. TM 1.54. Acquired by George Hewitt Myers in 1951.

The Textile Museum★

2320 S St. ⏰*Open year-round Tue–Sat 10am–5pm, Sun 1pm–5pm.* ⏰*Closed major holidays & 24 Dec.* 💲*$8 donation suggested.* 👣*Guided tours (1hr) available.* ✆*202-667-0441. www.textilemuseum.org.*

Founded in 1925 by George Hewitt Myers, this small private museum occupies a pair of town houses built by two renowned Washington architects. The building serving as entrance to the museum was designed in 1913 by the prolific John Russell Pope as a private home for Myers. The adjoining house was designed in 1908 by Waddy B. Wood, who later constructed the adjacent Woodrow Wilson House.

The museum focuses on the collection, study and preservation of handmade textiles and carpets. Its holdings comprise more than 19,000 textiles and rugs, primarily from the Near and Far East and South America, including an outstanding **pre-Columbian collection** from Peru. Changing exhibits present textiles from the US and abroad.

Less than a block east, the **Spanish Steps**, which connect S Street with Decatur Place, offer a quiet spot to sit and enjoy the lion-head fountain and seasonal plantings.

▷ *Return to Massachusetts Ave.*

Note the low complex of white buildings (nos. 2443-2445), which formerly housed the embassy of Venezuela, (now relocated to Georgetown).

▷ *Cross the avenue.*

Embassy of Japan

2520 Massachusetts Ave.

This Georgian Revival structure dominating a tree-lined cobblestone courtyard was built in 1931 for the Japanese government. The design, conceived by the architectural team Delano and Aldrich and reputedly approved by Emperor Hirohito, contains a hint of Oriental aesthetics in the delicately curved roofline. Note the depiction of a chrysanthemum, the imperial symbol of the Japanese emperor, that emerges from the balcony recess over the front entrance. The starkly modern chancery building to the right was added in 1986.

▷ *Continue on the opposite side of the avenue.*

At no. 2525 the Embassy of Turkey's chancery (1999, Shalom Baranes Assoc.) embodies traditional Turkish architecture with a contemporary look.

Islamic Center

2551 Massachusetts Ave. ⏰Open year-round daily 10:30am-4:30pm. Proper attire is required in visiting the mosque: arms, legs and women's heads must be covered and shoes removed. ✆202-332-8343. www.theislamiccenter.com.

This long white edifice, surmounted by a slender minaret, serves as a place of worship and instruction for the area's sizable Islamic population. Completed in 1957 with funds and materials donated primarily by the governments of Islamic countries, the center houses one of the first mosques in the country.

Operation of the Center

A board of governors, composed of the heads of Islamic diplomatic missions in DC, sets the center's policies. Prayer services are held five times daily. The call to prayer, traditionally chanted from a raised place by the muezzin, can be heard *(10am–5pm only)* from a loud-speaker on the minaret. Every Friday, the Muslim holy day, the faithful meet to pray. Daily worship services are also held here and marriages and funerals are performed in the mosque.

Visit

The limestone construction incorporates characteristic features of Islamic archi-tecture, including horseshoe arches, roof cresting and a 160ft minaret. The two-story buildings facing Massachu-setts Avenue house the library and the administrative offices. The double row of arches linking the two build-ings leads to a small courtyard with a pink marble fountain. Note the oblique alignment of the mosque's facade. Like all mosques, this building is oriented in the direction of Mecca. The **mosque** proper is an open square space flanked by colonnades ornamented in calligra-phy, and geometric and floral patterns (the Koran forbids the representation of human or animal forms). The lower parts of the walls are faced with 7,000 blue tiles donated by Turkey. The gifts from Egypt include the carved wood pulpit, or *minbar*. To its left is the niche indicating the direction of Mecca .

▷ *Cross the Charles Glover Bridge, a 420ft-long single-span construction (1940) that rises 75ft above a heavily wooded section of Rock Creek Park. Go to the corner of Whitehaven St.*

Embassy of Brazil

3000 Massachusetts Ave.

This edifice was built in 1909 by John Russell Pope. Inspired by Italian Renais-sance palaces, Pope designed four pro-portioned stories topped with a promi-nent cornice. The facade is punctuated by a recessed entry with two pairs of columns. The building, purchased by the Brazilian government in 1934, is the official ambassador's residence.

The dark-glass rectangular structure rest-ing on concrete legs at **no. 3006** houses the chancery. Erected in 1971 by the Bra-zilian architect Olavo Redig de Campos, it is one of the few contemporary buildings on Embassy Row.

Continue beyond the embassy of Bolivia *(nos. 3012-3014)* to the **Winston Churchill statue (1)** on the left. One of the great-est public figures of the 20C, Prime Min-ister Churchill was given honorary US citizenship in 1963 by President John F. Kennedy. Three years later, this statue by William McVey was unveiled.

British Embassy

3100 Massachusetts Ave.

This embassy complex (1931), designed by the British architect **Sir Edwin Lutyens** (1869-1944), resembles an early-18C English country estate. The building fac-ing the avenue is the main chancery—a U-shaped brick structure trimmed in white stone with steep roofs accented by tall chimneys. The ambassador's residence is linked to the rear of the chancery.

The nondescript office building rising to the west of Lutyens' building is the chancery annex. In 1957 the cornerstone for this addition was laid by Queen Elizabeth II.

Opposite, the **Kahlil Gibran Memorial (2)** commemorates the Lebanese-born (1883-1931) author of *The Prophet*.

THE ANACOSTIA RIVERFRONT

Somewhat off the beaten track, the banks of the Anacostia River host historic military installations and the southeast neighborhood known as Anacostia, an area rich in African-American history. Nationals Park, home of the city's baseball team, opened in 2008 and has initiated an infusion of new businesses and recreational venues into the area.

Highlights

> **Location:** See the map on page 221, in Additional Sights in DC section.
>
> **Timing:** Make advance reservations for the Navy Museum. Given the distances among attractions, allow one full day for a visit to this area.

A Bit of History
The Beginnings

The Nacotchtank Indians inhabited the area when Capt. John Smith explored it in 1608. Later explorers misheard Nacotchtank as "Anacostia," the name now applied to the eastern branch of the Potomac and its southeast shore. By mid-17C tobacco plantations, worked by black slaves, dotted the riverfront.

Thomas Jefferson had recommended that the land south and east of the river be included in the new federal district, as it offered a position from which to defend the city. The lower Southeast became the site of military installations, the first being the Navy Yard in 1799. With the demise of the tobacco economy, slaves were increasingly given or allowed to buy their freedom; by the early 19C the area had a large population of freed African-Americans. In addition, the liberal attitude of the federal circuit court toward black landownership and the rights of blacks encouraged many freemen to settle here.

The First Suburb

In the 1850s the area took on a suburban tenor with the establishment of Uniontown, whose row houses still stand along U, V, and W streets east of Martin Luther King Jr. Avenue. In 1862 Congress enacted a bill emancipating slaves in the District. After the Civil War a Freedman's Bureau was established under Gen. O.O. Howard, for whom Washington's **Howard University** is named. The bureau quietly purchased 375 acres in 1867 and resold it to African-American families eager to own land. Within a year 500 families lived here. In 1877 **Frederick Douglass,** abolitionist and one of the most prominent African-American figures in US history, moved to here.

20C

Throughout the first half of the 20C, Anacostia's demographics reflected a mix of black and white working-class residents, who lived in single-family homes. Low-income housing projects were built here in the 1950s and 60s. By 1970 the population of the area was predominantly African-American. The area suffered the serious social and economic problems afflicting many urban neighborhoods. In 1986 the district government designated Anacostia one of three development zones, and a line of the Metro was extended into the area.

Future Growth

A new stadium *(S. Capitol, First and N Sts. and Potomac Ave.)* for the **Washington Nationals** baseball team opened in 2008 to much fanfare and is expected to jumpstart new mixed-use waterfront development once the economy improves.

Frederick Douglass National Historic Site★

Known as Cedar Hill, this Victorian house was the last residence of African-American statesman, orator and abolitionist Frederick Douglass. The estate tops a grassy, shaded knoll overlooking the Anacostia River and the Mall area beyond, and serves as a perpetual monument to Douglass' ideals and spirit.

▷ **Location:** 1411 W St. SE. The site lies southeast of the Mall and south of the Anacostia River. By car: From Downtown, cross the 11th St. Bridge to Martin Luther King Jr. Ave. and turn left on W St.

🅿 **Parking:** Park *(free)* in the visitor center parking lot.

🎞 **Don't Miss:** The film *(17min)* about Douglass shown in the visitor center.

🕐 **Timing:** Allow 1hr for a visit.

A BIT OF HISTORY
Father of the Civil Rights Movement

Born into slavery in Talbot County, Maryland about 1818, **Frederick Douglass**, christened Frederick Augustus Washington Bailey, was the son of a black mother and an unidentified white father. As a boy he worked as a house servant in Baltimore, where he was taught reading and writing by the household's white mistress. However, as a young man he was sent to work in the fields and suffered physical deprivation and abuse at the hands of a notorious slave overseer. Later his owner allowed him to leave the fields and learn the trade of ship's caulker.

In 1838 Douglass escaped bondage and fled north, settling with his wife Anna Murray in New Bedford, Massachusetts. In 1841 he became involved with the Massachusetts Anti-Slavery Society and was soon a respected and well-known abolitionist and publicist. After the publication of his first autobiographical work, *Narrative of the Life of Frederick Douglass, An American Slave*, in 1845, Douglass departed for Europe. While abroad Douglass became a free man thanks to English sympathizers and friends who purchased his freedom in 1846. During the Civil War, Douglass exerted his efforts in recruiting black troops and in persuading Lincoln to legally end slavery. After the war he was involved with Reconstruction and moved to Washington, first settling in a row house on Capitol Hill, then, in 1877, on his Cedar Hill estate. During his years in Anacostia, Douglass received several presidential appointments to serve in district government.

In 1882 his wife died, and in 1884 his remarriage to Helen Pitts, a white woman, caused controversy but did not ultimately detract from Douglass' influence as a powerful spokesman for civil rights. In 1895, after attending a women's rights meeting, Douglass died suddenly of a heart attack at his home.

Frederick Douglass

National Archives 200(s)FL-22

Cedar Hill

The neat white house with its broad columned front porch was originally built as a speculative property in the late 1850s by John Van Hook, one of the developers of the area's first planned residential community, Uniontown.

When Douglass purchased the 9-acre estate from Van Hook, the house had never been lived in. Douglass expanded the property to 15 acres and added seven rooms to the rear of the house.

In 1900 Douglass' widow, Helen, founded the Frederick Douglass Memorial Association, which, in conjunction with the National Association of Colored Women, opened the house for tours.

The house was donated to the National Park Service in 1962; the park service restored the estate and opened the historic site to the public. Early 2007 saw the completion of a $2.7million preservation effort that, among other improvements, restored the house to its 1893-95 appearance.

VISIT

Visitor center open Apr–Oct daily 9am–5pm (rest of the year til 4:30 pm). Closed Jan 1, Thanksgiving Day & Dec 25. House visit by guided tour (30min) only, year-round daily 9am, 12:15pm, 1:15pm, 3pm, 3:30pm & 4pm (4pm is last tour during summer). (reservations encouraged ℘877-444-6777; $1.50 service fee). ℘202-426-5961. www.nps.gov/frdo.

The house is decorated with Victorian furnishings and memorabilia, most of which belonged to the family. The ground floor consists of a formal parlor and a family parlor, a dining room, kitchen, Douglass' study, a pantry and washroom. Note the rare Douglass portrait by Sarah James Eddy in the formal parlor. Douglass sat for the artist during a visit to Massachusetts. The second floor houses five bedrooms. Behind the house, a small reconstructed stone building served as a second study, which Douglass called "the Growlery."

Anacostia Community Museum

Located on the high ground of old Fort Stanton, a Civil War fortress now converted into a public park, this museum was conceived by the Smithsonian Institution as a neighborhood museum. Since its inception in 1967, it has focused on African-American communities, including Anacostia.

VISIT

Open year-round daily 10am–5pm. Closed Dec 25. ℘202-633-4820. www.anacostia.si.edu.

The museum holds a permanent collection of more than 6,000 objects dating from 1800 to the present, including photographs, furniture, works of art, musical instruments and textiles. Changing

Location: 1901 Fort Place SE. By car: From Downtown, cross the 11th St. Bridge to Martin Luther King Jr. Ave. and turn left on Morris Rd., which becomes Erie St. before ending at Fort Pl.

Parking: On-site parking is free.

exhibits on black history, culture and achievements are mounted year-round. The museum also sponsors a host of programs including an annual Mardi Gras arts festival, a Kwanzaa celebration and a concert series.

The museum permanently displays "Separate and Unequaled: Black Baseball in the District of Columbia," a popular exhibit exploring the time from Reconstruction to the 1950s when the city's baseball diamonds were segregated.

Congressional Cemetery

Ⓜ *Potomac Ave*

Established in 1807 by private investors, this grassy site above the river was created as the burial grounds for the new federal city. In 1812 the cemetery was deeded to nearby Christ Church, whose vestry allocated 100 plots for the burial of members of Congress, adding a further 300 in 1823. Congress bought more sites; provided funds for walls, a gatekeeper's house, vaults and other improvements; and renamed it the Congressional Cemetery. The many dog owners who walk their pets here help preserve the grounds.

VISIT

🕐*Open year-round daily dawn–dusk.* 🕐*Closed Jan 1 & Dec 25.* 🅿 ✆*202-543-0539. www.congressionalcemetery.org.*

- **Location:** 1801 E St. SE. By car: From Columbus Cir NE take Mass. Ave, NE, to 17th St. NE to E St. NE
- **Parking:** Street parking available near the gate.
- 🕐 **Timing:** About 1 hr
- **Don't Miss:** The Public Vault, the final resting place of three US presidents and two First Ladies.

Many prominent individuals involved with the history of the nation are buried on the 32-acre grounds. Notable among these are Civil War photographer Mathew Brady, "March King" composer John Philip Sousa (who was born in nearby Anacostia), and Push-ma-ta-ha, a Choctaw chief who served with Andrew Jackson in the War of 1812. In addition, more than 70 former members of the House and 20 former senators lie here.

Fort Lesley J. McNair

Ⓜ *Waterfront*

Strategically positioned at the confluence of the Anacostia River and the Washington Channel, this complex, dating back to 1794, is one of the nation's oldest military installations in continuous operation. Known by various names over the years—Turkey Buzzards Point, Fort Humphreys, and the US Arsenal—the post was renamed Fort Lesley J. McNair in 1948 in honor of the commander of the army ground forces who was killed in Normandy in 1944.

A BIT OF HISTORY

It was on this site in 1865 that four of John Wilkes Booth's fellow conspirators in the Lincoln assassination plot were imprisoned and hanged. One of them,

- **Location:** 4th and P Sts. SW. By car: Visitors must enter through the 2nd St gate two blocks from the Main Gate. Turn right on 2nd Street and the gate is on the right.
- **Parking:** Parking on base for visitors on military business.
- **Don't Miss:** Free summer Twilight Tattoo concerts by the U.S. Army Band.

Mary Surratt, was the first American woman executed by federal order. At the turn of the 19C, Maj. Walter Reed, who was instrumental in identifying the carrier of yellow fever, conducted research in the fort's military hospital. Occupying a 98-acre site, Fort McNair today is the headquarters of the US Army Military District of Washington and the home of the prestigious National Defense University.

VISIT

🕐 *The visitors' gate is open daily year-round. Visitors are allowed to drive or stroll only around the grounds.*
😊 *A photo ID must be presented for entry.* ♿ 🅿️ *Because the fort is an active military base,* 🔑 *buildings are open only to military personnel.*
The post is laid out in a long quadrangle with a central esplanade bordered by rows of brick houses that serve as residences for officers. At the southern tip of the grounds rises the **National War College** (1907), designed by McKim, Mead and White. Among the other noteworthy institutions on the post are the Industrial College of the Armed Forces and the **Inter-American Defense College** (1962). The Defense College trains senior officers from 19 countries in the Western Hemisphere.

Washington Navy Yard

Ⓜ *Navy Yard*

Once a prominent shipbuilding yard for the US Navy, this facility now serves primarily as an administrative center and as a historic precinct used ceremonially as the "Quarterdeck of the Navy." Two military museums open to the public are housed on the premises.

A BIT OF HISTORY

In 1799 the first secretary of the Navy, Benjamin Stoddert, authorized this shipbuilding yard as the US Navy's first shore facility. The prominent architect Benjamin H. Latrobe was commissioned to design the complex. The Navy Yard expanded rapidly until the British occupation of Washington in 1814. At that time the yard's commandant, Capt. Thomas Tingey, ordered the facility burned down, to avoid enemy takeover. The yard was rebuilt and continued ship production until the mid-1850s, when it began ordnance manufacturing.

By 1886 it was known as the Naval Gun Factory. The facility ceased operation in 1961.

VISIT

🕐 *The grounds of the Navy Yard are open daily year-round.* 😊 *A photo ID is required to enter the Navy Yard.*

▷ **Location:** 9th and M Sts. SE. Navy Yard. Navy Yard Metro Station (Green Line).
🅿️ **Parking:** Civilian cars are allowed on the ground only on the weekends. On Sat & Sun drivers must show vehicle registration and proof of insurance or rental agreement at the gate. A paid lot at 6th and M Sts. SE, is open during the week.

Navy Museum

Entrance at 11th & O Sts. SE. 🕐 *Open year-round Mon–Fri 9am–5pm; Sat-Sun & holidays 10am–5pm.* ✕ ♿ 🅿️ ✆ *202-433-4882. www.history.navy.mil.*
Housed in a cavernous workshop of the former gun factory, this exhibit hall was opened in 1963. Its permanent displays trace the history of the US Navy from the Revolutionary War through the space age. Among the highlights are an extensive collection of scale-model ships, including a 25ft-long, detailed model of a World War II landing craft (LSM). A number of gun mounts on display may be manipulated by visitors.
Permanently docked near the annex at Pier 2 is the destroyer **USS Barry**. The below-deck living and working quarters are open to the public.

Along with the countless treasures housed in Washington's many world famous museums and galleries, the capital city is also home to several off-the-beaten path gems. Often set away from the gleaming white marble of the monuments and the constant stream of people on the Mall, these attractions like Hillwood Museum, the Washington National Cathedral, The Kreeger Museum and The National Zoo can be found nestled among residential neighborhoods. While they might not be the sites most readily identified with Washington, DC, they by no means should be overlooked.

A Bit of History

Many of the Washington's current residential neighborhoods started out as summer communities where Washingtonians got away from the bustle of city life. During the 18th and 19th centuries and before automobiles were invented and car travel became popular for the masses, many wealthy city dwellers commissioned architects to design late Victorian frame houses much like the vacation homes found in New England at the time. President Grover Cleveland even summered in one of these picturesque tree-filled areas. Although his summer estate was demolished in 1927 his presence in the neighborhood remains to this day through its name, Cleveland Park.

Although the 22nd president's summer residence no longer stands many examples of similar types of homes do remain. The oldest example of this type of house still standing in Cleveland Park (and some say in the city) is the Rosedale estate (3501 Newark St, NW), built in 1794 by General Uriah Forrestre, an aide-de-camp of George Washington who became a Maryland congressman.

In the late 1890s electric streetcars began connecting Cleveland Park and other neighborhoods like it to Downtown and the area transitioned from summer retreat to "streetcar suburb." With time these suburbs became absorbed as part of the actual city. Sprinkled among many of them are historic homes and estates like Hillwood that now house museums or collections that can be visited by the public.

Highlights

1 Strolling **Hillwood**'s gardens after taking in the museum's Russian decorative arts collection (p224)

2 Gazing at the Great Pandas at the **National Zoo** (p226)

3 Taking a tour of the **Washington National Cathedral** (p228)

Neighborhood Treasures

DC's Metro rail system makes it easy for visitors to move away from the main tourist areas and explore other parts of the city. Many of the attractions like the National Zoo have their own station and tend to be an easy walk from the Metro stop. Signs pointing the way to sights of interest in residential neighborhoods can also be found along the way. Some of the smaller museums require a more significant walk or an additional bus ride or taxi fare.

City of Many Faiths

Diversity helps define the city's make up. Residents not only come from all ethnic backgrounds but also embrace a host of different faiths. Perhaps nowhere is this more evident than along the upper portion of 16th St. NW, where houses of worship for myriad religions line the famous street. Visitors of all religions tend to be drawn to DC's faith-based sites like the magnificent Washington National Cathedral and the churches on the grounds of Catholic University.

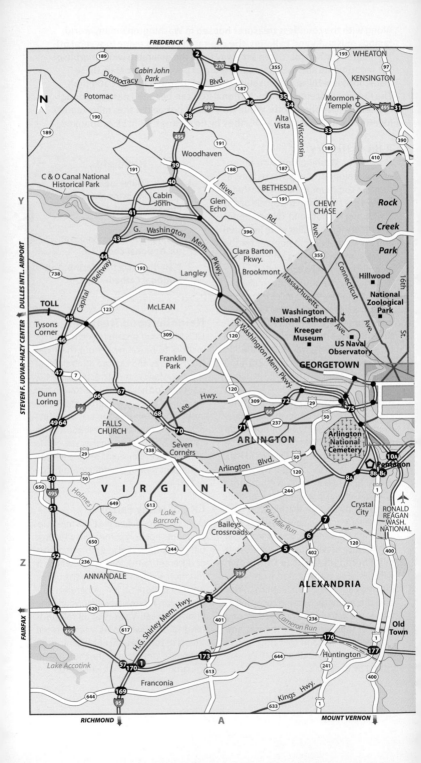

FREDERICK

A

WHEATON

KENSINGTON

Cabin John Park

Democracy

Blvd.

Potomac

Mormon Temple

Alta Vista

N

C & O Canal National Historical Park

Woodhaven

Glen Echo

BETHESDA

Rock

River

Rd.

Creek

Cabin John

CHEVY CHASE

Park

G. Washington Mem. Pkwy.

Clara Barton Pkwy.

Brookmont

Hillwood

Langley

National Zoological Park

TOLL

McLEAN

Washington National Cathedral

Tysons Corner

Kreeger Museum

US Naval Observatory

Franklin Park

GEORGETOWN

Dunn Loring

Hwy.

FALLS CHURCH

Lee

ARLINGTON

Arlington National Cemetery

Seven Corners

VIRGINIA

Arlington Blvd.

Pentagon

Holmes

Run

Lake Barcroft

Crystal City

RONALD REAGAN WASH. NATIONAL

ANNANDALE

Baileys Crossroads

Four Mile Run

ALEXANDRIA

H.G. Shirley Mem. Hwy.

Cameron Run

Old Town

Lake Accotink

Huntington

Franconia

Kings Hwy.

RICHMOND

A

MOUNT VERNON

STEVEN F. UDVAR-HAZY CENTER

DULLES INTL. AIRPORT

FAIRFAX

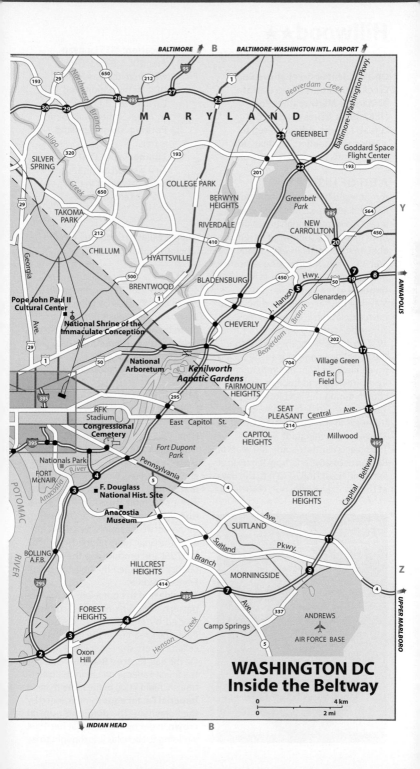

WASHINGTON DC
Inside the Beltway

Hillwood★★

M *Van Ness*

On a residential street above Rock Creek Park lies the 25-acre estate of Marjorie Merriweather Post (1887-1973), heiress to the Post cereals fortune. Administered by a private foundation, her mansion and grounds are open to the public.

A BIT OF HISTORY

A renowned businesswoman, hostess and philanthropist, Mrs. Post was also an avid collector. Though her columned brick mansion is somewhat unremarkable on its own, its interior holds 18C and 19C French furnishings and the most extensive collection of **Russian imperial arts**★★★ outside Russia. Marjorie Post accompanied her third husband, Joseph E. Davies, to Moscow, where he served as ambassador from 1937 to 1938. While they were there, the Soviet government was still selling art confiscated from the imperial family, aristocracy and Russian Orthodox church during the Revolution of 1917. The Davies purchased some of these treasures in the commission shops of Moscow and Leningrad.

The objects illustrate some 200 years of Russian decorative arts, from the reign of Peter the Great (1682-1725) to the days of the last Czar, Nicholas II (1868-1918),

> **Location:** 4155 Linnean Ave. NW. A 20min. (1mi) walk from the Van Ness/ UDC Metro station (Red Line). By bus: L1 or L2 bus to Tilden St then walk .5 mi.

P **Parking:** On-site parking is free.

○ **Timing:** Allow 3hrs. First view an orientation video *(14min)* at the visitors center.

when jeweler Carl Fabergé created his fabulous Easter eggs.

VISIT

○*Open Tue–Sat 10am–5pm (might be closed Jan).* Visit by self-guided tour *(audio tours available); guided tours of the mansion available.* ○*Closed major holidays.* $15. *Garden tours available in spring and fall.* P 202-686-5807. www.hillwoodmuseum.org.

Mansion

Hillwood displays the interior furnishings that reflect Mrs. Post's occupancy from 1955 to her death in 1973. In the entry hall, find a rock-crystal chandelier, Sèvres porcelain, portraits of Russian royalty, and 18C French commodes of wood marquetry, gilded bases and marble. The octagonal **Russian Porcelain Room** is lined with cases containing dinner services commissioned by Catherine the Great (who reigned from 1762 to 1796) and produced in the Moscow factory established by the Englishman Francis Gardner.

The oldest of the porcelains is a white pattern with pink rosettes, commissioned by Elizabeth I (daughter of Peter the Great) from the Imperial Porcelain Factory she established in 1744. Off the hall, the **Icon Room**★★ contains the finest Fabergé pieces in the collection, including two of the more than 50 **imperial Easter eggs** commissioned by the Romanovs. The **diamond nuptial crown**, worn by Alexandra at her 1894 wedding to Nicholas II, is thought to be

Imperial Easter Egg (1895) by Carl Fabergé

Hillwood Estate, Museum and Gardens

the only piece of Russian imperial regalia known to exist outside Russia.

Occupying much of the first floor are the **French drawing room**, appointed in Mrs. Post's favorite style, Louis XVI; and the **dining room**, featuring an inlaid-marble Florentine table with seating for 30. The long pavilion was used as a movie theater and for square dancing, an activity Mrs. Post enjoyed. The **Russian Liturgical Gallery** contains Russian Orthodox robes brocaded with silver and gold threads and a 24-carat **gold chalice** commissioned by Catherine the Great.

The bedrooms on the second floor include an Adam-style guest room with blue and white Wedgwood jasperware, and Mrs. Post's own Louis XVI room.

Grounds

Gardens surrounding the mansion include an informal flower garden, a formal French parterre planted in boxwood, a rose garden encircling a pillar marking Mrs. Post's grave, a Japanese-style garden, and a flowering pet cemetery. In the wooded area south of the mansion is a log **dacha**, a replica of a Russian cottage and the **Adirondack building**, a wood cabin that decorated Mrs. Post's retreat in the Adirondack Mountains of New York.

Hillwood's cafe serves a popular afternoon tea and will lend guests picnic blankets. Lectures, workshops, preschool tours, family days, gay community days and outdoor movies are among the many programs regularly held.

National Zoological Park★★

Ⓜ *Woodley Park-Zoo or Cleveland Park*

With plants and landscaped environments an integral part of its concept, this "biopark" exhibits more than 2,000 wild animals and serves as a research institution devoted to the study, preservation and breeding of threatened species. One-fifth of the 400 species represented here are considered endangered.

A BIT OF HISTORY

Created in 1887 as the Department of Living Animals, the precursor of this zoo was located on the Mall and featured such indigenous American mammals as bison, mule deer and lynx. In 1889 Congress appropriated funds for the creation of a true zoological park, to be administered by the Smithsonian Institution. A 166-acre tract above Rock Creek Park was purchased, and landscape architect Frederick Law Olmsted laid out plans for the new zoo. Because of disagreement

▷ **Location:** 3001 Connecticut Ave. NW. Use the accompanying map and take the zoo's main path, Olmstead Walk, which heads downhill from the visitor center; then follow Valley Trail back (⚠caution: it's a bit steeper, but has more shade). The Asia Trail, with its quarter-mile long path, showcases many animals that are new to the zoo.

🅿 **Parking:** There is a fee *($22 maximum)* for on-site parking.

🕐 **Timing:** Allow at least 2hrs plus time for a meal.

👪 **Kids:** The Giant Pandas are a highlight.

among zoo administrators, Olmsted's project was only minimally realized. Though it was an immediate success, the zoo was plagued with financial problems. Not until 1964, when appropriations for it became part of the Smithsonian Institution budget, was the zoo able to revamp and modernize its facilities.

Elephant Trails

As part of the zoo's campaign to save Asian elephants, the Elephant House is undergoing renovation. Phase one of the new Elephant Community Center is now open. This major development will expand and diversify the elephants habitat in order to stimulate natural behavior and hopefully increase the size of the herd. During construction the zoo's three elephants can often be seen in an outdoor area near the old building.

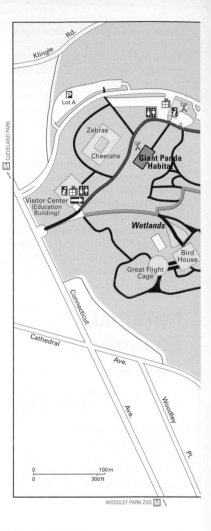

HIGHLIGHTS

Main entrance at Connecticut Ave. Grounds open Apr–Oct daily 6am–8pm; rest of the year daily 6am–6pm. Buildings open Apr–Oct daily 10am–6pm; rest of the year daily 10am–4:30pm. Closed Dec 25. (fee for parking) 202-633-4480. http://nationalzoo.si.edu.

The National Zoo's most famous residents, and some might argue its cutest, are its Giant pandas Mei Xiang (b.1998) and Tian Tian (b.1997). (*see sidebar*) The pandas, currently on loan from the China Wildlife Conservation Association, live in the zoo's new **Fujifilm Giant Panda Habitat**★★. Visitors can observe the two furry creatures playing, resting and eating in the 12,000 sq-ft outdoor exhibit, which was designed to mimic the pandas' natural habitat of rocky, lush terrain back in China. It includes rock and tree structures for climbing and grottoes, pools, and streams for keeping cool during DC's hot summer months. The indoor exhibit has also been expanded and contains more visitor viewing space and informational exhibits about the Giant Pandas.

Kids' Farm

One of the newest additions to the National Zoo, the Kids' Farm near the Rock Creek Park entrance and the bottom of the **Olmsted Walk**, allows young visitors to get up close to cows, donkeys, goats, alpacas, hogs, and rabbits.

Nearby at the Giant Pizza Playground, little ones can climb all over a 22-foot-wide rubber-surfaced pizza complete with a crawl-through olive. During the summer season (beginning in June) a free shuttle picks up visitors at Kids' Farm and drops them off at Panda Plaza/Bus Lot on the hour from 11am-6pm.

Reptile Discovery Center

Slimy scaly creatures abound at the Reptile Discovery Center where visitors can learn about the reptilian and amphibian world and view tortoises, alligators, Komodo dragons, and snakes. The number of people allowed in

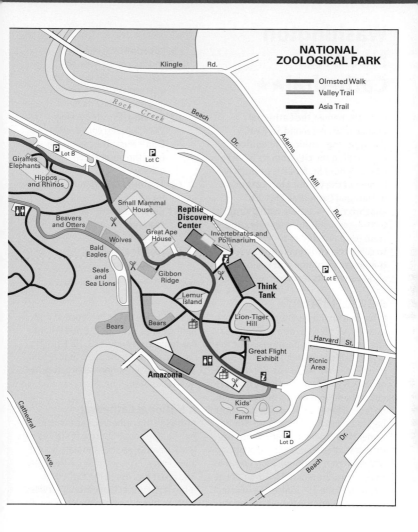

NATIONAL ZOOLOGICAL PARK

- Olmsted Walk
- Valley Trail
- Asia Trail

the indoor exhibit is limited so on busy days lines sometimes form under a shaded canopy.

The O Line

Don't forget to look overhead for orangutans crossing on the O Line, short for the Orangutan Transport System (OTS), a 490 ft system of towers and cables that allows the them to move between two buildings. Tower 1 is in the outdoor orangutan yard at the Great Ape House and Tower 8 is in the outdoor orangutan yard outside **Think Tank**★, an indoor interactive exhibit devoted to exploring what animals think about.

DC's Darlings

Giant Pandas Tian Tian and Mei Xiang have captured the hearts of Washingtonians. The breeding-age pair arrived in the US from China in December 2000 and produced their first offspring at the zoo in July 2005. Named Tai Shan, the cub returned to China in 2010. The People's Republic of China receives $1 million per year for the loan of the pandas; these funds help preserve the wild panda population.

Washington National Cathedral★★

Officially named the Cathedral Church of St. Peter and St. Paul, the imposing Gothic-style edifice overlooking the city from its 57-acre site on Mount St. Alban is popularly known as the Washington Cathedral or National Cathedral. This 20C anachronism—replete with flying buttresses, vaulting, gargoyles and stained-glass windows—was raised to celebrate Christian faith as well as the American nation and key figures and events in its history.

▷ **Location:** Massachusetts and Wisconsin Aves. NW. Take any no. 30s bus to the intersection of Wisconsin and Massachusetts Aves.

Ⓟ **Parking:** On-site parking *(fee applies except on Sun).*

👁 **Don't Miss:** The panorama from the observation gallery.

🕐 **Timing:** Allow 90min for a visit.

👥 **Kids:** The Darth Vader sculpture on St. Peter's Tower.

👁 **Also See:** US Naval Observatory.

A BIT OF HISTORY

In his plan for the capital, planner Pierre Charles L'Enfant proposed "a great church for national purposes," but the idea won little support, the new nation being committed to the separation of church and state. In 1893 Congress authorized the building but allocated no federal funds for the project; support had to be provided by private donors. Under the leadership of the Right Rev. Dr. Yates Satterlee, first Episcopal bishop of Washington, the foundation was able to purchase the Mount St. Alban site at the turn of the 19C. Satterlee insisted that the cathedral welcome all, regardless of faith or nationality, and that it be built in what he considered the only truly Christian architectural style—Gothic. The foundation stone was laid by President Theodore Roosevelt in 1907, before a crowd of 10,000. Services have continued here every day since 1912, when the first service was celebrated.

The cathedral, built primarily of Indiana limestone, was constructed by applying traditional techniques known to medieval European masons. Pneumatic tools and modern cranes accelerated the work. Thousands of people donated time, energy and money toward the construction, the furnishings and the landscaping. In a ceremony held in 1990, the final stone was set in place on the St. Paul Tower in the presence of President George H. Bush. The mid-Atlantic earthquake on August 23, 2011, put significant stress on the cathedral; repairs are ongoing but its general structure has been stabilized.

A National Cathedral

Although the cathedral is administered by the Episcopal Church, it strives to reach beyond religious and state boundaries. Every US president since Theodore Roosevelt has visited the cathedral. It has hosted special memorial services such as those for Vietnam War casualties, Iran hostages, Americans killed in the Persian Gulf War and victims of the September 2001 terrorist attacks. Several prominent figures are among the more than 100 Americans interred in the cathedral.

VISIT

🕐*Open year-round Mon–Fri 10am–5:30pm, Sat 10am–4:30pm, Sun 8am–4pm.* 👣*Guided tours (30min) year-round on the half-hour Mon–Sat 10am–11:30am & 12:45pm (Sat 3:30pm), Sun 1pm–2:30pm.* 💲*$10 donation suggested.* ✕Ⓟ. ✆*202-537-6200. www.nationalcathedral.org. Organ recitals Sun 5:15pm. Carillon recitals Sat 12:30pm.*

Exterior

Measuring 514ft long from west facade to apse, the cathedral is among the world's 10 largest churches in size. Crowning the crossing, the **Gloria in Excelsis Tower**, with its 53-bell carillon, rises 301ft and dominates the skyline northwest of Washington.

The **west facade**, designed by Philip Hubert Frohman, is flanked by two identical towers dedicated to St. Peter *(left)* and St. Paul *(right)*. The carved tympanum above the central portal was designed by Frederick Hart, also known for his Vietnam Veterans Memorial sculpture group on the Mall. The bronze gates of the central portal are decorated with scenes from the lives of Abraham and Moses, and a statue of Adam adorns the portal's *trumeau*, or central pillar. The centerpiece of the facade is the 26ft rose window—10,500 pieces of glass by stained-glass artist Rowan LeCompte.

Designed to carry rainwater away from the walls, the gargoyles and grotesques around the flying buttresses that support the vaulting of the nave reflect the whimsies that carvers were occasionally allowed to indulge. With binoculars, visitors can spot 📷 a sculpture of Darth Vader from the film *Star Wars* on the St. Peter Tower.

Interior

The narthex, just inside the west entrance, features inlaid seals of the 50 states and the District of Columbia on its floor. The nave extends some 565ft to the high altar and has three levels: an arcade of pointed arches; the gallery, or triforium, which bears the state flags; and the upper section pierced with windows (the clerestory). The vaulted ceiling soars 102ft—about 10 stories. Bays honor Abraham Lincoln *(to the left of the entrance)* and George Washington *(to the right)*. Halfway down the right aisle *(over the 5th bay)*, the cathedral's most popular stained-glass window, the **Space Window**, commemorates the first manned lunar landing in 1969. A genuine moon rock is fitted in the center of the large red disc representing the

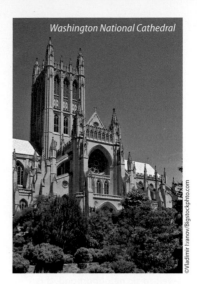

Washington National Cathedral

©Vladimir Ivanov/Bigstockphto.com

moon. Just past the Space Window is the tomb of President Woodrow Wilson. The four colossal pillars in the crossing provide support for the Gloria in Excelsis Tower. The pulpit, built of stone from England's Canterbury Cathedral, is still used every Sunday.

Above the high altar, the Jerusalem altar, is the **Ter Sanctus reredos**, a carved stone wall dominated by a representation of Christ in Majesty. To the left, note the Glastonbury Cathedra, a bishop's throne built of blocks from Glastonbury Abbey in England.

To the right of the choir, the War Memorial Chapel commemorates those who lost their lives for the nation. A statue of a young Jesus welcomes visitors to the Children's Chapel, which contains furnishings scaled down for youngsters.

Crypt

Access by the staircase on the north side of the choir.

This vast underground labyrinth extends under the entire main floor. Of particular note are chapels dedicated to the birth (Bethlehem Chapel), death (St. Joseph's Chapel) and resurrection of Jesus (Resurrection Chapel).

Among Americans interred here are Helen Keller (1880-1968) and her teacher Anne Sullivan. The crypt also houses the cathedral's visitor center.

Observation Gallery

7th floor. ⏱Open year-round Mon–Fri 10am–5pm, Sat 10am–4pm, Sun 1pm–4pm. Take either of the elevators in the narthex near the main entrance.

The gallery provides a **panorama** of Washington. The gallery's 70 windows offer a bird's-eye view of the flying buttresses that support the nave. A slide show and a small exhibit illustrate the history of the cathedral.

Grounds

The landscaped 57-acre site on which the cathedral stands, also known as the Close, comprises three schools, a college for clergy and the **Bishop's Garden**, which provides a fragrant haven of herbs, flowers and boxwood.

The Kreeger Museum★

Ensconced behind a high wall in a well-to-do neighborhood, this unadorned post-Modern mansion (1967, Philip Johnson) contains the formidable art collection of former residents David and Carmen Kreeger. Rife with 19C and 20C European paintings, the 200-piece collection includes African and 20C art.

A BIT OF HISTORY

A Washingtonian, Kreeger made his fortune in the insurance industry. An avid collector, particularly of works by European Impressionists and post-

▷ **Location:** 2401 Foxhall Rd. NW. Drive north on Massachusetts Ave. to Nebraska Ave. At the circle, exit Nebraska Ave. to the west. Turn left onto Foxhall Rd.

Impressionists, he hired Philip Johnson to build a house that could function as a museum and performance venue. After her husband's death in 1990, Mrs. Kreeger vacated the house. In 1994 it was opened to the public as a museum. The 24,000sq ft travertine dwelling comprises core modules of stacked cubes topped by barrel-vaulted ceilings. Most rooms have no doors. Designed

The Kreeger Museum

© Eileen Wold/The Kreeger Museum

as a concert hall and gallery, the Great Hall (22ft by 66ft) provides ample space for hanging art on its carpeted walls. Punctuated with floor-to-ceiling windows at each end, the hall opens onto a spacious terrace, the setting for outdoor sculpture.

VISIT

Visit by guided tour (90min) only, Sept–Jul Tue–Thu 10:30am & 1:30pm; reservations required. Optional tours Fri 10:30am & 1:30pm. Sat tours 10:30am, noon & 2pm (no reservations needed). *Closed major holidays.* *$10.* 202-338-3552. *www.kreegermuseum.org.*

Tours focus on one or two selected works in each room to illustrate historic trends, schools of art or specific techniques. Of particular interest are early works by Cézanne (*The Blue Vase,* c.1882) and van Gogh (*Bouquet of Zinnias,* 1886) that do not resemble the styles for which the artists later became known.

First-floor galleries house 19C and 20C European art. Paintings and small sculptural works grace the Great Hall.

Note Picasso's atypical *Café de la Rotonde* (1901). The dining room contains paintings by French Impressionists, including no less than nine by Monet.

The works of Corot and Mondrian are highlights of the library; the landing showcases paintings by Picasso, Miró, Man Ray and others.

On the lower level, one gallery is devoted to large acrylic works representative of Abstract Expressionism and Color Field painting. An alcove contains African art, primarily large wooden masks.

Upstairs, the terrace features larger sculptures by Henry Moore, Jacques Lipchitz, Isamu Noguchi and others.

"Sculpture on the Grounds" invites select artists to create a new installation on the east lawn every two years.

Kenilworth Aquatic Gardens

M *Deanwood*

Located on tidal marshland along the eastern bank of the Anacostia River, this peaceful haven in northeast Washington comprises some 40 diked ponds devoted to the cultivation of water lilies, lotus and other aquatic plants.

Location: Anacostia Ave. and Douglas St. NE. By car: Drive northeast on New York Ave. From New York Ave. take 295 South. Exit Eastern Ave. and turn right on Douglas St. (2nd right after exiting freeway). Continue on Douglas St. to the gardens' entrance.

A BIT OF HISTORY

Walter B. Shaw, a Civil War veteran, began the gardens in 1880. The lilies he grew multiplied so quickly that he began commercial cultivation. In the 1920s the gardens were popular for Sunday outings and were visited by presidents Wilson, Harding and Coolidge.

In the 1930s a dredging project proposed by the Army Corps of Engineers threatened the survival of the ponds.

To save them, the Department of the Interior purchased them in 1938. The 12-acre tract is currently administered by the National Park Service.

VISIT

Open Memorial Day–Labor Day daily 7am–5pm (rest of the year til 4:30pm). *Closed Jan 1, Thanksgiving Day & Dec 25.* 202-426-6905. *www.nps.gov/keaq.* *The blooms are most spectacular in the morning.*

Among the park's exotic flora are the **Victoria amazonica**, a water lily whose platter-shaped leaves grow as large as 6ft across, and that only blooms in the late summer and early fall. Also look for the **East Indian Lotus**. In 1951 seeds for this rare plant were discovered in a dry lake bed in Manchuria, and were subsequently germinated by the park service. Believed to have been 350 to 575 years old, they are among the oldest viable seeds discovered to date. The ancient lotus plants can be viewed in the pond directly behind the visitor center. The Victoria lilies are located in a pond at the far western end of the gardens, near the Anacostia River.

The delicate blooms here don't like the hot weather so in the summer come early before the heat of the day. Flowers close up when it gets above 89 or 90 degrees, and once closed won't open again until the next morning.

National Arboretum

This federally owned 446-acre tract on the slopes of Mount Hamilton is one of the largest arboretums in the country. Established by Congress in 1927, the arboretum opened to the public in 1947, when some 15,000 azaleas were in bloom. Today its hills and valleys are covered in evergreens, wildflowers, flowering trees and shrubs.

VISIT

Open year-round daily 8am–5pm.
Closed Dec 25. ♿ 🅿 ✆ 202-245-2726.
www.usna.usda.gov.

The **National Bonsai and Penjing Museum**★ (*open daily 10am–4pm*) is renowned for its collection of Japanese, Chinese and North American bonsai.

- **Location:** 3501 New York Ave. NE. By car: From downtown, drive northeast on New York Ave. and enter the service road on the right after crossing Bladensburg Rd. Another entrance at 24th and R Sts. NE.

- **Timing:** Allow 2hrs. The arboretum is designed to be toured by car. Nine miles of paved roads lead past the various gardens, collections and designated parking areas along the route.

The 2-acre **Herb Garden** comprises a formal knot garden; a rose garden with more than 80 varieties of "old" roses;

National Arboretum

© David Park/Dreamstime.com

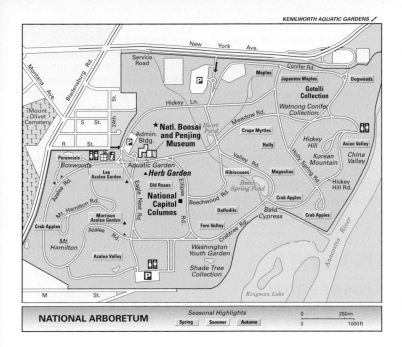

KENILWORTH AQUATIC GARDENS

NATIONAL ARBORETUM

Seasonal Highlights
Spring Summer Autumn

0   250m
0   1000ft

and 10 specialty gardens, where herbs are grouped according to their uses throughout history. Atop a bluff stand the **National Capitol Columns** that originally supported the east entrance portico of the Capitol prior to its expansion in the late 1950s. Pleasant stops along the drive include **Fern Valley**, the picturesque **Asian Valley** and the **Gotelli collection**, considered one of the finest groupings of dwarf conifers in the world.

National Museum of Health and Medicine

Previously housed on the grounds of Walter Reed Army Medical Center, this museum moved to a new 20,000sq ft building that opened in 2011 in celebration of the museum's 150 anniversary. With a collection of 25 million objects, the museum is an important repository of the country's medical past as well as an impetus to scientific inquiry and public education through its exhibits on contemporary health.

▷ **Location:** By car: Drive north on 16th St. into Maryland. Turn left on 2nd Ave. , then left on Linden Lane. By Metro: Exit at Forest Glen station (1mi from the museum), walk S on Georgia Ave., turn right on Seminary Rd., staying on the right side through next light; proceed to Linden Ln.

A BIT OF HISTORY

Begun during the Civil War by US Surgeon General William Hammond, the museum has advanced scientific knowledge through staff research conducted during wartime, epidemics and national tragedies such as the Lincoln and Garfield assassinations. As curator, Maj. **Walter Reed** (US Army surgeon 1851-1902) and his team identified the carrier of yellow fever, paving the way for the disease's control. In 1909 Maj. Frederick Russell successfully tested a vaccine for typhoid at the museum when it was housed at Walter Reed Medical Center.

VISIT

2500 Linden Lane, Silver Spring, MD. ◷Open year-round daily 10am–5:30pm.

◷Closed Dec 25. ♿ 🅿 ✆202-782-2200. www.medicalmuseum.mil ✋Some exhibits are not for the fainthearted. Exhibits depict medical progress through items ranging from Revolutionary War amputation implements to the medicinal leeches of modern microsurgery. Highlights include photographs of injured Civil War soldiers taken before and after facial surgery, microscopes dating from the late 16C to the 20C, and such artifacts as the lead bullet that claimed Abraham Lincoln's life.

US Naval Observatory

This naval facility is responsible for providing crucial astronomical and timing data to government agencies, the Navy and the country at large.

A BIT OF HISTORY

Originally established in 1830 in Foggy Bottom, the observatory was the first true scientific agency in the country. With its 26in telescope, Asaph Hall discovered the two moons of Mars in 1877. To avoid the detrimental noise, light and vibrations of the Foggy Bottom area, the observatory was moved in 1893 to a more secluded location on the upper portion of Massachusetts Avenue. Noted architect Richard Morris Hunt designed the main buildings.

Since 1974 a white brick Victorian structure initially built on the observatory grounds as the superintendent's house has served as the official residence of the vice president of the US *(○━not open to the public)*.

Today the observatory is responsible for calculating the positions of the solar bodies, measuring the earth's rotation, and determining precise time—the accuracy of which is vital for navigation and communications on earth and in space.

▷ **Location:** 3450 Massachusetts Ave. NW. By car: Drive north on Massachusetts Ave. past Embassy Row to visitors' gate at Observatory Circle.

🅿 **Parking:** Street parking available outside the entrance gate.

◷ **Timing:** Allow 2hrs. The tour is 90min and the video lasts 22min.

VISIT

♿♿Entrance at South Gate. ☞Visit by guided tour (90min) only, year-round alternating Mondays 8:30pm. 4- to 6-week advance reservations required: ♿see instructions online. ✋A photo ID is required for entry. Tour involves walking in darkness on hilly grounds. ◷Closed major holidays. 🅿 ✆202-762-1467. www.usno.navy.mil.

A video *(22min)* features the history of the observatory. Included on the tour is the **Master Clock** of the US and the U.S. Department of Defense, actually several rows of atomic clocks. The observatory also provides the timing data for individual GPS satellites and telephone modems. Visitors are given an opportunity to view the sky *(weather permitting)* through a 12in Alvan Clark refractor telescope.

Basilica of the National Shrine of the Immaculate Conception

Ⓜ *Brookland CUA*

A 20C blend of Byzantine and Romanesque styles, this massive Roman Catholic church is the official national tribute to Mary, the Mother of Christ and the patroness of the US. Official papal recognition of Mary as this country's patroness dates back to 1846, but it was not until 1914 that the plan for a national church for American Catholics was formulated, approved and designed. Construction of the crypt church began in 1920, and services have been held here since 1927.

▷ **Location:** 4th St. and Michigan Ave. NE.
🕒 **Timing:** About an hour.

VISIT

🕒 *Open Apr–Oct daily 7am–7pm. Rest of the year daily 7am–6pm.* 🗣*Guided tours (1hr) available.* ✕&🅿 ☎*202-526-8300. www.nationalshrine.com.*
Constructed of brick, granite, tile and concrete, the shrine follows the Latin cross design. Its dome is 108ft in diameter and 237ft in height. The **Knights' Bell Tower**—a gift from the Knights of Columbus—is surmounted by a 20ft gilded cross and stands 329ft high.

Among the adorned chapels in the **crypt**, note the Mary Altar (below the main altar) made of golden Algerian onyx. The side chapels are dedicated to saints, martyrs, the Good Shepherd, Our Lady of Bistrica and Our Lady of Lourdes.

Pope John Paul II Cultural Center

Ⓜ *Brookland CUA*

Opened in 2001, this modern, 100,000sq ft facility, designed by Leo A. Daly, was built to provide a haven for exploring personal faith in the new millennium.

▷ **Location:** 3900 Harewood Rd. NE., adjacent to Catholic University.
🕒 **Timing:** Allow an hour plus time for the 50min biographical film.

VISIT

🕒 *Open year-round Tue–Fri 10am–5pm.* 🚫*Closed major holidays.* ⊜*$5 donation suggested.* ✕&🅿 ☎*202-635-5400. www.jp2cc.org.*
The highlight of the main floor is the John Paul II Polish Heritage Room, which sheds light on Karol Joseph Wojtyla, the first non-Italian to be elected pope in 455 years. Among the keepsakes on view are a Tiffany clock, family photos, religious vestments, and downhill skis. Changing selections of art from the Vatican museums, accompanied by papal interpretation, fill the second floor. Ground-floor exhibits demand a high level of participation: interactive workstations, accessed by swiping a personal "smart card," cover everything from original sin to cloning. Visitors may also make virtual stained glass on a computer, collaborate on a song made from chimes or watch videotaped testimonials.

A recently acquired portrait of St. Thérèse of Lisieux (1907) by Celine Martin hangs in the chapel located on the entry-level.

George Washington Memorial Parkway along Dyke Marsh
between Alexandria and Mount Vernon
© Cameron Davidson/Alamy

As the focus of this guide is Washington, DC, we have limited our selection of excursions to nearby sights whose histories are closely related to that of the capital. The five excursions described in the following pages are concentrated within 36 miles of Washington and are accessible by car or public transportation. The well-organized visitor can take in two or more excursions in the same day *(expect long entry lines at Mount Vernon during the spring and summer)*. For longer excursions, the area offers a wealth of possibilities, including Baltimore *(40mi from DC)* and the vast Chesapeake Bay region in Maryland; and Manassas *(31mi)*, Fredericksburg *(53mi)* and Monticello *(near Charlottesville—115mi)* in Virginia.

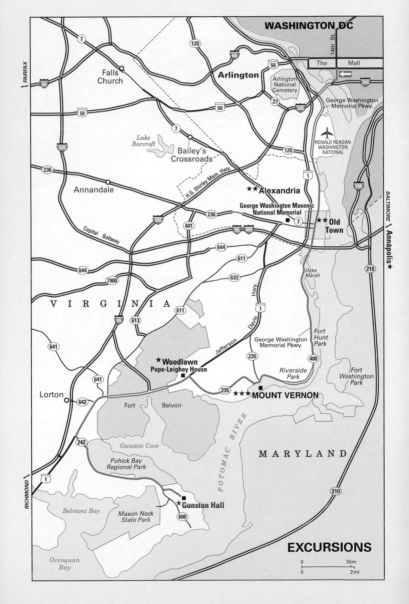

EXCURSIONS

Mount Vernon★★★

Map opposite

America's most visited historic estate, Mount Vernon sits on a grassy, shaded slope overlooking the Potomac River. Here, George Washington escaped the rigors of public office and enjoyed the life of a successful Virginia planter.

A BIT OF HISTORY
Family Heritage

The Mount Vernon property came into the Washington family in 1674 through a land grant from Lord Culpeper to John Washington, George's great-grandfather. The land passed through the hands of several descendants before Augustine Washington bought it from his sister in 1726.

In 1735 Augustine moved his family, which included three-year-old George, from Westmoreland County to the newly purchased Potomac property, then called Little Hunting Creek Plantation. The family spent four years here before again moving to a farm on the Rappahanock River. Records of the period, though sketchy, indicate that Augustine probably built a cottage near the location of the Mount Vernon mansion.

In 1740 Augustine deeded the Potomac property to his son Lawrence, George's elder half-brother. Lawrence renamed his 2,500-acre estate Mount Vernon, after a British admiral he had come to respect while serving in the Royal Navy. In 1743, when George was 11, his father died, and he came increasingly under the influence of his brother Lawrence. Married to Anne Fairfax, the daughter of William Fairfax, one of Virginia's wealthiest landowners, Lawrence moved in prestigious circles. George, whose upbringing until that time had been more practical than formal, was exposed to genteel colonial society at Mount Vernon.

When Lawrence died in 1752, the 20-year-old George took over the management of Mount Vernon, leasing it

- ▶ **Location:** 16mi south of Washington. **By car**: Leave DC by the 14th St. Bridge, take Exit 11A (for National Airport) and continue south on the George Washington Memorial Parkway. **By public transportation**: Take Metro to Huntington station; then board bus 101 (Fairfax Connector) for Mount Vernon. **By tour bus: Gray Line** has 4hr and 9hr tours daily; details from www.graylinedc.com or ✆ 202-289-1995. **By boat**: ℓ see *Spirit of Mount Vernon* under Sightseeing Cruises in *Planning Your Trip*. At Mount Vernon, use the map distributed at the ticket booth. First watch the 18min film on Washington in the Ford Orientation Center.
- ▣ **Parking:** There is plenty of free parking in the large on-site lot.
- ⊛ **Don't Miss:** The slave quarters, Washington's tomb and the Pioneer Farm.
- ⏱ **Timing:** Average round-trip driving time from downtown is 1hr. During peak season arrive early to avoid crowds; allow 3hrs for the mansion, grounds and Reynolds museum.
- ⚭ **Kids:** River cruises from the wharf (ℓ see *Planning Your Trip*).
- ℓ **Also See:** Woodlawn Plantation, 3mi east of Mount Vernon.

from Lawrence's widow. Though he eventually became the nation's greatest hero and its first president, Washington considered farming the "most delectable" occupation.

Mount Vernon

Mount Vernon Ladies' Association

The Gentleman Farmer

In 1759, after having distinguished himself in the French and Indian War, Washington married Martha Dandridge Custis, a widow with two children, John (Jacky) and Martha (Patsy). With his marriage to Martha, who owned some 15,000 acres in the Tidewater area near Williamsburg, Washington became one of Virginia's largest landowners. To accommodate his new family, Washington redecorated the simple 1.5-story farmhouse at Mount Vernon and added a full story to it. In 1761 his brother Lawrence's widow died, making Washington the legal owner of the estate. Over the years he increased Mount Vernon's holdings to more than 8,000 acres, which were divided into five independent but adjoining farms and worked by some 300 slaves. Washington believed that farms should be self-sufficient, and to that end he constructed outbuildings for such activities as blacksmithing, shoemaking, weaving and fish salting.

Washington enjoyed entertaining at Mount Vernon and was active in the social life of nearby Alexandria, where he owned a small town house. In 1773 he began an ambitious enlargement of Mount Vernon, adding two-story additions to the north and south sides of the house, the piazza on the east, the cupola and the curving colonnades. The project took almost 15 years to complete.

The Public Years

In 1774 Washington was elected one of Virginia's delegates to the First Continental Congress meeting in Philadelphia to protest British injustices. A year later the Second Continental Congress unanimously voted him head of its military forces, a position that would keep him engaged in war and away from Mount Vernon until 1783.

Returning home from the Revolution, Washington set about rejuvenating his farms and finances, which had suffered during the war. His fortunes were further drained by an endless stream of house guests, many of them uninvited strangers. For the next six years Washington devoted himself to farming, experimenting with crop rotation and introducing new plant varieties. He took great pleasure in his wife's two grandchildren, Eleanor (Nelly) and George (Little Wash). The Washingtons brought the two children to live at Mount Vernon after their father, Martha's son John, was killed in the American Revolution.

From 1789 to 1797 Washington served as the country's first president. During his two terms, he managed to return to Mount Vernon on 15 occasions, sometimes for only a brief visit and at other times for several months. Refusing public demands that he serve a third term, Washington retired for a final time to Mount Vernon in March 1797.

The Final Years

The last two years of his life were lived once more as a planter. On December 14, 1799, having spent a snowy day overseeing work on the grounds, Washington contracted quinsy, an acute inflammation of the throat. Doctors administered gargles and bled him four times with leeches, but to no avail. A day later he passed away in his bed at the age of 67. His body was interred in the old family burial vault overlooking the river. Two years later, Martha Washington was buried beside her husband.

After Washington

After Martha's death the mansion passed to Bushrod Washington, a nephew and Supreme Court justice. He bequeathed it to his nephew John Augustine Washington. When the latter's son, John Augustine Jr., came into possession of Mount Vernon in 1850, the estate was no longer agriculturally productive. Realizing the need to preserve the home but without the means to do so, John Washington sought to sell it either to the federal government or to the State of Virginia, but neither was in a position to buy it.

Instead, a woman in South Carolina, Ann Pamela Cunningham, began a grassroots effort to save the historic house. In 1853 she founded the Mount Vernon Ladies Assn. Through a public campaign, they raised the $200,000 necessary to buy the estate. The association has owned and operated Mount Vernon since 1858.

South of the upper garden, near the food court, the **Donald W. Reynolds Museum and Education Center** features interactive galleries filled with Washington memorabilia and a state-of-the-art theater. The museum boasts some 500 artifacts and documents that chronicle Washington's life. Three life-size wax models of Washington at ages 19, 45 and 57 are among the highlights of the exhibits. The crowning piece is a **bust of General Washington** executed at Mount Vernon by the French sculptor Jean Antoine Houdon. Videos are shown in the adjacent Education Center.

THE MANSION

🕐 *Open Apr–Aug daily 8am–5pm. Nov–Feb daily 9am–4pm. Rest of the year daily 9am–5pm.* ⊛*$17.* ♿*(partial)* ✕🅿 ✆*703-780-2000. www.mountvernon.org.*

The estate's main building is entered from the carriage side, opposite the river side, which boasts the well-known – columned piazza that is Mount Vernon's hallmark. The Georgian farmhouse is set off by a rust-red roof and curved colonnades connecting two flanking wings. A weathervane bearing the dove of peace tops its cupola. A facade of "rusticated board," a wood siding beveled and plastered with sand to resemble white stone, testifies to Washington's frugality; using real stone was much more expensive.

First Floor

The large **dining room**, or "new room," was the last addition to the house and is the most lavishly appointed. Here, as in the rest of the mansion, the decor is authentic to Washington's final years. Verdigris, a color favored by Washington, dominates the room and provides contrast to the ornate white woodwork around the Palladian windows and in the ceiling trim. The 21 side chairs are part of an original set made for this room by John Aitken of Philadelphia, who also crafted one of the mahogany sideboards. Washington characterized the ornate marble mantel, which was the gift of an Englishman, as "too elegant and costly… for my republican style of living."

The east-facing door in this room opens onto the piazza, which affords a pleasant **view**★ of the Potomac and the far Maryland shore. The center door in the piazza leads into the mansion's large central hall, whose pine paneling Washington had "grained" to resemble mahogany. Cross-ventilated from both the carriage and river sides, this hall was used for informal entertaining in the summer. On the south wall hangs a framed key to the Bastille prison in France, given to Washington by his French ally and friend, the Marquis de Lafayette.

Four rooms open off the hall. The small parlor used for informal family gatherings contains the harpsichord Washington ordered from England for his granddaughter, Nelly, who became an accomplished musician. Formal entertaining was done in the west parlor. The room retains its original ceiling molding, door and mantel pediments, and wall paneling. The small dining room is appointed with richly glazed verdigris walls and mahogany furnishings. Over the mantel is an original **engraving** of the Washington family by Edward Savage. A bedroom opens off this room.

Second Floor

A heavy "grained" staircase leads to five bedrooms off a central hall. More lavishly decorated than Washington's simple bedroom, these guest chambers reflect Martha's tastes. So many guests visited the estate that Washington once called his home "a well resorted tavern, as scarcely any strangers who are going from north to south, or from south to north, do not spend a day or two at it." The **master bedchamber** occupies a more private space in the south section. Simply furnished, this room contains the mahogany four-poster bed in which Washington died. The bedchamber also functioned as Martha Washington's office and contains the late-18C French desk at which she fulfilled her duties as an "old-fashioned Virginia housekeeper," as she called herself.

A narrow back staircase in this wing leads to Washington's own first-floor study. This large room contains many pieces intimately associated with him, including his desk and his presidential desk chair, which he brought back to Mount Vernon with him, and a terrestrial globe. The two wings attached to the mansion by curving colonnades house a kitchen *(south)* and quarters for white servants *(north)*.

THE ESTATE
Outbuildings

Twelve small dependencies are scattered along the lanes leading from both sides of the house. These structures re-create the operations of a self-sufficient estate, from the curing, spinning and laundry houses to the living quarters for overseers and slaves.

Grounds

Today the estate comprises 40 acres of landscaped grounds. The carriage entrance to the house is fronted by a sweeping bowling green bordered by stately trees. Several of the larger tulip poplars here were planted during Washington's lifetime. The **upper garden** on the north side of the bowling green is an ornamental flower garden, dominated by large boxwood hedges that date from Washington's day. An imposing reconstructed brick greenhouse forms the north side. Opposite the upper garden is the **kitchen garden**.

Two different burial sites lie beyond the stables. George and Martha Washington were originally buried in the old family vault, a brick-fronted underground crypt. In the years after Washington's death, Congress proposed enshrining his remains in the Capitol. However, after years of complications and delays, his relatives decided against it. In 1831 they erected the present **tomb** for George and Martha Washington, building it according to the wishes expressed in Washington's will. Beyond an iron grille, the couple's marble sarcophagi are visible within an open vault. Interred in the walls of the vault are 27 other family members. In front of the tomb are two marble obelisks in memory of Bushrod and John Augustine Washington, the 19C proprietors of Mount Vernon.

A path leads from the tomb to a shaded grove, where a small monument memorializes the slaves buried in unmarked graves at Mount Vernon.

Located near the wharf, a 4-acre **pioneer farm** features demonstrations of 18C animal husbandry, crop cultivation, brick making and timber transformation.

About 3mi south of Mount Vernon, via Route 235, Washington's **distillery** and **gristmill** are open to the public seasonally *(Apr–Oct)*. Demonstrations of whiskey-making and corn grinding are held daily.

Alexandria★★

Map p247

Situated just a few miles down the Potomac from the nation's capital, this enclave of historic homes and churches set along tree-shaded brick walks retains its colonial charm and an atmosphere of slow-paced Southern gentility. Alexandria's past is intimately bound with the founding of the country and with such preeminent Americans as George Washington, George Mason and Robert E. Lee.

A BIT OF HISTORY
The Town Is Created

The area now called Old Town, Alexandria traces its beginnings to the early 1700s, when a tobacco warehouse on what is now Oronoco Street spawned a settlement. Scottish tobacco merchants and Virginia tobacco planters petitioned the Virginia General Assembly to establish a town. In 1748 the assembly did so, and named it after the Alexander family, upon whose land the town was sited. The town was laid out in the grid pattern characteristic of 18C urban planning. A public auction was held for sale of the 84 half-acre lots. Over a two-day period, 42 lots were purchased. To ensure the growth of the town, a dwelling had to be built within two years of land purchase.

A Prosperous Seaport

For the next quarter-century, Alexandria flourished as a colonial seaport and trading center. By 1763 the port had outgrown its space and was expanding westward. It also grew eastward as land was filled on the marshy Potomac shoreline around present-day Union Street. Growth ended with the Revolution in 1775. During the war Alexandria was a pivotal meeting point for such leaders as George Mason, whose plantation was in the area, and George Washington, who maintained a house in town and a plantation eight miles down the Potomac. The townspeople were divided during the Revolution: some were ardent

Info: Ramsay House Visitors Center, King and Fairfax Sts; ☎703- 746-3301; www.visitalexandriava.com.

Location: Alexandria sits on the west bank of the Potomac River, 6mi SE of Washington. By car: Leave Washington by the 14th St. Bridge, take Exit 11A (for National Airport), and go south on the George Washington Memorial Parkway. By public transportation: Take Metro to King Street Station; then board eastbound DASH bus no. AT 2 or AT 5. Free shuttle runs along King St. from the Metro.

Parking: 1-day *(24hr)* parking permit available at Ramsay House Visitors Center.

patriots, while others resented the economic havoc war was playing with their lives. Battle threatened them only once, when British ships sailed up the Potomac, fired a few shots, then left. At the height of the war, in 1779, Alexandria was incorporated as a town.

Part of the New Capital

With the coming of peace, Alexandria's prosperity returned, and in 1789 the town's fortunes took a monumental turn when it was ceded by Virginia for the formation of the new federal city. Congress officially accepted it as part of the District in 1801. Alexandria's prospects were curtailed, however, by a congressional amendment that prohibited the construction of any federal buildings on the Virginia side of the river. Historians believe that this amendment was enacted at the instigation of President Washington, who owned Alexandria lands and feared allegations of favoritism. Nevertheless, the town had its heyday during the building of the new capital. Taverns, hostelries and businesses flourished, and the port became a major exporter of wheat, which had taken the place of tobacco as Virginia's cash crop.

In the early decades of the 1800s, Alexandria's fortunes declined as it lost trade to growing commercial centers in nearby Georgetown, Richmond and Baltimore. The town also incurred heavy debts in the building of the Alexandria Canal, which failed to stimulate the trade expected. Suffering economically from their association with the capital city and without representation in Congress, Alexandrians became disillusioned with their status as citizens of the nation's capital. In 1846 the County of Alexandria retroceded to Virginia, with whom it had always maintained strong social and political ties.

Civil War Years

From 1850 to 1860, with the coming of industrialization, a cotton gin and locomotive factory were built in town, and Alexandria once again thrived. Then federal troops moved in and occupied the town in 1861 for the duration of the Civil War, converting public buildings into Union hospitals and constructing a fort on Shooter's Hill, now topped by the granite tower of the George Washington Masonic National Memorial. During the Union occupation, Robert E. Lee, whose boyhood home still stands in Old Town, led the Confederate Army.

In 1870, soon after the war's end, Alexandria became an independent city, separate from the county of the same name (now called Arlington). Over the decades it spread west, annexing parts of the old county as it grew. Not until World War I did the town experience any real prosperity again, when the federal government constructed a torpedo factory on the waterfront.

During World War II, Alexandria benefited from the growth that infected the entire metropolitan area. Today the city encompasses nearly 16sq mi, with a population of about 140,000 (2010).

Elegant Enclave

In recent decades the Old Town quarter of the city has paid increasing attention to its architectural heritage, fostering an image of genteel provincialism. The city government carefully monitors the appearance of buildings in the historic district, which in 1969 was placed on the National Register of Historic Places.

Since the 1960s gentrification has overtaken what had been the working-class neighborhoods of the city. Professionals, lured by Alexandria's cachet, have bought and renovated the small colonials and elegant Georgians. Many now display the official metal plaques that designate buildings "of historic or architectural significance."

Today the city's waterfront is graced with parks, and restaurants and boutiques line King and Washington streets. At the foot of King Street, the **Torpedo Factory** has undergone a much-acclaimed urban renovation and now serves as an arts-and-crafts center, housing the shops and studios of visual artists.

⟶ WALKING TOUR
OLD TOWN★★
4mi. Map p247.

▷ *Begin at the corner of King and N. Fairfax Sts.*

Ramsay House Visitors Center

221 King St. ⟐*Open mid-Mar–Dec daily 10am–8pm (rest of the year til 5pm).* ⟐*Closed Jan 1, Thanksgiving Day & Dec 25.* ℘*703-746-3301. www.visitalexandriava.com.*

The north portion of this colonial clapboard incorporates the remains of the oldest structure in Old Town. Built in 1724 by William Ramsay, a Scottish merchant, the small house was moved to Alexandria soon after the town's founding. It now functions as the official visitor and convention center.

▷ *Turn left on S. Fairfax St.*

Stabler-Leadbeater Apothecary Museum

105-107 S. Fairfax St. ◷*Open Apr–Oct Tue–Sat 10am–5pm, Sun–Mon 1pm–5pm. Rest of the year Wed–Sat 11am–4pm, Sun 1pm–4pm.* ◷*Closed Jan 1, Thanksgiving Day & Dec 25.* ◉*$5.* ▣ ✆*703-746-3852. http://alexandriava.gov/Apothecary.*

An apothecary from 1792 to 1933, this shop has been restored to its mid-19C appearance. Shelving, cases, glass bottles and equipment used for preparing medicines and remedies are from the original store, which served as a supplier of pharmaceuticals in the area.

▷ *Cross King St.*

Market Square

Now modernized and dominated by a steepled city hall (1873), this square has served as the city's focal point since the mid-18C. It has been the setting for historic gatherings, including Washington's drilling of his Revolutionary troops.

Carlyle House★

121 N. Fairfax St. ☞*Visit by guided tour (45min) only, year-round Tue–Sat 10am–4pm, Sun noon–4pm.* ◷*Closed Jan 1 & Dec 25.* ◉*$5.* ♿ ✆*703-549-2997. www.nvrpa.org/park/carlyle_house_historic_park.*

Modeled after a Georgian manor house, this stone construction (1753) was built by John Carlyle, one of the Scottish entrepreneurs instrumental in founding Alexandria. Carlyle came to Virginia in 1741 as an agent for an English merchant, but he soon established his own trading concerns. He became a friend of George Washington, and a founding trustee of the town.

The mansion's hour of glory came in April 1755 when the British general Edward Braddock, en route to his ill-fated campaign against the French and Indians, headquartered himself here. During his stay he held the historic **Governors' Council**, at which five colonial governors met with Braddock in Carlyle House. He petitioned them for advice on military strategy and for financial support. The governors' contention that the colonists would refuse to provide funds to the British was an early sign of tension between England and the colonies.

Carlyle House

©R. Corbel/Michelin

When Carlyle died in 1780, his property passed to his heirs, but was eventually sold out of the family. In 1970 the Northern Virginia Regional Park Authority purchased the house and renovated it to its colonial appearance.

The two-story building, with a projecting central section and prominent quoins (or cornerstones), is topped by a hipped roof with two chimneys. Inside, the mansion is decorated in the style fashionable to its period. The popular tones of the day (verdigris, blue verditer and Prussian blue) predominate throughout the house. Note the fine woodwork cornices, pediments and paneling in the first-floor study and main parlor, the only two rooms that have retained their original architecture.

The second floor has bedrooms and an architectural exhibit room, where the restoration process is explained in captioned photographs and a section of the original rubble and mortar walls of the house is exposed. On the basement level is a servant's workroom containing various utensils of the day.

⊙ *A formal garden behind the house is laid out in parterres with brick walkways.*

Former Bank of Alexandria

133 N. Fairfax St.

This restored brick Federal structure is the oldest building (1807) in Virginia that has been continually used as a bank. Carlyle's son-in-law, William Herbert, served as the bank's second president and a director.

▷ *Turn left on Cameron St.*

The row houses in the **300 block (A)** of Cameron Street, representative of the early- to mid-19C architecture of the area, house the kinds of storefront shops for which Old Town is known. No. 309 has a side courtyard and loggia.

Gadsby's Tavern Museum★

134 N. Royal St. 👣 *Visit by guided tour (30min) only, Apr–Oct Tue–Sat 10am–5pm, Sun–Mon 1pm–5pm. Rest of the year Wed–Sat 11am–4pm, Sun 1pm–4pm.* 🕐 *Closed Jan 1, Thanksgiving Day & Dec 25.* 💲$5. 📞703-746-4242. http://alexandriava. gov/gadsbytavern.*

This tavern is one of the most celebrated hostelries from the early days of the country. Functioning now as a museum and restaurant, it is actually two joined brick structures. The two-story Georgian-style tavern dates back to about 1785; the three-story Federal-style construction was built as a hotel in 1792 by John Wise, a local businessman. Englishman John Gadsby leased the larger building from Wise in 1796, and in 1802 Gadsby also took over the smaller one, which he operated as a coffeehouse. The Federal-style building became the renowned Gadsby's Tavern. While the federal city was being built across the Potomac, Gadsby's Tavern frequently entertained its official-

dom—the Jeffersons, the Adamses and George Washington, whose town house was just a block away at 508 Cameron Street. For years an annual gala celebrating Washington's birthday was held in Gadsby's ballroom.

The buildings functioned as a tavern until 1878. They were restored to their original appearance in 1975 and reopened in 1976. The ground floor of the Federal-style building is leased as a commercial restaurant (*☕ see Address Book*). Much of the rest of the two buildings is devoted to a museum depicting the tavern as it appeared in Gadsby's day.

Visit – The first floor of the older building consists of an entrance hall and two public rooms. The larger room to the left is set as a dining room, with furnishings and food appropriate to the late 18C. The small dining room to the right contains a table set as it would have been for one of the private dinners that often took place here.

A large assembly hall dominates the second floor. Furnished with only a few chairs, this room was used by merchants to show their wares and by itinerant dentists to treat patients, as well as for social events.

Gadsby's famous **ballroom**, which occupies much of the second floor of the Federal building, was the scene of many elegant soirees. Its original paneling is now conserved in the Met-

Gadsby's Tavern Museum

visitalexandriava.com

ropolitan Museum of Art in New York. A musicians' gallery is cantilevered out over the ballroom.

The canopied beds and pleasant decor of the two bedchambers on this floor contrast sharply with the spartan accommodations in the small third-floor bedrooms, where travelers sometimes slept two or three to a bed.

Return to Cameron St. and continue west.

The modest clapboard building at **508 Cameron Street** is a recent reconstruction of the town house George Washington built as a convenient town office and lodging.

Turn right on North St. Asaph St.

At the intersection with Queen Street, note **523 Queen Street** *(the second house from the corner)*, one of the smallest houses in Old Town.

Among the mid-19C clapboards in the 300 block of North St. Asaph Street is an example of a **flounder house** (no. 311). This vernacular architectural style, which dates from the first half of the 19C, derives its name from the flat, windowless side of the house, resembling the eyeless side of a flounder fish.

At the next intersection note Princess Street *(on the left)*, which has its original cobblestone paving. The cobbles often came across the Atlantic Ocean as ballast for ships.

Continue to the corner of Oronoco St. and turn left.

Robert E. Lee's Boyhood Home★

607 Oronoco St.

Not open to the public.

Constructed in 1795 by John Potts, a business acquaintance of George Washington, this Federal town house soon became the residence of William Fitzhugh, a close friend of Washington.

Here in 1804, Fitzhugh's daughter Mary married George Washington Parke Custis, Washington's ward and the squire of Arlington House.

In 1812 Revolutionary War hero Henry "Light-Horse Harry" Lee, a friend of Washington and father of Robert E. Lee, rented the house from the Fitzhughs, who were relatives of Henry Lee's second wife, Ann Hill Carter.

Soon after, Lee was wounded in a Baltimore riot. Virtually bankrupt save for his wife's income, he sailed to Barbados in the Caribbean, reputedly to recover his health. Six-year-old Robert never again saw his father, who died away from home five years later.

Widowed, Ann Carter Lee relied heavily on her youngest son, Robert. The family lived here until 1825, with the exception of a four-year hiatus, during which William Henry Fitzhugh was in residence and the Lees occupied a family property at 407 N. Washington Street. Robert left his boyhood home in 1825 to become a cadet at West Point Military Academy. Unable to maintain a household without his help, Mrs. Lee moved to Georgetown.

The intersection of Oronoco and Washington streets is known as "Lee Corners" due to the cluster of Lee family residences. The Georgian building at 428 N. Washington Street was the home of Light-Horse Harry's brother, Edmund Jennings Lee, mayor of Alexandria from 1815 to 1818.

Lee-Fendall House

614 Oronoco St. (Enter on Washington St.) Open year-round Wed–Sat 10am–3pm, Sun 1pm–3pm. Closed Thanksgiving Day & mid Dec–Jan 1. $5. P 703-548-1789. www.leefendallhouse.org.

This clapboard house was built in 1785 by Philip Richard Fendall, a distant Lee relative who bought the half-acre lot from Light-Horse Harry Lee. Fendall successively married three different Lee women, and members of the Lee family continually lived in the house until 1904. Today the house is decorated in early-19C style, with many authentic Lee pieces.

Continue down N. Washington St.

Note the house at **no. 407**. Built by Charles Lee, another brother of Light-Horse Harry, this was the home in which young Robert E. Lee lived with his mother from 1817 to 1820.

Lloyd House
220 N. Washington St.
John Wise, who established Gadsby's Tavern, built this late-Georgian brick edifice as his residence in 1797. In the early 19C a succession of prominent Alexandrians lived in the house, including Benjamin Hallowell, a Quaker schoolmaster who briefly tutored Robert E. Lee. In 1832 the house was purchased by John Lloyd, whose wife, Ann Lee Lloyd, was a first cousin of Robert E. Lee. The house remained in the Lloyd family until 1918. In 1976 it became part of the Alexandria library system.

Christ Church★
Corner of N. Washington and Cameron Sts. (Enter walled graveyard from Washington St.) Open year-round Tue–Sat 10am–4pm, Sun 8:45am–1pm. Closed major holidays. Guided tours (20min) available. 703-549-1450. www.historicchristchurch.org. As the church may be closed for private use, it is advisable to phone before visiting.
Encircled by a high wall, the church grounds provide a haven where trees shade 18C grave markers. Both George Washington and Robert E. Lee worshiped in the brick and stone structure, with its pepperpot steeple. By tradition, presidents have come here to worship in Washington's pew on the Sunday nearest February 22, his birthday.
Construction of the church was completed in 1773. In its unadorned and luminous interior, a raised wineglass pulpit and a large Palladian window provide the focal point. Silver plaques mark the **pews** of Washington *(no. 60)* and Lee *(no. 46)*.

Return to Washington St., cross and walk down the 600 block of Cameron St.

In 1811 the Georgian brick dwelling at **611 Cameron Street** was home to Light-Horse Harry Lee and his family, including his three-year-old son Robert E. Lee. Thomas, the final Lord Fairfax of Virginia, lived in the imposing Federal-style structure at **no. 607** in the 1830s.

Turn right on South St. Asaph St. and walk two blocks, past the intersection with King St. Turn right on Prince St.

The large brick structure with Palladian windows, at the corner of Prince and Washington streets, is the **Federal District Courthouse** for Virginia's Eastern District. A number of nationally publicized trials, particularly involving Pentagon espionage, have been heard here. The statue (1889) (**1**) dominating the intersection of Washington and Prince streets commemorates Alexandria's Confederate dead.

Cross Washington St.

The Lyceum
201 S. Washington St. Open year-round Mon–Sat 10am–5pm, Sun 1pm–5pm. Closed Jan 1, Thanksgiving Day & Dec 24–25. $2 703-746-4994. http://alexandriava.gov/lyceum.
In 1834 Benjamin Hallowell *(see Lloyd House above)* interested his fellow citizens in founding a lyceum, or cultural center, and five years later this Greek Revival structure was built to house a library, lecture rooms and natural history exhibits. Many prominent 19C figures spoke here, including the orator Daniel Webster. After serving as a Civil War hospital, private home and office building, the building was restored in 1974.
Today it houses a museum featuring changing exhibits on state and local history.

Continue one block south on Washington St., then turn left on Duke St. and continue one block to South St. Asaph St.

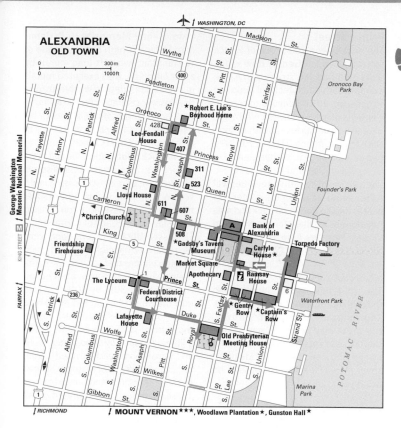

ALEXANDRIA
OLD TOWN

Lafayette House

301 South St. Asaph St.

⊶Not open to the public.

Built about 1815 by a shipping agent, this three-story brick building, with an elegant double doorway topped by a fanlight and flanked by lunettes, is a fine example of a Federal-style town house. In 1824 the Marquis de Lafayette stayed here during a state visit.

▷ *Continue down Duke St. two blocks to S. Royal St. Turn right and enter the brick gate marked no. 316.*

Old Presbyterian Meeting House

Between 300 block of S. Royal and S. Fairfax Sts. ◷Open year-round Mon–Fri 8:15am–4:15pm, Sun for services only. ◷Closed major holidays. ⴲ ☏703-549-6670. www.opmh.org.

Alexandria's Scottish immigrants established this church in 1772, contracting John Carlyle to oversee its building. It was the site of celebrations for Alexandria's Masons.

In 1799, at Washington's death, the church bell tolled for four days, and his public funeral service was preached here. In 1835 lightning struck the steeple and the ensuing fire virtually destroyed the church. Within two years it was rebuilt. The old flounder house manse inside the walled churchyard on the left was built in 1787.

The graveyard beyond contains markers for John Carlyle and other prominent Alexandrians. The sarcophagus enclosed by a wrought-iron rail on the north commemorates an unknown soldier of the Revolution.

(The box beside the sarcophagus plays a videotape on the church's history.)

▷ *From the church walk through the cemetery. Turn left (north) on S. Fairfax St., then turn right onto Prince St.*

Prince Street

The brick-paved 200 block of Prince Street is known as **Gentry Row**★, due to its dignified 18C structures. A fine example of this architectural period in Virginia, **no. 207** is believed to contain elements of a town house built by the George William Fairfaxes, Washington's close friends. At nos. 211 and 209 lived two of Washington's physicians, Dr. Elisha Cullen Dick and Dr. James Craik. The stuccoed, salmon Greek Revival **Athenaeum** (1852) on the corner was built as the Old Dominion Bank and now functions as a gallery for the Northern Virginia Fine Arts Assn. (◷*open year-round, call for hours;* ◷*closed major holidays;* ☎*703-548-0035; http://oha.alexandriava.gov).*

The architecture changes abruptly along the cobbled 100 block of Prince Street. Known locally as **Captain's Row**★, the street may derive its name from the 18C sea captain John Harper, who owned land along the north side of the street. Many of the original houses were destroyed in an 1827 fire.

▷ *Turn left on S. Union St.*

On the corner *(6 King St.)* is an early-19C warehouse made of brick and stone. End your tour at the **Torpedo Factory**.

ADDITIONAL SIGHTS
George Washington Masonic National Memorial

101 Callahan Dr. Ⓜ *King Street.* ◷*Open Apr–Sept Mon–Sat 9am–4pm, Sun 1pm –4pm. Rest of the year Mon–Sat 10am–4pm, Sun 1pm–4pm.* ◷*Closed major holidays.* ☛*Guided tours (1hr; $8) available daily.* ☞*$5.* ♿🅿 ☎*703-683-2007. www.gwmemorial.org.*

Crowning Shooter's Hill, this memorial to George Washington, the first master of Alexandria's Masonic Lodge, is a city landmark at the western end of Old Town. The granite building, topped by a tiered tower, is modeled after one of the Seven Wonders of the World—the lighthouse on the island of Pharos near Alexandria, Egypt. Begun in 1923, it took 40 years to complete.

Visitors enter **Memorial Hall**, dominated by a 17ft-high bronze **statue** of Washington. Two 46ft-long murals by artist Allyn Cox, who executed murals in the Capitol, depict Washington at the Masonic ceremony for the laying of the Capitol cornerstone, and with his fellow Masons at a religious service in Philadelphia's Christ Church.

The **Replica Room** *(down the hall to the left of Cox's cornerstone mural)* displays various Masonic articles associated with Washington, including the silver trowel and the Masonic apron he used while laying the Capitol cornerstone. The **Assembly Room** *(one floor below Memorial Hall)* has eight polished green granite columns that support the entire memorial. The 350-year-old Persian rug measures 30ft by 50ft, supposedly the world's largest rug made on a single loom. The 7-story tower houses a **museum** of Washington memorabilia, a library (◷*open by appointment only)* and 5 small rooms, each devoted to a different order or type of Masonry, such as the Knights Templar and Grotto Masons. These chambers are decorated in the Persian, Egyptian, Hebraic and medieval motifs symbolic of the specific orders. The top level opens onto an observation deck, with a **view** of Old Town.

Friendship Firehouse

107 S. Alfred St. ◷*Open year-round Sat–Sun 1pm–4pm.* ◷*Closed Dec 25 & Jan 1.* ☞*$2.* ♿ ☎*703-746-3891. http://alexandriava.gov/friendshipfirehouse.*

Organized in 1774, the Friendship Fire Company lists among its honorary volunteers statesmen, governors and presidents, including George Washington. The brick firehouse was completed in 1857. Though the company ceased fire fighting in the early 1870s, the Friendship Veterans Fire Engine Assn. maintains a ceremonial function.

Now city property, the building has an exhibit room *(1st floor)* with 18C and 19C fire-fighting equipment, including leather buckets and speaking trumpets. The meeting room *(2nd floor)* displays memorabilia relating to the company's social role in the community.

ADDRESSES

STAY

Alexandria & Arlington Bed and Breakfast Network – ℘703-549-3415 or 888-549-3415. www.aabbn.com. The cobblestone streets of Alexandria make staying at a bed and breakfast particularly inviting. If you're looking to stay in the tranquil pockets of Northern Virginia, the Alexandria & Arlington Bed and Breakfast Network maintains a listing of private homes and bed and breakfasts available for short- and long-term rentals.

$$$ Hampton Inn – 1616 King St. ℘703-299-9900. www.hamptoninn.com. 80 rooms. Ideally located just a short walk from Old Town's shops, restaurants and museums, the hotel occupies a pleasant red-brick building on King St. Its proximity to the nation's capital (20min from DC and a block away from the Amtrak station) adds to its appeal, as do the free breakfast buffet and free high-speed Internet access throughout the hotel.

$$$ Morrison House – 116 S. Alfred St. ℘703-838-8000 or 866-834-6628. www.morrisonhouse.com. 45 rooms. Built in the 1980s, and one of three Kimpton properties in Old Town, the Morrison House maintains the appearance of a Federalist-era townhouse while offering the service of an elite European inn. Furnished with period pieces and chandeliers, Morrison House features cozy four-poster beds against the backdrop of a decorative fireplace. At the hotel's dining spot, **The Grille**, American dishes draw on ingredients from area farms and artisans.

EAT

$$ Bastille –1201 N. Royal St. ℘703-519-3776. www.bastillerestaurant.com. **French**. Chefs Christophe and Michelle Pouteaux present a modern interpretation of classic French cuisine (think calamari beignets as appetizers, and scallops with roasted fennel and carmelized endives for an entrée) in a casual-chic setting. Their commitment to sustainable farming and reasonable prices enhances the attraction of this neighborhood bistro.

$$ The Warehouse – 214 King St. ℘703-683-6868. www.warehousebar andgrill.com. **Cajun**. One of Old Town Alexandria's most well-loved casual eateries greets diners with hundreds of colorful, smiling caricatures of local personalities. Creole alligator stew and creamy she-crab soup usher in a Cajun-accented menu rich with meat and seafood dishes. A pleasingly old-fashioned caramel custard provides a rich finishing touch.

$$$ La Bergerie – 218 N. Lee St. ℘703-683-1007. www.labergerie.com. No lunch Sun. **French**. Housed in a historic brick warehouse near the river, elegant La Bergerie serves a tempting array of French dishes and Basque regional specialties. Crystal chandeliers sparkle above the comfortable dining room, where attentive servers monitor casual lunches and intimate dinners. Order a raspberry or hazelnut soufflé for dessert before diving into the savory roasted elk tenderloin topped with cracked cardamom, or classic Dover sole.

$$$ Gadsby's Tavern – 138 N. Royal St. ℘703-548-1288. www.gadsbystavern restaurant.com. **American**. One of the few remaining 18C dining establishments in the US, this tavern is aptly suited to the cobblestone streets of Old Town. Costumed servers and entertainers amuse, as patrons dine by candlelight on colonial favorites such as fried oysters and George Washington's duck. The attached museum provides a glimpse into the history of the port city.

$$$ Majestic Cafe – 911 King St. ℘703-837-9117. www.majesticcafe.com. Closed Mon. No lunch Sat & Sun. **American**. The pink and blue neon signs that loom over colonial King Street join the 1700s and the 1930s in peculiar harmony. The Majestic Cafe serves up a tasty selection of stylish American favorites. Start off with the house-made chicken liver paté on toast points. Move on to the home-style meatloaf, or braised short ribs with parsley potatoes, accompanied by a frosty glass of egg cream.

George Washington Birthday Parade

visitalexandriava.com

CALENDAR OF EVENTS

Listed below is a selection of Alexandria's popular annual events; some dates may vary each year. For more information contact the Alexandria Convention and Visitors Assn. ℘703-746-3301 http://visitalexandriava.com. Unless otherwise indicated, the area code for all numbers is 703.

Late Jan

Robert E. Lee Birthday Celebrations
Lee-Fendall House ℘548-1789, www.leefendallhouse.org

Mid Feb

George Washington Birthday Celebrations:

Birthnight Banquet and Ball
Gadsby's Tavern Museum ℘746-4242

Revolutionary War Encampment & Skirmish
Fort Ward Park ℘838-4848

Parade
Old Town ℘829-6400, www.washingtonbirthday.net

Early Mar

St. Patrick's Day Parade
King Street
www.ballyshaners.org

Apr–Oct

Doggie Happy Hour
Hotel Monaco ℘549-6080, www.doggiehappyhour.com

Late Apr

Historic Garden Week Tour
Old Town ℘804-644-7776, www.vagardenweek.org

Mid May–early Jun

Armenian Festival
℘202-586-5562

Late May

Memorial Day Jazz Festival
Waterfront Park ℘746-5418

Early Jun

Civil War Camp Day
Fort Ward Park ℘746-4848, www.alexandriava.gov

Mid Jul

USA & Alexandria Birthday Celebration
Oronoco Bay Park ℘746-5592, www.alexandriava.gov

Late Sept

Tour of Historic Homes
Old Town ℘683-5544, www.thetwig.org

Mid Nov

Historic Alexandria Antiques Show
Holiday Inn Hotel and Suites, Old Town ℘549-5811, www.historicalexandriafoundation.org

Early Dec

Scottish Christmas Walk
Old Town ℘549-0111, www.campagnacenter.org

Mid Dec

Historic Alexandria Candlelight Tours
Old Town ℘746-4242, www.alexandriava.gov

Annapolis★

Set on the south bank of the Severn River, Annapolis, capital of Maryland, is known for its history and its harbor. The former dates back to 1649, when Virginia Puritans established Arundel Towne along the Severn. The latter is located at the heart of the historic district and shelters hundreds of yachts and sailboats tied up at City Dock. The dock is the departure point for water taxis and sightseeing cruises of Chesapeake Bay.

A BIT OF HISTORY

Named in honor of England's Queen Anne, Annapolis became the seat of colonial government in 1695. Founding fathers laid out the new capital with the 1779 Georgian-style **State House**★ *(center of State Circle ℘410-974-3400; www.msa.md.gov)*—which served as the US capitol between 1783 and 1784—occupying the highest point, while **St. Anne's Church** *(Church Circle ℘410-267-9333; www.stannes-annapolis.org)* was given the second-highest site. The rest of the town spread out on narrow streets from these structures, symbolizing the key positions of church and state. In the 18C Annapolis reigned as Maryland's premier port, as well as the colony's cultural capital.

Today the city's economy revolves around tourism, state government and the US Navy.

Info: Annapolis & Anne Arundel County Conference & Visitors Bureau, 26 West St.; ℘410-280-0445; www.visitannapolis.org.

Location: Annapolis is located 36mi east of Washington. By car: Take US-50 East to Exit 24 (Rowe Blvd.); proceed on Rowe Blvd., crossing College Creek Bridge; stay in the right lane; Rowe will split into Northwest St.; look for signs to Visitor Center. By public transportation: Take the Metro to New Carrollton, then bus (infrequent) or taxi to downtown. Main Street is the historic city's hub.

Parking: Gotts Garage on Northwest St., next to Visitors Bureau.

Don't Miss: A boat cruise on the harbor (for cruise information, contact Visitors Bureau above).

Kids: The ship models at the US Naval Academy.

SIGHTS

Hammond-Harwood House★★

19 Maryland Ave. Visit by guided tour (40min) only, Apr–Oct Tue–Sun noon–5pm (last tour 4pm). Nov–Dec

Annapolis State House

www.VisitAnnapolis.org

Tue–Sun noon–4pm (last tour 3pm).
$7. 410-263-4683 ext. 16.
www.hammondharwoodhouse.org.
This outstanding example of the Georgian style (1775), with its bowed wings, is the work of William Buckland. One of the country's first and foremost architects, Buckland emigrated from England in 1755. A joiner by trade, Buckland had a keen eye for detail, and the elaborately carved rose garlands above the entryway fanlight and the ornate woodwork and plaster ornamentation within are glorious proof of his skill. Inside, the tall arched window above the staircase is modeled on one found in London's Church of St Martins-in-the-Fields.

Chase-Lloyd House★

22 Maryland Ave. Visit by guided tour (20min) only, Mar–Dec Mon–Sat 2pm–4pm. $4. 410-263-2723.
Built for Samuel Chase, a signer of the *Declaration of Independence*, this imposing three-story brick Georgian home (1774, William Buckland) is best known for its **entrance hall** featuring a split, cantilevered staircase and a tall Palladian window. Only the first floor and the garden are open to the public as the rest of the house has served as a home for elderly women since 1890.

US Naval Academy Chapel
©Joseph Justice/iStockphoto.com

William Paca House

186 Prince George St. Visit by guided tour (45min) only, late Mar–Dec Mon–Sat 10am–5pm, Sun noon–5pm. Call for winter hours. $10. 410-990-4543. www.annapolis.org.
Patriot and signer of the *Declaration of Independence*, lawyer William Paca based his design of this brick town house (1765) on the Georgian principal of attaching wings to the main structure with short corridors called "hyphens." The **gardens** behind the house have been restored to their 18C appearance.

US Naval Academy★★

Armel-Leftwich Visitor Center, 52 King George St. 410-293-8687.
Visitor Center open Mar–Dec daily 9am–5pm, rest of the year 9am–4pm.
Closed Thanksgiving Day & Dec 25.
Guided tours available.
photo ID required; $9.50.
410-293-8687.
www.navyonline.com.
Midshipmen study to be officers in the US Navy and Marine Corps on a peaceful, 338-acre campus along the Severn River and College Creek.
In 1850 the five-year-old Naval School became the official undergraduate college for the US Navy. Today, competition is fierce to be one of the 4,000 midshipmen who gets a rigorous and free education at the academy.
A guided tour of "the Yard," as the grounds are called, includes massive **Bancroft Hall**, the 1906 Beaux-Arts structure in the center of campus that covers 33 acres and boasts 5mi of corridors. Few buildings in Annapolis rival the glorious gold-domed US Naval Academy **chapel**★★ (1908, Ernest Flagg), modeled after the Hotel des Invalides in Paris. In the chapel's eerily lit crypt, the remains of the nation's first naval hero, John Paul Jones, are interred in a black marble sarcophagus.
After the tour, visit the Preble Hall **museum**, where you'll find a collection of **ship models**★★ made in England during the 17C and 18C and other artifacts.

Gunston Hall ★

This colonial Georgian estate was the home of **George Mason** (1725-92), a respected thinker whose writings influenced the course of the Revolution and the development of the young Republic.

A BIT OF HISTORY

During the Revolutionary period, George Mason wrote the **Virginia Declaration of Rights** (May 1776), which stated "that all men are by nature equally free and independent and have certain inherent rights... namely... pursuing and obtaining happiness...." Mason's friend Thomas Jefferson echoed this wording in the *Declaration of Independence* (July 1776). Mason opposed the original Constitution because it had no Bill of Rights and did not call for the immediate abolition of the slave trade. His opposition was influential in the adoption in 1791 of the first 10 amendments to the Constitution, commonly known as the Bill of Rights. A fourth-generation Virginian, Mason inherited considerable family landholdings when he was 10. In 1755 he began constructing Gunston Hall. He served as a county justice, member of the Virginia House of Burgesses and a delegate to the Constitutional Convention of 1787. Father of nine children, Mason died at his home in 1792. His estate remained in the family until 1866. After a succession

> **Location:** Gunston Hall lies 22mi south of Washington. By car: Follow directions to Woodlawn. Continue south on US-1 and follow signs.

> **Timing:** Average round-trip driving time from downtown: 1hr 30min. Allow 3hrs, including 11min film about Bill of Rights.

of owners, it was deeded to the Commonwealth of Virginia.

MANSION

Visit by guided tour (45min) only, year-round daily 9:30am–4:30pm. Closed Jan 1, Thanksgiving Day & Dec 25. $10. (partial) 703-550-9220. www.gunstonhall.org.

The unembellished brick facade is offset with quoins, or cornerstones, of local buff-colored Aquia sandstone. The carriage entrance features a pedimented portico with a fanlight above the door. The river entrance portico is a semioctagonal porch with graceful ogee arches. The interior of the house is noteworthy for its mid-18C carved **woodwork** executed by English craftsman **William Buckland**, a carpenter-joiner who arrived in Virginia in 1755.

In the central hall, Buckland used pilasters, chair railings and a double arch

Gunston Hall, Palladian Room

Courtesy of Gunston Hall

offset with a pine cone finial. The Masons' bedroom opens off the left of the hall, and directly across from it is the **Chinese formal parlor**, the only surviving room in America featuring the scalloped Chinoiserie woodworking of the colonial period.

GROUNDS

Beyond the house on the south side is a small frame schoolhouse, a reconstruction of the one in which the nine Mason children were tutored. A gravel path connects the schoolhouse to the family **graveyard**, where 16 family members are buried. The two raised sarcophagi contain the remains of George Mason and his wife, Ann.

A double row of magnolias and cedars lines Magnolia Avenue, the carriage approach to the house. On the river side, an impressive boxwood allée leads through **formal gardens** to an overlook above a garden terrace. A mile-long walk through a wooded area leads to the river.

Gunston Hall sponsors a host of events year round that help bring history alive for visitors. In December guests can experience "Plantation Christmas" by taking a ride in horse-drawn carriage and by nibbling on period recipes prepared in the hearth kitchen. Gunston's sponsors several highly regarded family programs and the annual kite festival in March will make your heart soar.

Woodlawn★

This gracious Federal-era estate reflects the refinement of its original owners, Lawrence Lewis and Nelly Custis Lewis. Favored relatives of George Washington, whose own Mount Vernon lies only three miles away, the Lewises brought to their home many of the furnishings and memorabilia of the original Washington estate when they moved into the completed north wing in 1802.

A BIT OF HISTORY

In 1797 Lawrence Lewis, Washington's nephew, came to Mount Vernon to serve as his uncle's personal secretary. There he met **Eleanor** (Nelly) **Parke Custis**, the granddaughter the Washingtons had raised. After a quiet courtship, Nelly and Lewis were married in 1799. Washington ceded a 2,000-acre tract west of Mount Vernon to them on which to build their home. Washington died less than a year after the wedding; in 1802 Martha Washington died, the year in which the Lewises moved into the completed north wing of Woodlawn.

When Lawrence died in 1839, Nelly went to live with her son. In 1846 Woodlawn

- ▷ **Location:** Woodlawn lies 19mi south of Washington. By car: Follow directions to Mount Vernon. Continue 3mi west on Rte. 235 and follow the signs to Woodlawn. By public transportation: Take the Metro to Huntington station and transfer to a 9A (Fort Belvoir) bus to Woodlawn; tell driver to stop there for you.
- ⏱ **Timing:** Average round-trip driving time from downtown: 1hr 30min. Allow 2hrs for a visit.

was offered for sale, and was subsequently owned by private owners and a foundation. In 1957 the estate became the property of the National Trust for Historic Preservation.

VISIT

The Mansion is closed for renovation until spring 2013. The grounds and Pope-Leighey House remain open.
🍂*Visit by guided tour (35min each house) only, Fri–Mon 10am–5pm,*

Pope-Leighey House

© Thomas A. Heinz/Corbis

every 30min (last tour 4pm).
🕐*Closed Thanksgiving Day & Dec 25.*
💷*$15 .* 🅿 ✆*703-780-4000.*
www.woodlawn1805.org.

MANSION

Prominent architect Dr. William Thornton was involved in the construction of the house. The structure has a two-story central core with symmetrical one-story wings that are connected to the main house by hyphens.

Decorated as it might have been during the Lewises' lifetime, the house contains furnishings that belonged to the family, including several furnishings from Mount Vernon. Opening off the center hall are a parlor and living room. Adept musicians, Nelly and her daughters often gave performances on the harp and piano that still dominate the parlor. The fire screen was embroidered by Nelly.

Off the living room the master bedroom holds personal items of the Lewises.

The one-story hyphens connected to the center house were kitchen and work areas in the Lewises' day. They now hold a reception room *(south side)* and an educational space *(north side)*, which were added at the turn of the 19C. The two wings connected to the hyphens are used as administrative offices.

The second floor contains four bedrooms and a linen room, all of which open off a central hall.

The **grounds** are graced with large trees and boxwoods. The parterred garden is noted for its roses.

POPE-LEIGHEY HOUSE

This small, L-shaped house in a wooded setting is one of the few publicly accessible examples of what the 20C's most eminent American-born architect, **Frank Lloyd Wright** (1867-1959), called his "Usonian" architecture—functional, simply designed homes affordable to middle-class Americans.

Built in 1941 for Loren Pope, a journalist in nearby Falls Church, Virginia, the 1,200sq ft, five-room house cost roughly $7,000. The Leigheys bought the house from the Popes five years later. When it was threatened with demolition because of highway construction in 1964, Mrs. Leighey donated it to the National Trust for Historic Preservation, which moved it to its current site.

The house contains the furniture that Frank Lloyd Wright designed for it and is built only of cypress, brick, glass and concrete, following the Wright tenet to use as few materials as possible and to respond to the surrounding environment—again showing how Wright was ahead of his time.

Junction of 7th Street NW and H Street NW at night
© Philip Scalia /Alamy

Where to Stay

Party lines aside, the city's range of accommodations is sure to please both discerning diplomats and budget-minded backpackers. Swank boutique hotels, charming guest houses and grande-dame luxury establishments provide sanctuary to the thousands of families, journalists, politicians and international visitors who come to the capital each year. Most hotels are located in the Downtown and Georgetown areas, while less-expensive rooms can be found in the Dupont Circle and Adams Morgan neighborhoods.

USEFUL CONTACTS

For **price-shopping** and to find available rooms during the high season, consider using a rooms broker like Hotels.com *(www.hotels.com)*, Expedia Travel *(www.expedia.com)*, Capitol Reservations *(www.capitol reservations.com)* or Quikbook *(www.quikbook.com)*.

RATES

The properties listed below were selected for their ambience, location and/or value for money. Prices reflect the average cost for a standard double room (two people) in high season (not including any applicable city or state taxes). Room prices may be considerably lower in off-season, and many hotels offer discounted weekend rates.

> **$$$$$** over $350
> **$$$$** $250-$350
> **$$$** $175-$250
> **$$** $100-$175

CAPITOL HILL

$$$ Capitol Hill Hotel – *200 C Street, SE.* 📞*202-543-6000 or 800-814-5983. www.capitolhillhotel-dc.com. 152 suites.* Nestled on a quiet residential street in the shadow of the Capitol, this hotel is well-situated for seeing sights on or near the Hill: the Capitol building is just two blocks away. The fully renovated property offers roomy accommodations and modern amenities. Free high-speed Internet access is available throughout the hotel, and all rooms have flat-screen TVs, DVD players and either a kitchen or kitchenette. Many suites are pet-friendly. A complimentary breakfast buffet is available every morning.

$$$ Hotel George – *15 E St. NW.* 📞*202-347-4200 or 800-546-7866. www.hotelgeorge.com. 139 rooms.* George Washington is the father of this country and Hotel George is the father of this, the city's modern hotel scene. When the hip boutique hotel opened in 1998 its vibrant colors and minimalist interior made it an instant success with guests, and, much to the chagrin of traditionalists, brought the modern hotel trend to town. A short walk from Union Station, Hotel George houses the popular see-and-be-seen **Bistro Bis** (**$$$**) restaurant.

$$$ The Liaison Capitol Hill – *415 New Jersey Ave. NW.* 📞*202-638-1616 or 866-246-2203. www.affinia.com/ Liaison. 343 rooms.* The newly renovated guest rooms present a cool, modern and muted complement to the lounge-style lobby with its oversized pop art portraits of world leaders. Throw in after-hours cocktail parties on the rooftop deck, and the result is a tip-to-toe study in contemporary lodging. Request in-room spa treatments or order from a dream menu that includes

Hotel George

©David Phelps Photography/Kimpton Group

magnetic therapy pillows, and even sound pillows equipped with ultra-thin speakers for your MP3 player. The rooftop pool is the place to cool off in summer and the sidewalk deck is great for people-watching.

$$$ Phoenix Park Hotel – *520 N. Capitol St. NW. ℘202-638-6900 or 800-824-5419. www.phoenixparkhotel.com. 145 rooms.* Situated between Union Station and the US Capitol, Phoenix Park pairs a convenient location with generous amenities and live Irish entertainment. The welcoming exterior harkens back to an 18C Irish manor, while the lively downstairs Dubliner Pub draws a steady crowd of Capitol Hill staffers.

DOWNTOWN

$$ Channel Inn Hotel – *650 Water St. SW. ℘202-554-2400 or 800-368-5668. www.channelinn.com. 100 rooms.* Billed as Washington, DC's only waterfront hotel, Channel Inn offers comfortable, affordable rooms with views of the Washington Marina. Seafood restaurants and DC's fresh-fish market neighbor the property. From the balconies of the guest rooms you can watch sailboats, yachts and fishing boats glide past. Bargain weekend rates are sometimes available online.

$$$ Henley Park Hotel –*926 Massachusetts Ave. NW. ℘202-638-5200 or 800-222-8474. www.henleypark.com. 96 rooms.* This hotel's Tudor-style exterior and meticulously restored rooms reflect the classic elegance of Washington's earlier days. Gargoyles and lead windows guard the entrance to this charming property.

$$$ The Madison – *15th & M Sts. NW. ℘202-862-1600 or 800-424-8577. www.themadisondc.com. 367 rooms.* Billed as a modern adaptation of historic Washington, the hotel offers rooms and suites with a light and bright setting. Located just a few blocks from the White House, The Madison puts you near major attractions, the Metro and restaurants.

$$$$ Morrison-Clark Inn – *1015 L St. NW. ℘202-898-1200 or 800-332-7898. www.morrisonclark.com. 54 rooms.* This turn-of-the-19C mansion seems misplaced in Downtown's business

John Jacob Astor Suite, St. Regis Washington, DC

©Starwood Hotels and Resorts

district. Past the antiques-filled parlor, with lace curtains and burgundy wall coverings are three styles of accommodations. Choose from neutral-toned Neoclassical, opulent Victorian and country-style distressed woods and wicker. The restaurant's Southern-style specialities make it a national favorite.

$$$$ Renaissance Mayflower Hotel – *1127 Connecticut Ave. NW. ℘202-347-3000 or 800-228-7697. www.renaissance mayflower.com. 657 rooms.* A perennial favorite of frequent visitors, the Mayflower flaunts the splendor of Washington's golden age along busy Connecticut Avenue. The lobby of this luxury hotel is graced with Federalist furniture and gilded accents, while the guest rooms recollect the genteel elegance of a distant era with their marble bathrooms and antique accents.

$$$$ St. Regis Washington, DC – *923 16th St. NW. ℘202-638-2626 or 877-787-3447. www.stregis.com. 182 rooms.* The landmark St. Regis looms over Washington's thriving business district with an air of distinction. Since Calvin Coolidge cut the ribbon for the hotel's grand opening, prime ministers, presidents, royalty and celebrities have frequented the luxurious hotel. The 2008 multi-million dollar renovation touched every interior space, including the guest rooms that now seamlessly blend modern function with classic form. The hotel butlers help travelers with everything from unpacking to dinner reservations to tea service.

$$$$ Willard InterContinental – *1401 Pennsylvania Ave. NW. ℘202-628-9100 or 866-487-2537. www.washington. intercontinental.com. 345 rooms.* A bastion of Washington tradition, the Willard towers over Pennsylvania Avenue as it has for more than 150 years. Inside, the magnificent Beaux-Arts lobby recalls an earlier age of opulence and political mystique with its grand columns and glittering chandeliers. The Round Robin Bar has served many a president mint juleps and potent brandies. The bright rooms sport a tasteful, antique-dotted decor; many provide views of the Washington skyline. The hotel's Red Door Spa offers weary travelers a way to detox and de-stress before heading home.

$$$$$ Hay-Adams – *800 16th St. NW. ℘202-638-6600 or 800-853-6807. www.hayadams.com. 144 rooms.* With a view of the Executive Mansion from its location across Lafayette Square, the lauded Hay-Adams is closer to the White House than any of the city's grande-dame hotels. Steeped in Washington lore, this elaborate, Renaissance-inspired beauty repeatedly houses world leaders and discerning travelers. During the days leading up to his 2009 inauguration, President Barak Obama and his family stayed at the historic property.

$$$$$ W Washington DC – *515 15th St. NW. ℘202-661-2400. www.starwood hotels.com. 349 rooms.* The swank and opulent yet funky W is aglow with all things modern. Splashes of bold color accent the contemporary black-and-white interior while guest rooms feature waterfall showers, iPod docking stations and built-in leather chaises. But the most in-demand real estate in the hotel is the rooftop where the outdoor terrace lounge offers up-close city and White House views that look like they belong on a postcard.

FOGGY BOTTOM

$$$ Hotel Lombardy – *2019 Penn-sylvania Ave. NW. ℘202-828-2600 or 800-424-5486. www.hotellombardy.com. 160 rooms.* Restored to reflect its original 1929 character, Hotel Lombardy is located just four blocks from the White House in the center of Washington's business district. Luxurious bedding complements the densely woven orien-tal rugs and sleek chrome bath fixtures. Technological amenities coexist with the quaint ambience of this bastion of traditional Washington, DC hospitality.

$$$ The Melrose Hotel – *2430 Pennsylvania Ave. NW. ℘202-955-6400 or 800-635-7673. www.melrosehoteldc.com. 240 rooms.* The allure of this Foggy Bottom property is largely the oversized guest rooms bedecked in hues of yellow and blue and equipped with writing desks and marble baths, as well

---

What you should know about Washington, DC hotels:

♦ Quoted rates do not include the city's substantial **hotel tax** of 14.50 percent. For example, with a quoted room rate of $139, you will actually pay $159 for that night's stay.

♦ Rate categories shown should be taken as a general guideline only. **Rates** can be higher or lower depending on season, day of the week and volume of advance reservations.

♦ Guest **parking** will cost, on average, from $15 to $45 per day.

♦ **Pet owners** should contact hotels directly or peruse www.petswelcome. com for a list of establishments that are dog- and cat-friendly.

♦ In-room **telephone charges** can range from 50¢ to as much as $2 for local calls. Some establishments will charge as much as four to five times the usual rate for long-distance calls. Even using a long-distance calling card can sometimes incur connection fees. When checking in, be sure to ask the price for local calls and connection fees for toll-free numbers. When in doubt, use your cell (mobile) phone or, as a last resort, the pay phones off the lobby.

as original art commissioned for the hotel. Several rooms include queen sleeper sofas. The Melrose's location within walking distance of the Kennedy Center and Georgetown makes its sunny, cheery rooms a DC bargain.

$$$$ The Fairmont Hotel – *2401 M St. NW. 202-429-2400 or 866-540-4505. www.fairmont.com/washington. 415 rooms.* The great outdoors reigns at the Fairmont, as sunlight pours through the glassy atriums where trees flourish. Ample guest rooms are clothed in elegant furnishings and sunny hues; posh executive suites are tailored to suit business travelers and to accommodate small meetings. Located on the fringes of Georgetown, the Fairmont provides easy access to shops and restaurants.

The Fairmont Hotel

©Fairmont Hotels & Resorts

$$$$$ Ritz-Carlton – *1150 22nd St. NW. 202-835-0500. www.ritzcarlton.com. 300 rooms.* This luxury Washington hotel brings sought-after amenities to the West End. The wood-paneled lobby features comfortable seating and a fireplace. Bathed in pale yellow and moss green, the elegant rooms show off plush bedding and include business perks like dual-line telephones and high-speed Internet connections. Guests enjoy privileges at the Sports Club/LA fitness center.

GEORGETOWN

$$$ Georgetown Inn – *1310 Wisconsin Ave. NW. 202-333-8900 or 888-587-2388. www.georgetowninn.com. 96 rooms.* Combining European elegance and colonial charm, this inn sits along bustling Wisconsin Avenue in the heart of Georgetown's tony shops and restaurants. Luxurious marble bathrooms and pillow-top beds welcome guests back after long days of sightseeing.

$$$ Georgetown Suites – *1111 30th St. NW. 202-298-7800 or 800-348-7203. www.georgetownsuites.com. 220 suites.* Sitting just minutes from historic Georgetown's shops and restaurants, this all-suite hotel is perfect for families and long-term visitors. The two buildings, located half a block from each other, hold spacious suites equipped with kitchenettes. Rates include free Wi-Fi and a complimentary continental breakfast.

$$$ Hotel Monticello of Georgetown – *1075 Thomas Jefferson St. NW. 202-337-0900 or 800-388-2410. www.monticello hotel.com. 57 rooms.* Situated just footsteps from the historic C & O Canal and lively Wisconsin Avenue, the Monticello makes an excellent base for exploring Georgetown. The hotel offers ample, newly renovated rooms, complimentary breakfast, and a new rooftop claiming views of Washington Harbour and Georgetown.

$$$ The Latham Hotel – *3000 M St. NW. 202-726-5000 or 800-583-7591. www.thelatham.com. 133 rooms.* With a prime Georgetown location that houses Citronelle, one of Washington's most popular restaurants, the hotel boasts comfy, yet elegantly appointed rooms and rambling suites with generous amenities—each sure to please their occupants. No doubt Georgetown's only outdoor rooftop pool will too.

$$$$$ Four Seasons – *2800 Pennsylvania Ave. NW. 202-342-0444 or 800-819-5053. www.fourseasons. com. 222 rooms.* With an unassuming brick exterior, this upscale hotel earns its distinguished marks with luxurious furnishings and impeccable service. Expansive rooms and suites feature custom-designed furniture, original artwork and refrigerated private bars. Guests can take advantage of the state-of-the-art fitness center, the two-lane indoor saltwater lap pool and the tranquil day spa.

DUPONT CIRCLE

$$ Hotel Tabard Inn – *1739 N St. NW. 202-785-1277. www.tabardinn.com. 40 rooms.* A Dupont Circle institution, this hotel radiates character with its twisting staircases, stained-glass lamps and antique furnishings. Rooms vary in size and decor; some share bathrooms. The plush couches and overstuffed chairs in the lounge are great places to unwind over cocktails. The restaurant's acclaimed contemporary fare can be savored in the simple dining room or on an enclosed patio. A continental breakfast is included in the room tab. Many of the specialty herbs used in the kitchen here come from its rooftop garden.

$$$ Dupont Circle Hotel – *1500 New Hampshire Ave. NW. 202-483-6000 or 800-534-6835. www.doylecollection.com. 327 rooms.* A rebranding and extensive renovation of this hotel turned it into a contemporary gem in a can't-be-beat location. Well-designed guest rooms feature Frette bed linen, heated bathroom floors and ergonomic work station. The restaurant's sidewalk patio overlooking the area's famous circle becomes in-demand real estate once

the mercury begins to rise. Called the Level Nine experience, the exclusive top floor acts like a hotel within a hotel with its own private elevator, concierge and lounge.

$$$$ Hotel Palomar – *2121 P St. NW. 202-448-1800 or 877-866-3070. www.hotelpalomar-dc.com. 335 rooms.* This modern, 10-story property bustles, especially late afternoons when patrons enjoy complimentary wine and hors d'oeuvres in the sleek lobby. Guest rooms are large, sporting contemporary furnishings, colorful wall art and high-tech gadgets. The full-service, on-site restaurant, **Urbana** (**$$$**), serves up primarily Northern Italian dishes.

$$$$$ Jefferson Hotel – *1200 16th St. NW. 202-448-2300. www.jeffersondc.com. 99 rooms.* Built as a grand private residence in 1923, the Jefferson dazzles with its established reputation, impeccable service and classic exterior. The top-hat clad doormen reopened the doors to the Beaux Arts jewel in 2009 after an extensive renovation.The small historic hotel became DC's first Relais & Châteaux property in 2010. The hotel's namesake is evident throughout, from the spa treatments based on botanicals grown in Thomas Jefferson's Monticello gardens to the Jefferson-signed documents incorporated into the rich decor.

ADAMS MORGAN

$$ Adam's Inn – *1746 Lanier Place, NW. North of the Dupont Circle district. 202-745-3600 or 800-578-6807. www.adamsinn.com. 26 rooms.* This pleasant B&B, housed in three old town homes, prides itself on its homey atmosphere and reasonable rates. A computer room with a public terminal, a television lounge and a guest kitchen complete with a tea and coffee station are a few of the welcoming touches. A continental breakfast is served every morning in the breakfast room and, weather permitting, can be enjoyed outside on the small patio or in the garden. Some of the rooms have shared bathrooms.

Dupont Circle Hotel

The Dupont Circle Hotel/The Doyle Collection

Where to Eat

Many attractions in DC have on-site eating facilities *(indicated in the Sights in this guide by the symbol* ✕*)*. Picnicking is permitted on the Mall. In warm seasons snacks are available from kiosks on the Mall or from street vendors along Independence Avenue. Union Station, the Old Post Office (Pennsylvania Ave. & 12th St. NW) and the Shops at National Place (Pennsylvania Ave. & 13th St. NW) house eateries for all tastes and budgets. Upscale establishments on K Street and Connecticut Avenue offer formal dining, while the large waterfront restaurants on Maine Avenue SW specialize in seafood. Many Asian eateries are located in and the Arlington–Clarendon area, while the vibrant Adams Morgan neighborhood hosts a wide variety of ethnic restaurants; Hispanic and Ethiopian cuisine in particular. Fashionable dining can be found along 14th Street, while H Street NE is destined to be the next "in" spot. The venues listed below were selected for their ambience, location and/or value for money. Rates indicate the average cost of an appetizer, an entrée and dessert for one person (not including tax, gratuity or beverages). Most restaurants are open daily—except where noted—and accept major credit cards. Call for information on reservations and opening hours.

$$$$	over $75
$$$	$50-$75
$$	$25-$50
$	less than $25

CAPITOL HILL

$$ Capitol City Brewing Company – *1100 New York Ave. NW.* ℘*202-628-2222.* *www.capcitybrew.com.* **Pub**. Casual and comfortable, the District's oldest microbrewery since Prohibition serves simple bar tastes in a restored historic building. Beer fans can try a Sampler of the in-house brewery blends. Servers promptly bring soft, warm pretzels for patrons to munch on while perusing

---

Eating Out in DC

Smoking is not allowed in Washington, DC restaurants or bars. Although **jackets** may not be required, gentlemen might feel more comfortable wearing one in the more expensive restaurants. **Reservations** are highly recommended. **Gratuities** are generally not included on the bill; a tip of 15 to 20 percent is considered standard.

the menu. Giant sandwiches and capacious salads rejuvenate patrons after a day of sightseeing. For dessert, share the massive Monumental Brownie.

$$ Tortilla Coast – *400 First St. SE.* ℘*202-546-6768. www.tortillacoast.com.* **TexMex**. Wayward Texans have come here for potent margaritas and spicy tastes of home since 1988. Cleanse your palate with the Stars and Stripes margarita, a blend of traditional and strawberry margaritas laced with Blue Curaçao. Spinach and mushroom enchiladas and soft tacos satisfy vegetarians, while southwestern flavors star in hickory barbecue chicken fajitas.

$$ White Tiger – *301 Massachusetts Ave. NE. No lunch Sat.* ℘*202-546-5900. www. whitetigerdc.com.* **Indian**. Just footsteps from Union Station, the tropical decor and Raji mystique of White Tiger seem a far cry from the nearby steak houses. The menu weighs heavily on lighter, northern Indian fare, with impeccable tandoori chicken or lamb dishes and savory naan bread. Outdoor seating makes this restaurant a favorite of Capitol Hill employees.

$$$ Bistro Bis – *15 E St. NW.* ℘*202-661-2700. www.bistrobis.com.* **French**. Located in the stylish Hotel George, this decisively French bistro swarms with political figures. Washington celebrities hover around the zinc bar and nestle into cozy leather booths, while three dining levels complement the contemporary offerings. The seasonal menu here changes according to market availability.

©Gwen Cannon/Michelin

Georgia Brown's

WHITE HOUSE AREA

$$ Georgia Brown's – *950 15th St. NW.* ☏*202-393-4499. www.gbrowns.com.* **Southern**. This well-appointed restaurant pushes Dixie cooking to new heights by combining standard Southern ingredients in unusual ways and adding artistic flair. Try the she-crab soup before moving on to an entrée of "head-on" shrimp with spicy sausage and creamy grits or Southern-fried chicken. The vegetarian plate includes a large black-eyed peacake and fried green tomatoes. Peach cobbler à la mode is the signature dessert.

$$ McCormick & Schmick's – *1652 K St. NW.* ☏*202-861-2233. www.mccormick andschmicks.com.* **Seafood**. This upscale (but not pricey) restaurant, with a score of establishments nationwide—and three locations in DC—is renowned for its exceptionally fresh and varied seafood. The menu typically features a dozen kinds of shellfish as well as a wide array of fish. Request menu items grilled or sautéed to your taste.

DOWNTOWN

$ Nooshi – *1120 19th St. St. NW.* ☏*202-293-3138. www.nooshidc.com.* **Asian**. Nooshi features sushi on its menu, fusing Malaysian, Japanese, Indonesian, Thai and Chinese variations of noodles. Select from udon, ramen, egg, chow fun, and then select a preparation style—the frenzied cooks do the rest. The savory satays and spicy *tom yum* soup are worthy introductions to a quick, simple meal.

$$ Rasika – *633 D St. NW.* ☏*202-637-1222. www.rasikarestaurant.com. Closed Sun.* **Indian**. This DC hot spot pulls diners in with its sophisticated setting and contemporary Indian cuisine, served as small plates. Start with a pomegranate margarita, then order the much-talked-about appetizer *palat chaat* (crisp baby spinach) with sweet yogurt, tamarind and date chutney. For your main course, try a tandoori dish or the signature black cod. End your meal with the carrot halwa with cinnamon sabayon or the date and toffee pudding.

$$ Zaytinya – *701 9th St. NW.* ☏*202-638-0800. www.zaytinya.com.* **Mediterranean**. This very popular restaurant near the National Portrait Museum draws DC-ites to its large, whitewashed dining levels, accented with Aegean blues. The mezze-based menu offers Greek, Turkish and Lebanese seafood, meat, and vegetarian options, accompanied by puffy pita bread and oil. Try the skewered lamb (Adana Kebab), the black cod, and the falafel, to sample each option. The muscat-soaked apricots make a great finale to your meal.

$$$ The Caucus Room – *401 9th St. NW.* ☏*202-393-1300. www.thecaucusroom.com. No lunch Sat–Sun.* **American**. This restaurant is the consummate Washington steakhouse, where power players disappear into the dark wooded interior to down a tender steak and a glass of merlot. Truly a bipartisan venture, The Caucus Room is partially owned by Republican Haley Barbour and Democrat Tom Boggs, and boasts a colorful William Woodward mural of a jovial donkey and elephant amicably enjoying a lavish feast. Generous portions and impeccable service justify the high prices.

$$$ DC Coast – *1401 K St. NW. www.dccoast.com. No lunch Sat–Sun.* ☏*202-216-5988.* **Contemporary**. A bronze mermaid sculpture greets hungry locals at this popular Downtown restaurant. Housed in an Art Deco-era bank, the contemporary dining room features lantern-style chandeliers, oversized oval mirrors and spiral-shaped booths. Chef Jeff Tunks' tri-coastal specialities (Mid-Atlantic, Gulf and West) include a roasted pork chop with mustard greens, the evening's soufflé and Chinese-style smoked lobster.

$$$ Elisir – *427 11th St. NW. 202-546-0088. http://elisirrestaurant.com. No lunch Sat. Closed Sun.* **Italian**. From the olive oil and infused sea salt tasting to the branzino carpaccio, served in a cigar box and smoked at the last minute, the dishes that Chef Enzo Fargione presents are both refined and whimsical. Inspired by a visit to the Cold Stone Creamery ice-cream parlor, the cubed veal carpaccio shows the craft of a chef who combines levity with high culinary art. Try the decadent potato gnocchi with smoked Maine lobster or the roasted veal filet with pan-seared veal sweetbreads.

$$$ 701 – *701 Pennsylvania Ave. NW. 202-393-0701. www.701restaurant.com. No lunch Sat–Sun.* **Contemporary**. Tucked behind the Navy Memorial, 701 recalls the elegance of an upscale supper club, with its piano music and vast selection of vodkas and caviar. The fresh fish selections are dramatic preludes to performances at nearby Shakespeare Theatre. For elegance at an affordable price, try the pre-theater menus, or stop by for dessert after the performance.

$$$ The Source – *575 Pennsylvania Ave. NW. 202-637-6100. www.wolfgang puck.com. Closed Sun.* **Asian Fusion**. This restaurant's architectural details pay homage to its home in the Newseum, but the menu deserves the headlines. To start, try the spicy tuna tartare served in sesame meso cones, or the tandoori arctic char with cucumber raita, pickled beets and tomato chutney. Move on to soft shell crab (in season) in angry sauce or lamb duo of soy-marinated chop and tenderloin stir-fry. Finish with avocado-pistachio ice cream or the yuzu and lime tart.

$$$ Vidalia – *1990 M St. NW. 202-659-1990. www.vidaliadc.com. No lunch Sat–Sun.* **Southern**. With upscale versions of shrimp and grits and chicken and dumplings, Vidalia is an oasis of Southern comfort food in Washington's bustling business district. The restaurant's sunny yellow walls match

The Source

©Zain Deane/Michelin

the warm cornbread and refreshing lemonade that accent a summer lunch. Try the signature roasted Vidalia onion in season, and close your meal with sticky pecan pie paired with bourbon-laced ice cream.

U STREET CORRIDOR, DOWNTOWN
$ Ben's Chili Bowl – *1213 U St. NW. 202-667-0909. www.benschilibowl.com.* **Chili**. Ben's is common meeting ground for DC's African-American community and young urban dwellers alike. Sloppy chili dogs, thick milkshakes and fries loaded with cheese and bacon have proven to be universal pleasers in this Washington dining landmark. The interior retains the nostalgic charm of a 1950s diner, while modern business lunchers swivel around on the barstools during their mid-day power meal.

FOGGY BOTTOM
$$$ Kinkead's – *2000 Pennsylvania Ave. NW. 202-296-7700. www.kinkead.com.* **Seafood**. Chef Bob Kinkead's innovative combination of sauces and ingredients makes his award-winning American brasserie one of the premier seafood restaurants in the city. Choices from his daily changing menu may include pepita crusted salmon with crab, shrimp, corn and chili ragoût.

GEORGETOWN
$ Rocklands – *2418 Wisconsin Ave. NW. 202-333-2558. www.rocklands.com.* **Barbecue**. For an inexpensive meal in Georgetown, follow the sweet smell of hickory smoke up Wisconsin Avenue to Rocklands. Traditional barbecue staples,

from ribs and pulled pork to jalapeño cornbread, are deftly handled here.

$$ Bangkok Joe's – *3000 K St. NW. 202-333-4422. www.bangkokjoes.com.* **Asian**. At this casual, welcoming eatery close to the water, it's best to focus on the tasty menu of made-on-the-spot dumplings and creative spring rolls. With flavor combinations like lobster, pine nuts and butternut squash, these aren't your average Asian appetizers.

$$ Clyde's of Georgetown – *3236 M St. NW. 202-333-9180. www.clydes.com.* **American**. With several locations in the Washington metropolitan area, cheery, saloon-like Clyde's has burgeoned into a Washington legend. Casual diners can opt for traditional burgers, sandwiches and chili, while patrons with greater expectations can select from a lengthy list of fashionable cocktails and fresh seafood catches.

$$ Old Europe – *2434 Wisconsin Ave. NW. 202-333-7600. www.old-europe.com. Closed Mon.* **German**. One of Washington's only German restaurants, Old Europe draws a healthy contingency of beer and schnitzel lovers who find solace in few other locales. The walls are covered, as anticipated, with steins and wooden crests that create a perpetual air of Oktoberfest.

$$ Old Glory – *3139 M St. NW. 202-337-3406. www.oldglorybbq.com.* **Barbecue**. Don't miss this fun, lively barbecue joint perched on the busy Georgetown corner of M Street and Wisconsin Avenue. Settle into a booth, and a server will promptly arrive to powerfully "brand" your table with a purposeful slap of an iron stamp. Each table comes equipped with regionally inspired sauces. Mosey up to the lavish hickory bar boasting the largest selection of bourbons in DC. Tuesdays are trivia nights

$$$ 1789 Restaurant – *1226 36th St. NW. 202-965-1789. www.1789restaurant.com. Dinner only.* **American**. This Washington fine-dining legend is named for the year in which nearby Georgetown University was founded. Its country-inn setting and seasonal American menu have assured its longevity. Start with the foie gras or beef crudo two ways and move on to a main course of Alaskan halibut or rack of lamb. Complete your repast with the 1789 chocolate coin—a concoction of caramel, chocolate and whiskey.

DUPONT CIRCLE

$ Pizzeria Paradiso – *2003 P St. NW. 202-223-1245. www.eatyourpizza.com.* **Pizza**. Tucked inside a tiny row house near Dupont Circle, Pizzeria Paradiso serves up one of the best pizzas in the nation's capital. Delicate crust and fresh ingredients are the key. The exceptional crust soaks in a rich, smoky flavor from the wood-burning oven, as the fresh mozzarella melts over a bed of thinly sliced roma tomatoes. A second roomier location is in Georgetown, *3282 M Street NW. 202-337-1245.*

$$ Kramerbooks & Afterwords Cafe – *1517 Connecticut Ave. NW. 202-387-1462. www.kramers.com.* **International**. A longtime favorite with literature lovers and cafe-goers, this Dupont Circle institution combines a well-stocked bookstore with a bar and restaurant. Entrees range from filet mignon or Tuscan lamb chops to seared sushi tuna or Thai-steamed mussels. There's a changing selection of microbrewery draft beers and a wine list. If you're in the mood for simply kaffeeklatsching, the coffee and dessert menu is extensive.

$$$$ Restaurant Nora – *2132 Florida Ave. NW. 202-462-5143. www.noras.com. Dinner only. Closed Sun.* **Contemporary**. America's first certified organic restaurant is housed in an updated 19C grocery store off Dupont Circle. Chef Nora Pouillon's menus reflect what is in season and fresh each day and may feature delights such as chilled garlic vichyssoise, Amish rabbit roulade and Alaskan halibut. DC diners have praised her innovative organic creations for 20-plus years.

LOGAN CIRCLE/14TH STREET

$$$ Estadio – *1520 14th St. NW. 202-319-1404. www.estadio-dc.com. No lunch Mon–Thu.* **Spanish**. Wrought-iron accents and chairs fit for conquistadors embrace patrons in a night of Iberian immersion. This tapas restaurant serves up a mix of old-school classics with

Estadio

©Zain Deane/Michelin

inventive New World small plates like crispy duck breast with beluga lentils. Kick off the meal with a cocktail of elderflower, orange-thyme or crushed strawberry. End it with a slice of divine manchego cheesecake.

$$$ Pearl Dive Oyster Palace – *1612 14th St. NW. ℘202-319-1612. www.pearldivedc.com. No lunch Mon– Thu.* **Cajun**. Adding a delightful dash of New Orleans to DC, Pearl Dive pulls in an often-raucous crowd to its casual setting of exposed brick walls and lone chandelier to feast on the likes of oysters, seafood gumbo and crawfish etouffee. After dinner, head upstairs to the Black Jack bar for cocktails and a game of bocce in the back room.

ADAMS MORGAN

$ Lauriol Plaza – *1835 18th St. NW. North of the Dupont Circle area. ℘202-387-0035. www.lauriolplaza.com.* **Mexican**. A popular eatery, Lauriol Plaza keeps pitchers of margaritas flowing freely during happy hour. Fabulous fajitas and other Tex-Mex mainstays are joined by Puerto Rican and Latin American selections on the extensive menu. With ample outdoor dining, Lauriol Plaza sizzles on summer evenings.

$ Saigonnais – *2307 18th St. NW. ℘202-232-5300. www.dcnet.com/saigonnais.* **Vietnamese**. Located in the heart of

Adams Morgan, Saigonnais tantalizes with aromatic Indochine creations. Stylish and simple, the spring rolls are crisp and flavorful, while the assembly-required, pork-filled crepe rolls offer a challenging prelude to the lemongrass chicken and other generous dishes.

$$ Mama Ayesha's – *1967 Calvert St. NW. ℘202-232-5431. www.mamaayeshas.com.* **Lebanese**. Middle Eastern delicacies have been served at this restaurant since 1960 when Mama Ayesha Abraham first opened it, honing recipes she brought with her when she immigrated to the US in the 1920s. Start with a variety of hummus or a fattoush salad before feasting on kabobs. Bigger appetites will be whetted by the daunting baked lamb shank. Dinners conclude with a cup of sweet Arabian coffee and decadent baklava.

WOODLEY PARK

$$ Lebanese Taverna – *2641 Connecticut Ave. NW. ℘202-265-8681. www.lebanesetaverna.com.* **Lebanese**. One of the most popular restaurants in Woodley Park, this taverna teems with young professionals and outdoor-cafe enthusiasts. Large groups create their own servings from the hummus bar before tucking into a savory array of mezze: a spread of hors d'oeuvres, paired with warm, soft pita bread that emerges from the wood-burning ovens.

Entertainment

Not that many years ago, Washington was equated with a lackluster night scene, with the exception of U Street and perhaps Adams Morgan. Downtown DC pretty much closed up at night, save for the scant restaurant trade. But today, the capital city boasts a wide array of options for entertainment, especially after dark. Classical music lovers, club goers, jazz enthusiasts and dance fans can find almost every venue here, from concert halls to mega-dance floors to intimate lounges. And not just in DC, but in Georgetown, Tysons Corner and areas nearby as well.

PERFORMING ARTS

Washington provides visitors with a great diversity of performing-arts offerings year-round. Highly respected dance, symphony and opera performances are held primarily at the Kennedy Center. Located in Vienna, Virginia, just 30 minutes from Washington, **Wolf Trap** is the country's only national park dedicated to the performing arts. Visitors can enjoy a relaxing dinner under the stars on the grounds or bring a picnic for concerts, dance, jazz, opera and other performances from late May to early September. In the DC area, several dozen live-performance **theaters** mount a variety of stage productions performed by travelling Broadway companies and acclaimed regional and local groups. DC's main theater district centers on E Street between 7th and 15th Streets NW (the National, Warner, Ford's and Shakespeare theaters), while the Arena Stage along the southwest waterfront presents classic and contemporary drama in its new complex. U Street's Lincoln Theatre where Duke Ellington and Ella Fitzgerald once brought down the house is experiencing a second renaissance. Popular rock and alternative **music** are performed at intimate and large-scale nightclubs

Tickets

As some of the more popular events sell out months in advance, it is advisable to buy tickets early. Full-price tickets can be purchased directly from the venue's box office or from one of the brokers listed below; a service charge of 10 percent or more may be added to the ticket price. Ticket brokers sometimes have tickets available when the box office is sold out, but expect to pay a substantial service fee. Hotel concierges may also be able to help secure tickets. Theaters sometimes reserve a limited number of seats for full-time students, seniors and active-duty military personnel (identification may be required).

Tickets.com (☎888-223-6000; www.tickets.com) takes phone and online reservations for selected events and sights in DC and environs. Major credit cards are accepted. The service charge added to the price of each ticket varies, depending upon the event.

Ticketmaster (☎202-397-7328 or 800-551-7328; www.ticketmaster.com) outlets are conveniently located throughout the area; call or check online for locations. Major credit cards are accepted. A convenience charge is added to the ticket price.

TICKETplace offers tickets for selected events on the day of the show at half price, plus a service charge of 12 percent of the full face-value of the ticket. Purchases must be made in person (major credit cards only) from the box office at 407 7th St. NW (open year-round Wed–Fri 11am–6pm, Sat 10am–5pm; ☎202-393-2161; www.cultural-alliance.org).

John F. Kennedy Center for the Performing Arts

© Carol Pratt/Kennedy Center

as well as at stadiums and other large venues throughout DC, northern Virginia and neighboring Maryland. Area bookstores, coffee houses and other locations host **public readings** or talks by both established and up-and-coming authors throughout the year. For a detailed listing of events, consult the *Washington City Paper (distributed Thursday)*, *Washingtonian* magazine, the "Weekend" supplements in the Friday edition of the *Washington Post* and in the Thursday edition of the *Washington Times,* or the free publications listed in this guide under *Planning Your Trip.*

CLASSICAL MUSIC

National Symphony Orchestra
The John F. Kennedy Center for the Performing Arts, 2700 F St., NW. ☏*202-416-8100. www.kennedy-center.org.*
The National Symphony Orchestra makes its home at the Kennedy Center where it puts on a full season every year in addition to performing throughout the city and around the world. The annual NSO Capitol Fourth Concert on the West Lawn of the Capitol is a favorite among locals and tourists who arrive hours before to put down a picnic blanket to secure a good spot for the show which always

concludes with Tchaikovsky's 1812 Overture and a fireworks display.

Strathmore
10701 Rockville Pike, North Bethesda. ☏*(301) 581-5100. www.strathmore.org.*
The award-winning Baltimore Symphony Orchestra and National Philharmonic perform regularly at the stunning light-filled Music Center located on the tree-lined Strathmore campus in suburban Maryland. Pitch-perfect adjustable acoustics make Strathmore a wonderful place to hear your favorite symphony or concerto. Every Wednesday evening at 7 pm enjoy music under the stars during Strathmore's free outdoor summer concert series.

DANCE

John F. Kennedy Center for the Performing Arts
2700 F St. NW. ☏*202-467-4600 or 800-444-1324. www.kennedy-center.org.*
World renowned dance companies such as the Alvin Ailey American Dance Theater, Bolshoi Ballet and the Martha Graham Dance Company have graced the Kennedy Center stages over the years. The American Ballet Theatre performs a full-scale production of the *The Nutcracker*

here every December to sold out audiences.

THEATERS AND COMPANIES

Arena Stage
1101 6th St. SW. 202-488-3300. www.arenastage.org.
Arena Stage has become the largest theater in the nation dedicated to American voices. Now located in the Mead Center for American Theater, it is the second largest performance arts complex in DC after the Kennedy Center. The first not-for-profit theater in the US, this 60-plus-year-old company is considered an important pioneer in the regional theater movement.

Ford's Theatre
511 10th St. NW. 202-347-4833. www.fordstheatre.org. Tickets for performances can be purchased online at www.fords.org.
After President Abraham Lincoln was assassinated in 1865 at Ford's Theatre, the stage went dark for many years. It opened again in 1968 following a massive restoration. In 2009 the theater unveiled the results of a second major renovation that included a new lobby, new seats, upgraded sound and lighting systems, renovated bathrooms and enhanced accessibility for patrons with disabilities. The historic look and feel of the theater, including the now infamous presidential box, remain intact and preserved.
A full performance schedule keeps the curtain going up most nights. The plays and musicals presented here embody the cultural patrimony of the nation. *For day tours of the theater and museum, see Ford's Theatre in the Downtown chapter.*

John F. Kennedy Center for the Performing Arts
2700 F St. NW. Guided Tours Available. Tickets and information: 202-467-4600 or 800-444-1324. www.kennedy-center.org.

A "living memorial" to the 35th US president, the Kennedy Center ranks as one of the country's leading cultural institutions. The performances that take place in the six theaters housed here are as diverse as the people who buy tickets to see them and include full-production operas, Broadway shows, dramatic plays, family performances and comedies. The highly acclaimed National Symphony Orchestra also makes its home here. Eighteen enormous crystal chandeliers (a gift from Sweden) dangle from the impossibly high ceiling in the regal 630ft-long Grand Foyer. A bronze bust of President Kennedy sits in the red-carpeted foyer. Don't leave without looking up at the collection of flags in both the Hall of State and the Hall of Nations. During intermission, stroll outside on the terrace for a beautiful view of Georgetown and Virginia over the Potomac, and before the curtain goes up, grab a bite to eat at the cafe upstairs that offers an impressive view of the city.

Studio Theatre
1501 14th St. NW. 202-332-3300. www.studiotheatre.org.
Dedicated to showcasing the talents of contemporary playwrights, the Studio Theatre produces an eclectic mix of productions ranging from the serious to the sublime. Joan Didion, Neil LaBute and August Wilson have all had their work performed on the four stages here.

NIGHTLIFE
DOWNTOWN

Ozio
1813 M St. NW. 202-822-6000. www.oziodc.com.
Marketing itself as a "cigar and martini lounge," Ozio paints a tempting picture of urban chic to Washington's international crowd. It's got the martini menu and lingering cigar smells to match, though the splashy murals and muted walls detract from its loungy qualities.

There is also a no-smoking dance floor if that's more your scene.

H STREET CORRIDOR, DOWNTOWN

Rock and Roll Hotel
1353 H St. NE. ☎*202-2388-7625. www.rockandrollhoteldc.com.*
Washington's music scene crowds the Rock and Roll Hotel for its live edgy music on the ground floor and its theme rooms upstairs. But don't unpack while you are up there. Despite its name, the hotel does not take overnight guests but instead is named as a tribute to places like the Savoy in London and the Chelsea in New York. Even though you can't check in, you don't have to go home to sleep on an empty stomach. The hotel just added a menu that features choices like "up on your knees" ham and cheese, and chicken and waffles for brunch.

U STREET CORRIDOR, DOWNTOWN

Black Cat
1811 14th St. NW. ☎*202-667-4527. www.blackcatdc.com.*
Live-music lovers flock to the Black Cat for a sneak preview of some of rock's rising stars. With an ample space that can hold 550 fans, the Black Cat is readily packed with pierced and tattooed punk- and alternative-music fiends. The familiar U Street haunt is co-owned by former Nirvana drummer and current Foo Fighter Dave Grohl.

Bohemian Caverns
2001 11th St. NW. ☎*202-299-0800. www.bohemiancaverns.com.*
One of DC's best jazz spots in the days of Duke Ellington, Bohemian Caverns reopened fairly recently with a fresh new look and a pleasing lineup of performers. Three levels were added above ground. An upscale restaurant occupies the main level, while live music trickles up from the refurbished caverns below.

GEORGETOWN

Blues Alley
1073 Wisconsin Ave. NW. ☎*202-337-4141. www.bluesalley.com.*
Few Washington nightlife places have enjoyed the success and notoriety of Georgetown's Blues Alley, which has been praised by *New York Times* critics and Dizzy Gillespie alike. Since it opened in 1965, Blues Alley has touted itself as "DC's Best Jazz Supper Club" and is worthy of the distinction.

Sequoia
Washington Harbour, 3000 K St. NW. ☎*202-944-4200. www.arkrestaurants.com.*
Yachts and sporty racing boats sidle up to the Georgetown waterfront on warm summer evenings to enjoy the dockside night scene. A constant stream of music wafts from the docked boats into the bar, where DC's "bold and beautiful" down beer and margaritas in the two-level glass-front restaurant and its River Bar.

Third Edition
1218 Wisconsin Ave. NW. ☎*202-333-3700. www.thethirdedition.com.*
This Georgetown mainstay served as the backdrop for the 1985 movie *St. Elmo's Fire* and has hosted many a beleaguered college student since it opened in 1969. On Wednesday through Saturday nights, a dance party erupts on the upper level, leaving the mellow downstairs beer-sippers and game-watchers in the wake of pop and rock classics. In the summer (and winter, at management's discretion), a lively Tiki Bar opens to offer one of Georgetown's few opportunities for outdoor nightlife away from the riverfront.

DUPONT CIRCLE

Eighteenth Street Lounge
1212 18th St. NW. ☎*202-466-3922. www.eighteenthstreetlounge.com.*
Celebrity residents and visitors are often spotted in this lounge, one of Dupont Circle's most coveted

Eighteenth Street Lounge

©Maria Izaurralde, http://www.mariaizaurralde.com

night spots. Bouncers stand guard over the beautiful property—a historic mansion once home to Teddy Roosevelt—and maintain a strict admissions policy. Leave the jeans, sneakers and ballcaps at home.

Gazuza
1629 Connecticut Ave. NW. ☎202-667-5500. http://gazuzalounge.com.
Sleek furnishings and outside seating overlooking busy Connecticut Avenue have placed Gazuza on the Washington nightlife map. The chic ambience and enviable property don't engender a sense of exclusivity, though; Gazuza's Dupont Circle location attracts a healthy mix of revelers seeking house music, hookah and trendy cocktails.

ADAMS MORGAN

Habana Village
1834 Columbia Rd. NW. ☎202-462-6310. www.habanavillage.com. Closed Sun–Tue.
Forget the embargo on Cuba, Habana Village does its best to re-create the island in DC. Sultry and sexy characterize all three stories of the club, where women never pay cover charges, and even shrinking violets move from the wall to dance the salsa,

rumba and bolero. Come for salsa lessons and live music on weekends, when bartenders pour mojitos by the hundreds.

Madam's Organ
2461 18th St. NW. ☎202-667-5370. www.madamsorgan.com.
"Sorry, we're open" reads the mural outside, just below a busty redhead's boldly painted portrait. The bright colors and brazen sarcasm of Madam's Organ have made it one of the most familiar sites in DC. Inside, it's just as quirky. Take the stairs up to Big Daddy's Love Lounge and Pick-Up Joint, but beware… it's aptly named.

TYSONS CORNER, NORTH VIRGINIA

Iris Lounge
8300 Tyco Rd. ☎703-760-9000. www.irisloungeva.com.
This large, multipurpose venue is quite the hot spot. It's a restaurant and lounge with billiards rooms and a members-only cigar room. On weekends the place transforms into a nightclub, when its glass-enclosed Rocky Patel cigar room hangs above the dance floor, serving up hand-rolled cigars and 20-year-old single barrel scotch.

Shopping

Visitors to Washington can find everything from specialty shops and boutiques in Georgetown to established department stores situated in and around Downtown. Scattered throughout the city are several enclosed malls featuring multilevel arcades and offering a wide selection of shops, restaurants and movie theaters. Some of the more exclusive malls (Willard Collection, Mazza Gallerie and The Collection at Chevy Chase) house boutiques of internationally renowned designers.

Galleries, antique shops and bookstores can be found in the neighborhoods of Adams Morgan, Dupont Circle and around Eastern Market on Capitol Hill. Fashionable Connecticut Avenue from K Street to Dupont Circle presents fine shops and specialty stores. In Old Town Alexandria, visitors can find an array of gift and antique shops and galleries.

DOWNTOWN AND VICINITY
DEPARTMENT STORES

Macy's
1201 G St. NW. ℰ202-628-6661. www.macys.com.
The fabled New York City department store set up shop Downtown following the demise of Hecht's, DC's last local department store chain. Name-brand sportswear for men, women and children along with dressier attire can be found on the multi-level store along with a good selection of housewares, cosmetics, shoes and jewelry.

H&M
1025 F St. NW. ℰ202-347-3306. 1025 F St. NW. www.hm.com/us
The Swedish H&M clothing store took DC by storm when it first opened in town, bringing the world of affordable, trendy clothing to a region once plagued by navy blue pinstripes and boring business suits. This location sells clothing and accessories for women, men and children and tends to get very crowded during lunchtime on weekdays with shoppers browsing before heading back to the office.

SHOPPING MALLS

Union Station
50 Massachusetts Ave. NE. ℰ202-289-1908. www.unionstationdc.com.
You don't need to plan a rail trip to experience DC's glorious Union Station. Designed by Daniel Burnham, the magnificent 1907 Beaux-Arts landmark now houses one of DC's most popular shopping and dining complexes. Familiar retailers like The Body Shop and Ann Taylor join speciality shops like Appalachian Spring, devoted to American crafts, and Alamo Flags, which sells flags and an array of other patriotic merchandise.

SPECIALTY SHOPS AND DESIGNER BOUTIQUES

Nana
3068 Mt. Pleasant St. NW. ℰ202-667-6955. http://store.nanadc.com. Closed Mon.
An adorable little shop with a cult following, Nana's sells vintage-inspired casual women's clothing from up-and-coming designers as well as a carefully selected number of vintage pieces. All the new items adhere to the owner's standards of being ethically made. The purses are among the most popular find here.

GEORGETOWN
SHOPPING MALLS

Shops at Georgetown Park
3222 M St. NW ℰ202-342-8190. www.shopsatgeorgetownpark.com.
Fashionistas and bargain hunters alike will find something to bring home at The Shops at Georgetown Park, a mall right in the heart of the area's shopping district. The popular women's clothing and houseware shop Anthropologie draws a big

crowd as does the hip, wallet-friendly department store H&M. Other stores here include J. Crew, Express and Comfort One Shoes. A food court on the lower level gives weary shoppers a place to rest their feet.

SPECIALTY SHOPS AND DESIGNER BOUTIQUES

Urban Chic
1626 Wisconsin Ave. NW. ℰ202-338-5398. www.urbanchiconline.com.
Well-dressed Washington women come to Urban Chic for stand out pieces for work and play from an array of established and up-and-coming designers like Rebecca Taylor, Milly, For All Mankind, BCGC and Autumn Cashmere. The boutique also carries men's and children's designer labels.

Dean & Deluca
3276 M St. NW. ℰ202-342-2500. www.deandeluca.com.
Your inner Julia Child will thank you for stopping in Dean & Deluca although she probably won't want you to leave this culinary dream store. Gorgeous produce, exquisite cheeses, fine wines and beautiful kitchen wares fill the shelves of the shop that also sells fresh coffee, pre-made sandwiches and pastries.

Georgetown Cupcake
3301 M St. NW. ℰ202-333-8448. www.georgetowncupcake.com.
People line up along the street for gourmet cupcakes crafted by sisters Sophie LaMontagne and Katherine Kallinis. The small shop rotates flavors daily including favorites like red velvet, key lime and chocolate ganache. The sweet treats can be packed up to go but chances are you won't be able to resist them long enough for them to make it home.

Annie Creamcheese
3279 M St. NW. ℰ202-298-5555. www.anniecreamcheese.com.
Annie Creamcheese proves that anything old can be fabulous again.

This glitter-filled vintage shops sells designer pieces from days gone by. Browse the ever-changing selection of clothing and accessories from the 1940s through the 1980s.

CONNECTICUT AVENUE / DUPONT CIRCLE
BOOKSTORES

Politics & Prose Bookstore & Coffeehouse
5015 Connecticut Ave. NW. ℰ202-364-1919. www.politics-prose.com.
One of the most successful independent bookstores in the country, Politics & Prose caters to a well-read and politically savvy clientele with its knowledgable staff and hand-picked selections. Prominent authors make a point of stopping here to read their latest books and sign copies for the crowds. The children's section downstairs is well stocked and every spring raises caterpillars into butterflies that the young readers help release. The Monday morning storytime *(on hiatus in summer)* for the toddler set is astanding room only affair. Done up with mismatched furniture, the coffeehouse in the basement serves coffee, drinks, sandwiches, salads and a vegan soup of the day. With a purchase, you will be given the code that lets you access the coffeehouse's wireless connection.

Kramerbooks & Afterword Cafe & Grill
1517 Connecticut Ave NW. ℰ202-387-1400. www.kramers.com.
Located right off Dupont Circle is Kramerbooks, a monument to books, coffee and late-night dining. The front of the store houses an array of current and classic literary titles and in the back the cafe serves food, wine, beer and dessert into the early hours of the morning. Outdoor seating is a popular choice during the summer and the store always seems to have something going on.

Museum Shops

Washington's countless museums translate into countless museum shops where gems and treasures can be yours for the price on the tag. If you are on the prowl for something truly different to take home pop into the gift shops attached to just about every museum, big or small in town.

The National Building (401 F St. NW; 202-272-2448; www.nbm.org) is the place for ergonomic office supplies and refreshingly original selection of gifts like nut and bolt salt and pepper shakers, Bauhaus building blocks and buildings of the world Christmas ornaments. The International Spy Museum (800 F St. NW; 202-393-7798; www.spymuseum.org) stocks spy gadget and disguises, while the National Gallery of Art (Constitution Ave. between 3rd and 7th Sts. NW; 202-737-4215; www.nga.gov.) is the place for art-inspired jewelry, scarves, prints and notecards. The lesser-known Textile Museum (2320 S St, NW; 202-667-0441; www.textilemuseum.org) is a treasure trove of exquisite handstiched items from around the world.

SPECIALTY SHOPS AND DESIGNER BOUTIQUES

Proper Topper
1350 Connecticut Ave. NW. ☎202-842-3055. www.propertopper.com.
Flirty frocks, glitzy gifts and, of course, a huge hat selection make Proper Topper one of DC's best-loved independent shops. The unusual and the pretty fill the sweet little store that first came on the scene in 1990.

Tiny Jewel Box
1147 Connecticut Ave. NW. ☎202-393-2747. www.tinyjewelbox.com.
The Tiny Jewel Box is three glorious floors of things that sparkle, shine and make you smile. For more than 75 years the store has been selling Washingtonians creatively set jewelry, antique pieces and unusual gift items.

MARYLAND
SHOPPING MALLS

Westfield Montgomery Mall
7101 Democracy Blvd. ☎301-469-6000. http://westfield.com/montgomery.
Anchored by Nordstrom department store, Montgomery Mall outfits many a teenager and grown up in the DC area. Popular stores here include Old Navy, Sephora, Lucky Brand Jeans, J. Jill and Forever 21. Dining options at the food court range from fast food to

crab cakes and fresh fish at Legal Sea Foods restaurant.

SPECIALTY SHOPS AND DESIGNER BOUTIQUES

Luna
7232 Woodmont Ave. ☎301-656-1111. www.shopluna.com.
A steady stream of regulars pops into this Bethesda boutique on any given day to browse its selection of flirty jeans, tops and dresses perfect for lunch with a girlfriend or a night out on the town. The always changing selection of fun statement jewelry, much of it reasonably priced, can make just about any outfit pop.

VIRGINIA
SHOPPING MALLS

Tysons Corner Shopping Center
1961 Chain Bridge Rd. ☎703-893-9400. www.shoptysons.com.
This massive center is the place to go for serious retail therapy. Popular department and chain stores here include Bloomingdale's, Nordstrom, Lord & Taylor, the Gap and L.L. Bean. The smaller **Tysons Galleria** *(2001 International Drive; 703-827-7730; www.tysonsgalleria.com)* mall across the road houses more upscale choices like Neiman Marcus, Saks Fifth Avenue and Versace.

Sports and Recreation

SPECTATOR SPORTS

DC is a great town for sports fans with a national baseball, football, hockey and basketball team to cheer on. Tickets for sporting events such as those in the charts below can usually be purchased at the venue itself or through **Ticketmaster** (☎800-745-3000; www.ticketmaster. com). When games are sold out, you can sometimes get tickets through a ticket agency (see the Yellow Pages of the phone directory) but expect to pay a premium.

WHERE TO GET A WORKOUT

The **National Capital YMCA** is open only to YMCA members and guests of members (1711 Rhode Island Ave. NW ☎202-862-9622; www.ymcadc.org). The **fitness centers** listed below allow nonmembers to use their facilities (weight rooms, aerobics classes and pool, if available) for a nominal daily fee ($10–$25). Members of IHRSA should ask if they are entitled to a lower daily fee.

FITNESS CENTERS

Washington Sports Club

18 locations in DC, MD & VA. ☎202-332-0100. www.mysportsclubs.com. Washington Sports Club has 18 clubs throughout the region where members can sweat their ways to health and fitness. The club offers a special 30-day membership for $30 at a club of your choosing, ideal for travelers coming to town.

City Fitness

3525 Connecticut Ave. NW. ☎202-537-0539. www.cityfitnessgym.com. Close to the Cleveland Park Metro, this local gym offers cardio equipment, free weights, weight machines and fitness classes. A one month membership is available.

SPAS

Nusta Spa

1129 20th St. NW. ☎202-530-5700; www.nustaspa.com.
A 5,000 square-foot full-service spa for men and women, Nusta marries indulgence and a commitment to the environment. Non-toxic, rapidly renewable and recycled materials were employed in the spa's construction and technicians use organic, non-toxic products during face and body treatments.

Red Door

1401 Pennsylvania Ave. NW. ☎202-942-2700. www.reddoorspas.com.
The Elizabeth Arden Red Door Spa at the Willard InterContinental offers a full line of treatments that pamper the body and soul. Popular offerings include the Red Door signature massage, phyto organic rescue facial and the cream and sugar body scrub. Red Door has a second DC location in Chevy Chase (5225 Wisconsin Ave. NW; 202-362-9890) as well as a spa in Bethesda (10213 Old Georgetown Rd; 240-644-1319) and Tysons Corner (8075 Leesburg Pike; 703-448-8388)

The Spa at the Mandarin Oriental

1330 Maryland Avenue. SW. ☎202-787 6100. www.mandarinoriental.com/ washington/spa.
Just walking into the tranquil spa at the luxurious Mandarin Oriental spa is enough to lower your blood pressure. The soft colors, aromatherapy candles and tranquil music lull you into a state of relaxation from the minute you step inside this oasis of relaxation. Guest can enjoy the amethyst steam rooms, experience showers, relaxation areas; a vitality pool and ice fountain (for female guests) , and a sauna and plunge pool (for male guests). A package in honor of the famous cherry blossoms includes a cherry body scrub, a foot massage and a cup of hot cherry tea to complete the experience.

Philadelphia Philies v
Washington Nationals
at Nationals Park

© Mitchell Layton/Getty Images

PROFESSIONAL SPORTS

Sport/Team	Season	Venue	✆Information/Tickets
🏐 Baseball (AL) Washington Nationals	Jun–Oct	Nationals Park SE	Info: 202-675-6287 & Tickets: 800-745-3000 www.nationals.mlb.com
🏈 Football (NFL) Washington Redskins	Sept–Dec	FedEx Field Landover, MD	Tickets: 301-276-6050 www.redskins.com
🏒 Hockey (NHL) Washington Capitals	Oct–Apr	Verizon Center 7th & F Sts. NW	Tickets: 202-397-7328 http://capitals.nhl.com
🏀 Basketball (NBA) Washington Wizards	Nov–Apr	Verizon Center 7th & F Sts. NW	Info: 202-661-5000 Tickets: 202-661-5050 www.nba.com/wizards
🏀 Basketball (WNBA) Washington Mystics	May–Aug	Verizon Center 7th & F Sts. NW	Info: 202-266-2200 Tickets: 877-324-6671 www.wnba.com/mystics

HORSE RACING

Racetrack	Season	Event	✆Information
Laurel Park	Oct–Mar	Thoroughbred racing	301-725-0400 www.marylandracing.com
Pimlico	Mar–Oct 3rd Sat/May	Thoroughbred racing Preakness Stakes	410-542-9400 www.marylandracing.com
Rosecroft Raceway	Year-round	Harness races	301-567-4500 www.rosecroft.com
Charles Town Races	Year-round	Thoroughbred racing	800-795-7001 www.ctownraces.com

POLO

Venue	Season	Event	✆Information
Lincoln Memorial Polo Field	Jun–Oct Wednesdays 5pm Saturdays 1pm	local tournaments	www.americaspolo cup.com

INDEX

INDEX

INDEX

W

Z

STAY

EAT

MAPS AND PLANS

THEMATIC MAPS

MAPS AND PLANS

COMPANION PUBLICATIONS

NORTH AMERICA ROAD ATLAS

 A geographically organized atlas with extensive detailed coverage of the USA, Canada and Mexico. Includes 246 city maps, distance chart, state and provincial driving requirements and a climate chart.
 Comprehensive city and town index
 Easy-to-follow "Go-to" pointers

MAP 583 NORTHEASTERN USA/ EASTERN CANADA

 Large-format map providing detailed road systems and including driving distances, interstate rest stops, border crossings and interchanges.
 Comprehensive city and town index
 Scale 1:2,400,000 (1 inch = approx. 38 miles)

MAP 761 USA ROAD MAP

 Covers the principal US road network and presents shaded relief detail of the overall physiography of the land.
 Features state flags with statistical data and state tourism office telephone numbers
 Scale 1:3,450,000

MAP 582 MID-ATLANTIC, ALLEGHENY HIGHLANDS

 Mid-Atlantic, Allegheny Highlands at 1:500,000 is a fully indexed map in the Michelin Regional USA series for motorists and tourists which is comprised of three maps at 1:2,400,000 covering the USA and southern Canada and two maps at a more detailed scale of 1:500,000 which cover the north-eastern seaboard from northern Virginia and DC to Southern Maine.
 Interstates or state highways are mapped with details of the number of lanes, intermediate driving distances, toll roads and rest areas. Minor and un-surfaced roads are also shown, as are ferry routes and airports. Scenic routes are highlighted where applicable.
 Native Indian land and land belonging to the U.S military are clearly designated on the maps, as are state capitals and boundaries, border crossings and time zone limits. Minimal grey relief shading is shown, as is each State's highest point of elevation. National and State forests and parks are clearly demarcated with variable green shading and other state lands are detailed in the legend.

★★★ **Highly recommended**
★★ **Recommended**
★ **Interesting**

Sight symbols

Walking tour with departure point and direction

Church, chapel	Panorama – View
Synagogue	Building described
AZ B Map co-ordinates locating sights	Other building
Other points of interest	Small building
Statue, monument	Lighthouse
Fountain	Cemetery described – Other

All maps are oriented north, unless otherwise indicated by a directional arrow.

Other symbols

Interstate Highway　　US Highway　　Other Route

Highway, interchange	Visitor information
Toll road, bridge	Hospital
Tunnel with ramp	Gift shop
One way street	Restrooms – Restaurant
Pedestrian street – Steps	Elevator – Escalator
Airport – Subway station	Parking – Post Office
Train station – Bus station	Railroad passenger station
Ferry: cars and passengers	Gate
Ferry: passengers only	Golf course – Stadium
Sight of special interest for children	Harbor cruise

Abbreviations and special symbols

Embassy: described – mentioned　　Japanese cherry trees

YOU ALREADY KNOW THE GREEN GUIDE, NOW FIND OUT ABOUT THE MICHELIN GROUP

The Michelin Adventure

It all started with rubber balls! This was the product made by a small company based in Clermont-Ferrand that André and Edouard Michelin inherited, back in 1880. The brothers quickly saw the potential for a new means of transport and their first success was the invention of detachable pneumatic tires for bicycles. However, the automobile was to provide the greatest scope for their creative talents.

Throughout the 20th century, Michelin never ceased developing and creating ever more reliable and high-performance tires, not only for vehicles ranging from trucks to F1 but also for underground transit systems and airplanes.

From early on, Michelin provided its customers with tools and services to facilitate mobility and make traveling a more pleasurable and more frequent experience. As early as 1900, the Michelin Guide supplied motorists with a host of useful information related to vehicle maintenance, accommodation and restaurants, and was to become a benchmark for good food. At the same time, the Travel Information Bureau offered travelers personalised tips and itineraries.

The publication of the first collection of roadmaps, in 1910, was an instant hit! In 1926, the first regional guide to France was published, devoted to the principal sites of Brittany, and before long each region of France had its own Green Guide. The collection was later extended to more far-flung destinations, including New York in 1968 and Taiwan in 2011.

In the 21st century, with the growth of digital technology, the challenge for Michelin maps and guides is to continue to develop alongside the company's tire activities. Now, as before, Michelin is committed to improving the mobility of travelers.

MICHELIN TODAY

WORLD NUMBER ONE TIRE MANUFACTURER
- 70 production sites in 18 countries
- 111,000 employees from all cultures and on every continent
- 6,000 people employed in research and development

Moving
for a world

Moving forward means developing tires with better road grip and shorter braking distances, whatever the state of the road.

CORRECT TIRE PRESSURE

RIGHT PRESSURE

- Safety
- Longevity
- Optimum fuel consumption

-0,5 bar

- Durability reduced by 20% (- 8,000 km)

-1 bar

- Risk of blowouts
- Increased fuel consumption
- Longer braking distances on wet surfaces

forward together
where mobility is safer

It also involves helping motorists take care of their safety and their tires. To do so, Michelin organises "Fill Up With Air" campaigns all over the world to remind us that correct tire pressure is vital.

WEAR

DETECTING TIRE WEAR

The legal minimum depth of tire tread is 1.6mm. Tire manufacturers equip their tires with tread wear indicators, which are small blocks of rubber moulded into the base of the main grooves at a depth of 1.6mm.

Tires are the only point of contact between the vehicle and road.

The photo below shows the actual contact zone.

NEW TIRE

WORN TIRE
(1,6 mm tread)

If the tread depth is less than 1.6mm, tires are considered to be worn and dangerous on wet surfaces.

Moving forward
means sustainable mobility

INNOVATION AND THE ENVIRONMENT

By 2050, Michelin aims to cut the quantity of raw materials used in its tire manufacturing process by half and to have developed renewable energy in its facilities. The design of MICHELIN tires has already saved billions of litres of fuel and, by extension, billions of tons of CO2.

Similarly, Michelin prints its maps and guides on paper produced from sustainably managed forests and is diversifying its publishing media by offering digital solutions to make traveling easier, more fuel efficient and more enjoyable!

The group's whole-hearted commitment to eco-design on a daily basis is demonstrated by ISO 14001 certification.

Like you, Michelin is committed to preserving our planet.

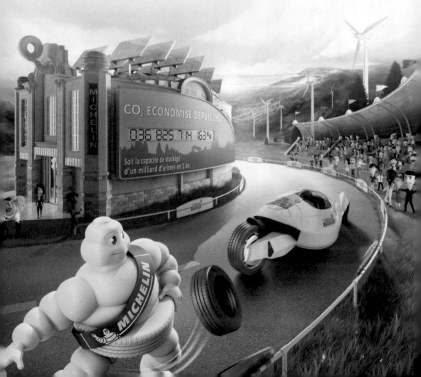

CO2 ÉCONOMISE DEPUIS 1992

036 825 714 163 %

Soit la capacité de stockage
d'un milliard d'arbres en 1 an.

Chat with Bibendum

Go to
www.michelin.com/corporate/en
Find out more about
Michelin's history and the
latest news.

QUIZ

Michelin develops tires for all types of vehicles.
See if you can match the right tire with the right vehicle...

Solution : A-6 / B-4 / C-2 / D-1 / E-3 / F-7 / G-5